Hey Littl
    Guess on...
past 50 (oops 30) HA HA There
is no more little
        Big Hugs
        Shelley

Familiar Stranger's...A mother's Story

by

Shelley Cowell

authorHOUSE®

AuthorHouse™
1663 Liberty Drive, Suite 200
Bloomington, IN 47403
www.authorhouse.com
Phone: 1-800-839-8640

First published by AuthorHouse 9/3/2009

ISBN: 978-1-4343-1746-9 (sc)

Printed in the United States of America
Bloomington, Indiana

This book is printed on acid-free paper.

Familiar Strangers

Walking our life paths with blinders
Looking past or through instead of at
Never knowing those closest to our hearts
Never seeing our lives or loves

The face is familiar, the soul is a stranger
The eyes are the path to the soul, to the heart
Never looking into the eyes we refuse to see the soul
When will we stop looking past and look at
When will we see and feel the soul

The peace, the love, the connection cannot be
We cannot love or be loved 'til we see
See the soul, feel the life and the love
It is out of our grasp like the dove
So we travel our paths as **FAMILIAR STRANGERS**

FAMILIAR STRANGERS lonely and scared
Unable to fill the empty gaps we live
Unable to fill the empty gaps we feel
Strangers trying to feel like family
Family being strangers, **FAMILIAR STRANGERS**.

Author: Shelley Cowell

Dedicated to:

all the mothers of the world
who do not understand their
children....take the time to see
them, really see them. Talk to
them, not at them.

Shelley Cowell

Introduction

Born July 28, 1932 in Ottawa, Canada ... Suzanne's father George Whittenby, career soldier, fought in both wars. Her mother Anna, social climber, war bride, lonely and bitter from life's hardships, hated the world and all it had to offer.

Suzannes' mother was a strict, hard woman who raised her children heavy-handedly. Her motto: spare the rod was to spoil the child. Life was hardship and if you weren't hard too, it would crush you. To toughen up her children was to love them and prepare them to survive a cruel world. Status, wealth and respectability, were the things that were never to be forgotten or a very harsh price would be paid.

Suzanne spent her life with no doubt in her mind that her mother hated and loathed her. What her mother hated and loathed the most was the love between Suzanne and her Daddy. Suzanne was beautiful and brilliant, she could do no wrong. At least not in her fathers' eyes ... in her mothers' eyes, she could do "NO RIGHT ".

Everything changed far too quickly when she met and fell in love with Ray Briar, the "much-too-old-for-her" suitor. He came from dirt poor exfarmers who lost everything in the Great Crash of '29. They were poor, uneducated, with no social standing, no culture, and on top of all that, he was eight years her elder. He was everything that Suzanne's mother hated, which was why Suzanne fell in love, got pregnant and married in that order.

They lived in total poverty with no help from her parents, which was the way Ray wanted it. He had a lot of old-fashioned pride, he would be the one to provide for his family even if it meant holding down two jobs, which it did.

Seventeen and pregnant for her second child, lonely and scared, they survived in a tiny trailer with not so much as running water; everything seemed hopeless. That is when she was alone. When Ray was with her, she was in love and none of it mattered. But he was so seldom home.

Once her second child came she tried her hardest to love that child, but all she could see was the incredible burden that one more child would bring. She was so tired, so sick and tired. How would she ever manage? How could they ever survive as a family?

Ray found them a farmhouse that would give them a home, a real home. He was in heaven; he loved and missed life on a farm. What was heaven to him was pure HELL to his young wife, who had lived in town all her life. She dropped deeper and deeper into a depression feeling there was no way out.

That is 'til her mother passed away and they moved into her parents' home with her father. She began rekindling old friendships, hanging out with her school chums instead of Ray who wasn't used to sharing her. More and more, each hurting the other as much as possible until something had to blow and it did.

Suzanne soon discovered that Ray and her father had sheltered her from the real world. She made one mistake after another, finally leading to the worst nightmare of her life. One she would never be able to block out of her memories. She knew she had to have Ray back he would keep her safe he had always protected her, but he couldn't protect her from herself or the destructive path she had to follow.

Chapter One

A mother lay in her hospital bed holding the baby she'd just given birth to. She looked far older than her eighteen years, already tired of life and what it had to offer. Looking at the perfect angelic child in her arms, she was a child of helpless innocence. She didn't feel the bonding warmth of a mother who had waited and anticipated the coming of a miracle.

She could only look at the child with exhausted worry, another burden, when the weight she already bore was more than she could stand. What was she going to do now? All she could think about was how badly her husband wanted to have a son. He was the eldest son of the eldest son of a long line of eldest sons. He was obsessed with carrying on the line.

The only line she could see was poor dirt farmers and not even that since the depression took all the farms. Farmers they were and always would be. They were men and needed not only land to prove it. It seemed as if he couldn't be a man until he had a son. Now he was stuck with not one, but two girls to support.

She knew her husband loved her and would try hard to pretend that it didn't matter, that it really wasn't somehow her fault. His lips would be smiling, as his eyes would be full of disappointment. There was no doubt in her mind that her husband wouldn't waist time before he started pressuring her to try again.

Her mind wandered from her husband, to what she was going to do when she got home with this little bundle. They resided in a, tiny trailer that they rented from a friend. It wasn't even a proper house-trailer; it was a camper, without so much as the luxury of running water.

They were very lucky the trailer was parked near a small restaurant. The owners were kind enough to let them haul water whenever they needed it. She often wondered how much was kindness and how much was pity.

It had been a very long and bitter winter. She was thankful it was February and spring would be just around the corner. Summers in the trailer were surprisingly pleasant, that is except for hauling water. This would be twice the burden now with two babies only eighteen months apart.

As she closed her eyes she pictured rows and rows of diapers hanging on the line. It was almost impossible to get clothes dry in the winter, after they hung outside, they then had to be spread out all over the trailer to thaw then ironed dry.

It seemed to her that there was never enough, they were all either hanging on the line, frozen, or dirty. That was when she had only one baby what was she going to do now that she had two that would dirty them twice as fast.

She was really wishing she'd had a baby shower like with Anna, her first baby. It seemed so unfair to only have a shower for the first one, when you need so much more for two.

Even if there had been a shower there would be no one to come to it. She had lost touch with all her friends when she married Ray.

He really had become her life. She would never go to her so-called family that was certainly out of the question. She would never give them the satisfaction... as far as they were concerned life was wonderful and she wanted for nothing.

They had hated Ray right from the start. Her mother could be so viscous, nasty and hurtful. Her mother couldn't say Ray's name without putting lowlife in front of it.

How could her father have fallen in love with her in the first place? There was certainly nothing lovable about her. All the pictures of her mother as a young girl showed her to be a great beauty. Surely that wasn't all she was? Surely her father couldn't be so shallow as to stay all these years for beauty alone.

Suzanne had been told all her life, she was the image of her mother. To her that wasn't much of a complement. She prayed real hard that didn't include personality. She would end it all, if she had to end up as hard and cold as her mother. After giving it about thirty seconds of thought she knew she could never be that evil. The devil himself was probably scared of her mother.

Having terrible thoughts about her mother made Suzanne hate herself. There had always been great waves of distention bordering on hatred. Although it was never said and barely thought, because, after all, a mother was supposed to love her daughter. Or was that simply an illusion created by television and books?

How could she help but look down at the baby in her arms and wonder if they would love or like each other. She tried to remember a time when her mother and her didn't hate each other. The best she could come up with was a few moments of tolerance. There were no moments of warmth or love. Never was her mother proud or accepting of Suzanne or anything she did.

Her mother was always filled with disappointment for her youngest daughter. Even when she had accelerated in school one year, then completely skipped a grade the next year, putting her in classes with kids two years her senior.

Truly believing her mother would have to be proud now, she was so excited she ran as fast as she could. She would have to acknowledge Suzanne's worth now. After all, she was going to high school next year, a whole two years early.

Suzanne burst into the back door to the kitchen; her mother could be heard screaming at the top of her lungs, stopping instantly Suzanne had to try to catch what the upset was about, praying it wasn't anything she had done or caused.

She thought about waiting for a better time. A time when her mother wouldn't be so hostile, but unfortunately there would be no better time. There was never a time when her mother wasn't screaming.

Suzanne was sure it had to be a vast exaggeration but, at the moment, couldn't remember a time when it wasn't true. Standing paralyzed deciding what to do, the decision was made for her. It was too late, her mother saw her. She couldn't escape the wrath that was about to descend on her. Every instinct she had told her to run, but she couldn't she was frozen. Suzanne learned at a very young age that running made everything so much worse.

Aware of her mother standing over her screaming wildly, but unaware what about, she had learned long ago how to tune her out. Since most of the time she was totally irrational anyway. Even when she did listen, it never made any sense. Her father told her it was because her mother was a cockney ghetto girl, who learned to scream from birth.

... "YOU ARE NOT LISTENING...!" she could hear, all too late. There was a sting in her cheeks as she went flying across the room and landed up against the back door.

She put her hands over her head; she knew this was only the beginning. She had to protect her face. If any of the blows, kicks, or punches left a mark that couldn't be hidden under her clothes, she would not be allowed out 'til she healed; that would be more than she could bare.

With the slamming of her mother's door, the beating was over, at least for now. Her four brothers and one older sister busied themselves making everything perfect for when their mother would reappear. It would only be moments before their father would come home from work.

She could tell them both her news at the supper table, it was the only safe time and place in their household. Everything had to not only be proper, but perfect. That included everything from place settings to manners. Her mother grew up in total poverty, but her father was a blue-blood Brit from the best of schools. It was an obsession with her mother to prove to her husband, Suzanne's father, that she could be every bit as blue-blooded as his family.

Everything was right on schedule, the table was set, and supper was ready. Mother was calm, and Suzanne prayed... "PLEASE LET EVERYTHING GO WELL" ... With so many children, there was always someone for mother to be angry at.

Her father walked in the doorway at the exact same time everyday. It wasn't always that way, there was a time when her father was in the armed forces, and everything was crazy, you'd come home from school, the house would be packed ... they would be moving... end of discussion.

JUST LIKE THAT!! No good-byes to friends simply move. Suzanne often wondered, back in those days, if her parents knew in advance and didn't feel the need to tell any of the children.

It was two years ago that her father took the job as a civil servant in a small town and left the Force forever, settling his family on Lake Erie's shore. Somewhere in the back of Suzanne's mind she was still waiting for the next move.

... "SO FAR, SO GOOD. "... Praying as hard as she could... "PLEASE DON'T LET ANYONE DO ANYTHING WRONG..." It took so little to upset the apple cart. She still felt chills going through her as she remembered a time when her mother stabbed a fork into the back of her hand for not holding the knife correctly while cutting her meat.

With that, she figured she had better get her news out quickly. Why was she so scared? This was good news. There was no way of knowing if it was good news 'til her mother reacted. It was not the present reaction of the moment a person had to worry about, it was later when her father wasn't around.

Now, all Suzanne could do was watch for the little subtleties: a smirk, a frown, and sometimes the way her breathing changed. In her fear and anticipation she blurted it out. She would be going to highschool next year. Suddenly fear filled her every thought. Did she seem boastful? Did she sound like she was telling instead of asking?

Nothing was worse than cornering her mother like it was all decided and there were no choices. Her father was pleased and excited wasting no time in telling her how proud he was.

This was no surprise to Suzanne; after all she was not only daddy's girl but DADDY'S princess. She was also aware of the fact that there was something about her father calling her princess that brought out extreme loathing in her mother.

As much as Suzanne wanted to hear all the praise her father could give her, she wished he would stop. She could see her mother quietly seething, like a black cloud looming over. The storm wasn't far behind and it would be bad.

The only good thing was that if her father thought it was good then her mother would, verbally at least, go along with him. So quietly, very deep inside, she felt great pride and bubbled with the excitement of it all.

It wasn't 'til after school the next day that she realized how crazed her mother really was. Her mother was already waiting by the door when she came in ... "YOU THINK YOU'RE SO MUCH BETTER ... YOU THINK YOU'RE SO MUCH SMARTER ... DADDY'S LITTLE PRINCESS ... WELL YOUR HIGHNESS ... YOU NEED TO BE DRAGGED OFF THAT THRONE OF YOURS "...

With every word she spoke came another blow, a kick, a punch, dragged by the hair into the bathroom, another kick.... "HOPE YOU AREN'T TOO GOOD TO SCRUB TOILETS .... PRINCESS "...

Suzanne couldn't decide which hurt more, the blows or the hated tones of her voice. She never really understood why her mother hated her so much. Now that she was older, she could see it as pure uncontrolled jealousy, something Suzanne would never inflict on her children. She would love her children.

As this affirmation lingered on the edges of her mind, her eyes fell on the helplessness of her newborn child filling her with feelings of burden and dread. Truly believing that once she got home she would feel more love, she was just so tired. After all, a mother has to love her own daughter.

Her own mother, who was as nasty and as cold as they came, loved her. She had often told her how much she loved her. She only "SPANKED "her to help her be a better person. That had to be love. Her mother explained to her many times, that it is the mothers that don't hit their children that don't love them enough to care how they turn out.

Suzanne glanced at the clock realizing her husband would be there soon, she must hurry to get ready. Ray only had forty minutes to spend with her and eat his supper before he went on to his second job. This merely brought her thoughts back to all the hardships.

Her husband was already holding down two jobs and they were barely getting by. She would not discuss any of this when he got there, after all he was already doing all he could do to provide for them. Besides she wanted to enjoy the peace and serenity of the hospital while they still could. There was time enough to worry after she got home.

As soon as Ray walked through the door Suzanne could see how tired he was. Barely even glancing at the baby in the bassinet he was too tired to even pretend to be pleased. Too tired to open the bag lunch that he brought from home, he gave her a sweet kiss hello, then sat in the only available chair in the room.

As she started to talk to him about naming the baby she realized he was sound asleep in the chair. Watching him sleep Suzanne could see he was starting to look old. His hair was receding; the worry lines around his eyes were deep with heavy dark circles around them. While only Twenty-six, he looked far older.

Totally exhausted, he still had at least six more hours at his second job, then back up at five a.m. for his day job. She looked at him with guilt and sadness, feeling that somehow she had gotten him into this with her desperate need to get away from her mother; a desperate need to be loved, to feel needed and worthwhile.

Her thoughts drifted to a different time ...She was a shy, yet bubbly fifteen year old, full of life. Most of her friends were seventeen and older, giving her a maturity beyond her actual years. When she smiled the little girl in her shone through. Ray met Suzanne through his cousin who was dating a classmate. It never once entered his mind that she wasn't at least the same age or older than her friend Jane. Jane was never very bright so it was easy for Suzanne to appear the older of the group.

Suzanne was a striking beauty. She had the kind of looks that made everyone want to stop and stare, to touch her to see if she was real and not a porcelain doll. It was however her intelligence and regal aura that attracted Ray. He was very good looking himself and had all the charm it took to collect a full harem of followers, but rarely did they have looks brains and personality.

This girl had everything he ever wanted. He knew halfway through the first date he was going to marry her. At twenty-three he was ready for his own family. He had already been supporting his father's family for years.

All she had to do was smile at him and he would melt into a puddle at her regal feet. He never did learn how to say no to her. When they met she had just finished grade eleven. She spent most of their first date telling him about her father's plans for her to go to college.

Ray listened to every word with complete fascination and adoration; he had never known anyone who could either have the money or the intelligence for college. No one in his family had even finished high school.

When he was younger he prayed he would be the first but there were six children to feed and a father that couldn't work. So it fell on his very young shoulders to support his entire family. After all he was the eldest son and it was his duty to step in where his father couldn't.

Forced to quit school in grade nine after the accident crippled his father, it took him no time to find a job on a commercial fishing boat. He soon learned how to be a good fisherman. The first lesson was to carry scotch to work with him. It was an unpopular drink so there was little chance of the other fishermen helping him drink it.

Suzanne's mother's favorite expression for this much-too-old-for-her-daughter, man, was... "CRADLE-ROBBING, LOW-LIFE, DRUNKEN FISHERMAN "... For their first several dates they were forced to sneak away to where they weren't likely to run into any of her family or their friends.

Saying she was out with Jane was usually an acceptable excuse and not too far from the truth since they near always double-dated. Unfortunately the only place for them to go was parking or strolling in isolated areas. If any of her brothers or sisters had seen them, they would have taken great pleasure in divulging her deception.

Once her parents discovered she was dating, all "HELL " broke loose. Her mother was in an uncontrolled rage ... the worst Suzanne had ever seen. Her mother's ranting and raving she could handle, it was her father's reaction of total disappointment that hurt the most. She had never lied to or deceived her father before. It broke his heart she chose now to do it.

Now she would be allowed to date Ray openly, since there really was no way of keeping them apart. However her mother did do everything in her power to make their dates as miserable as possible. Most of the time Suzanne was crying so hard they could only go parking so Ray could console and comfort his princess.

Ray very quickly became her protector, her knight in shining armor. Ray loved the way he felt when he was with her, being her protector, her knight. He felt important, he felt needed and loved, she needed him and he would be there for his princess.

By the time she went back to school in September for her final year, they were very much an item with no doubt in her mind they would be together forever. There was strong pressure from her father for her to prepare for college. He hoped that the separation would put a wedge between the two. Sure a little space would bring her back to her senses not to mention people her own age and social standing.

Ray was far beneath her station and would never be more than he was at that moment. Suzanne's mother would continue to openly hate

Ray. Somehow in disappointing her father she pleased her mother, almost feeling closeness to her that had never been there before.

She missed being Daddy's girl, now that she was Ray's princess that was all she would need. At least that was what she told herself to console her wounded soul.

She wanted to share her happiness with her Dad the one person who had always been there for her. Now she was forced to keep everything from him. Everyday she felt the weight of her lies to a father she had never so much as kept a secret from before.

It was New Years Eve, their first New Years together. Suzanne had saved all her babysitting money for a new grown up gown and was going to wear the high heels her best friend had loaned her. She had spent days practicing how to walk in them and now she was ready... ready for the most important night of her life.

Her older sister who normally was cruel and hateful even offered to do her hair in a french knot. It was a very grown up look and Suzanne was thrilled that Ray was the one to escort her on her first grown up night out.

Things had been fairly peaceful between her and her mother, so much so that Suzanne had let her guard down. Her heart went into her throat as she heard Rays knock at the door. Taking a deep breath she began her slow nervous walk across the room.

She could hear her mother's screams from the other side of the room, "SLUT... WHORE" ... grabbing at a handful of hair she dragged Suzanne to the floor, clawing at her new dress and ripping it. Her mother was still kicking when Ray walked in.

Stopping, the physical blows, the verbal obscenities could still be heard as Ray carried her to the car. Suzanne was crying uncontrolled, Ray had not realized how terrifying Suzanne's life really was. Ray knew Suzanne's mother was sharp-tongued, but he didn't know of the physical attacks. Suzanne had never told him.

She was ashamed a piece of her believed she deserved the beatings, they were her fault somehow. If Ray knew how bad she was he would not want her anymore. She couldn't stand life if Ray wasn't in it, if he quit loving her as her father had.

They spent most of the night holding onto each other. He promised, no matter what he had to do he would try to find some way to get her away from all of it. He would give her a better life.

As he held her in his arms consoling and promising, trying to undo all the pain her mother had caused, give her hope for better times, they began to melt together to become one. They were making love, it seemed only natural... and there was no doubt they were making love.

He moved very slowly, very gently, with every movement he worried about hurting her. He had never been with a virgin before, and it scared him. She had no fear, she had no doubt, this was right and she knew it coaxing him to go on. Afterward they held each other so close they couldn't tell where one ended and the other began.

From that moment on they were one, and no one would ever come between them. The princess had found her Prince Charming, but could they possibly live happily ever after? Does love conquer all? We all know life is never as simple as that. But to a girl who will be sixteen in only four days ... fairy tales do come true.

She hated to wake Ray; he was so tired, he would be angry if she didn't. They could not afford to lose even one days pay. When he awoke he gave her a long gentle hug and a sweet kiss, his way of apologizing for sleeping through their entire visit.

He walked over and stared into the bassinet. He couldn't believe how perfect and beautiful she was. It made him think of his first daughter. She came two months early, weighing two pounds and four ounces, looking very much like a drowned rat at birth. Even at a year-and-a-half, it was pretty clear she would take after his side of the family. The men were all handsome but the women were plain.

This little Angel was her mother and grandmother all over again. As he stood staring at his new daughter, Suzanne asked again, what should we call her? ... "SHE LOOKS LIKE AN ANGEL TO ME!" ... so Angel it will be. Maybe if they got lucky her personality would grow into her name. With that, he looked at his watch and ran out the door, yelling he loved her and would see her tomorrow.

She wished to herself that he would stay for her parent's visit, she dreaded having to deal with them alone. Her mother was barely through the door..." WHAT WILL YOU DO NOW? " ... Only her mother could make such a statement sting so deeply. Suzanne knew that behind that statement was ... "YOU MADE YOUR BED NOW LIE IN IT. "...

Grandpa gazed down at the sleeping Angel and smiled a smile Suzanne hadn't seen in a long time. He said ... "MY GOODNESS, IT'S MY PRINCESS ALL OVER AGAIN" ... The words cut her deeper than the sarcasm she had to endure from her mother.

The little girl lost way deep inside of her wanted to shout at him ... " THAT IS MY NAME ... I AM YOUR PRINCESS ... DON'T YOU REMEMBER?"...

That night she cried herself to sleep, the nurses were glib, everyone gets baby blues after childbirth. But she knew she was crying for the little girl lost deep inside of her. For Daddy's girl, the princess that fell from grace. She knew that little girl was gone forever, never would she surface again. It was time to grow up and be a wife and mother.

When Ray came to see Suzanne the next day, something was different but he wasn't sure what. It was as though something was missing from her eyes when she looked at him. He could feel her sadness even if he couldn't understand it.

Suzanne was never able to explain things she felt deep inside, especially the little girl feelings. To him it was all foolishness that he really didn't have time for even if he could understand what she was talking about.

She had long since learned to keep these feelings to herself, to push them deep down inside. She had to get on with taking care of her family. To Ray, the girls and him were her family. Why should it matter what her parents said or did? But it did matter, Suzanne wasn't sure why, but it did.

Suzanne had told Ray she was homesick and missed Anna their oldest daughter. She was sure she would be fine after she got home. That's what she told herself, in reality she dreaded going home, she knew there would be nothing but never ending work and loneliness. One more thing she could not divulge to Ray.

How could she tell him she missed him, that she couldn't stand the loneliness and the isolation, when he was doing it all for her? She knew he was exhausted all the time; he wasn't working two jobs because he wanted to, but because he had to.

Whenever she tried to talk to him about her feelings of loneliness, she would convince herself she was being that selfish spoiled child her mother had always told her she was. So she let it go, holding it in, pushing it deeper inside.

Her mother picked her up at the hospital the next day while Ray was at work. As the car moved into the driveway that led to the run down trailer, her mother sighed and shook her head, as she had every time she pulled up to the trailer. Grandma carried the baby while Suzanne carried the luggage. As Suzanne put the key in the lock she dreaded what would be next.

She prayed Ray had at least kept the house tidy. No such luck, Ray loved her and provided for her, but he never did a dish, a speck of housework or anything else that could be construed as women's work.

... " MY GOD SUZANNE COULDN'T YOU FIND SOME WAY TO FIX THIS PLACE UP ... IT'S BAD ENOUGH YOU LIVE IN A SQUALOR, DOES IT HAVE TO BE A STYE AS WELL... "Thank God Ray's mother came in with Anna. Suzanne scooped her up and covered her face with kisses. ... "MOMMY MISSED HER LITTLE GIRL SO MUCH... "

Her mother would leave right away; she was always worried that people might see her at the trailer and think she knew people that lived that way. She also felt it was beneath her to spend time with Ray's mother. After all Ray's mother was an illiterate country girl. It was disgusting the way she gushed over Anna. She would not tolerate spoiled grandchildren.

Suzanne felt a sigh of relief when the door closed and she could hear her mother pull out of the driveway. Her mother was right, Ray's mom was uneducated; she only went to grade two.

Back in those days farm folk could not see the sense in education for females. She was one of the warmest and most caring people she had ever known. A true lady who never put on heirs or made anyone feel worthless. She had been wonderful and helpful from the beginning; Suzanne had been accepted into her family from the first time she met them.

Suzanne thought about it and could not think of any time that Ray's mom ever showed anger or rage. For that matter she never even seemed to show tension or even sternness. The years of hardship from living through a depression with a husband that could not work, while raising six children, showed on her face.

Ray had told Suzanne when they first met how his father was working in a factory; Ray was only thirteen at the time... the roof of the factory caved in. He had been saved, but his legs were not leaving him an invalid. In those days there was no disability, compensation or welfare. Ray's father almost never talked, spending all his time sitting in a chair staring out the window.

Suzanne felt sorry for him; it must have been unbearable for him to watch his children and wife trying to support his family. Whenever Suzanne was there for supper, she would try not to eat. She always worried there would not be enough for everyone else.

Ray's mom handed her a casserole that she had made, sure that Suzanne would not feel like cooking. Suzanne was hesitant to take it. Things were difficult since they no longer had Ray's earnings to support the family. Ray's mom was always generous and kind perhaps too kind when her own family was always on the edge of hungry.

She had once taken her last loaf of bread to a homeless family wandering down the street. Suzanne had trouble understanding this, her mother had always told her that street people got what they deserved, that they were lazy and shiftless and refused to get jobs. Yet

Ray's mother had nothing but empathy and compassion for the poor souls.

Grateful for the casserole, Suzanne thanked her mother-in-law for thinking of it. Her own mother, who could afford it, hadn't thought of it. She often felt it was Ray's mom, who should be snubbing hers, she was far better than Suzanne's entire family.

What made her mother the way she was? She came from one of the poorest hardest slums in England. She should understand, she should feel sympathy for the hardships of life since she felt them herself. But she had clawed her way out of that slum so could anyone else and if they didn't it was because they were lazy and deserved to be there.

Suzanne grew up not knowing any relatives beyond her parents. Her paternal relatives had disowned their son, her father the day he married her mother. She was beneath his station, he had been educated in the best schools England could offer, and he had no business consorting with ghetto trash.

It was his family's blue-blooded attitudes that forced the young couple to leave England and settle in Canada. He refused to raise his family in such narrow-minded bigotry.

The young bride thought she would be pulled out of the ghetto and welcomed into England's royalty with open arms. Maybe that is why she had raised her family with so much anger and bitterness.

Her father had given them a very comfortable life even during the great depression. They never wanted for anything. He was a high-ranking officer in the Canadian Armed forces; it was very prestigious but not prestigious enough for Suzanne's mother.

Suzanne did not even know that poverty or hardship existed except in stories that she really never believed. That is 'til she met Ray. Poverty was something in some distant land, some third-world country like in the pictures on the wall at her Sunday school.

Suzanne was glad to be alone at last. The baby was asleep, so she could spend some time reading stories to Anna. The dishes would wait. There was a special bond between Suzanne and Anna. She had felt it from conception.

That pregnancy was different, it was special, and Suzanne could feel the love and connection as the new life grew in her stomach. She would read her stomach stories, talking to it long before the birth. Suzanne wished she could have those feelings for Little Angel. From the beginning she felt burden and dread, then adding guilt for not wanting the pregnancy making it all the more stressful.

Anna climbed up on her mommy's knee in the big overstuffed sofa that nearly filled the entire trailer. Suzanne and Ray both slept on the sofa. There was no room for a bed. There was barely room for the crib that the girls would have to share once Angel outgrew the drawer that would hold her for now.

Suzanne and Anna drifted off to sleep with the book still in their hands. That was how Ray found them when he came in from work at four p.m. It gave him a special feeling of warmth to see his girls so peacefully snuggled up together. He lifted Angel out of the drawer where she slept and sat on the floor beside the sofa.

He had a little time alone to get to know the newest member of his family. Somehow there was something different about this baby. Something in the eyes, they seemed old and serious. Even at a mere few days old they seemed to talk, to draw him into them.

Suzanne loved that the first thing she could see when she opened her eyes was Ray holding his daughter, counting her fingers and talking baby talk as though they both knew exactly what they were saying. Ray was a wonderful natural father she wished he had more time for them. She wished he had more time for her. That he could be a real part of their family instead of just a paycheck.

He looked up at her and smiled... "YOU DID GOOD SHE'S BEAUTIFUL... "This gave her a wonderful feeling of warmth. This would be the first opportunity they had to talk. She loved it when they were alone. Nothing seemed to matter when they were in each other's arms.

It was as though they were transported to a different place and time, a world of their own. Suzanne could not see the hardships, all she could see was Ray and how much he loved her. It made her feel warm and safe, like when she was a little girl with her Daddy.

That is, when they were together. When they weren't together all she could see was the squalor and hardship of the life they had together. The endless work, all the things they had to go without, things she wanted for her little girl. Even a book for Anna was a hardship.

When she wasn't thinking of it herself, she always had her mother to remind her of how crappy their life was. What a failure Ray was for not providing a better home for his family. What kind of a man lets his family live with such poverty.

With Ray working two jobs, averaging between sixteen and eighteen hours per day, it seemed she was always alone. All Ray had to do was walk in the door, wrap his strong arms around her, and it would all magically disappear. She believed in Ray with all her heart and in her heart she knew this was only temporary. All she had to do was hold on and give him time to get them through it.

Ray looked around the trailer sighed, and rolled his eyes trying hard to be cool and stern. Instead he looked like the cat that swallowed the canary. He couldn't contain himself any longer... "WE HAVE A HOUSE!!"...

Suzanne was so excited she didn't even wait for details, they really didn't matter. The only thing that mattered was real rooms, running water, and most important of all, a bathtub. There were times when Suzanne thought she would sell her soul to soak in a hot tub.

The house had been sitting empty for several months and was in need of a lot of repairs, but was still livable. There was nothing Ray couldn't do. He was handy around the house something his young wife greatly admired. Her father was a paper-pusher and had trouble even changing a light bulb.

The best part about getting the house was that Ray had worked a deal; he traded a rent discount for repairs and upkeep. This meant Ray wouldn't have to continue working two jobs and hopefully Suzanne would have some relief from the babies.

Ray had taken the night off work, to drive out and see their new home. He talked the entire trip nonstop; she had never heard him say so much. It was usually Suzanne who liked to chatter, probably because she spent so much time alone. She wondered if they would now be able to get a phone. That really would be heaven, or at least a piece of it.

The drive seemed to take forever; Ray explained to her how there was a lot of land with it so he could farm during the day and keep his evening job at the factory. She didn't hear much, but she did hear canning, chickens, and a cow?!.. Had she heard that right?... He wanted her to be a farmer's wife?

The further they got into the country the more uncomfortable Suzanne felt. She was a town girl. The idea of being in the country so isolated, scared her. But she hadn't seen Ray this excited since their wedding day how could she tell him she hated the idea? Not the entire idea, she liked that she would have real rooms. If she could get Ray to throw in a phone maybe it wouldn't be so bad. Who knows, maybe she would learn to like it.

Pulling into the driveway, she strained to see the houses of her nearest neighbors. The silence that hung in the air haunted her like a ghost. She liked the security of knowing she had people close by. It seemed to her that if she were a mass murderer this was the kind of place she would choose to mass murder in.

Ray was so filled with excitement he couldn't see his wife's apprehension. It never even occurred to him that what was exciting to him may be scary to Suzanne. Being raised a farm boy who was forced to move to town only after his father's accident, he never did get the farm out of his soul.

Ray looked around with his rose-colored glasses firmly fixed over not only his eyes but his good sense. Which Suzanne was sure had totally left him. He saw a large farm house with flourishing crops and a few farm animals... she saw a run-down shack that needed a lot of work. She saw isolation, loneliness and a life she knew nothing about... "CHICKENS!" ... indeed.

Like he would be around to take care of them. Who was going to plow, plant and hoe, let alone harvest the Damn thing? Ray had no time now and here he wants to double his work- load. Never did it occur to him Suzanne could be of little or no help in this venture.

Chapter Two

Suzanne couldn't bring herself to burst Ray's bubble; they couldn't stay in the trailer, not with two babies. Rundown or not isolated or not it was better than the trailer. Anything was better than the trailer, they would make it a home their home.

So move they did, after hitting every second hand shop and relative for furniture. They even managed to get a small bed for Anna, who grinned from ear to ear at the prospect of being a big girl.

Ray had swung to an evening shift so they could spend the day moving in. By the time Ray had to leave for work everything was piled in the middle of the living room. That was fine with Suzanne she found that Ray mostly got in the way. She was excited to set up her first real home.

Suzanne rushed around the house trying to unpack as fast as she could. She wanted everything perfect when Ray walked through the door; something she had learned from her mother. The only way to keep your man was to have everything perfect at all times. In the trailer she couldn't show Ray what a good housekeeper she really was.

The time passed quickly, it was ten. Ray was due home in about an hour and a half. She had enough time to unpack one more box. Then she could fix him his first dinner in their first home, or at least their first home that was firmly attached to the ground.

Angel began crying. It was only seconds before the crying had built into screaming. It was time for her bottle, Suzanne prayed Angel would eat fast; she still had so much to do before Ray got home. While Suzanne heated the bottle the cries built into hysteria; Suzanne could feel her anger building at Angel's impatience.

As Suzanne opened the door nothing felt right, the hairs on the back of her neck stood up. She turned on the light and stood in horror as she looked into a crib filled with rats; the largest, fattest, meanest rats that anyone could have ever conjured up in their worst nightmare. Grabbing at a pillow she began swinging at them in an attempt to get them away from her babies.

They weren't afraid of her; they arched their backs and held their ground. Her screaming intermingled with Angel's, then Anna's began to chime in, as the noises and rats turned their new home into a house of horror.

She tried to reach for Angel as one of the four-legged creatures jumped onto her arm, feeling the sting of its teeth she tried to shake it off. Wrapping a blanket around her arm she tried again, this time with success. She had a grip on Angel and wasn't letting go.

Making her way to Anna, she could feel them on her legs and feet, the room was full of them. As Anna stood up she dove at the safety of her mothers arms. Blind with the hysteria of the moment, Suzanne ran through the house all of them still screaming and crying uncontrollably. She was frenzied trying to get out, to get her babies to safety.

Once outside, she realized they couldn't stay out, she didn't even have shoes on her feet. Something she realized as soon as she calmed down enough to feel the snow melt between her toes. The only other shelter within walking distance was the old wind torn barn. God knew what horrifying creatures were in there!

Very slowly she worked her way back onto the small closed in front porch. Locking the front door between the house and the porch as if she thought rats might be able to turn the knob. At this point nothing was rational.

Frantically ripping open boxes she wasn't even sure what she was looking for. The first box she opened was full of old coats and clothes; she pulled out the coats and made a bed, lifting Anna into it, she then handed Angel to her, covering them with coats leaving one out for herself.

In another box she found Ray's work socks and pulled on a couple pairs. There were three boxes marked "kitchen ", Suzanne dug through all of them hoping to find something she could use. She finally found a carving set, they had received as a wedding gift. Holding the knife in one hand and the oversized fork in the other, she felt no safer, but couldn't let go.

Poor Anna, Angel was still screaming. Suzanne picked up the box with her babies and lifted them as high as she could, setting it safely on top of another pile of boxes. Climbing up beside it herself she hugged and rocked the cardboard cradle trying to calm and comfort her babies.

She had to maintain calm, be in control as feelings of hysteria consumed her. If she were ever going to get her girls to stop screaming she would have to talk calmly and make them feel everything was all right.

That was what a puzzled Ray was greeted with as he walked through the door; Suzanne curled up on top of a bunch of boxes, rocking her babies. Through a flood of sobs and tears Suzanne managed to get her story out. Ray arrogantly patronized her, sure it was all a vast exaggeration that he could take care of in a minute.

He unlocked the door; half laughing to himself that Suzanne thought she could lock the rats out. He was sure it was the hysteria of a prissy town girl; a farm girl would have known what to do about a stupid little rat.

Tears once again streamed down Suzanne's face as she begged Ray not to go into the house she just wanted to get as far from this house as she could as fast as she could. Big tough macho man thinks he can handle twenty or thirty rats. What was he going to do, ask them politely to leave, thank them for coming?

Maybe he could explain to them that his wife didn't like rats, they would surely get up and leave if they knew they weren't wanted. The more Suzanne thought about it, the angrier she got that Ray not only didn't believe her, but thought it was all a big joke.

Ray didn't have to go too far into the house before he found Suzanne's rat in a box in the kitchen. He was relieved that he found the little beggar quickly. He grabbed a cast iron frying pan figuring he would simply whack it. Moving closer he saw three more, then one of them jumped on his back.

That was enough for Ray he was out of there; it was more than he could handle. Still white and shaking he ran to the porch locking the door behind him. Suzanne had already moved herself and the girls to the car where she smugly awaited her husband's apology. He silently listened to Suzanne's rantings as they drove to his mothers.

Standing at the door half -dressed and no shoes Ray's mom was sure the house had burned down. She was almost relieved to hear that it was merely rats. To Suzanne it would have been better if the house had burned down at least then she would never again have to go back.

Getting up with the sun Ray and his brothers grabbed their guns and went rat hunting.

The first thing they did was blow smoke bombs under the house to scatter the little critters. Ray had never seen so many they were everywhere, both inside and out. Ray and his brothers started shooting as fast and as much as they could, not bothering to take the time to aim rats were everywhere they were bound to hit them.

Ray was sure anyone driving by would think war had been declared. In Ray's eyes it was war and he wasn't going to be the loser of this battle. While the boys were busy shooting outside Ray filled all the holes he could find with rat poison then hammered pieces of tin over each opening.

The hardest job was disposing of the carcasses; the brothers talked it over then decided the only recourse was to burn them as the ground was still too frozen to dig graves. As bad as it was going to smell it was definitely the more sanitary thing to do.

Who knows what kinds of diseases they were carrying. The way they were attacking the night before, they could have even been rabid.

It was a very long day of cleaning up the mess, burning bodies and repairing holes in the walls and floors from both the rats and the shooting.

As unpleasant as the job was, Ray loved every minute of it. It had been a long time since he had been one of the guys doing guy things. They laughed, teased, joked and swore, not once having to apologize to the ladies. It was a great day for Testosterone. They were men and loved proving it.

Camping out in the living-room drinking beers and reliving the prime of their highschool days ... all their dates were great beauties who always said yes to their undeniable charms; the football games were all won; and when they went hunting they always got that moose or better yet, the great Bear.

Not a single rat had been seen all night. To be safe, the last thing Ray did before picking up Suzanne was to grab three or four wild cats from friend's farms for the barn. With a lot of apprehension Suzanne allowed herself to be talked into going back to the house.

In her mind she was dragged kicking and screaming with little other choice. All Ray's promises and reassurances didn't convince her. Rats were rats. They were tricky and sneaky and she knew they were out there somewhere hiding in the dark corners.

Suzanne cringed every time she opened a cupboard door, a drawer or even turned on a light. She had not told Ray but if he was working late, she would turn every light in the house on long before the sun was going down and they would stay on until he walked through the door. Even the lights in the girl's rooms had to stay on. She wasn't walking into a dark room not knowing what was there hiding in the corners waiting for her.

She would never again live in a house with no phone. The next time something happened she was going to be able to call for help. She would never again feel so alone and helpless. Ray wanted them all to live on an island detached from the rest of the world, and the people who inhabited it, she liked the world. She liked having friends, and people to talk to.

She hated being in that house alone, so much so that she adjusted hers and the babies sleeping habits to Rays shift work. If he worked night shift, she would do everything she could to keep her self and the girls awake. They would all sleep together. There was no way she could close her eyes without Ray there to keep her safe.

That is, when Angel allowed them to sleep, mostly the newest member of their family screamed and cried at all times. She would drop off to sleep only long enough to build up her strength to scream longer and louder.

Suzanne didn't know what to do; she would put Angel in her crib and close the door. Trying to pretend she couldn't hear her babies' hysteria and panic. This would go on sometimes for the entire time Ray was gone.

Suzanne often curled up on the couch her trembling hands held tight to her ears tears streaming down her face as she was engulfed with helplessness being pushed to the edge of an insanity only a mother could understand.

The only thing that seemed to pacify Angel was when Suzanne was carrying her around. To Suzanne, that only confirmed that her Daddy had spoiled Angel far too much. Suzanne wasn't about to give into it. She was in control not some spoiled baby that needed to learn just who the boss was.

Insisting this wasn't normal behavior for a baby this small, Ray made Suzanne take the baby to the doctor, something had to be wrong. They never had any of these problems with Anna.

While at the doctors, not only was there no screaming, but Angel slept peacefully as though she didn't have a care in the world. The doctor couldn't find a thing wrong to make matters worse he couldn't see how such an Angel could be any trouble at all.

They weren't home for more than moments when Angel started her screaming again; Suzanne was at the end of her rope. She handed her baby to Daddy and went to bed, where she seemed to be spending most of her time of late.

Suzanne kept thinking that Angel would have to reach a point of exhaustion and drop off to sleep. The only one to get exhausted was Suzanne. Ray tried to hold the baby to rock and comfort her but Suzanne insisted he leave her in the crib where she would scream with terror and hysteria.

He had to believe that Suzanne knew what she was talking about but it broke his heart to hear his Angel crying, it broke his heart to fight with his wife about it. It was a woman's place to know these things.

He knew how to put food on the table he didn't begin to understand why a baby screamed. A small piece of him began to believe what Suzanne was saying, that he had spoiled this little thing that seemed to so desperately need him.

Suzanne was at the end of her rope, she couldn't continue like this much longer. Ray only had one more shift to put in then he would be home for two days and could take over the house giving his wife a much-needed break.

The minute he walked through the door he could hear Angel screaming, a sound he had gotten used to coming home to. This time it was different, this time he could hear Suzanne screaming ... "SHUT UP! ... SHUT UP! ... I CAN'T STAND IT!! ... SHUT UP!!...

Running into the girl's bedroom, Ray could see Suzanne standing over Angel with a pillow. He grabbed her hands ... " WHAT ARE YOU DOING!? "... He knew what it looked like and prayed he was wrong.

Suzanne dropped the pillow and sat on the floor crying exhausted sobs. Ray was filled with a feeling of helplessness. He hated to see his girls in so much pain and had no idea how to make it all better.

Why couldn't he fix this, there had to be an answer, something, anything that would bring peace back to his household. He had never known what to do when a woman cried and now he had a house full of crying females.

He picked Suzanne up in his arms, cradling her, comforting her as he carried her to her bed. After a gentle kiss on the cheek he laid her down and tucked her in assuring her everything would be alright. He would find a way to fix this... he would. Ray felt responsible for all of this. He had left Suzanne alone too much. He should have found a way to help her more, to be there for her.

Angel stopped crying as soon as he picked her up. Ray had a long Daddy-daughter talk with her as if she could understand every word. He calmly explained to her that Mommy was worn out and he had a lot of work to do. Maybe she would be content if she were able to watch him; to not be alone. The only answer was to drag her crib into the kitchen then lay her in it so he could talk to her as he worked.

Ray started doing dishes and making supper, at the same time talking and singing to Angel as he worked, Anna following him along trying to mimic everything he was doing, Daddy's little helper.

By the time he was done sweeping and vacuuming Angel was sound asleep with out screaming herself into exhaustion. It was a calm, peaceful sleep, the sleep of an Angel. This gave him opportunity to fix Suzanne a plate and lay in bed with her while she ate.

The room was filled with a heavy silence neither of them able to speak. He had never seen Suzanne's eyes filled with such sadness. It was as though she were lost in another world. The silence continued filling the room until it was time to go check on Anna and run her bath. As he walked toward the door he turned and told Suzanne how much he loved and needed her.

She was his entire world; he had no life without her. She was his life, his only life. He had two days at home he would handle everything. If Suzanne wanted to spend every minute of it in bed, that would be fine with him.

He wanted her to be all right and he would do whatever it would take for that to happen.

Ray was worried, Suzanne had not spoken, she hadn't even acknowledged his presence in the room nor anything he was saying. She had become a shell, an empty shell.

What kind of mother could do such a thing to her own baby? Being tired was no excuse. What if Ray hadn't come home when he did, how far would she have gone? It was the not knowing the answer to that question that upset and worried her the most.

Ray held her in his arms until she fell asleep. Then he quietly slipped out and did the supper dishes with his favorite helper. By this time Angel was awake, but she didn't wake up screaming.

It didn't take long to occur to Ray that it was the rats; she was scared to be in that room. Such a simple thing, why hadn't either of them thought of it sooner? He carried his baby daughter into the front room where the two of them watched television.

Ray continued chattering away to her explaining about football and everything they were doing wrong. Ray was a devout couch coach and very good at this profession. She looked up at him with her wide-eyed beauty; Daddy had her that was all that mattered.

She loved to hear Daddy's voice. She always stopped crying as soon as she heard it. Suzanne could only wish she had that kind of power over Angel. When Ray looked up he saw Anna peaking around the corner waiting to see if Daddy would smile at her, or tell her to go back to bed. She got the smile she was hoping for and came running into his arms.

Anna on one knee Angel on the other, Ray tried to remember when he last had time to sit this way with his girls. He promised them that they would do this more often, things were going to change. Daddy would be around more from now on, he would make the time for all the girls in his life. He then promised himself that he would keep all his promises.

It was hard explaining to a little girl that Mommy was tired and they would all try hard to make things easier for Mommy. Anna looked up, at her Daddy... "ANGEL BAD, ANNA GOOD GIRL "... Ray tried to find a way to explain to Anna that Angel wasn't a bad girl, she was being a baby. All babies cried it was just a matter of finding out why.

Daddy was going to try to fix everything so that Angel didn't have to cry all the time, then Mommy wouldn't be so tired. The first effort was to leave Angels crib in the kitchen, at least long enough to test his theory.

Suzanne thought it was all so ridiculous. He was encouraging her to be weak. If she had a fear they should force her to face it. To Ray this was a cruelty, something his mother-in-law would think of.

His mind was made up; Angel would stay in the kitchen and there would be no discussion.

Suzanne's mother picked her up for a doctor's appointment. It was Suzanne's first time out of bed in a couple days. Even with days of bed rest she seemed to get even more tired.

The doctor didn't give her the news she either expected or wanted to hear... Suzanne was pregnant again and would need a couple more days on bed rest. She had half suspected but didn't dare seriously think about it.

Ray would be pleased; there was another chance at the son he so desperately wanted. When she arrived home she went to bed not saying a word. Somehow, she thought if she didn't say the words maybe it wouldn't be real all the time knowing deep in her heart it was.

She couldn't stop thinking of what happened with Angel what if ... what if ... she really didn't want to hurt Angel. She just wanted her to stop. That wasn't the full truth either. What she wanted was for Angel to not "BE "but to have never been. She didn't hate her she just didn't want her.

What if she had these same feelings for this child? What if she was only capable of loving one child? She so wanted this pregnancy to be some terrible joke or maybe a bad dream that she would wake up from any moment.

Unfortunately it wasn't a joke and she was wide awake. It was not going away and she needed to face it and deal with it. She could hear her mother's favorite, nasty expression ring through her head... "YOU MADE YOUR BED, LIE IN IT..." It seemed to Suzanne her mother had been saying that to her or about her all her life.

Ray could see the change in his wife but didn't know what to do. All he could do was walk on eggs and keep the girls out of Suzanne's hair as much as possible. There had to be something he could do to pull her out of her depression.

He was looking at her; she was looking at herself. He could not remember the last time she laughed, let alone smiled. Ray would give almost anything to see the little girl smile that would cover her entire face whenever he entered a room. She had become no more than a shell, going through the motions of a day to day routine.

He knew that the only thing that would work was to get her away for awhile. She needed a break; to feel like a person again, not a mother, not a wife or homemaker, but a pampered spoiled little girl.

It would be early June before he could even get a short amount of vacation time. That would give him a month and a half to put something spectacular together. It would have to be a secret, not only would it be more exciting but he worried if she could handle the disappointment if he couldn't get the time.

He was very secretive the entire trip to Toronto. He talked about everything except where they were going or what they were doing. Neither of them could feel good about leaving the kids with Suzanne's mother, but there was no one else who could take the kids for the full ten days.

The Royal York was the best and the finest hotel in the Toronto area. Even as Ray was pulling into the parking lot Suzanne was sure it was all a joke. She kept expecting him to laugh and pull out of the lot.

Even when he went so far as to walk in the front door and pretend to check in, she expected him to turn back. When he didn't she was in shock; following him, hoping that if it was all a dream she would never wake up.

As they stepped off the elevator Ray scooped her up in his arms and carried her the rest of the way. She curled herself around him like being carried was the most natural thing in the world. They melted together, they were always meant to be one. For the first time in a long time, she renewed the feelings she had when they first started dating. She knew why she fell in love with this man.

There were no babies, no diapers, no rats, no farm, and most important there was no isolation and no feelings of loneliness. She was born for this life, it fit her like a glove; unlike Ray who never knew how to dress, what to say or even which fork to use.

Knowing how much Ray hated all this made her love him all the more. Ray excused himself using going for cigarettes as an excuse. That was fine, she was in heaven, spinning circles and hugging herself. This gave her the opportunity to check out every detail of the room. She didn't want to miss a thing, especially feeling like an only child at Christmas.

To Suzanne it was Christmas and Ray was Santa Claus. He walked through the door with the biggest most beautifully decorated box she had ever seen. She sat on the bed with the box on her lap, not wanting the moment to end.

The box was far more beautiful than anything that could be inside of it. It was Ray that finally ripped open the box, as he grinned from ear to ear like a Cheshire cat. Paralyzed, she sat staring not blinking, breathing, or making a sound. Maybe if she didn't move, the moment wouldn't pass and time would stand still.

A small tear escaped and trickled down her cheek. Now it was Ray that was concerned, what could he have done wrong? He got one of his sisters-in-law to help him pick it out. But really they were all farmers wives and knew nothing about style and fashion. He stammered out an apology, he so wanted everything to be perfect. Suzanne dove on him, covering him with kisses, about a hundred all on his face. It was a game they played when they were dating; a game he loved. He finally got to see that little girl he once knew, his princess was back.

There were tears all over her face as she took the dress out of the box. Raising it ever so slowly, paying attention to every detail. Her eyes spotted the spaghetti straps then moved down to the beaded bodice that had been designed to hug the body. She wondered if she could still wear this style after two babies and a third one on the way in six months.

The skirt was full and shear with many layers of cherry red material. Under the dress in the same box was a matching handbag and heals.

It was all so perfect, every detail. But the most perfect of all was the theater tickets to "THE KING AND I ".

Suzanne dove on Ray, wanting to make love to him. She wanted to feel him deep inside of her. Most of all she wanted to feel like they were new lovers. For the moment, nothing existed outside of them.

She knew Ray must have spent their entire savings and she didn't care. She felt like she had stepped into a fairytale and she was Cinderella at the Ball, Ray was her romantic Prince Charming and nothing was too good for his princess.

Looking into Suzanne's eyes, Ray could once again see the little girl spark he fell in love with so long ago. The look in her eyes, the spark of life and the recapturing of their passions all made the efforts worthwhile.

That night Suzanne did not think about her girls. She didn't think about the house. She didn't think about her pregnancy, she didn't even care how much it all cost. She was swimming in more love than she had ever felt for their entire relationship and nothing else mattered. For one night she was the Princess.

After they left the Royal York they went on to a friend's cottage. They would be able to spend a week getting to know each other with no kids, no pressures, only the two of them in love. They gave each other a promise that they would not discuss anything that came anywhere near kids or worries.

Only two days passed when they received a frantic call from Suzanne's mother. It was Angel... she had not eaten or drank since they left. Not crying or fussing in any way, she lay very still, staring with sad empty eyes. The doctor couldn't find anything wrong with her; however, if she didn't start eating soon she would have to be hospitalized.

Suzanne didn't believe a word of this. She was sure it was her mother's way of making her life miserable, as she had always done everything she could to make Suzanne as unhappy as possible. She had never for Suzanne's entire life allowed her to have anything that might be good or fun in anyway. She hated that Suzanne might even have a moment of happiness.

Ray couldn't believe how Suzanne was reacting to this. He knew they had to get back right away. He was frantic for the five-hour drive and really couldn't understand why Suzanne had this attitude and wasn't worried. He was worried enough for both of them.

Suzanne bounced back and forth between blaming her mother and blaming Angel. She acted like she thought this five-month-old baby was doing this on purpose. Ray thought maybe Suzanne had a case of temporary insanity and would come to her senses once they got home and found out what was going on.

He would never say it out loud, but he felt she was being incredibly selfish. He was seeing a new side of Suzanne or maybe it was always there and he never noticed.

Suzanne walked in the house and picked up her children without saying a word to her mother, giving her a very cold, dark glare. It was Ray who went back into the house to talk to Suzanne's mother. She swore she didn't make it up and they should call the doctor tomorrow.

By the time Ray got out to the car, Suzanne was holding Angel who was drinking a bottle, half starved unable to get it down quickly enough. He couldn't believe how cold and angry Suzanne looked. She wanted to scream at someone but couldn't figure out whom.

Suzanne had about all she could take of Angel and all her spoiled fussy behavior. Couldn't sleep in the bedroom, can only sleep in the kitchen, can't sleep with the light off, so the light stays on twenty four hours a day, now the...." LITTLE PRINCESS "... is too good to be left with a sitter for a couple days.

Suzanne knew that all this anger she felt for Angel was totally irrational, selfish and extremely childish. As she stood looking into the mirror talking to herself trying to get a grip on her emotions, it was her mother's face she saw in the reflection.

She saw that evil glare that glassed over look of insanity that her mother would get before backhanding her into next week. It scared Suzanne, to think she could become her mother, and now she stood staring at her scariest trait.

She took a deep breath and walked into the next room. First, she gave Ray a long, strong hug and apology, he was right they should have come back. Her next step was to go into the kitchen and get Angel. She gave the baby a sweet, gentle kiss and promised to try hard to love her more. Suzanne wondered why this baby was so hard to love. Why couldn't it come naturally like it did with Anna?

She sat in the oversized rocker, Anna on one knee and Angel on the other. As she rocked, she told Anna her favorite fairytale. Ray looked at his three girls and sighed a sigh of relief, everything would be alright now.

Everything was always so simple for Ray, so black and white. Ray not only had no grey in his life, he had no understanding of why Suzanne's entire life was always in the grey. There was always a "BUT "...things could never be simply exactly as they were.

Even though the trip was cut short it was worthwhile. Suzanne seemed calmer, even the girls seemed better. After the winter and the spring they had put in, the summer went well; they were closer than they had ever been as a family.

Suzanne was handling the new pregnancy at times she almost seemed pleased about it.

The new baby was due near Christmas; a son would be the perfect gift. They wouldn't even consider the possibility of a girl, or at least Ray wouldn't. Suzanne couldn't think of anything else.

The summer disappeared all too fast. As the days shortened and the weather cooled, Suzanne busied herself doing all the canning from their garden. She may have hated farm life but she loved having fresh vegetables. Even when money was tight there was always something to eat. Her mother even came to help her several times.

Suzanne was surprised at small moments of closeness, little minuscule specks of understanding and respect, fleeting, but there none the less. With the beginnings of understanding was hope. Hope that one-day forgiveness and approval would follow. Well, maybe Suzanne wasn't quite ready for that, but they had reached a point of tolerance and that was half the battle.

As the winter grew closer she could feel the winter blues creeping up on her. Suzanne never understood why she got so emotional and depressed in the winter, maybe because she had spent the last three winters as big as a house, due to chronic pregnancy. She was only half way through and she was already sick to death of being pregnant.

It seemed to her that every pregnancy and every winter was harder to handle. She was spending more and more time in her bed. Ray tried to talk to her. She was... "JUST TIRED" ... and went back to bed. Suzanne couldn't see any reason to talk to Ray. He wouldn't understand. No one understood.

Suzanne spent much of her time feeling sorry for herself, pulling further and further away from everyone. She needed to be alone. It seemed to Ray that was all she ever said to him...

"LEAVE ME ALONE... "

Very slowly, very subtly, they were pulling further and further apart. Ray could feel something was missing. He missed that little girl bubble of excitement. He could not remember the last time she laughed.

Occasionally he would get a controlled smile, a subtle longing. There were even times she seemed to be peaceful. Ray wished he could crawl inside of her and see what was behind the sadness in those eyes.

For Ray, life had gotten so much better. It was exactly the way he wanted it to be; his girls and a farm. He was finally making enough money at the factory that he only needed one job, giving him more time to help Suzanne.

This pregnancy seemed to take so much out of her, leaving her tired all the time. He told himself everything would be better once the baby came. He was sure it was only hormones; all women get emotional while pregnant. The mood swings would stop after the baby came. Wouldn't they? At least that was what he hoped and prayed for.

The day finally came... Suzanne gave birth to a bouncing baby ... GIRL. Suzanne was thankful she wasn't a gambler because she sure had no luck in her life. Ray smiled a brave smile and said a girl was better. He'd had lots of practice with girls. He wouldn't have known how to deal with a boy anyway.

Ray and the girls spent Christmas alone that year; Suzanne was anemic and had to stay over in the hospital. She came home three days later and Ray fixed a surprise dinner. Ray spent as little time as possible in the kitchen; Suzanne could not help but smile as he made his way around this strange territory. She did feel good that he cared enough to try. Suzanne never knew if the meal was good or bad, she enjoyed every bite with love.

The next couple years flew by without any dramatic incidents. Anna was getting ready to start kindergarten, Angel could not understand why she could not go; they had always gone everywhere together. Alice, the youngest, was almost potty trained. Suzanne dreamed about how good life would be with no diapers in it. It would certainly be a touch of heaven.

Chapter Three

They all went to Suzanne's mothers for Easter that year, but somehow things were different. Her mother was very quiet, almost withdrawn. She didn't even criticize Suzanne, although Suzanne spent the entire meal waiting for it to come. She worried more that the criticism wasn't there.

During the drive home Ray and Suzanne couldn't help but discuss how tired and old her mother had become in what seemed like a short period of time. Suzanne didn't spend any more time with her mother than she had to, but she knew something was wrong.

She would call her Dad as soon as she got home. She could grill him for information that she knew her mother would not divulge. Her mother would have simply brushed her off as it was none of her business or anyone else's.

Her father couldn't tell her much; all he could tell her was that his wife, her mother was tired all the time. Suzanne knew what that meant when she was tired but doubted that was her mother's problem.

Her father knew that his wife had gone to the doctor, but had not confided in him as she never confided in him. They had quit speaking except for dire necessity or social gatherings to save face, most of their marriage was a big farce, fabricated to keep face in the town.

Many years ago he had made a serious mistake a mistake he could never take back, but refused to regret. He had loved her deeply and if she had lived, it would have changed all their lives.

AFFAIR!... WHAT AFFAIR?... NOT MY DAD!!... WHEN? ... HOW?... WHO?... this had to be a joke. Her dad would never have done anything like that. Her mind was flooding; full of the thousand questions she wanted the answers to.

These weren't strangers, they were her parents, and she knew nothing about them. How could she have spent her life in the same house as these people and not have known any of this? She searched her memories trying to remember some hint or clue.

Was that why her mother was so desperate for things to be perfect for her father? Why she always quit yelling as soon as he came through the door? Her mother lived by propriety and that was all they were allowed to see.

Always holding her head high, always in control, it was no one's business what emotions she felt or what difficulty she had in her life. Her father was hesitant to discuss any of it. Suzanne had to know she would keep prying 'til she got the answers she needed.

This was her family, her life, she had grown up with a hateful mother and she had the right to know why. It was her business, and she would have answers. Her father started the explanation with.... the affair had happened before Suzanne was born, it was with the Aunt, Suzanne was named after, they had all come from England together shortly after their marriage.

Even then she was a screamer, all the time. She was always so angry completely different than her sister. Her sister was gentle and kind, he couldn't help but fall in love with her. When she died in childbirth it nearly killed him, he couldn't stand that he had lost her.

At the time there was no other choice but to go back to his wife, who punished him for his indiscretion all these years. He allowed this as a retribution for his guilt. He was filled with guilt for his lost love, guilt for his disastrous marriage. He had hurt so many people.

What happened to the child? Suzanne had to know, but he refused to discuss the matter any further, she would never know that her mother was her aunt and that because of his indiscretions she had to be raised by a woman that hated and resented her. Suzanne was a constant reminder to her mother that her husband didn't love her.

This new insight into her mother's heartache, answered some questions for Suzanne, but raised many others. She tried to get her father to fill in more details to discuss it further. He was adamant he had said all he was going to say on the matter and never wanted to hear about it again. He was already regretting telling her what he had told her.

It was only a few months later that Ray and Suzanne were startled out of their sleep at two a.m. by a banging on the front door. They lay very still in bed, holding their breath, in hopes that whoever it was would go away.

There was something about a knock in the middle of the night that always put chills in a person's bones. On the second knock, Angel woke up crying. They had no choice, they had to go down and answer it.

Ray stumbled around trying to find something he could use as a weapon, finally settling for the broom from the hall. Suzanne wondered how long it would take to get help this far out. They knew the entire thing was ridiculous, no burglar or mass murderer would bother to knock; but they were still spooked and being cautious.

When he finally got to the front door he could hear a familiar voice in a whispered yell. It was Suzanne's father. Ray wasn't prepared for what he saw. His father-in-law looked terrible. It was obvious that he had been crying.

Suzanne's Dad had survived two wars and the Depression; he was one of the strongest men Ray had ever met. Ray couldn't even imagine what could be bad enough for this rock to crumble.

Ray watched him as he staggered over to a chair and collapsed into it, breaking into uncontrolled sobs. Ray had never seen a man cry, he didn't know how to handle it. He wanted to leave the room, to get away from whatever it was. He felt even more helpless than he did when Suzanne cried and she was a girl; it was expected from her.

Suzanne ran to her father, desperate to know what was going on. She hated to see him weak; he had always been strong. She could not, her entire life; remember seeing either her father or her mother show the slightest sign of emotion.

Her father grabbed at his youngest daughter, holding her so tight she thought she would snap in two. Suzanne began crying as hard as her father, begging him to tell her what was wrong, what was happening? He squeezed the breath out of her as he forced out the words he didn't want to accept ... "SHE IS DEAD... "

Relieved to leave them alone Ray went to make coffee, any excuse to escape the discomfort that he was being swallowed up by. He was no good with emotional outbursts. He didn't know how to act or react. Ray could never figure out if it was better to be strong or comforting. Was he expected to fall apart with them? The entire situation made him very uncomfortable.

By the time he came back they had stopped crying enough that they could talk. Suzanne's father didn't understand what happened. His wife had sent him out with a long list of chores that had to be done, no different than any other time. She liked to keep him busy so he would be out of her hair. He often thought she made the "TO DO LISTS " ... up to get rid of him for a few hours of peace.

Pay bills, get groceries, drop this off, pick that up, etc... It kept him busy and away from the house most of the day. When he finally got home she was in bed so he didn't disturb her. He wanted to let her sleep; she had been so tired. He busied himself putting away the groceries and making dinner, thinking it would be a nice surprise, something he rarely did.

When he entered her room carrying a tray he called out to her, then he yelled. She wouldn't answer. Even when he shook her, she wouldn't answer. He had no idea how long she had been dead. He had left her alone at least two hours after he got home. If only he had checked her when he first got home ... maybe he could have saved her ... maybe she was still alive ... if only.

By the bed he found two empty pill bottles and a note only saying ... "I AM SORRY..." He called the doctor he had to know... "WHY!!!"... She had a script for pain pills and sleeping pills. The doctor told him she had cancer and would have died a long and agonizing death.

They had been married forty years and she couldn't tell him she was dying. She owed him that much, he should have been allowed to make things right, to apologize, to tell her he loved her. How could he be so blind? How could he know so little about the woman he shared his life with?

They had quit sleeping in the same bed together many years before, but they still shared their lives or should have. He sat silently, staring. Suzanne knew he was trying to make sense of it all, trying to figure out how they got to this point. When had they become strangers?

Eventually he drifted off to sleep; Suzanne knew he couldn't go home. He had never been in a house alone his entire life. She wondered how he would deal with this. All her brothers and sister were married and gone off on their own.

Suzanne wondered why her family wasn't closer, more like a real family. She couldn't remember ever feeling like they were a family, even when she was a little girl. She had memories of friends going on family outings and get togethers.

She always thought they were odd for wanting to spend time with their family. She tried to stay as far away from her family as she could. The only time they got together as a family was when her mother insisted. For some social gathering; to put on whatever pompous act her mother wanted to perform for the neighbors or church. Even Ray's family had regular family reunions that everyone actually seemed to enjoy.

Suzanne thought she would never fall asleep. It was without a doubt the longest night she had ever put in. She was drowning in all the pain and hurt she had spent a lifetime trying to push deep down inside of her. It was erupting like a volcano that had brewed for many years. Now there was no stopping it from pouring out, no end of hot burning lava.

Suzanne was filled with guilt, she should be concentrating on the good not the bad and painful. The harder she tried to remember the good times the more the bad consumed her. Suzanne was sure there had to be some time when they were happy together. There had to be good memories somewhere, a time without pain, a time when they were all a family.

It made her even angrier that she could only think of the bad, the painful, and the hated. Now she hated her even more. She hated her for dying before Suzanne could find out why her mother hated her so much. How dare she leave everyone in so much pain?

Wasn't it like her, the final big pain, devastating everyone in one fell swoop? Suzanne felt she would never find the answers. That she would never be at peace inside, she would never know the answers to her pain.

The next morning Ray left Suzanne and his father-in-law sleeping while he made the appropriate calls. He knew neither his wife nor his father-in-law was capable of it. Ray looked through the address book, trying to decide whom to call first, as he realized what a nightmare this funeral was going to be. He had never known a family so torn apart, so full of petty jealousy and anger toward each other.

Suzanne had not spoken to her sister in over five years. Ray was never sure why. They were both too proud and stubborn to let things go. Even the brothers never spoke to each other. He had to be careful; if he called the wrong person first there would be bad blood.

The only way of doing it was by seniority. Then if anyone got their nose out of joint he could say he went from oldest to youngest. It was already bad enough that his father-in-law came to them first.

They all hated Suzanne because she had always been Daddy's little girl, Daddy's princess. Almost every disagreement Suzanne had with her siblings someone spouted out the hated words with sharpness and pain; the same tone her mother had always used.

Ray no sooner started making calls than there were knocks at the door. The house was full of Suzanne's family in no time. They were all angry and at each other's throat. Ray stood numb, how could they call themselves a family.

Ray decided to leave all the chickens in the coupe pecking at each other while he got his girls out of the range of fire. He packed his three princesses up and took them to the park where he stayed all day. As he watched his two little girls playing in the sand he thanked God they liked each other and prayed they always would.

On the way to the park, he stopped at a pay phone to call his mother. He needed to be reassured there were people in the world that loved each other and had rational thought. Every time he spent more than a few consecutive moments with Suzanne's family, he was thankful for the family his parents raised him in.

As he drove home, he prayed as hard as he could that everyone had left. After all, how long could so many people who hated each other stay under the same roof? Pulling into the lane he could see all the cars and thought about turning and running, but the girls were tired and needed a nap. He decided to bite the bullet and go in.

When he walked in the door, it was far too quiet, almost a haunting quiet. Suzanne and her sister were hugging and talking through buckets of tears; her brothers were shaking hands and patting each other on the back.

Ray shook his head, sure this had to be a strange dream he could wake himself from. As he looked around, the table was covered with more food than he had ever seen casseroles, salads, cold chicken, cakes and desserts of all kinds. Everyone stayed well into the night. Ray had never gotten to know Suzanne's family as there had always been too much anger to get through.

Mostly he did what he could to keep her as far from them as possible. Now that he was sitting and talking to them, they weren't half bad. He started to believe it wouldn't take much to be friends with any of them.

On the last day of the viewing, after everyone else had left; Suzanne asked Ray to leave her there alone... she needed to speak to her mother.

Ray looked at her like she was crazy, he shouted... "YOUR MOTHER IS DEAD, YOU CAN'T BRING HER BACK ... YOU CAN'T CHANGE THE PAST "...

He hugged her and begged her to let her mother go. Suzanne had unfinished business and Ray would have to understand. If he could not understand then he should trust that she was doing what she had to do.

Ray would never say it out loud, but in his heart he was glad and thankful that his mother-in-law was gone. She had caused everyone that ever got close to her no end of pain. He had always wondered why she had no guilt or remorse about any of it.

There were times he felt she enjoyed seeing people hurt and the one she liked to hurt the most was Suzanne. Anyone else would have put something in the note that would give loved ones some sort of peace of mind. Not her, she would be a hurtful bitch right to the end.

As Suzanne stood beside the coffin looking at her mother so still and quiet; all she could think about was how sad it was that her mother had to be dead before anyone could get a word in. They all had words to say to her, words of heartache and pain held in for years.

Was her mother now rolling in her coffin at what her family actually had to say to her? Was she up there some where feeling and hearing the pain her family had. Pain she had caused. Did she now as a spirit have any regret or guilt for that pain?

There was a little girl deep down inside of Suzanne that still needed her mother's love and approval. She had always wanted her mother to be proud of her and if she couldn't have that, then she at least wanted her mother to like her.

To Suzanne her mother liking her was far more important than love. To her, love was not important. Her mother told her she loved her all the time. Even when she was beating her, she told her she loved her.

Mass murderers, thieves, and wife beaters all had people that loved them, but they weren't liked. Being liked, now that was what was important; that was what made a person special.

That had been her goal with her mother for what seemed to be her entire life, now it was too late. She would never make her mother like her, be proud of her. She would never prove to her mother that she was someone worth spending time with, someone she could like, someone special.

What was more important than even that were the unanswered questions ... " WHY?! "... Why was she such a disappointment to her mother? Why did her mother dislike her so much? Why didn't her mother make some kind of effort to get past all the anger she felt for Suzanne or at least tell her what she did to cause her mother to dislike her so much for her entire life?

Suzanne tried hard to remember when it all started. Was it one particular thing she had done and her mother never forgave her? No matter how far back Suzanne went, the anger and the hatred was always there. Occasionally she could remember moments of cold tolerance, but never pride or a sense of liking the person Suzanne had become.

As she looked into the open coffin she was overcome with hysteria... "WHY DID YOU HATE ME??... WHEN DID IT START?? ... WHAT DID I DO?? " ... It was at that moment her father came into the room and put his arms around her.... "IT WASN'T YOU PRINCESS... SHE HATED THE WORLD "...

He hoped that maybe now she could find some peace, maybe they could all find peace.

He wanted all his children to let go of the pain or they would end up as angry and hateful as their mother had been. He wanted to remember her as a young girl. As she was when she was still full of life and hope; before she had been beaten down with heartache.

That night Suzanne and her father sat up all night talking. It seemed to Suzanne she was talking to a stranger, listening to stories about a bigger stranger. Her mother had been brutally attacked and raped while still no more than a very young girl. She had nightmares all her life and never got over it.

Her father then went on to tell her how she had grown up in one of the hardest ghettos in England. Her father was a drunken abuser of the entire family. He forced her to work at a very young age and to give the money to him so he could maintain his drunken stupor. There was never a time that they weren't cold, hungry and filled with fear.

Her father explained these things to her so she could understand her mother's hardness and obsession with being socially acceptable. There were some things however he could not bring himself to tell her. Family secrets that were too embarrassing or too painful to tell.

Secrets that would make her hate him forever. She would never know that someone else was her mother. That it was her aunt who had bore his illegitimate child; that his wife had agreed to take the child, but could never love her.

Suzanne was a constant reminder of her husband's disloyalty and betrayal. How her own sister, a sister she had rescued from the slums and a life too horrific to think about ... returned the good deed by trying to steal not only her husband but her entire life. Bringing shame and disgrace to her household.

Suzanne didn't need to know his shame or feel it. Why should she be ashamed of who she was? She had been made out of love and he had always loved her and her mother. Perhaps he loved her more because she was the only thing left of her mother.

He had many regrets to hurting the people in his life he was supposed to love, but he never regretted having Suzanne as part of his family. His only real regret was that she had been raised with such hatred and anger, that she had to be punished over and over again for his indiscretion. He should have stood up to his wife, forced her to treat his princess better.

Somehow Suzanne got a new understanding of her mother that night. For the first time in her life she was able to feel something for her mother other than hatred ... pity was what she was now filled with.

She was filled with all kinds of emotions, none of them were love. Why couldn't someone have told her years ago? Maybe they could have built on this and understood each other. Why did her mother have to die before they could get to know each other? Why couldn't her mother have confided in her? Let someone, anyone in.

Her mother believed you lived the life you were given and do the best you can with it. Anything else would be whinny weakness. Weakness was something she could never tolerate. She hated people who were always trying to get someone to feel sorry for them by whining and crying about things that happened to them in their life. Did whining make it go away? Did it change anything?

It only made you weak for people to walk on you. In her mother's mind, she wasn't beating her children she was doing them a favor by strengthening them and preparing them for the hardship of the world. A world that was sure to stomp all over them if they weren't strong enough to stand up to whatever it dished out. She truly believed she would have been doing her children a disservice to coddle them.

For the first time in as far back as she could remember, Suzanne slept that night and slept well; no thrashing, no nightmares, solid peaceful sleep. As Ray lay in bed with Suzanne, watching her sleep, he could see a calm sort of peacefulness in her sleep, a calm that had never been there before. Maybe everyone could get on with their lives now.

Chapter Four

Suzanne's Dad had stayed with them since before the funeral. She knew he could not go back into that house alone. They offered for him to move in with them... it was foolish for them to pay rent when he owned a house big enough for all of them.

Ray couldn't argue, he could see the hope in Suzanne's eyes he knew how badly she wanted this. She had always wanted this from the first night they had spent on the farm. So they all prepared to move into the home Suzanne had grown up in.

Suzanne was filled with many emotions. She could hardly wait to get back to town. The first thing she would do was have all her old friends over for coffee. She had been incredibly lonely for the past two years. It was a quiet suffering. How could she tell Ray that he and the girls were not enough?

The more Ray listened to Suzanne chatter with excitement, the more the move to town scared him. She was full of excitement with the prospect of reuniting with her school girl friends. He had Suzanne to himself and liked it that way. He knew even if she didn't there was no time for friends; she had three girls and a husband to take care of. She had her time with giggly girls when she was in school, now it was time to grow up and be a mother and a wife.

Ray stood in the driveway taking one last look. He thought about the garden he wouldn't work in, the woods he wouldn't hunt in with his brothers. He listened to the silence he would never hear again. He smelled the air, clean country air that he had wanted his girls to grow up in. As he got into his car and drove away he tried to reassure himself the move was only temporary, that he would save the money to buy his own farm. That was what his mind told himself over and over but his heart sank, as he knew the truth. The truth was that Suzanne hated the farm and would never allow him to move her back onto another one.

What kind of life would his girls have in town? He wasn't sure about the two little ones, but Anna took after his side and loved the farm. He would miss most of all the time he spent with his girls helping him on the farm. They loved to pull the weeds and gather eggs; they were a family working the family farm together.

Suzanne could see the sadness in Ray's face and knew he would hate it in town. No more than she hated it on the farm for the past two years. She had taken her turn of being lonely and miserable; it was his turn to give a little, to adapt to her way of life. It was her time for some happiness.

Her girls were not going to be uneducated country girls. They would have all the charm and polish they could only get by not only living in town, but, in the best neighborhood around the best people. They would have all the polish her mother had tried so hard to get into her. It would be different if they were boys, girls needed breeding and she was the one who could see to it they got it.

That first day home was such a whirlwind of emotions and excitement. There was something about being back in her own room; she was twelve years old again.

When Ray climbed in bed with her, she felt like they were doing something bad and sneaky. She couldn't stand the thought of her Daddy hearing them together. Being married didn't help, in her heart she was still Daddy's little girl and now that they were back under his roof it was all reconfirmed.

Her mother had to be rolling over in her grave. If there was any way she could come up from that grave to voice her disapproval and haunt them to their own grave Suzanne was sure she would... It was over a week, before she could even make love to Ray, even then she wasn't comfortable with it, but was sick to death of putting him off.

Suzanne was in nostalgia heaven. She spent her day's playing cards with her Dad and her girlfriends, talking about old school days. When Suzanne got together with her friends, it was nonstop laughter, everyday.

Ray wondered why she couldn't be that happy with him. She never had time for him anymore, at least not alone. She totally denied this, after all she was always home. She never went anywhere. Not even when her friends begged her to go out with them on girls' night outings.

He didn't like her to have friends and hated to see her happy. She felt like she had lots of time for him but he wanted all of her time and energy. It seemed to her that he was trying to suck all the life out of her and make her into an old lady before her time. Suzanne had all her friends and her Dad to agree and support her.

Ray started feeling, it didn't matter if he came home from work or not. Once in a while he would stop at the local bar for a quick one after work. At first it was one every once in a while, then a couple one day a week, then a couple days a week, then everyday as long as he was home for supper.

Who cared!? Suzanne sure didn't seem to notice ... or care. If she didn't care then why should he? After all she had lots of company that she liked a lot better than his. It was obvious to Ray that she simply didn't need him any more; she had Daddy to put the roof over her head and friends for company. There was simply no place for him in her new world.

It took about a year for Ray to become a full-fledged alcoholic. He was a heavy drinker when Suzanne met him, but he hadn't touched a drop since they were married almost seven years ago. Suzanne couldn't figure out where all this drinking business was coming from.

It was actually a slow and gradual progression but to Suzanne who hadn't been paying attention, it seemed to happen over night. She was having too much fun with her friends to notice he had become invisible in the household. In self defense or perhaps for revenge he started coming home later and later, drunker and drunker.

They fought nonstop, neither was willing to budge or even accept responsibility... "IF YOU SPENT MORE TIME WITH ME I WOULDN'T HAVE TO DRINK!"..." IF YOU DIDN'T DRINK I WOULD BE ABLE TO STAND BEING WITH YOU " ... They were both wrong and they were both hurting.

In reality it was three little girls that hurt the most. Neither of them had time for parenting. Anna missed her story at bedtime, Angel missed being rocked, and sweet Alice didn't have much of a chance to get used to anything.

Suzanne's Dad tried to fill in some of the gaps, but to the girls it wasn't the same. They loved their grandpa but they missed and needed Mom and Dad, who seemed to only have, time for fighting and screaming.

Suzanne eventually reached a point where she preferred it if Ray did not come home. The very sight of him made her sick. The constant smell of old cigarettes and booze repulsed her. His very touch made her skin crawl. There was nothing more disgusting than being pawed at by a slobbering drunk.

He had lost that gentle sweetness he had when they were making love. Now it was a wrestling match... him grabbing at her... her pushing him away. Once in a while she would force herself to lie down with him, thinking it was her duty. But couldn't remember the last time she enjoyed being touched by him. For one fleeting moment she remembered back to a time when she couldn't get enough of him.

She wanted to be lost in the memory of that time a time when she not only enjoyed his touch and his company...." HE " was all she could think about when he wasn't with her. Why was he doing this at a time when everything was so good? They had everything they could ever want. Suzanne believed life would be perfect if only Ray would quit drinking and go back to the way he was when they were first married.

Ray didn't know how it happened, but his father-in-law had taken everything away from him... his wife, his home, even his girls. He had no home to go home to and no one who cared if he was there.

The girl that he rescued and protected didn't need him anymore. She had Daddy to do all that. What did she need him for? She didn't even seem to need him for sex. All she ever did was push him away.

Ray wondered whom she was sleeping with if it wasn't him. She must be getting it somewhere; she used to be so passionate. There was a time when Ray couldn't keep up with her. Now he had to practically beg her and guilt her into lying down with him for a few minutes.

Even then she acted like he couldn't finish quick enough. Probably so she could get back to her friends, whoever they were. Ray was sure there had to be something going on. One thing was sure; it was something that didn't include him.

With the help of her Dad, Suzanne learned to drive. With a new license in tow she had a new freedom an independence she had never felt before. No longer was she a little girl dependent on her Daddy or her husband to take her anywhere. No longer would she have to beg Ray to drive her someplace that he may or may not approve of. From now on if she wanted to GO, she went!

To celebrate this new found freedom her friends dragged her to an out of town bar. If Suzanne had gone to one in town, she took the chance of having to deal with a drunken Ray in public in a town where people knew them both.

Suzanne had never been in a bar, nor even drank for that matter. Ray had always told her only tramps looking to get picked up went to bars. It was certainly no place for married women or women with any kind of moral caliber.

Suzanne knew Ray must be wrong... all her friends went into bars and they weren't looking to be picked up. They went to dance and laugh, to have a good time and feel good.

Suzanne wasn't sure what she expected when she walked through the door that night. She felt scared and excited all at the same time.

She wasn't even half way across the parking lot; she could feel and hear the air filled with music and laughter.

She could feel her adrenaline pumping as her heart made its way into her throat. Her hands were trembling as her palms began to sweat. She wasn't this nervous the first time she made love to Ray.

When they got inside they all were asked for I.D. It made her feel good that she still looked young. But then, she was young, she had just turned twenty-three. She had married Ray when she was only sixteen that seemed like a hundred years ago.

Her friends picked a little table near the dance floor. When the waiter came, Suzanne didn't have a clue. All she knew about drinking was how bad it smelled on Ray and she was pretty sure anything that smelled that bad had to be awful.

One of her friends ordered her a Planter's Punch, a strange combination of fruit juices with a kick. She liked that it went down easy, too easy. Her friends warned her to slow down on the second one. Suzanne found it hard to believe she could get drunk on fruit juice.

A nice looking gentleman came over and sat down beside her, he was drawn to her great beauty. He took her hand and stared deep into her eyes. She was scared and embarrassed yet somehow delighted.

Pulling her hand away she said she was married. She could see how that would be easy to forget in a place like this ... she almost forgot it herself. One of her friends told him to shove off, it was girls night ... he kissed Suzanne's hand and left.

The girls giggled and laughed, teasing Suzanne at his hoakiness, Suzanne also laughed, but in her heart she was drawn to the hoakiness. It was that hoakiness that drew her to Ray. That is the old Ray, the romantic lover Ray that she loved more than anything else in her life.

She liked that a stranger was treating her like an attractive woman. She had spent her entire life being Daddy's little girl then Ray's little princess. Ray was her knight, protector to the helpless little girl that needed to be rescued.

It was now clear to Suzanne that Ray and her father had not protected her from life but held her prisoner, keeping her the little girl that they needed her to be so they could feel manlier. There was an entire world out there that she had never even imagined she could be a part of.

All that was about to change she was an adult now, an adult that could not only live in the real world but experience and enjoy all that it had to offer. Suzanne danced, laughed, then danced some more. She fell on the floor in giddy drunkenness, loving every embarrassing moment.

She even went so far as to dance with a total stranger, a fast one of course. She was sure it would be all right as long as they didn't actually touch. Now she understood why Ray went to the bars so often, it had been a long time since she had felt so good or laughed so hard. He could have shared the fun and brought her once in a while.

The only thing she could figure was that he didn't want her to have any fun. Didn't he try to keep her on the farm away from the rest of the world and all this fun? She knew she had to find a way of doing this again, even if she had to sneak out.

It seemed to only be a blink 'til the night was over and a very tired waitress was trying to nudge them all out the door. It was one of the other girls that drove home that night pouring Suzanne into her front door and onto the couch.

———

Ray crawled through the door a little before midnight, not too worried about Suzanne being mad. More sure she wouldn't even know he was gone. Staggering through the dark house he tripped his way up the stairs to their bed. Maybe if he woke her up slow she wouldn't be too mad to snuggle.

It had been such a long time since they simply held each other and drifted off to sleep in the warmth of each other's arms. Ray had trouble remembering the last time they even slept facing each other. He had been making love to a very cold back for a long time. It seemed like it was at least as long as they had lived in her father's house.

For a moment his mind and heart went back to the farm, he missed it so. He missed how they were a family. They weren't a family any more just a bunch of strangers living under the same roof, but not in the same worlds.

He couldn't believe Suzanne wasn't there. He kept wandering from room to room as though it were all a bad joke. He kept asking his father-in-law whom he dragged out of bed… Where she was?! Who she was with?

This was crazy, in all the years they were married never had he come home and not found Suzanne waiting for him. By one a.m. he was a crazy person. Now, it was almost two a.m.; he had already called all of her friends, hospitals and the police.

Only driving less than a week, anything could have happened. Once he ruled out accident or death, he started to get angry. The anger became rage. How dare she leave him worrying? How dare she be screwing around with God knows who? "WHO "…that was the big question. Who was she seeing behind his back…? Suzanne's father couldn't listen to this drunken raving any longer; he went to bed to worry in private.

By the time she came through the door so drunk she had to be carried, he wondered who got her that way? Who put that smile on her face? Who got her so turned on? She certainly had not been in that lovin' mood for him, at least not for a very long time. The more that he thought about it the more enraged he became.

Suzanne was still in a silly mood. She was in such a silly mood that she didn't see the black evil rage that had consumed Ray. Stone cold, he stood glaring at her.

She staggered over to him to give him a hug and kiss. She was actually in the mood for some playful loving for a change. He raised his hand; she fell to the floor, feeling a sting in her cheek she had not felt since before her mother died.

He heard her scream and fall to the floor… Did he do that? Could he have done that? He went up the stairs to his room and closed the door. Standing with his back tight to the door, he had to contain himself, to stay away from her until he could think, regain his control and calm himself down.

How could he have raised a hand to any woman? He had always hated men who hit or bullied women... something had to give, they were destroying not only each other but their family and future together.

Ray went into his daughter's rooms; he needed to see if they had heard, if he had scared them. Anna was sound asleep. She could sleep through anything. He gave her a gentle kiss being very careful not to wake her.

Alice was also sound asleep. It was Angel, now she was Daddy's little insomniac. She hated any yelling or confrontation of any kind. For some reason she was more emotional and sensitive than any child he had ever met.

He knew right where to find her. He opened the closet door and there was his "LITTLE ANGEL ", she had pushed herself as deep into the back of the closet as she could. In the security of the darkness she was hugging the stuffing out of her rag doll.

Angel looked so scared and worried it was as though someone had put old ladies eyes on this little girl. Even at four years old she carried the weight of the world on her shoulders. He crawled into the back of the closet beside her. She curled in close to him, with a small tear in her eye she begged... "DADDY PLEASE DON'T HURT MOMMY ... DON'T MAKE HER CRY"...

One thing about Angel she could really rip a guy's heart out. After a big hug he held onto her promising her that the fighting was over. He would never hurt Mommy ever again. With that he carried her to bed tucked her in and read her a story 'til she fell asleep. Angel had so much trouble letting go and sleeping, but she seemed pretty peaceful for now.

Once Angel was asleep Ray went back and packed his suitcase. He really didn't know if he could stand being without his girls, but he did know he couldn't keep going like this. They were strangers to each other; he hated the monster he had turned into.

Suzanne was passed out cold on the couch. He tried several times to write her a note, but nothing seemed appropriate. He slipped out quietly without a word, half afraid she might see him and he would have to face the shame and guilt of what he had done and what he had become.

His mother-in-law had always been right he was a low-life drunk and Suzanne was too good for him. All he could do now was tuck his tail between his legs and crawl off. He loved her enough that he knew he had to protect her from himself. He was no longer her knight, he had become the dragon. A fire breathing dragon that spread pain and destruction to all that got close.

Suzanne woke as the sun was rising, her head was pounding, and her body ached. She thought if this was a hangover she would never drink again. Looking around the room she could see her mother's curio table on its side with a broken leg. Her father would never forgive her.

Sitting on the side of the couch, she could see Angel curled up on the bench by the front window, rag doll in one hand and blanket in the other. As Suzanne watched Angel she could feel that sadness that seemed to always surround her.

The only time Angel sat in the window was when she was waiting for Daddy to come home and tuck her into bed for the night. Suzanne had given up trying to figure Angel out a long time ago. She was a strange kid that did stranger things; there were other things to deal with right now.

Suzanne got up and walked into the bathroom to splash water in her face. She had a black eye and a cut across her cheek. She didn't remember Ray hitting her that hard; she must have hit the corner of the table when she went down. All at once she was filled with anger. How dare he treat her this way? She did nothing that he hadn't done to her a hundred times in the past year.

He can go to the bar every night, drunk every night... she's not allowed to have fun even once? The more she thought about it the angrier and more indignant she felt. He was going to hear about it when he got up.

For now, she would take a long peaceful bath before anyone woke up. Then maybe she could discuss it all calmly instead off screaming at him. It seemed to her that all they ever did was yell and slam doors.

While she lay in the tub she wondered how everything got in such a mess.

All the little things were gone. They never kiss hello or goodbye, they never snuggle on the couch watching television. They had quit holding hands and they certainly never talked or did anything as a family anymore.

These were all the things she would discuss with Ray as soon as he got up. Things definitely had to change and she couldn't do it alone. He would have to quit drinking so much and start acting like he's part of the family.

Feeling refreshed after a long soak in the tub, she was now ready to confront Ray. While making breakfast for the girls she started planning their talk. Maybe it would be best if they went for a drive alone, that way she could get everything out with no interruptions.

It had been so long since they had been alone. A picnic lunch so they could make a day of it, lying on the beach talking and snuggling. That's what she would do... let Ray sleep and have everything ready when he got up.

Suzanne sent Anna to get the other girls to come eat their breakfast. Angel would not come. She wasn't leaving the window ... " NOT NOW ANGEL!... I AM TOO TIRED TO DEAL WITH YOU AND YOUR STRANGE MOODS ... "She was waiting for her Daddy.

After explaining to her that they were going to let Daddy sleep, Suzanne attempted to pick her up and carry her to the table ...All Hell broke loose, Angel was kicking and screaming like she was being murdered. Suzanne had no choice but to give in.

She had learned a long time ago that Angel was not only the most stubborn child in the world but also the most difficult to understand. Ray was the only one that could ever do anything with her. She would have to leave her 'til her Daddy got up.

One more thing she needed to discuss with Ray. He was going to have to start disciplining that child. It was ridiculous that he was the only one Angel would listen to. Angel was a touchy subject between

Ray and Suzanne ... Ray saw her as her name inferred, a perfect little Angel that never did anything wrong.

But then she never did do anything wrong when Daddy was around. He was sure Suzanne didn't understand Angel and picked on her unfairly.... Could there be bad chemistry between mother and daughter? Angel was only four years old and Suzanne was her mother... Aren't mothers supposed to love their daughters?

Suzanne tried many times to explain to Ray it wasn't that she didn't love Angel ... she simply didn't know how to deal with her. Suzanne didn't understand it herself. There was something about Angel that always made Suzanne angry. If she could not understand her own feelings how could Suzanne begin to understand what Angel was feeling.

It was close to noon and Ray still had not come downstairs. Grandpa had gathered up the girls to take them to the park. All except Angel who still refused to leave the window except to run real fast to the bathroom and back even faster as though someone would steal her spot while she was gone.

Suzanne's Dad didn't say a word about the broken table or the black eye that could not be hidden no matter how much makeup Suzanne put on it. He had heard the fight and decided to stay out of it. He couldn't decide who was right. He couldn't take a side. In his mind they were both wrong and the only losers were his little granddaughters.

Angel fell asleep staring out the window. Suzanne figured it would be a good time to deal with Ray, not knowing what kind of mood he was going to wake up in. But she figured he had better be apologetic or at the very least humble.

The bed was still made; it hadn't even been slept in. She went to see if he had slept in the girl's room, like he had done so often when she wasn't in the mood to be pawed at. Then back into the bedroom, like maybe she mislaid him and could find him if she looked hard enough.

Suzanne ran outside in her slippers and nightgown looking up and down the street for his car ... "THAT SON OF A BITCH! ... "Who did he think he was… leaving like that? As if she were the one who did something wrong. If he thought she would come crawling to him…

"NEVER… NOT EVER…" She did nothing wrong…nothing!! It was he who owed her the apology.

She couldn't even begin to count the number of times she sat home waiting for him to stagger in from the bar. She could not believe she spent the morning feeling guilty, trying to plan a nice day for the two of them.

She would show him. Not only was she not going to crawl and call him first, but she would go to the bar as often as she wanted. If he wanted a war he would get one. A torrent of anger and emotions continued to consume her.

She now understood why Angel was determined to not leave the window. Angel would just have to get used to the idea that Daddy was gone. She wasn't Daddy's spoiled little girl anymore. The princess would have to come off of her throne and act like the rest of the family.

Suzanne had decided, she would get all that spoiled behavior out of her if it killed them both. The war was on and her Daddy wasn't there to save her. Suzanne was exhausted, she couldn't fight anymore she couldn't think all she could do was go to her room and cry herself to sleep.

When the phone rang Suzanne refused to answer it. If Ray wanted to talk to her he would have to come and do it face to face. It would teach him a lesson to worry, then he would have some idea how she felt when he didn't come home from work. She wanted to see how he felt to be crazy with worry.

Suzanne would have her father send him away when he did finally show up. There was no doubt in her mind that he would show up, at least not much doubt. He would come crawling back; he loved her and wouldn't be able to stand life without her at least that was what she hoped.

Ray's mother begged him to go back home, or at least call, he wasn't being fair not explaining to Suzanne why he left. To sneak off in the middle of the night and not even say goodbye to the girls. How could he? She had raised him better.

What his mother did not understand was that he didn't leave because of anything Suzanne had done. He left because he was scared of what he had become. He loved Suzanne and didn't want to hurt her or the girls. If she really loved him, she would understand and be there when he was ready to come home, no matter how long it took.

With Ray gone, Suzanne started going to the bar far more regularly. She went at least twice a week and even went in the afternoon once in a while. It became her second home. She even went so far as to get a job as a waitress. She liked serving the customers. She could talk to everyone, and she had a new set of friends, even male friends.

She loved the way they flirted with her, making her feel pretty and desirable. When she was at work she did not have to think about Ray or the girls, she could be herself. She didn't have to be someone's wife or someone's mother, or even someone's daughter. It seemed to Suzanne that she had spent her entire life being somebody's something.

Ray had only been gone one month and Suzanne had managed to get on with her life without him. She started to date a guy from the bar. His name was William; not Will, not Willie, not Bill or even Billy. It was William and he got very intense if anyone called him anything else. Even total strangers got the message very quickly.

Suzanne thought his intensity was ridiculous and uncalled for however he was very attentive and doted over her. She only saw him at the bar. He never came to the house. She thought it would be too confusing for the girls and she didn't think her father would approve. Especially after the fight they had about her working the bar.

She still had not called Ray and he had not called her. He did however call and talk to the girls while Suzanne was at work. Suzanne was surprised how little she had thought about Ray. She hardly even missed him, except at night.

Then it was the old Ray she had missed. The Ray that was sweet and tender that held her in his arms and made her feel safe and loved.

But then she had missed that Ray for years, at least now she wasn't constantly doing battle with his evil drunken twin.

Out with William a few times, she still wasn't ready to have sex, she had only been with Ray her entire life. The thought of being with someone else scared her. It was a line that once crossed could not be erased, an act that could never be taken back if it were wrong.

She had to be sure, sure of William and sure of how she felt about Ray. She would have to face whether or not the separation that was never discussed was to be permanent. She simply wasn't ready to think about that step let alone deal with it.

One night after work, William stuck around to have a few drinks while Suzanne closed the bar. They sat and drank, she was feeling pretty good. William dropped coins in the jukebox, choosing a soft schmaltzy song.

They seemed to melt into each other, slow dancing across the empty dance floor. For the first time in a long time Suzanne felt totally relaxed and comfortable. For the first time in a long time she wasn't a wife or mother she was Suzanne a desirable lady.

William kissed her, a slow gentle kiss that she couldn't help but return. The slow gentle kisses made their way to her cheek, her ear, covering her neck. His kisses became harder, more passionate, he was hurting her. She tried her hardest to pull away, but he was holding onto her too tightly.

She whispered softly that he was hurting her and that she wasn't ready for this. As she looked into his eyes she could see a cold meanness that she had never seen before. She gathered up all her strength and yelled as she tried to push him away...

"I SAID NO! ... I MEANT NO!! "... He slapped her in the face still holding onto one arm ... " DON'T GIVE ME THIS SHIT ... YOU KNOW YOU WANT IT ... YOU HAVE BEEN LEADING ME ON FOR WEEKS ..."

Suzanne began to cry ... "NO!! ... I SWEAR I WASN'T ... I THOUGHT WE WERE FRIENDS, I THOUGHT YOU CARED..."

The more she cried, the stronger he got. He knocked her feet out from under her and dove on top of her.

Suzanne screamed and kicked and cried, he seemed to be blind to all of it. She managed to get hold of the leg of a chair and pull it down on him. He lost his grip on her for a moment. She tried to move as fast as she could but it wasn't fast enough. He caught her by the ankle and was right back on her ripping at her clothing.

He was consumed with anger and went at her with hatred in his voice... " HOW DARE YOU ... HOW DARE YOU ACT LIKE YOU NEVER WANTED IT, LIKE I AM SOME KIND OF MONSTER ... YOU THINK I AM GOOD ENOUGH TO BUY YOU DRINKS, BUT NOT GOOD ENOUGH TO TOUCH YOU ... YOU ARE NOTHING BUT A LITTLE COCK TEASE ... YOU HAVE BEEN ASKING FOR THIS..."

After he was finished he got up and dressed like nothing happened. He slowly walked toward the door and left as though it was any other night. Not looking back at her or saying a word; he simply left.

As Suzanne lay on the floor in a crumpled ball, a piece of garbage William was through with and now discarded, her body trembled as the tears then sobs welled out of her uncontrolled. He was right this was all her fault, she went too far. She should never have led him on. She knew she had driven him to this act of uncontrolled passion and perhaps revenge for his frustrations and rejection.

For the first time since he walked out of her life Suzanne wished Ray were back. She not only wanted but needed him. She needed him to put his arms around her and make it all go away. She needed him to make her feel safe again, to feel like everything was going to be all right.

Suzanne continued to think about how much she missed him and the special bond they had, she couldn't help but let the tears pour out of her. She didn't want to stop them; she couldn't have even if she had tried. She needed to cry, to get it all out. She wasn't crying for what William did to her but what she had done to Ray and their family.

How could she be so stubborn? She should have called him a long time ago. Maybe if she had ... none of this would have happened. For the sake of stubborn pride she had now lost all her pride and most of her dignity.

Maybe it wasn't too late, maybe she could still salvage what they once had as a married couple. Why hadn't he called her, she knew he loved her so why hadn't he made any effort to get back home? He had to still love her, how could he simply stop, she hadn't.

Suzanne got up off the floor only after she was sure William had left. When she heard his car drive away she knew it would be safe to leave. She got up very slowly and with great difficulty as pain shot through her entire body.

She made her way into the bathroom, to look into the mirror; she had to see the horror of the last hour. She needed to fix the memory into her brain to never escape to never forget what happens to stupid little girls that stray too far. Ray had warned her about men in the bar, she refused to listen. Suzanne was sure she knew better, well here was the evidence of just how much she did know.

Her face was covered in blood; her eye was already beginning to swell shut. Washing the blood from her face, she fixed herself the best she could. Luckily her coat was long enough to cover her torn clothes. She would have to come up with some believable story about her face.

Suzanne knew she could never speak of this, not ever, not to anyone. She would be too ashamed, too embarrassed, Ray would never forgive this. If she were ever to have a chance of putting her marriage back together Ray could never know of this.

It was close to four a.m. when Suzanne finally came through the door. She had to be very quiet not to wake anyone. She had no idea what she was going to tell her father, but it would have to be good and convincing.

As she sat on the couch reliving the evening, running it through her mind over and over, trying to determine what she could have done different. His face was in her head; she would likely never again close her eyes and not see him coming at her.

From the corner of her eye she could see her Angel curled up in the window. The only place she slept since her Daddy walked out. The only place she would sleep 'til he returned. This had been a major war between the two of them. Suzanne was in no shape to deal with who was more stubborn… tonight Angel was.

Suzanne went into the bathroom and ran a hot bath, so hot it almost burned the skin off her. The same skin she now wished she could crawl out of. She had to get the filth of the evening off. A scrub brush would scour away all signs of William.

If she could have found some way of removing her skin she would have done just that. No matter what she did she couldn't get clean enough. She couldn't get the smell of his sweat and sperm off her body and out of her nostrils.

All the soaps and perfumes she had could not make it go away or even cover it up. As Suzanne lay in the hot tub, she started to cry all over again. Suddenly she stopped, there would be no more tears, no more feeling sorry for herself.

Her mother was right, life was hard and if you weren't hard right along with it..." IT WOULD CHEW YOU UP AND SPIT YOU OUT " … Something terrible happened, now it was over … the only thing left to do was get over it.

Suzanne slept late that morning she didn't get up 'til noon. She was very lucky her father loved to get the girls their breakfast and take them to the park almost every morning. Her father was pretty wonderful and she rarely treated him fairly and never told him how much she loved and appreciated him.

After she woke up she stayed in bed still trying to decide on the best story to not only tell her Dad but the entire world and everyone in it. There was no one who wouldn't ask or stare at that face; it would take a good lie to be believed.

The one thing Suzanne did know was that she could never tell the truth not even to her closest friends. Everyone would think she got what she deserved. They all told her about William, she thought they were wrong, she wouldn't listen she knew better than any of them. She was always flirting with him.

All her friends warned her about leading him on, giving him the wrong impression. She was enjoying the attention too much. She picked up the phone and called into work, she was too sick to work for a couple days, it was a good time to practice her story. The only way it would work was if she gave the same story to everyone...

She had a car accident on the way home last night, nothing too serious. Her boss could hear the panic in her voice and asked if she was all right. Suzanne assured her she was just a little shaken up and bruised her head hit the steering wheel.

That wasn't what her boss meant; William had been in the bar since it opened still pretty drunk from the night before. He was bragging to all that would listen, what a tease Suzanne had been but that he had taught her what happens to teasers. There was only one way to handle them and he knew it.

She hoped that Suzanne wasn't foolish enough to sleep with such an obvious jerk. Suzanne assured her that she had seen through William and told him so last night; he was just blowing smoke because she rejected him. She was so convincing she almost believed it herself. She would be sure to avoid William like the plague here on out.

After she got off the phone she felt even more embarrassed and ashamed, if that were at all possible. How could she be so stupid? Why couldn't she see what everyone else saw?

When her father got home and saw Suzanne's face he was upset and angry, he was sure those drunks from the bar must have beat her up. She explained to him that she was too tired to drive home, so a friend drove and they got into an accident, hitting her face on the windshield.

None the less, if she hadn't been working so late it still would not have happened... "DON'T WORRY DAD IT WON'T HAPPEN AGAIN "... she would make sure she got enough sleep from now on and be more careful.

She couldn't spend all day taking care of the girls, fighting with Angel, and still be able to work all night. She didn't need to work, he had enough money put away to support them all. He didn't want her in that bar anymore, maybe the next time she would be hospitalized or even worse. He couldn't even bring himself to say all the things that could be worse. It was horrific enough having the thoughts pass through his mind.

Suzanne loved her father but she had to make him understand... " I KNOW YOU WANT TO TAKE CARE OF ME ... I AM NOT DADDY'S LITTLE GIRL ANYMORE ... I AM AN ADULT WITH A FAMILY TO TAKE CARE OF AND SUPPORT " ...

He knew she was right and that he had no place interfering in her life, but she was making such a big mess of it. He promised to stay out of it as long as Suzanne would promise to talk to Ray and start making some effort toward getting their life and family back together.

Suzanne sat down with a cup of tea as she watched her girls; it was as though it were the first time in a long time she had taken the time to really look at them. Anna was the little mother, the one who washed the girl's faces and brushed their hair. She even picked out their clothes. As Suzanne really gave it thought it was Anna that potty trained Angel by dragging her kicking and screaming to the bathroom every time she went herself.

Angel was all sentiment, emotions and sensitivity. Easily hurt, easily upset, yet filled with a hard and stubborn strength that had no end. Once the war began, Angel never surrendered or lost the battle. She would fight 'til her last breath then she would wake up the next day and continue the fight as though it were still the same moment.

Like that business with sleeping in the window, Suzanne couldn't begin to count how many times she had taken Angel out of that window, only to find her right back there. Suzanne yelled at her, spanked her, locked her in her room and yet she stubbornly went back each and every time.

Sometimes Suzanne could see her laying in the window glaring at her as if daring her to do something about it. Angel was capable of giving the evilest of glares. She was five and a half years old and she could send chills through any adult with a glance. That is of course, except Daddy, because she loved her Daddy.

Alice sweet Alice, there was no other way of describing Alice her youngest daughter. She had a gentle kind of shyness that made all who ever met her love her. There was no easier child to love. She never seemed to want or need anything; she would just let everyone love her. Unlike Angel who was almost impossible to love and could totally drain a person emotionally and physically.

As Suzanne looked at her girls she realized there was one thing missing... Ray! There can't be a family without a Daddy and it was time for this Daddy to come home. She got her girls dressed in their best Sunday dresses. Even Angel cooperated once she knew she was going to see Daddy.

He was due home from work at four, it was only two now. The extra time would be spent visiting with Ray's parents. Suzanne was scared to death; she had not seen her in-laws since Ray went home. She had no idea what Ray had told them about why he left, or even if they knew about her being a barmaid.

She pretty much made up her mind not to ask any questions if they didn't. What she really hoped was that they didn't know, she wasn't even real sure how much Ray knew. She was fairly sure her father wouldn't be the one to tell him.

Alice was right up on grandpa's knee, Anna was in the kitchen helping grandma bake cookies and Angel took her spot in the front window waiting for her Daddy to appear. Suzanne sat quietly in a chair running through her mind all the things she wanted to say to Ray. She was thankful that Ray's parents were the kind of people not to pry.

Suzanne knew everything she wanted to discuss and what she wanted to say she simply didn't know how to say it. Even though Ray had no right to hit her she still had to take some of the responsibility for this mess.

Ray was right, she did put her friends first, her father first, the girls first, but never Ray first. She had neglected him, let her family fall apart. She had done all she could to push him away; as far over the edge as possible it was no wonder he cracked.

When Ray's car pulled into the drive, Suzanne walked slowly toward him with a mixture of excitement and apprehension. A fear of the unknown, for the first time since she met him she couldn't second guess him... would he be glad to see her?... would she be forced to face his rejection?...would he be able to see into her soul and know she had betrayed him in the worst way?

It wasn't 'til that moment that she realized how much she missed and loved him. As she got closer to the car she could see he wasn't alone, he had a woman in the car with him. How dare he? Is this why he didn't call? He had probably been seeing her the entire time. He probably left her to be with this tramp.

Suzanne ran to the passenger side of the car, grabbed the woman by the hair and dragged her out. She didn't need to ask for or hear an explanation there wasn't any that could explain a man who would leave his wife struggling with his babies while he picked up with someone else.

The two of them fell to the ground kicking and screaming in the worst catfight Ray had ever seen. Ray grabbed hold of Suzanne, while his brother grabbed the other woman, the two of them were still screaming at each other as Ray dragged Suzanne into the backyard... "WHAT?... ARE YOU TOTALLY INSANE?...WHY ARE YOU ATTACKING TOTAL STRANGERS? "...

Suzanne started screaming back at him ... "TOTAL STRANGER?... TOTAL HOME WRECKER YOU MEAN? ... YOU LEFT ME FOR THAT? ... SHE ISN'T EVEN PRETTY AND SHE IS ALMOST OLD ENOUGH TO BE YOUR MOTHER ... IF THAT IS WHAT YOU WANT I WILL GET MY GIRLS AND LEAVE ... I WAS FOOLISH TO HOPE YOU MIGHT STILL WANT TO BE A FAMILY " ...

Ray grabbed her and held her as tight as he could, he kissed her long and hard with a passion that had been restrained and held inside for a very long time. As he was trying to hold her and kiss her she started to pound him in the chest with both her fists and yelling...

"HOW DARE YOU TRY TO MAKE LOVE TO ME WITH YOUR GIRLFRIEND IN THE FRONT YARD ... GO KISS HER! ... "

Ray looked at her and started to laugh ... "DON'T YOU KNOW HOW MUCH I LOVE YOU ... I COULD NEVER MAKE LOVE TO ANYONE BUT YOU ... SHE IS MY AA's PARTNER"...

Suzanne looked at him puzzled and confused ... "SHE IS YOUR WHAT??"... Ray explained to her that he left because he was scared of hurting her. Ray knew after he had hit Suzanne that his drinking was totally out of control. He had to do something, he was no good to anyone the way he was.

He wanted Suzanne to go in the front yard and meet his new friend Liz but she was far too embarrassed. So Ray apologized on his wife's behalf and took her home. Ray went into the house and gave each of his girls a big kiss and hug.

It was all he could do to get Angel to let go of him long enough for him to go back in the backyard and talk to Suzanne. With the girls following his every step he knew he would never be able to talk to Suzanne this way. They would need a little time alone.

He asked his mother to watch the girls while they went for a drive. She was more than happy as long as it got Ray back home where he belonged. She was sick of his moping.

While driving to the lake, Ray looked at Suzanne, why had he not noticed how beat up she was? Where did that black eye and fat lip come from? She had huge worry lines, big bags under her eyes... she looked so old and tired.

He hated for his little princess to look like an old beat up ally cat. She told him the only thing she could... the same story she had told her Dad. He said ... "YOU MEAN YOU ARE STILL GOING TO THAT PLACE" ... She said ... "NO!... IAM WORKING THE BAR AS A WAITRESS. "

Suzanne wondered what he thought she was using for money all this time he was trying to find himself. Ray figured there must be a better, safer job. He didn't want to fight but there was a lot to talk about.

Suzanne and Ray were like total strangers. They had so many things to talk out even after a couple hours of talking the only thing they could agree on was that they loved each other and didn't want to be apart.

After picking up the girls they went out for supper. It was so good to be a full family again. Angel insisted on sitting on Daddy's knees the entire meal. Suzanne decided she could let it go for the moment but it was definitely one of the... "Have to discuss topics".

They drove the girl's back to Ray's mothers, where they would spend the night. Not only hadn't they seen their grandchildren for a long time but Ray and Suzanne needed a night alone.

Anna the big girl promised to help grandma. Alice gave Mommy and Daddy big hugs goodnight and climbed up on her grandpa's knee. Angel took a screaming fit, grabbed hold of Daddy's neck and couldn't be pried off.

Ray was about to suggest they take her with them when he saw the look on Suzanne's face. Instead he suggested they should stay long enough to tuck the kids into bed before they go ... that was bad enough. He could see the tension building in Suzanne.

It was always Angel ... this time Ray could understand, after all, it took her a whole month to get her Daddy back. She couldn't be blamed for not wanting to loose her Daddy now that she had him back; it had to seem like an eternity to such a little heart.

He picked her up and carried her up to one of the bedrooms, laying her on the bed he read her a story and laid down quietly beside her 'til she fell asleep. No such luck, she was with her Daddy and she was staying awake to make sure he didn't leave her again.

Suzanne was getting impatient, he swore to Angel that he would be back and he would never leave her again, she simply had to be a good girl and spend just one night at grandma's house.

As Ray pulled out of the driveway, he could see his Angel's face pressed tight to the glass of the bedroom window, big alligator tears streaming down her cheeks. He wondered if it wouldn't have been better if she were in a back bedroom, but then she still would have been in agony he just would not have had to see it.

There had to be some way of making her more secure, a way for her to feel safe and trust in her entire family. She seemed so scared all the time. It broke Ray's heart to think that almost every time she really needed him he was gone. It was no wonder that she had no trust or feelings of security within their marriage.

Ray and Suzanne spent the night making love, talking and making love some more. They finally fell to exhaustion in the comfort of each other's arms and the security of each other's undying love and devotion.

That night Suzanne awoke in a cold sweat reliving "THE " night, her worst nightmare, every blow, every cutting word as though it were all happening again and again. How many times would she have to live through it?

With tears in her eyes, and a body that would not stop trembling she squeezed into Ray as tight as she could holding him with all she had. She had to get over this, what would she tell Ray if he were to notice how scared she was all the time.

It was the accident surely an accident would cause this kind of nightmare and trauma. Once again she squeezed Ray in his sleep, this was where she belonged, where she was safe... nothing bad could ever happen to her as long as Ray was holding her.

Waking up in each others arms they made love again then showered together it was as though they were afraid to be out of each others sight in case it were all a dream they could wake up from.

Suzanne called her Dad, Ray called the girls. Angel wasn't screaming, but she was very quiet and withdrawn a sort of hold her breath 'til her Daddy comes through the door state of limbo. She did however manage a small amount of breakfast. Ray figured that for Angel that was a good sign.

The reunited couple went home packed a picnic lunch, picked up their girls and went to spend the day at the beach. It was time to be a family again and what better way to start. They talked non-stop telling each other anything and everything. From now on there would be no secrets, at least that was what they promised each other.

Ray would never know about William, Suzanne would take that to her grave. It just didn't happen Suzanne refused to think about it or let it affect her in any way. It was no more than a very bad nightmare… a nightmare that would never stop coming back to haunt her.

Suzanne and Ray accomplished a lot that day. They learned to talk, they learned to let each other in on what they were feeling, but most of all they learned to put each other first. Suzanne agreed to only see her friends while Ray was at work, they would be gone by the time he got home. Ray agreed to never drink again and come home after work.

That didn't mean he wouldn't once in a while go back out, but he would take Suzanne with him. From now on their socializing would be as a couple; never again would he leave her home alone.

Last but not least Suzanne promised to give up her job at the bar; she was more than welcome to work if she wanted but not in a bar. She acted like it was a big sacrifice; she loved Ray so much it made her happy to sacrifice for his happiness and well being. If it made their marriage stronger she would do it.

Now she had a ready-made excuse to give her boss, she was trying to save her marriage. Truth be known she dreaded going back. She couldn't ever face William and everyone he may have told. She was thanking the Gods when Ray put his foot down and told her to never set foot in that place again.

Everyone knew how jealous and unreasonable Ray was, how he was so old fashioned he didn't want any wife of his in a bar. It would never occur to any of them she was too embarrassed and ashamed to show her face there ever again. If Ray hadn't put his foot down she would have found some other excuse … any excuse that kept her out of there.

Chapter Five

They walked into the large gym together, holding hands. Suzanne was very quiet as she watched Ray go from person to person shaking hands with some, hugging others. It seemed so strange for him to be so friendly with people she was only meeting for the first time. He had an entire life outside of hers.

A life she could not understand, a life she would never be a part of. She could go to the meetings with him but she would never have that feeling of sharing, of common ground, of common heartache. Filled with feeling of jealousy and not knowing exactly what she was jealous of. Maybe it was simply that they all had a piece of Ray that wasn't hers and she wanted "ALL" of him.

Consciously she knew she was being incredibly childish, subconsciously she wanted to grab Ray by the hand and drag him out of there. How could strangers do more for him than she could? Was that it? She wanted him to change for her; she wanted to be the one to save him. Their love should be enough to conquer all.

For the first time she had a look into Rays loneliness as he watched her laugh and fit into friends he had nothing in common with. Her eyes were open, this time it was her that was the outsider and she didn't like it, didn't like it one bit.

Sitting on a chair, squeezed in with several others sitting in rows like a bunch of sheep lined up for sheering she was filled with a silent wonder for what she was doing there. Ray was holding her hand tight enough that it had fallen asleep long ago.

The sweat from his palms started to make her hand slippery. However, she could still feel Ray's trembling within hers. She cupped her other hand over his, trying to show support even if she didn't feel it. In truth, it all seemed incredibly ridiculous to her. They didn't need all this, nor did they fit into this kind of world.

These were mostly low-life dredges, the kind of people her mother would abhor. She listened to story after story of heartache and abuse, the depths of despair that dragged them all through the gutter. How low they had all sunk before they could begin to put things back together.

Most of them had lost everything. Through it all she couldn't help but think of her mother, how she had loathed these kinds of people. She often said they all got what they deserved and they deserved nothing. In her opinion they didn't even deserve the air they breathed.

In her mother's mind, drunkenness was for the weak of character. They were too weak to control their own lives so they lived inside a bottle, then blamed the bottle for everything in their life that was wrong.

All they needed was willpower. They drank because they wanted to drink, so if they were starving, homeless, on the street that too was their choice. No one should pity or help them. Did they pity or help all the people in their life? The same people they abused beat and belittled, whipping all self-esteem out of them. Pity the people that loved them, that were hurt by them.

Suzanne had always known what a drunk was. It was someone who couldn't hold a job, who abused and beat his wife and children. It was the guy who had his head on the bar passed out cold. Those people who sleep on the street hugging the paper bag with a bottle not so successfully hidden. The one thing a drunk wasn't was Ray.

She wondered why Ray felt the need to come to AA's. He wasn't like those people. He didn't drink for most of their marriage. His drinking was only out of control the last little while and that was because of her and her neglect of him.

If she were not spending all her time with her friends he wouldn't have been drinking. It was all her fault she drove him to it. He wasn't a falling down drunk like these people, he never missed work, and he always supported his family.

Ray stood on the stage to tell his story. Suzanne was sure he had nothing to say and what he did say was bound to be pretty boring compared to other stories, what could he say? "MY NAME IS RAY... I TREAT MY FAMILY WELL AND WORK VERY HARD. " ...

Ray started to tell his story ... why didn't she know any of this? He talked about how he started at age fifteen; he never went a day without a drink in those days. He was out of school and supporting his family while all his friends were allowed the luxury of being school kids. He was an adult and drank with adults to prove it.

After he met and started dating his wife her parents thought he was a low-life drunk. Suzanne was so much in love she couldn't see what was all too clear to her parents. He learned to hide his drinking and only drank small amounts in the shed or in his car.

He talked about all his hiding spots and how good he got at concealing his problem. Mostly he got good at hiding his problem from himself, lying to himself. It wasn't until he hit Suzanne that he couldn't continue to lie to himself or anyone else.

Being the cowardly drunk that he was, he let his wife take the blame for everything. She believed everything was her fault, if she paid more attention to him he wouldn't drink. The truth was, he had a problem long before he met her. If she had not come along, it would have consumed him a lot sooner than it had.

He looked down at Suzanne and said ... "THANK-YOU" ... Thank-you for loving me, thank-you for believing in me and most of all thank-you for not giving up on me. They both had tears in their eyes. Suzanne never loved Ray more than at that moment. They had been together all those years and they had been total strangers.

What was it that stopped them from letting each other in? Why couldn't they share their fears? She knew they had to start getting to know each other, really know each other. She loved him for letting her in on his darkest secrets, but she could never tell him hers.

He'd hate her. What she had done was unforgivable and Ray was only human. He may or may not forgive the act but he certainly would never forget it or get it out of his head. Some secrets had to be kept. She was protecting him from unbearable pain by not telling him.

Suzanne had not menstruated since that night. She was sure she was pregnant, if anyone knew the feeling of pregnancy she did. All the signs were there, she didn't need a doctor to tell her. There was a deep gnawing inside of her, way deep in the pit of her stomach; lurking doubts, not knowing if this child was Ray's or William's.

It really didn't matter how much the facts haunted her she would go to her grave before she would admit there was even the slightest chance this wasn't Ray's baby. Ray would never ever have a reason to question it.

William and Ray's appearance were very close physically; they had similar physiques, hair and eye color. She had decided not to tell him anything until she had missed at least one more period. She couldn't avoid telling him. Since his newfound sobriety he paid closer attention to everything.

He straight out asked her why she had not had a period since they had gotten back together. She told him she was about two weeks late but she wanted to wait until she knew for sure. He was even more excited than she expected him to be. He always saw pregnancy as a trophy to his manhood.

Suzanne on the other hand saw it as a major burden. This time it would be different because Ray was different. This time he would be there for her. This time they would do it together. She wondered how many of the pains he would feel when she was in labor.

The next nine months went fairly quickly. Ray was true to his word; being there for her throughout the entire pregnancy. He waited on her hand and foot until it made her crazy. Talk about going from one extreme to another, Suzanne wasn't real sure she could stand it much longer.

The only relief she got was when she signed herself up for night school. She took a course in accounting. Once the baby was born she would also take a course in bookkeeping, then another in management. She was always good in school, especially with numbers.

It was time to start thinking about having a future even though they were doing well and there was no doubt in her mind that they would be together forever. It was time she started doing something to prove herself. She wanted to feel like she was more than a wife or baby factory. She wanted to know who she was outside of everyone else and their expectations.

Suzanne thought life was good, with everything falling into place just as she needed it. That is except for the occasional nightmare that always took her by surprise, torturing her otherwise wonderful life.

Ray wasn't drinking, she loved school, and they were all getting closer as a family, even Angel was cooperating. She couldn't think of one thing she would change in her life. This was the life she had always wanted.

It was a cold March day when Suzanne went into labor. This time was different; she was actually looking forward to having this baby. The first pain was at home right after supper around six o'clock, and the most perfect boy ever born was in the doctors arms by nine.

Ray barely had time to get to the hospital from work. When he did look into the face of the son he'd waited so long for, he couldn't talk. He stood staring, with the pride of a peacock, at the face of ... "RAYMOND EARL BRIAR JUNIOR" ...

She felt good, Ray felt good, wasn't it nice to go through a pregnancy that everyone wanted. When it was time to go home the baby had to stay because he wasn't gaining weight They tried to explain it to her but the only thing she really understood, was don't worry they would run tests. How could this be, her other children were all healthy.

Suzanne went back to the hospital the next day to be with the baby. When the doctors informed her that the tiny helpless baby she had just given birth to, had a heart defect, they would have to operate immediately.

Suzanne cried... "HE'S TOO SMALL ... YOU CAN'T OPERATE ON A BABY THAT SMALL!! "... All they said to her was that the baby would die if they didn't.

As she looked down on Raymond Earl the fourth, she thought about how tiny and helpless he looked and how helpless she felt. It took every bit of strength she had to compose herself and hold onto her emotions. She had to call Ray, and she had to be calm when she did.

She couldn't talk to him directly so she left a message with the office secretary for Ray to meet her at the hospital after work there was no sense in worrying him at work. She was worried enough for both of them.

For the first time since the night she was raped, she thought about William and wondered if this was hereditary. Maybe this affliction was common in his family and this was William's son. She tried to push the idea out of her mind, but she kept thinking about all the people who would be hurt if any of this was divulged.

If the doctors didn't say it was a family trait, she wouldn't mention it either. She really wished there were some way of knowing without having to tell anyone. She couldn't go to some strange doctor and say this child may or may not be my husband's.

Even if they did blood tests they would have to also test the men in question. William was lower than slime and he would never make claim on a son of hers. She would not have him in her or her son's life. She didn't even want to think about what it would do to Ray that the son he had been trying to make was in reality another man's.

As she paced and worried outside the operating room doors a thousand things went through her mind. She thought about what her mother would say if she were still alive ... " IF HE DIES, HE DIES, LIVE WITH IT ... IT'S NOT LIKE YOU CAN'T MAKE ANOTHER ONE " ...

Suzanne could always count on her mother for the cruelest of attitudes. Mostly what she said was true, she was just so incredibly cold about what came out of her mouth. Why was she thinking about her mother at this time, she should be thinking only of little Ray.

It seemed like forever, but Suzanne finally saw Ray walking almost at a run down the hall. She could see he was as worried as she was. She ran into his arms crumbling into tears, sobbing and crying uncontrollably. They melted into one, feeling each other's pain and heartache.

Ray was trying to ask her if their son was dead, a question that wouldn't leave his thoughts and fears, a question that he couldn't quite make pass his lips. Suzanne reached up and touched those lips gently. She couldn't bear it if he spoke the words out loud. Somehow the act of saying it out loud may make it come true.

Suzanne wasn't superstitious but she wasn't taking any chances either. She told him between sobs that he was still in surgery. They wouldn't know anything for some time; all they could do was wait and pray.

Suzanne fell asleep with her head on Ray's lap; this had always been where she was safe. Everything had to work out; her knight in white armor had come to fend off all bad things. Nothing bad could ever happen to her when Ray was there to keep her safe.

She opened her eyes to see the surgeon standing over her looking grim and exhausted. She held her breath, praying as hard as she could. He told her even though the surgery was over, it would be several hours before they would know much.

All they could do now was wait. Suzanne felt like she had stepped into a bad soap opera. Poor Ray didn't know what to think or feel he stood around trying to make some sense of it all.

He had a look on his face that broke her heart, as though someone had stolen his Christmas. He'd waited a lot of years for his son. He loved his girls very much, but a son that was very important not only to Ray but to his father, his family name. It wasn't fair. The girls were all so healthy and uncomplicated he took it for granted that it had to be that way.

He called his parents and Suzanne called her Dad. They all came to the hospital to wait with them. It was the first time Ray had seen his father leave the house in many years. He didn't even go out in the yard anymore.

As Ray watched his father that evening in the hospital, it occurred to him for the first time that his father was getting very old and tired. He could see this written into every wrinkle and worry line that cut deep into his brow.

This may very well be his father's last chance to see his name carried on. His brothers had boys but it had to be the eldest son of the eldest son. He needed to know before his time came that the line would be carried on, that someone would be head of their clan long after he had gone.

The family here in Canada numbered close to two hundred members, all technically under Ray's fathers care. When he passed then Ray would inherit the family responsibilities. In days gone by the head of the family settled all family quarrels, approved all weddings, approved the sale of properties and was a pall bearer at all family funerals.

His was the final word for the entire family and not to be disputed. Now it all changed, the head of the family was more or less a figure head, but still important much like the Queen of England. The most important responsibility they still held was to keep up the family Bible which held all the names past and present of their vast family tree. The Bible came to Canada with the original family, six generations of births, deaths, and marriages had all been recorded.

Suzanne admired the way Ray's family kept such careful account of their family heritage; it seemed a huge responsibility for a baby who was already struggling for life. So many people were holding such great expectations of such a little guy.

Baby Ray ended up spending three months in the hospital, but it was worth it as he was totally healthy and out of any danger. Suzanne regretted missing so much of his newborn stage. She loved holding and rocking a newborn. They were so helpless and tiny; it gave her a feeling of keeping them safe.

Suzanne had a very strong mothering instinct, something her mother never had. The day the baby came home, they had a huge family party. Everyone was there from both sides to dote over the only son. He was the baby that would carry on the line.

Men!... such a commotion. They didn't have all this excitement when the girls came home. To hear Ray tell it, one would think he had made and delivered this baby all by himself ... girls were O.K. but a "SON "... now that was something. Suzanne laughed to herself as she thought how Ray could be a real man now that he had a son.

Not that he wasn't a real man before or any different a person in any way. Ray's father had his chest out with the pride of a peacock. It seemed to Suzanne that this little guy knocked ten years off Ray's Dad's life. It gave him new hope, a reason to hang on, it gave them all new incentive.

The next couple years were good for all of them especially Suzanne who was continuing to go to school. She breezed through the hardest of courses as though it were no harder than breathing.

Ray was constantly reminded that he had no more than a grade nine education staring him in the face. He'd always been good with his hands and a hard worker; intellectually he simply couldn't keep up. Suzanne had tried many times to talk to him about school, to include him in conversations when she had friends over. He was out of his element and no one felt it more than Ray.

Although he was very proud he was also overwhelmed. He felt like he wasn't good enough and never would be. His wife was never going to be that little woman, country girl that he thought he wanted. He was proud to have such an intelligent wife; he just wished he could keep up with her.

She was leaving him behind and he knew it. It would only be a matter of time before someone smarter took her away. Every time she brought class mates home for study sessions he was even more aware of this. Suzanne tried hard to include him and bring him into conversations.

Mostly this made him feel stupid and inadequate. He had no clue what they were talking about. Suzanne was proud of Ray, the way he was so devoted to his children and her. The way he never complained about her school and her friends coming over to study. She thought about how much they had been through and how lucky she was to have Ray in her life.

All this was true, it was... then why did she also have feelings of embarrassment creep into her head every time Ray appeared around her friends? If he wouldn't always dress like a farmer, she had bought him nice clothes, why wouldn't he wear them? He could be so stubborn.

He complained they didn't suit him; he wasn't comfortable enough in them. Why couldn't he just make the effort, he had no idea how important it was to her, how embarrassing it was to have her friends think she had married a backward farmer? It was such a simple thing, why couldn't he do that for her?

His outer appearance was only the small part of her problem. Ray had a knack of always saying the wrong thing at the wrong time. Somehow he always managed to come off as totally uneducated.

As hard as she tried to bring the conversation to something he knew, it became clear he knew very little. Suzanne really didn't understand when she had met Ray he seemed so mature and worldly. She loved to listen to him talk. Now she just prayed for his silence.

Suzanne finally finished her schooling, she could now write her own ticket. She graduated the top of her classes, in office management, accounting, bookkeeping and a few extra courses in sociology and one in psychology.

Ray couldn't understand why she had to study all that head stuff to be a secretary. All it did was cause a lot of trouble. She was constantly analyzing everything, him, their marriage, the kids, her life. None of it seemed good enough for the great Suzanne, who had suddenly become bigger than life, at least bigger than their life together.

While preparing and sending out resumes, her only real worry was her lack of experience. Out of twenty resumes, twelve called her for an interview. Out of twelve interviews seven called her back for a second interview; out of those seven there were only three that truly tweaked her interest.

One in particular was a posh hotel with a lot of class, far more classy than she could ever hope to be employed in. It was about a forty-minute drive away. That wasn't a problem she loved the idea that it was far enough that they would never know Ray. He wasn't likely to show up at work to embarrass her.

She wasn't sure she could ever have the kind of poise and dignity it would take to deal with people of that social standing. The wardrobe alone was out of her reach, but she did want it, it was all she could think about.

Her mother had told her all of her life she was a slob and would never make it in social circles. Now she wished she had listened to her mother and paid attention to all she was trying to teach her. All the things her mother had tried to pound into her were suddenly important.

She hated her mother for years for always riding her about her hair, her clothes, how she lived, where she lived even who she had associated with. Now she was wishing her mother was around to teach her and give her pointers.

Her father laughed and said..." WHO DO YOU THINK TAUGHT YOUR MOTHER"? She was born a ghetto girl that didn't even know how to use the proper silverware. He began teaching her, she had to learn proper formal etiquette, formal place settings, how to present herself, how to greet people with dignity. He even taught her how to walk across a room as if she were born to royalty.

They had hoped that his family would love and accept her if he smoothed out the rough edges a little. But they hated her even more for pretending to be something she wasn't and never would be. Now he found himself teaching his daughter all the things he had years ago walked away from.

As Ray watched Suzanne transforming into a new lady of class and refinement, a dignity that had always been there surfaced to the top. She far out classed him and Ray knew it.

How could he not worry? He knew he could never voice these worries out loud Suzanne was sure to say he was trying to keep her down. She wanted this so much and had worked so hard, what right did he have to hold her back?

It was her right and her destiny, but was it Ray's? When she went for her third and final interview at the Hotel Royal, she was ready, she was more than ready. She looked great, she had attitude and confidence. She was made for this and it would be hers.

Ray knew she would get the job, why not she was perfect for it. He knew this and hated it. He wanted to turn the clock back; he wanted his sweet little wife back. The young naive girl that thought he was the smartest greatest man on the planet.   He was her white knight that saved and protected her from the rest of the world.

None the less he took a deep breath gave her a big kiss for luck and pretended he was as excited as she was. It was all so confusing, he wanted to be supportive, he wanted her to be all that she could be.

At the same time his heart sank knowing he would never be able to keep up to her in this new and scary world. He knew he was loosing her. They were traveling in different directions pulling them further and further apart.

Ray not only couldn't keep up with Suzanne but his girls were all zooming past him. Anna was in grade three and had her first crush on a boy in her class. It wasn't that long ago he put her on his knee and read her fairy tales. All grown up she had to do everything herself and for everyone else as well. She took care of everybody, she was the little mother.

Ray could see his own mother in her; that soft, gentle female born to be a mother ... All the features he wished Suzanne had. Anna was the same in school, steady and true. She brought all her homework home and did it all with no questions or reminders.

Angel on the other hand was as different as she could be. She was a dreamer, not only were her feet not on the ground, but her head was in the clouds. Even at the grade one level Ray could see how school was going to be a problem for his angel.

She was extremely bright and was a fast learner that is when she allowed someone to teach her. Mostly she thought she already knew everything, it was a wonder she didn't get up and teach the class herself. It was very frustrating to her teacher and even more frustrating for Ray and Suzanne, who were continually being called to the school for conferencing on how to handle their child.

All Suzanne could say was ... "IF YOU FIGURE IT OUT TELL US, WE HAVE NEVER HAD CONTROL." Her Daddy had some control but Suzanne had none. Anna loved that Angel was always in trouble and that she was the good girl.

Alice was starting kindergarten and won everyone's heart right off the bat. She was one of those kids that people couldn't help liking. Ray junior, called R.J., was now walking and getting into everything. There was no doubt he was Daddy's boy, they went everywhere together. After all, he couldn't learn to be a man if he didn't spend time with men.

When Ray's Dad passed away that year, peacefully in his sleep, Ray's family reacted to his death so differently than Suzanne's family when her mother had passed. His death seemed to bring a warm peaceful closeness to the family.

It wasn't that any of them were glad he had died, but they were at ease with his death. They didn't have anger, pain and unspoken guarded thoughts that had been pushed down and away for many years.

Ray's family dealt with things as they came up. There were no long time grudges. They had disagreements as any family, but they fought them out and made up then and there. Ray was stoic both at the funeral and afterward. His father wouldn't suffer anymore he could have peace. His eldest son had an eldest son, so it was time.

It wasn't long after the funeral before Ray's mother came, the car filled with boxes. Ray never dreamed the extent of the responsibility that he would inherit from his Dad. His mom sat with him, going over every detail of his newly inherited position.

First was the family Bible, which held the heritage of the family tree. Every time there was a birth, a death, or a marriage, it had to be entered with the date. In the case of a death he would have to go back to their birth to enter it.

She showed him how to enter his own father's death and where the birth of his son had been entered. She also explained to him that he would have to attend all family reunions. All family changes for the year that were reported needed to be recorded. There were reports of family business and family land that had to be discussed as well as handling any family disputes.

Next was the stack of deeds to family owned property, they would all go over into his name now that his Dad was gone. Ray was confused and overwhelmed ... Why hadn't his father taught him all this over the years.

Ray had always believed that being the eldest son of the eldest son was more or less a title with no real responsibilities, this was the twentieth century. Why was his family still living in the dark ages? Ray would be sure when it was time to pass it all onto R.J. his son would be prepared better than his father had prepared him.

As he looked through the piles of deeds he realized that they were properties that his cousins and uncles had lived on and worked for lifetimes. It would make more sense to sign each property over to the person living on it.

His mother couldn't believe she was having the same conversation with her son that she had with her husband many years earlier. Ray had to understand that it wasn't as easy as he made it sound. Much of the property was acquired by the family many generations ago, even though some of the properties were lost during the depression, what remained belonged to the entire family and everyone worked them together.

Ray remembered as a kid and a younger man going to family farms with all the other cousins and uncles. He thought it was a big party or reunion, it wasn't work, it was fun getting together with the family. He figured they all helped each other because they were neighborly and family stuck together to help each other.

Ray looked through the property list, most of which were working farms, why had he and his immediate family lived as paupers? Why had he and his brothers worked so many odd jobs trying to sustain his father's family, keep food on the table utilities on and rent paid? Why hadn't his father allocated farmland for them to live on and work? If they were head of the family why then were they the poorest family in the clan?

Ray tried his hardest to understand frustrated with the memories of the hardships they endured his entire life he couldn't help but lash out at his mother for the first time in his entire life.

He didn't understand and would never understand there was nothing she could say to make it all acceptable. With tears in her eyes she begged him to listen, to let her explain. Once Ray's father could no longer work the farm that Ray had been born on, it was no time before he lost it to the bank shortly after the crash.

How could he take a farm from another family member? He was already riddled with guilt, he had lost the farm and in his opinion his manhood. He had already lost so much she couldn't nor would she ask him to give up his pride. He would never have been able to hold his head up if he even suspected they knew.

No one in the family ever knew how hard things had been nor would they now know. As far as the family was concerned they chose to live in town because it was easier on his disability. They had asked many times, but Ray's father always assured them all was well.

Suddenly so much of his childhood came clear. There was so much he never understood.

There had always been some unspoken resentment held for the rest of the family that they never helped them after the accident. Ray had never understood how they could all turn their back on the head of their family.

It was all too much to absorb all at once. His head was spinning there was too much to do, to know. He thought all his life he had come from a simple honest family. No secrets, no games, now he discovers his entire life was a secret.

His mother tried to get him to go past it, he had other things to worry about he couldn't get stuck on his childhood. What they did or did not do to prepare him was in the past. Maybe they should have told him more, to prepare him but it was her husband's decision and she honored it even when she didn't agree.

He had to next take responsibility for the family heritage, memento's, family photo's antiques passed from one generation to the next. All of this was from another time. Ray felt like he had stepped into a time warp of some kind.

There were portraits of some very grim looking characters, he couldn't help but wonder why everyone looked so hard and miserable in the olden days. Surely there would have been a day here and there that made them happy or put a smile on their faces? Obviously not the days the pictures were painted.

Ray was upset he began to grumble, he wanted her to take it all to someone else. He didn't want this, he didn't want to know the family secrets or control other peoples lives. For the first time in his life he saw his mother angry.

There was no ... "GIVE THE JOB TO SOMEONE ELSE "... this was what he was born for. It was his birthright, his responsibility and his duty, no one else's. His father should have prepared him for this but since he didn't, Ray would have to deal with it. The only thing Ray could do was be sure R.J. was better prepared.

Ray spent the next several months visiting his uncles and cousins and all the deeded property the family owned. He went over the history of the farms to find out who was living on them and how long, as well as who was working them the most.

He was well aware that neither he nor his brothers had been to a family planting or harvest for years. To him this made it all the more ludicrous, he worked the least and yet all the farms and properties were in his name.

Ray spent months, stewing and contemplating trying to be sure he was doing what was best for all concerned. His mother would have to understand. It wasn't right for him to hold deeds for land someone else put their life's sweat into.

It was time to call a family meeting, all the heads of households were called together. He was signing over pieces of land to the family member that lived and worked the property most. There were a few larger farms that were split and divided among cousins. They had worked all the farms all their lives and really did deserve to own something, even if it would be small farms in comparison to other farms.

For the first time since she met Ray's family, Suzanne had to witness uncontrolled anger from Ray's mother. She accused him of turning his back on generations of family tradition. He was breaking the family up; he had no family pride or loyalty.

To have it all in one family name kept them together as a family. She couldn't imagine anyone going to work a farm that they didn't have a piece of. Now instead of being a unit they were all fragmented.

As it turned out, she was right. Ray couldn't believe how right she was. All the cousins and uncles got busy caring for their own lands. There were no more family gatherings for planting or harvests. One of his uncles sold his property almost as fast as it had been put into his name. It was to become a subdivision.

Ray had spent a lot of restless sleepless nights trying to do the right thing, trying to be fair and honest to his entire family. He believed he was doing the right thing at the time, yet it all blew up in his face. He wished he could take it all back that he had listened to his mother.

They had always been a very close family, he never expected everyone to pull apart at least not so quickly. He looked down at his son playing on the floor and thought about how he had stolen his heritage, his right to be head of a family.

It was all gone now, except the memories of how it used to be. Ray felt like he was mourning two deaths that year; the death of his father and the death of the family. Even the family reunion was small that year. Half the number that usually attended and they had to be coaxed and dragged.

Suzanne could see the pain that Ray was going through, feeling helpless to comfort him. There was nothing she could do to make things better for him. It was hard for her to understand what he was feeling. Her family had never been around. She couldn't remember meeting aunts, uncles, cousins or anything else. How could she help him when she couldn't fully understand the loss?

Chapter Six

It was difficult for Suzanne to be supportive when her own life was so good. She was getting everything she ever wanted. It was almost impossible to look sad and sympathetic when she wanted to burst with excitement and enthusiasm for her new life.

She was now the assistant manager at the best hotel in the city. She even liked the long drive. It gave her calmness, time to think and get things together before and after work.

It was especially good on the days when she was fighting with Angel. All the fighting bothered Suzanne, but she could never find a way of avoiding it. The older Angel got the more the fights escalated into something completely out of control.

Angel always seemed to have such a chip on her shoulders, as though she was mad at the world. Suzanne wished she could crawl inside her head and see what her daughter was thinking when she gave those evil glares that always put her mother in such a rage.

There were days when Angel was spending every waking moment grounded to her room. As fast as Suzanne let her out, they were right back in the middle of a war, and right back into her room Angel would go.

It was not unusual for Angel to eat every meal alone in her room. She was without a doubt the most stubborn child, she never learned by her mistakes and she never gave in. She would take a spanking and still not back down. Suzanne felt constant defiance.

Ray couldn't stand it when Suzanne and Angel got going and he really hated it when Suzanne started hitting Angel. His mother had raised six children under very difficult circumstances and had never once hit any of them. Suzanne's answer to that was that his mother didn't have to raise Angel.

Suzanne wondered why they ever named her Angel when she was anything but. She was sure Angel was a devil child. Maybe Angel was a payback in life for all the tortured fights she had with her mother.

Her mother loved to scream at her ... " I HOPE YOU HAVE A CHILD AS ROTTEN AS YOU ARE SOME DAY ... " Angel was the answer to her mother's curse all those years ago. Even if Suzanne didn't quite remember being as bad as Angel always seemed to be.

Between the age of five and six Angel seemed to change somehow. A haunting kind of change, she quit crying. Suzanne was spanking her for refusing to do her chores. The more Suzanne spanked her the harder and colder the hated glares became.

She would simply stare her mother down with an evil look of hatred and stubbornness. The more Angel stared Suzanne down the more Suzanne hit her determined to break her will, determined to win.

It went far beyond a spanking to an insanity that could not be held back. Ray grabbed Suzanne holding her back while he screamed at Angel to go to her room and stay there until he came for her.

This enraged Suzanne all the more. How dare he interfere? That was why she was so spoiled to begin with. She would listen to her mother if Ray hadn't insisted on spoiling her and interfering every time Suzanne tried to discipline her. He always let her get away with everything.

How was Suzanne to ever get any kind of control if Ray kept interfering? He always set her up to be the bad guy, the bad guy who got stuck doing all the discipline. Of course Angel loved Daddy more; Daddy never spanked or even scolded her. Whatever Angel wanted Daddy would give.

This time it was Ray that was out of control, screaming at her that she went too far. She would have killed her if she'd kept going. Suzanne was still enraged... didn't he see that look Angel was giving her; total disrespect and defiance...

Ray grabbed Suzanne shaking her trying to get some sense into her..." SEND HER TO HER ROOM; DO NOT BEAT ON HER..." Suzanne yelled at Ray ... "I DO NOT BEAT HER, I SPANK HER..." Ray interrupted ... "NO! YOU BEAT HER ..."

For the first time since he had laid eyes on her Ray could not stand the sight of her, he had to get away from her. He needed time to think, to figure this out. Ray crawled deep into the back of the closet, Angel's safe place, her hiding spot. He knew that was where she would be.

Angel looked so scared and so helpless hugging her rag doll as she curled up in a ball in the corner. Ray could barely see her as she hid in the dark, he was thankful for this. It broke his heart to feel her tremble as he held her in his arms. He could feel her fear and heartache and was helpless to take it all away, to make her pain disappear.

How could he fix this, he loved them both so much? How could he stand by his wife and still love and protect his little Angel? In many ways Suzanne was right Angel should be minding her. This all began because Angel was too stubborn to do a job that would have taken her ten minutes. He carried her into the bathroom and put cold compresses on her red and now swelling welts.

There was no doubt she was going to be covered with bruises. She would have to stay home from school for a few days, while grounded to her room, including meals. This was no hardship to Angel she liked being alone, besides she was never really alone.

Her father asked her why she didn't take out the garbage like her mother asked. Angel explained to him that it wasn't her turn, Mommy wouldn't let her explain. How come Anna never got spanked when she didn't do her jobs? Ray tried to explain to Angel that when Anna was given a job to do she did it. She didn't get all stubborn and turn it into world war three.

Even if it were Anna's job couldn't Angel do it because her mother asked her to ... "NO, DADDY I WAS BUSY DOING MY OWN JOB

... THE DISHES ... "Ray didn't know what to say, Suzanne was harder on Angel; she did pick on her unfairly.

Anna and Alice never got spanked; they also didn't go out of their way to make everything more difficult. Ray was so frustrated in this situation he could see they were both right they were both wrong. Suzanne had to stop hitting Angel ... when you leave marks you have gone too far.

Suzanne was happiest when she was at work. She had all the power, all the control. The manager liked to stay in his office as much as possible, leaving her to handle everything ... and she loved it.

It wasn't just the power or being in charge, she was good at what she did ... She could look at her mother in the grave and say, see mother ... "I AM NOT WORTHLESS OR USELESS.... "

All her life her mother made her feel as though she were a complete disappointment. She loved that feeling of being good at something. Suzanne loved her work so much she used any excuse to work long hours and not have to go home.

There were times when she would work late into the night, then tell Ray they had an emergency and it was too late to drive home so she would grab a room at work. Suzanne had no control at home. Angel had more control than she did.

Ray had forbidden Suzanne to physically discipline Angel. Angel was to be sent to her room to stay 'til Ray got home to handle the problem. Suzanne couldn't believe it, Angel could treat her with total disrespect and defiance and Suzanne was to do nothing.

She wondered what she was doing there. She obviously had no purpose in the family. Anna did all the mothering, Angel did all the controlling and Ray did all the spoiling. She wasn't needed there; she had no control, no purpose.

Nothing she did was right. She felt like she did when her mother was alive. She was the same screw up she was as a little girl. She couldn't do anything right then and she wasn't doing anything right now.

Suzanne hadn't been home for three days, excuse after excuse by phone. Ray decided to go to the hotel to see her. It seemed to him that was the only way he would see her. As soon as he walked through the door he knew he had made a mistake. He felt like a backward, hick farmer.

He knew it was a posh, upper-class establishment, he just didn't know how far above him the place was. He thought she meant regular people dressed up. These people even walked and stood differently. He could feel them staring at him wondering how he got in.

Ray could see Suzanne across the room talking to a group of well-dressed patrons. She fit in so well, she was one of them, and he wasn't. He wished there was a way of getting her attention without going over to her. He grabbed a bellboy as he was passing by and sent him over to get her.

When she turned to look at him her face fell, betraying her embarrassment. He could actually feel the shame she felt. He wondered what she would tell people. He knew by the look on her face, she wouldn't be introducing him as her husband. It suddenly became very clear that no one at her work even knew she had a husband.

Suzanne walked up to him rushing him back out to the parking lot like he was no more than an unwanted delivery boy. She ducked him behind a parked car in an attempt to camouflage their familiarity. That was fine with him; the less time he had to spend with those snobs the better he liked it.

He asked her if she had told those people he was her husband, she was flushed with embarrassment ... "WHAT DO YOU EXPECT... YOU COME HERE DRESSED LIKE A FARMER ... AND EXPECT ME TO NOT BE ASHAMED OF YOU ... WHAT ARE YOU DOING HERE? ..."

Ray stood looking at the total stranger that he once loved more than life itself wondering the same thing himself. What was he doing there? ..." IN CASE YOU HADN'T NOTICED YOU HAVEN'T BEEN HOME FOR THREE DAYS ... I HAD TO COME SEE IF I STILL EVEN HAD A WIFE... "

Suzanne stood shaking her head commenting sarcastically ... "VERY FUNNY... YOU KNEW WHERE I WAS ... I CALLED

YOU EVERY DAY.... THIS JOB IS IMPORTANT TO ME ... WHEN I HAVE AN EMERGENCY I HAVE TO STAY AND HANDLE IT... "

Ray was getting pretty disgusted with her attitude ... "WHAT ABOUT THE EMERGENCIES AT HOME? ....WHAT ABOUT YOUR JOB AS A WIFE AND MOTHER? ... WHY DON'T YOU TRY BEING PART OF THE FAMILY? ..."

Ray had all he was about to take, she had not been part of the family for a long time, how dare she act like he was the bad guy?..."I DO NOT MIND YOU WORKING A NORMAL EIGHT HOUR DAY, BUT A MAN WANTS HIS WIFE AT HOME AT NIGHT ... HAS IT NOT OCCURRED TO YOU THAT YOU ARE NOT BEING FAIR TO YOUR DAD...

She was being selfish and he had to find a way to get her to think of the effect this had on the entire family. All she ever thought of was herself and what she needed, she barely knew she was even part of a family..."HE IS GETTING TOO OLD TO WATCH THE KIDS DAY AFTER DAY BECAUSE YOU CAN'T BE BOTHERED TO COME HOME... "

Suzanne didn't want to discuss it any further she wasn't about to argue it out in the middle of the parking lot where everyone could hear them. She had a job to get back to and what she really wanted was for Ray to leave before anyone figured out they knew each other.

There was no further discussion she turned her back and walked away as though she were dismissing a subordinate. To Ray she had just poured salt in the wound. She did however promise to be home for supper.

That wasn't going to do Ray much good he would be gone to work by then and she would be asleep by the time he got home. She already knew that when she said it. That was the plan, to escape all this 'til she was calm enough to discuss this all calmly, hopefully Ray could do the same.

By the time Suzanne did get home she was still pretty upset with Ray. She sat down to discuss it with her father before she had to start supper

... "CAN YOU BELIEVE HE CAME TO MY WORK LOOKING LIKE A FILTHY FARMER ... LIKE AN UNEDUCATED HICK ... HOW DARE HE? ... HE KNEW MY JOB WAS IMPORTANT TO ME ... HE KNEW IT WAS A HIGH CLASS HOTEL ..."

Her Dad looked at her with total disbelief. This attitude and snobbishness was the very reason he walked away from his family, his country and all the classes full of foolish judgements. The classes always acted like they were so high above the rest of the world, when all they really were was small minded, petty people.

Just as Suzanne was now being small minded and petty, not to mention incredibly selfish! For the first time ever he was ashamed of his daughter and her attitudes. It broke his heart to see what she had turned into. How did this happen, hadn't she learned anything from her mother?

Suzanne couldn't believe the way her father was talking to her, she was sure he, of all people, would understand. He came from that world, why didn't he understand how she felt? How important it was to her job to maintain the classes.

Angel came running in interrupting, Suzanne wasn't in the mood to deal with her. She tried to brush Angel off telling her to go play. She couldn't, she needed to ask her grandpa something. Suzanne was already on the edge but this was enough to push her over it.

Suzanne was trying to have an adult conversation with her father and she wasn't about to compete for his attention. Especially with this spoiled attention-seeking child. This once, she wasn't going to have her own way. All the attention did not have to be toward her.

She sent Angel to her room ... Angel refused. That was it; she was not going to wait for Ray this time, she would handle this herself ... right now ... "YOU WILL GO TO YOUR ROOM RIGHT NOW YOUNG LADY ..."

Angel knew her mother was on the edge but she had to explain ... "BUT MOMMY IF I GO TO MY ROOM I CAN'T DO MY JOB AND DADDY WILL BE MAD AT ME... "Suzanne grabbed Angel by the hair and dragged her to the stairs, screaming at her all the way...

"YOUR DADDY IS NOT HERE! ... HE WILL NOT SAVE YOU THIS TIME PRINCESS ... HE IS NOT IN CHARGE AND NEITHER ARE YOU ... I AM IN CHARGE ... YOU WILL LEARN TO LISTEN TO ME ... IF IT KILLS US BOTH ..."

... "BUT MOMMY...!" Suzanne could not believe she was still arguing. She hit Angel again then kicked her ... She wasn't stopping; she hit her and hit her again. It made her crazy that Angel wouldn't cry that she had the arrogance to stare her down.

To Suzanne that was just more defiance, Suzanne's father got up and grabbed at her trying to hold her so Angel could get away. He yelled for her to go in the upstairs bathroom and lock the door. As Angel ran up the stairs, he fell to the floor grabbing at his chest...

"CALL AN AMBULANCE I CAN NOT BREATHE ... OHH GOD! ... IT HURTS ... HURRY! ... PLEASE HURRY. "

When the ambulance arrived they gave him oxygen and rushed him to the hospital under lights and sirens. Suzanne didn't know what to do. She had to get to the hospital; she had to be with her father. What could she do with the girls? Would they let her in the hospital with children Ray had to come home from work, he had to watch them so she could go.

That lady next door that was always sticking her nose in everyone else's business was at the door ... "COULD SHE HELP?"... This time she could help, someone had to stay with the kids 'til Ray got home. Suzanne had to get to the hospital.

In an attempt to keep everyone calm the neighbor lady got them at the table eating sandwiches, but there was no Angel. She couldn't find her. Anna and Alice said Angel was a bad girl so she had to stay in her room ... she was always bad.

The neighbor made her way up the stairs calling out for Angel, there was no answer. Now she was getting worried, something didn't feel right. Angel was nowhere. Not in her room or her sister's room, she wasn't in the bathroom either. Anna yelled for her to look in the back of Angel's closet; she liked to hide there when she was in trouble.

When she opened the closet door she was horrified. There was this tiny little thing, curled up in a ball looking scared to death. As her eyes adjusted to the darkness she was sure this innocent little child was covered with bruises and blood.

As she attempted to bring her out of the closet Angel fought and cried, her mother would be mad if she came out. The neighbor hated going through the cupboards and drawers but she had to find a flashlight, she had to get a better look at this child... what could have happened?

It broke her heart to see her she almost wished she hadn't looked. She was covered completely, old bruises, new bruises, welts, a bloody nose, and cuts on her face and arms. There was a huge gash by her left eye that was beginning to swell.

This was something out of a horror movie. She had never seen anything like this. Closing her eyes she made every attempt to keep the tears from escaping. It did her no good; she could still see the tiny face covered with blood and fear, even from behind closed eyelids. This sight would never leave her, not ever.

Leaving Angel, afraid to touch her, to move her, she went to the phone first for an ambulance, then the police. Something had to be done and done now. She wasn't about to wait for a parent, she wouldn't be able to live with herself if she didn't do something to assure the safety of this child.

Pacing nervously in front of the door, where were they? Why weren't they there? Anna jabbered about Angel always being in trouble, she was always a bad girl. She turned trying not to be furious with Anna; no one was bad enough to deserve that. But Anna was sure Angel was, she was always bad. It made mommy crazy she was so bad.

... "SO IT WAS YOUR MOMMY THAT HIT ANGEL "... Anna told her she had to because Angel never listened. The neighbor wanted to know if anyone else in the family was bad enough to get hit ... "NO, WE LISTEN TO MOMMY ... WE ARE GOOD ... AREN'T WE ALICE ... "Alice was too shy to talk, she merely shook her head in agreement.

When Ray pulled into the drive he saw police, social service and ambulance that was just pulling away. The police were trying to ask him questions. He didn't want questions he wanted answers … "WHAT IN THE HELL HAPPENED HERE AND WHERE IS MY WIFE … MY FATHER-IN-LAW…"

His only thought was to follow that ambulance to find out if his family would be alright and what was really going on … "MY WIFE WOULD NEVER TRY TO KILL HER FATHER OR HER DAUGHTER "…There had to be more to this, there had to be. He couldn't imagine what kind of explanation Suzanne could possibly come up with to explain this mess away.

It looked like Angel needed stitches by her eye and had a possible broken arm. They wouldn't know about internal damage until they got her to the hospital. Police and Children's Aide were still throwing questions at him all at once. He had no idea what happened.

They told him they had already talked to the other children and there was no doubt that his wife did all the damage. As there was no doubt that he had never raised a hand to any of the children. This was the only reason the other children were not removed from the home.

They were going to follow him to the hospital where they could get statements from the doctors. There was no doubt that his wife would be arrested. He begged them not to arrest her that he could work this out, that he would get her help.

Ray could hardly stand to look at Angel nor could he take his eyes off her as he tried not to believe what they saw. She looked like one of those kids on the news from the other side of the world that had been injured during an air raid.

He was still trying to talk them out of arresting Suzanne… He would take time off work to protect the kids … she wasn't a monster; she never touched the rest of the children. Angel was rebellious and hard to handle. Grabbing him firmly the officer swung him around hard forcing him to look at his daughter… "DOES ANY CHILD DESERVE THIS? … NO CHILD COULD BE THAT BAD…"!

"NOT A MONSTER!!... SHE WAS ALMOST BEATEN TO DEATH THEN LEFT TO DIE..." From what the other children had said, she almost killed her own father because he tried to interfere. If her father died she could very well be charged with manslaughter, as well as child endangerment and child abuse.

Ray couldn't believe this was happening he felt like he had stepped into the "Twilight Zone or the Outer Limits" ... If he had, he hoped the show was over soon. He knew Suzanne would never hurt her father, or the children, intentionally anyway.

The fact was that the father-in law had a massive coronary trying to stop her. Why would anyone do that kind of damage to such a tiny little thing? There was no excuse... in his heart he agreed, there was no excuse.

They were trying to explain to him that the only way the other children could remain in the home would be if his wife were not. At least, not until after her court appearances then the judges would be the ones to lay out guide lines. They figured she would spend one night in jail, then she could make bail arrangements in the morning. She still would not be allowed with the children unless accompanied by a social worker.

Ray loved Suzanne very much, she was his life, and his children had to come first, no matter how much it hurt. He had to protect Angel. he had let Angel down. He hadn't protected her when she needed him. Why hadn't he seen this coming and stopped it? How could he have let things get so far out of control?

Suzanne paced up and down in front of the intensive care doors, unable to sit or even relax for a second, not until she knew. Surely someone knew something. She would never forgive Angel if her father wasn't all right.

Why did he have to interfere? Couldn't he see how bad Angel was? That child had to be disciplined; he was just like Ray always taking Angel's side. Why couldn't they see how much they were spoiling her into complete uncontrolled behavior?

For a mere moment Suzanne drifted off to her own childhood... Why didn't he ever interfere when her mother was hitting her? Why hadn't he ever protected her? Those were unfair beatings, and he never did anything then. But he can protect Angel who is plain spoiled rotten. Her best trait is being able to manipulate the men in her life. Why was it that no one could see?

From the corner of her eye she could see a stretcher come in with a small child on it, accompanied by police, there must have been an accident of some kind. Poor child she looked so little on the stretcher, barely visible with the circus that accompanied her.

The last one in was Ray, thank God, Suzanne had never needed him more than at this very moment. As she watched he seemed to be hanging back with the police, he seemed so upset? Was Ray somehow connected with the accident? In his hurry to get to the hospital had he hit this small child?

It wasn't Ray that came to her, it was the police... They were right in her face ... " YOU HAVE THE RIGHT TO REMAIN SILENT..." as they were talking they started to put handcuffs on her. She looked at Ray her eyes begging for help. He couldn't even look at her... "WHAT IS GOING ON? ... WHAT ARE THE CHARGES? "...

The police attempted to drag out a confused dazed Suzanne, as she passed the stretcher she could now clearly see the small child that she had hardly recognized 'til this very moment. She was covered in blood and bruises, her right arm was braced, there were loose bandages around her head and most of her tiny body.

... "I DIDN'T DO THAT ... I ONLY SPANKED HER ... SHE MUST HAVE FALLEN OR SOMETHING AFTER I LEFT..." Suzanne was frantic to explain the unexplainable, there was a big mistake. She had to find a way of getting the police to understand that. She wasn't the bad guy; she could never do all this not even to Angel.

...."THAT SITTER MUST HAVE DONE SOMETHING... SHE WAS FINE WHEN I LEFT FOR THE HOSPITAL... YOU MUST BELIEVE ME... RAY! YOU BELIEVE ME ... DON'T YOU!? ... I WOULD NEVER ... I'M NOT A MONSTER... WHY ARE YOU TREATING ME THIS WAY?... "

Suzanne didn't believe that the neighbor could do this but it was the only thing she could think of. Unless Angel fell down the stairs, or maybe she threw herself down the stairs to get even more attention than she already gets. It was all grasping at straws but that was all she had.

The police didn't say a word beyond reading her rights, they didn't even discuss it, how could they, how could anyone? Ray knew what they were thinking ...it was the same thing he was thinking. The difference between Ray and the police was that he knew and loved Suzanne.

He knew she wasn't the monster they thought she was. Normally she would never hurt anyone, especially her family, things just got out of control. She lost her head, if she hadn't been so mad at Ray this would never have happened. She didn't mean it; he knew she could never have meant it.

He looked down at Angel and realized how the entire situation was insane ... Suzanne was insane, she had to be, and no normal person would do this. How could he love someone that was capable of this?

As the doctor worked on Angel, Ray asked one of the nurses if they would check on the condition of his father-in-law. They would all feel better knowing he was safe. He could reassure Angel that everything including her favorite grandpa was all right.

He finally had a chance to talk to Angel and try to find out what had happened without pushing her too much. Angel cried as her story spilled out, she was simply trying to tell her Grandpa something important. She couldn't go to her room she had chores to do.

Her Daddy had told her she had to get them done; he would have been mad at her if she went to her room and didn't get them done... "WHY WOULDN'T MOMMY LET ME TALK? ... I WASN'T TRYING TO MAKE HER MAD... I DIDN'T MEAN TO BE BAD.... SHE WOULDN'T LET ME TALK ... I AM SO SORRY DADDY..." tears suddenly welled out of her in an uncontrolled heaving.

... "WHERE IS GRANDPA? ... I HAVE TO SEE GRANDPA ... I HAVE TO TELL HIM I AM SORRY ... I DIDN'T MEAN FOR HIM TO GET HURT ... I DO NOT WANT HIM TO HATE ME...I

REALLY DID TRY TO BE GOOD…PLEASE DON'T HATE ME DADDY? … PLEASE, PLEASE DON'T HATE ME …"

Ray hugged her, trying not to move her for she was a broken china doll. He was afraid of hurting her, of breaking her more … " I COULD NEVER HATE YOU … YOU ARE MY ANGEL … IT WASN'T YOUR FAULT BABY … IT REALLY WASN'T… DON'T EVER THINK FOR EVEN ONE MOMENT THAT IT WAS … MOMMY DOESN'T MEAN TO HURT YOU, SHE IS SICK AND NEEDS HELP …"

She looked up at him with the saddest eyes he had ever seen … " MOMMY HATES ME DADDY … SHE HAS ALWAYS HATED ME … I TRY HARD FOR HER TO LIKE ME … I TRY HARD TO BE GOOD … IT JUST MAKES HER HATE ME MORE…"

Ray could hardly stand to hear what she was saying; his heart was crumbling into little bits as the delusions of his happy home shattered his reality. Suzanne did hate Angel he knew that, he had seen it himself but refused to acknowledge it…

"DON'T WORRY PRINCESS, WE WILL GET MOMMY A GOOD DOCTOR, SO SHE CAN LEARN HOW TO LOVE YOU …"

The doctors came back and told Ray that his father-in-law was out of danger for now, but they were going to keep him in intensive care for twenty-four hours to be safe. Ray could go in but he wasn't to upset him in any way.

When Ray went in he wasn't prepared for how terrible he looked. He had aged ten years in the blink of an eye. Ray told him Suzanne was at home with the kids. He smiled a weak smile of disbelief…" GOOD TRY… I HEARD THE POLICE OUTSIDE OF THE DOOR… HOW BAD IS IT AND DO NOT LIE TO ME … START WITH ANGEL, IS SHE ALL RIGHT? " … Ray begged him to relax and not worry they could talk after he was stronger. Ray needed to understand it was the not knowing that was keeping him from relaxing.

Ray told him everything, every detail. About Angel's broken arm, her stitches and the other cuts and bruises, and how the police believe if he hadn't stopped Suzanne she would have killed Angel. Ray had gone this far, his father-in-law might as well hear it all, he told him about Suzanne's arrest.

He looked at Ray with sad tired eyes ... "THIS IS ALL MY FAULT ... IF I HAD STOPPED HER MOTHER YEARS AGO... SUZANNE WOULDN'T BE THIS WAY..."

It was mostly all hidden from him but he could see the bruises, he could feel the fear and tension every time he walked through his door after work....".HER MOTHER WOULD BEAT HER AND BEAT HER ... IT DIDN'T MATTER HOW MUCH SUZANNE BEGGED, HER MOTHER WOULDN'T STOP UNTIL SUZANNE WAS DOWN ON THE FLOOR IN A CRUMBLED BALL ... "

Such sadness and heartache surrounded this family. Now this man tired from all the heartache and guilt he carried for most of his life, was trying to carry it all alone. It was a heavy burden that no one should carry alone. There was always more than one guilty person when these things happened.

Ray would not allow it, it wasn't his fault. Not alone anyway, there was a lot of guilt to be spread around and some of it fell on Ray's shoulders. They both saw what was happening and should have stopped it.

As his father-in-law continued his story, Ray didn't interrupt nor did he stop him. Ray knew if there was to be any healing this man had to get some of the guilt that weighed on his heart off or surely it would break from the burden he carried in it.

... "I'D COME HOME FROM WORK, THERE WOULD BE A SILENT HEAVINESS SURROUNDING THE HOUSE... I COULD FEEL THE FEAR AND YET IT WAS EASIER TO PRETEND ALL WAS WELL... I TOLD MYSELF IT WAS MY IMAGINATION ... I WOULD STAND THERE NOT KNOWING WHAT TO DO ... WHEN IT CAME DOWN TO IT I WAS AS SCARED AS THE KIDS WERE ...

Ray could barely stand to look at the heartache in the eyes of his once strong father-in-law. Tears continued to stream down his face as he struggled to relieve himself from the pressure of holding so much in for so long.

..."WHEN I SAW SUZANNE BEATING AND KICKING ANGEL SHE LOOKED LIKE HER MOTHER ... IT SENT CHILLS THROUGH ME ... I KNEW IT WAS TIME TO PUT A STOP TO IT ... ANGEL DIDN'T DESERVE THIS ... TELL HER GRANDPA IS SORRY... GRANDPA LOVES HER... TELL HER SHE IS A GOOD GIRL ... WHY DIDN'T I STOP THIS SOONER? ... WHY DIDN'T I SAVE SUZANNE ALL THOSE YEARS AGO? ..."

Tears filled his eyes and covered his face, the heartache welled up into his throat till he couldn't talk any longer, and all he could do was wallow in the heartache he could not escape or avoid.

Ray walked out of the intensive care, ran into the washroom, locked the door and fell to the floor sobbing uncontrolled into his hands. Angel didn't cry anymore, he would cry for her and for everyone else.

Once the tears started he didn't know how to shut them off. He cried and sobbed until his entire body hurt. He cried until he thought he couldn't stand it, then he cried some more.

Ray had to get a grip, he had to stop, and he couldn't let Angel see him this way. While Angel was getting her arm set Ray called the police to see how soon he could get in to see his wife and what arrangements had to be made to get her out as soon as possible.

They told him he would have to wait 'til morning. She had already called a lawyer and nothing could be done until the next day. He asked them if they could tell her that her father was out of danger.

He dreaded having to call the family, especially Suzanne's. He decided to simply tell them their father was in the hospital. Their father could fill in the details if he wanted them to know. The hard part was calling his mother; she would have to know all the details.

He would need her to stay at the house for a few days; she would need to know why Suzanne wasn't home, why his father-in-law wasn't. Ray didn't want to answer all the questions she was going to ask.

His mother had always been wise and intuitive; she instinctively knew not to ask any questions. Her son needed her and that was enough she would pack a bag and go to the house they could discuss it after things calmed down. She could feel his pain and heartache even as he spoke on the phone. He didn't need to tell her the details he hurt and that was all she needed to know.

Ray was thankful when he got home that his neighbor didn't ask many questions. She simply said she was sorry, she didn't know what else to do. He thanked her and assured her she had done the only thing she could. He told her to never feel guilty for rescuing a helpless child. The truth was she probably saved Angel's life.

Maybe now Suzanne could admit she had a problem and get some help. He was relieved that the other kids were all asleep, he needed to be alone, and he needed to think. Or maybe what he needed was to not think. Not think about any of it.

How could he do that? As hard as he tried he couldn't do anything but think? It all ran through his mind over and over, haunting him like an unwanted apparition... the faces of Angel, Suzanne and his father-in-law, so much pain, so much heartache.

When his mother came in, Ray was sitting in a chair staring straight ahead; she knew he wasn't ready to discuss it. She took off her coat and went into the kitchen. She came back out with a sandwich and a coffee for the son she didn't know how to help.

She knew her son well, and knew he wouldn't have even thought about supper. He was still trying to wake up from the nightmare he was living. None of this could be real, normal people didn't almost kill their own children or their father's.

Normal people didn't get thrown in jail ... that was for low-life dogs and thieves. Not people like Suzanne; she was a good, caring wife and mother. She just went too far, cracked under the pressure, she didn't mean it; she wasn't that monster that the police thought she was.

Ray dissolved in the tears that once again poured out of him. This time he had his mother's arms to sob into and comfort him. She gently caressed his head trying to make it all better not knowing what to say or do. There was only one thing to do ... BE THERE.

Ray was able to compose himself enough to tell his mother what happened. She sat in silence 'til he was done, allowing him to tell his story not speaking 'til he invited her advice.

Ray's mother needed to know if she had always hit the kids. Ray tried to explain it all to his mother with great difficulty ... something he didn't understand himself. He started with the fact that she didn't hit the kids, she only hit Angel.

To Ray's mother it didn't make any sense to only hit one child, you were either a hitter or you weren't... " MOM, I HAVE SEEN THEM TOGETHER, IT IS LIKE THEY HATE EACH OTHER ... IT'S NOT ALL SUZANNE AND IT'S NOT ALL ANGEL ... THEY BOTH HAVE TO PUSH EACH OTHER OVER THE EDGE ...

Ray was trying his hardest to make his mother understand something that even he couldn't begin to understand. There was no understanding; this was part of a nightmare, a nightmare that he wanted to wake up from....

"ANGEL HAS THIS NEW IRRITATING THING SHE HAS STARTED DOING... SHE STANDS STARING, GUNNING SUZANNE DOWN WITH HURTFUL, DIRTY GLARES ..."

It broke her heart to listen to the pain and the heartache of her son as he tried to make excuses, but there was NO excuse. She listened as he continued ... "SHE DOESN'T CRY OR ANYTHING, SHE STANDS IN DEFIANCE ALMOST AS THOUGH SHE WERE DARING SUZANNE TO DO SOMETHING ABOUT IT "

A broken hearted mother listened to her son pour his heart out about all the heartache he had been living for a long time"... I DON'T KNOW MOM ... I JUST DON'T KNOW WHAT TO DO ... I DON'T WANT TO LOOSE MY WIFE ... I HAVE TO PROTECT MY CHILDREN. "

He was barely able to hold back the tears that had sat on the edge of his eyelid all night. Inside, he was still in that bathroom at the hospital crying his heart out. How could any of this be real?

Ray's mother agreed with one thing, the children had to be protected at all cost. Once social services took them he would never get them back. He had to hold together as much of the family as possible. She would stay and help with the kids as long as he needed her.

She liked the idea of being needed and having someone to care for again. She had been lonely since her husband passed on. Ray gave his mother a hug and told her he loved her. He couldn't remember the last time he told her that.

As he hugged her he was thankful for the kind of person she had always been. She taught him calmness and levelheaded behavior. He was lucky he had always known his mother loved him no matter what he did.

He thought about Angel and Suzanne and found it inconceivable that two generations could grow up feeling only hatred and contempt from their own mothers. He couldn't imagine the emptiness of not feeling a mother's love.

While Ray lay in bed that night he worried about Suzanne, he worried about Angel, he worried about his father-in-law, and he wanted a drink. He wanted to crawl inside a bottle and stay there until this was all over with and he had his family back.

Now what? Where do we go from here? He needed to talk to Suzanne; he couldn't handle all this alone. There were too many things to think about; too many decisions, too many problems, he couldn't think anymore.

He felt so tired and so weak. It was as though someone had reached inside of him and pulled out his best parts. He had never felt so alone, so scared. His family was falling apart and he couldn't do anything to stop it.

For the first time since he was a kid, he knelt at the side of his bed and began to pray. He prayed harder than he had ever prayed. He begged God to heal his family and bring everyone home safely.

Mostly he prayed for Suzanne to find some way to love Angel before it was too late for both of them ... Too late for Angel to forgive her mother, too late to keep Angel from doing this to her own child...

"PLEASE GOD BREAK THE CHAIN OF ABUSE ... "Let both Suzanne and Angel heal, physically and emotionally. He ended his prayer by asking God to watch over all of them and keep everyone safe from fear.

As they slammed the cold, iron barred door shut; Suzanne tried to tell them it all had to be some kind of mistake. She loved her father, she loved her children, even Angel who made her crazy, all she did was spank her. Her own mother had hit her much harder, many times. Everyone spanked their children.

Angel must have done something after she left for the hospital and was using it to get attention. They didn't know Angel and how manipulative she could be when she wanted attention, especially with her Dad and her Grandpa.

Tomorrow she would talk to Ray and clear everything up. Once she had a chance to explain, everyone would realize this was a mistake, a huge mistake. She could clear it all up tomorrow. Surely everyone could see she wasn't a criminal.

Jail was a terrible place to be. It was cold and uncomfortable; they didn't even give her a blanket. The lights stay on all night and it's never quiet. Suzanne curled up in a corner and pulled her legs inside her baggy sweater in an attempt to get warm.

She would never be able to stand more than one night in this Hell. She desperately wanted a hot coffee; a hot anything would be good. She hadn't eaten since lunch and wondered how long 'til breakfast.

Every time she drifted off to sleep she would drift right into the same nightmare and wake up in terror. Her mother was standing over her, punching and kicking her over and over. It was so real; Suzanne could feel every blow as if it were being struck then and there.

Each time she woke up she had tears in her eyes. She huddled herself into a ball, began rocking and crying ... "DADDY WHY COULDN'T YOU HAVE STOPPED HER? ... WHY DIDN'T YOU SAVE ME? ... WHY ANGEL AND NOT ME? " ...

She thought about the last words he had said to her ... "I AM ASHAMED OF YOU" ... It replayed through her head over and over again. That one statement hurt her more than any blow her mother had ever struck.

For that night, Suzanne was eight years old again. That child she had pushed down inside her many years ago kept trying to crawl back up to the surface. That little girl deep inside of her was filled with a sadness that Suzanne could hardly bear.

She couldn't believe how painful it was for that child to come to her conscious thought. She couldn't stand it. Why now?... when she needed to be strong. It was more pain than she could stand, filling her with the pain and emotions of a lifetime of heartache and struggle.

Consumed with an irruption of emotions Suzanne screamed as loud as she could...

"LEAVE ME ALONE.... GET OUT OF MY HEAD.... YOU HURT ME MY ENTIRE LIFE DO YOU HAVE TO HURT ME IN YOUR DEATH... QUIT HAUNTING ME MOTHER ... GO AWAY LITTLE GIRL ... BOTH OF YOU LEAVE ME ALONE!! " ...

Suzanne still hadn't realized the little girl wasn't her daughter. It was the little girl that got lost inside her so many years ago. The one Suzanne refused to acknowledge because she was too weak. She always fell apart, always crying when Suzanne needed to be strong.

She wanted to go to sleep and stay asleep. Couldn't she have one night of peace with no haunts or nightmares? Suzanne was so tired; however she didn't dare let herself fall asleep. Once the nightmares started they would stay to plague her all night.

It was without a doubt the longest night she had ever put in. The sun wasn't quite up when they brought her a semi-warm coffee and a burger of some sort with nothing on it. In the holding cells that was what was served for every meal because no one ever stayed long. Mostly overnight, which was what she hoped for?

She did manage to beg a second cup of coffee out of them. She brushed her teeth with her finger, having never felt so grungy and disgusting. It was as though they all went out of their way to degrade her as much as possible. How dare they, treat her like a criminal. They would all be sorry once she cleared all this up.

Shortly after nine, her lawyer showed up, Paul Andrews he was court appointed. Lawyer Paul Andrews was a tall strikingly handsome man that caught Suzanne's eye the minute he walked into the room. She couldn't speak, she didn't know what to say she hated that this man would think she was a criminal.

Lawyer Paul tried to go over all the charges, things had to be sorted out before they went into court. As her lawyer rambled off the charges, she knew, he must have the wrong client...

"ABUSE... ENDANGERMENT... POSSIBLE INVOLUNTARY MANSLAUGHTER "... if her father didn't make it.

He showed her statements from the neighbors. Suzanne believed there was a possibility that the neighbor did something and didn't want to take responsibility for whatever she did. Maybe Angel fell down the stairs in her care, being afraid she would get into trouble she made up a story.

Suzanne continued reading statements from her children, her father, and the police officers on the scene, social workers and lastly the doctors that treated both Angel and her father. Mr. Paul Andrews asked her if there was a possibility she lost her head and didn't remember things. She couldn't imagine why these people were saying these things. It couldn't be the way they said ... that would make her a monster.

Her lawyer asked her to submit to psychiatric assessment. She wasn't crazy, why was everything blown so far out of proportion. She may not understand what was happening but the one thing she did know was that she wasn't crazy.

Paul Andrews was trying to explain to her it wasn't because she was crazy, agreeing to assessment would accomplish two things; it would buy them more time and the judge would look at her more sympathetically if she was taking responsible steps to help herself. She hated the idea but would go along with it.

She was led into the courtroom with a guard on each side of her. She wondered why they were being rough, so pushy. Couldn't they see she wasn't a criminal? She wasn't like the others, this was all a mistake.

The judge mumbled something, her lawyer mumbled something else; she was ordered to stand, to sit. She was moving like a robot or a wind up toy. It was all a dream. She was in a daze, and none of it made sense.

The next thing she knew someone took off the handcuffs and she could leave. Paul led her into a small conference room where he tried to explain to her what had happened. She was let out on her own recognizance with several stipulations.

It was at this point that her lawyer asked her a real strange question... "DID SHE HAVE A PLACE TO STAY?" ... of course she had a place to stay... "AT HOME OF COURSE! ... WITH HER FAMILY WHERE SHE BELONGED "...

That was when he told her she couldn't go home; not until all the court dates are over and the judge orders it ... "I CAN'T GO TO MY OWN HOME? ... I CAN'T SEE MY FAMILY? " ... "YOU ARE NOT TO BE ALONE WITH YOUR FATHER OR YOUR CHILDREN UNDER ANY CIRCUMSTANCES" ...

Suzanne couldn't understand this, she hadn't hurt any of her other children ... She didn't even believe she had hurt her Dad, and Angel, at least not on purpose anyway. She was free to go to work and do almost anything else as long as she showed up for the court dates.

Her court date wasn't for three months and she would have to be a perfect upstanding citizen with complete calmness. There could be no scars on her character at all. It would be vital that she appear both cooperative and upstanding.

Suzanne was finally released, escorted to her home by a social worker and her lawyer to pick up what she would need. She was never to come home without the social worker. Suzanne could not believe how cold and unfriendly the worker was.

Suzanne always thought they were supposed to be friendly and helpful. She went out of her way to make Suzanne feel like a criminal. Quickly Suzanne packed her things then sat down to explain things to her children. The social worker watched her every move, listened to every word she spoke.

Why didn't anyone understand that she would not hurt her children? She desperately needed to see Ray, but he was at the hospital with Angel ... "GOD FORBID!... ANGEL SHOULDN'T COME FIRST TO HER DADDY ... HE SURE WASN'T TOO WORRIED ABOUT HIS WIFE. "

For once she wanted someone to worry about her, to be there for her. Nobody rescued her when her mother beat her ... but because it was Angel suddenly it is all a big dramatic deal.

She asked her lawyer the rules, she needed to go to the hospital and talk to her Dad. It would not be allowed. Maybe if he wanted to see her, only after he was stronger, maybe a letter or a phone call. Even that had to be approved by the judge.

Suzanne went to her mother-in-law, thanking her for coming. She wanted to explain, to beg her to understand and not hate her. The words just didn't come to her, how could she ever explain this. It broke Suzanne's heart to hear the coldness in her tone.

Ray's mother had always been both kind and warm, more so than her own mother. The kind of warmth she wished her mother had had. Now Suzanne had probably lost all her respect and love never to get it back again...

Maybe Ray could explain once he understands what's going on. Suzanne could explain things to him, make him understand then he could make his mother understand. In time she could win back their trust and love, she simply needed time for them to understand.

As hard as Suzanne tried, she simply couldn't understand what all the commotion was all about. Angel couldn't have had more than a couple bruises. Her own mother had hit her harder...many times.

Nobody cared that Angel had been completely disrespectful and deserved what she got. That was what Suzanne had to get both Ray and his mother to understand. If Ray hadn't spoiled Angel for her entire life this would never have happened. He always took Angel's side.

Suzanne wondered why she had to be the bad guy. There was no way Angel was going to win, not this time. Angel had the whole world feeling sorry for her but Suzanne knew the truth. There was no way she would push Suzanne's buttons ... she refused to feel guilty.

The most important question, would she be allowed to be alone with Ray. Suzanne was thankful she could spend as much time as she wanted with him as long as the kids weren't there. She pressured her mother-in-law into calling the hospital, to have Ray meet her at the coffee shop on Division Road.

Suzanne was so scared of facing Ray. Yesterday she was treating him like he was an embarrassment, and now it was her causing the embarrassment. Yesterday seemed like a hundred years ago ... was it really yesterday? She gave all her children a big hug that would have to last her a long time.

She told her lawyer she would take a room at her place of employment until she had a better idea of what she was going to do. She would call him with more details when she had everything worked out.

Force of habit; she hated to make final decisions without discussing things with Ray. Nothing could be definite till it had his approval. She had done nothing without Ray's input since she was a teenager and she wasn't about to start now. She didn't always do what he said but she did always listen.

While waiting for Ray, she tried to run the events of the night before through her mind. She was still unable to get her mother out of her head. She hated to think of her mother as it always hurt too much. Suzanne had to find a way to get her out of her head.

It was rare for her not to get a lump in her throat and feel tears well up in her eyes every time she thought about her mother. Until now she had been successful at pushing it all back inside. The past couple days were different. Her mother was inside her head at all times. Her mother was haunting her, and not about to stop.

Suzanne had already been at the coffee shop over an hour. She was scared to death Ray wouldn't come; that he didn't want to see her again. Or even worse, that he hated her and was disgusted by what they say she did.

After three cups of coffee and several trips pacing from window to window trying to spot Ray's car, she gave up and called the house. Maybe he never got the message. Maybe her mother-in-law couldn't find him.

It had taken her some time to get the message to Ray. But he was now on his way. He was anxious to speak to Suzanne. To find out from her what had happened. As hard as he tried he couldn't come up with an excuse for what she had done. Not this time, it was unforgivable.

He couldn't imagine what she had to say to defend herself. He desperately needed to hear something, anything that would make this all right. He needed to know he wasn't in love with a monster.

Finally she got a glimpse of him walking up very slowly, head down, looking exhausted and forlorned. Suzanne had never seen him this way. He looked beaten down, like he had lost his dream and all hope of ever attaining it.

When she finally saw him he looked so much older, she didn't remember the deep worry lines in his brow or the crows feet around his eyes. For the first time in a long time she was looking at him long and hard. Had she made him that old?

Several moments of heavy silence passed before either of them could start awkward conversation. Suzanne began telling Ray she hadn't hurt Angel that much ... something must have happened after she left. Angel was trying to play him for extra sympathy. She babbled on, not knowing what she was saying; it was like her tongue and lips were on automatic pilot.

Suzanne hadn't even realized that she was doing all the talking, Ray sat in complete silence, staring deep into her eyes like he was trying to see what was behind them. He still didn't understand what happened. How did this happen? What was she thinking? Angel was her daughter, how could she have hurt her that way?

Suzanne started making excuses... she didn't hurt her that much ... "IT WAS ONLY A SPANKING! " ... Something had to have happened after she left.

Ray stopped her ... " SUZANNE, I TALKED TO THE KIDS, TO YOUR DAD, THEY TOLD ME EVERYTHING ... DO NOT LIE TO ME ... PLEASE ...ADMIT TO THE TRUTH.!!.. "

She had to start facing the truth and the truth was that she needed help. If he couldn't get her to face the truth about what happened, then she could never be helped or get better... "

SUZANNE!!... YOU HAVE TO GET HELP ..."Suzanne wanted to know about her father, but what she wanted most was to change the subject. Was he all right? Did he hate her? Would he ever forgive her? Ray handed her a letter from her Dad, which she put in her purse to read later when she was alone.

She was scared of what it might say. If he said he hated her and never wanted to see her again, she would have to be alone to read that. Suzanne looked at Ray and said she wanted to be alone with him so they could talk more freely.

They drove to the nearest motel, not for sex but to talk ... They talked about Suzanne's Dad, they talked about jail; they even talked about the neighbor and Ray's Mom. Not once had Suzanne even asked about Angel.

As Ray listened to her talk it suddenly occurred to him everything she talked about was about her or how things pertained to her.   She didn't worry whether or not her father was going to die, she only worried if he still loved her. She didn't worry about what she had done; she worried about what others thought of her. Instead of worrying how Angel was, she worried about how much grief Angel was bringing her.

Ray could not believe that Suzanne actually blamed Angel for starting all this trouble. She blamed her father for interfering and she blamed the neighbor who must have done something to Angel after Suzanne left for the hospital.

There was lots of blame to go around. That is to everyone except Suzanne who was only doing what she had to do. He couldn't stand to listen to her any longer. He tried his hardest to block out her words, he didn't want to face what kind of person she had become. This was the only person he had ever loved. She was his life, his love.

Ray's rose colored glasses fell to the floor and shattered. For the first time he was seeing Suzanne for who she really was. He didn't like what he was seeing or being forced to accept. Had she always been this way? Why hadn't he ever noticed these traits before?

Ray had to get out of there; he couldn't listen to what she was saying. He gave her the excuse that he had to get back to the hospital. He looked at her with a new coldness that Suzanne had never seen or felt before.

She could feel it chill her to the bone as she heard Ray's voice ask her.... "YOU AREN'T EVEN GOING TO ASK ABOUT ANGEL... ARE YOU? " ... She looked at him with anger and frustration ... " ANGEL?! ... IT'S ALWAYS ABOUT ANGEL... ANGEL IS FINE! ... WHY IS EVERYONE ALWAYS SO WORRIED ABOUT THAT CHILD? ... I AM YOUR WIFE ... ARE YOU NOT WORRIED ABOUT ME? ... I HAVE LOST MY FAMILY, MY HOME, MY FATHER... I COULD BE GOING TO JAIL ... WHY? BECAUSE A SPOILED CHILD WOULD NOT LISTEN ..."

Ray didn't want to even bother answering or discussing any of it. He knew he had to find some way of opening her eyes, she had to see ... " I CAN WORRY ABOUT HER AND STILL WORRY ABOUT YOU ... YOU MAY BE MY WIFE BUT ANGEL IS MY DAUGHTER ...

YOU ARE AN ADULT ... SHE IS A HELPLESS CHILD ... YOU HAVEN'T EVEN SEEN HER ... YOU DON'T KNOW WHAT KIND OF DAMAGE YOU DID ... COME WITH ME I AM GOING TO TAKE YOU SOME PLACE... "

Suzanne filled with hesitation and apprehension as she stepped into Ray's car. She knew right away what direction he was going in, what he wanted her to see. He didn't understand she wasn't allowed to go to the hospital. It was an order from the judge, if she were caught it would go against her when she went back to court, they would probably throw her right back in jail if they caught her.

Ray had it all figured out, Angel wouldn't see her, but she needed to see Angel. He had to take the chance that no one else would see her

121

either. This was the only way, if she didn't see what she had done now; while the damage was evident then she would never accept what she had done. That she needed help.

She was a monster; she was the selfish spoiled brat, not Angel. Suzanne had to see and accept this. It was the only way, Ray knew if they were ever to fix this she had to see. He was desperate for her to step back into the real world without her rose colored glasses and excuses.

Ray took Suzanne into a small observation room with one-way glass. She sat down and started to look around the playroom. There were a half dozen kids playing in the middle of the room, all various sizes, getting along with each other well. They could see three other children watching television.

In the far corner of the room was a chair by the window, in it sat a sad, lonely looking child. Suzanne couldn't see her very well as she was curled up in a ball hugging something. Likely it was her favorite doll or stuffed animal. Suzanne remembered being that young and that sad. She remembered when her only friend in the world was her teddy.

There was something familiar about this child; Suzanne couldn't take her eyes off her. She felt as though she were watching herself at that age. She began to realize that the child she watched was her own Angel... holding that ugly rag doll.

The same rag doll that Suzanne threw away after replacing it with a more beautiful doll. A doll Angel refused to play with, a doll that cost Suzanne a lot of money. It was only one more example of Angel's ingratitude. Angel was far too big for that old rag doll. That would be going back into the trash where it should have stayed in the first place.

Suzanne couldn't believe the way she was sitting there looking so sad and pathetic, so she could get more attention from her Daddy. As Ray walked over to Angel her eyes lit right up she never got that excited to see Suzanne. He picked her up and gently sat in a chair near the mirror with Angel in his lap.

They were going to play a game, counting all the bruises and bandages. There was a grand total of twenty three bruises, ten dressings and bandages, a broken arm, a cracked rib and six stitches across her cheek that he hoped wasn't going to scar.

Suzanne was still telling herself that Angel had to have fallen after she left. Suzanne remembered Angel running up the stairs she could have easilly lost her footing and fallen back down them.

That would cause the kind of damage that Suzanne was seeing. It was the only thing that made sense. Why couldn't everyone see that it made sense that way? Angel just wasn't telling anyone because this way she got more attention from everyone. Or maybe she was afraid of getting into trouble, Suzanne needed to speak to Angel to get her to tell the truth.

As Ray was driving Suzanne back to her car at the coffee shop, she tried to talk to Ray about the possibility that Angel needed to tell the truth, that she had fallen after Suzanne left. If anyone could get Angel to tell the truth Ray could. People needed to know that Suzanne couldn't have done all that damage. She wasn't the monster they were making her out to be. She wasn't!

Ray drove in silence; Suzanne could feel the coolness between them. She knew Ray was taking Angel's side and didn't believe her. If she couldn't convince Ray who loved her and knew her better than anyone how would she ever convince strangers. Angel had won again as Angel always won.

When Ray dropped off Suzanne he couldn't kiss her goodbye, he couldn't even stand to look at her. When she got out of the car he stared straight ahead and coolly stated ... "GET SOME HELP ... YOU NEED IT ... YOU DID THAT TO HER AND THE SOONER YOU CAN ADMIT IT, THE BETTER OFF WE'LL ALL BE ..."

She shook her head and walked away. Ray knew she didn't believe any of it. What hurt and upset Ray the most was that she still had not shown any remorse or regret for what she did to Angel or even admitted that just maybe she actually caused this damage.

He went straight home he had to spend some time with his other children. Anna was the first one to ask questions. She wanted to know if the police took Angel away because she was a bad girl.

Ray brought all the kids together, R.J. sat on his knee, with Anna and Alice on either side. This was really hard for him. What do you say?... MOMMY HAS A PROBLEM AND SHE NEEDS TO SEE A SPECIAL KIND OF DOCTOR. NONE OF THIS WAS ANGEL'S FAULT ... SHE IS NOT A BAD GIRL ... "Anna looked at him very puzzled. She was bad; Mommy had said it all the time.

Anna continued to argue with Ray ... "ANNA YOU ARE ARGUING WITH ME RIGHT NOW. DO YOU DESERVE FOR ME TO HIT YOU? ... WELL NEITHER DID ANGEL ... NO ONE DESERVES TO BE HIT ... NOT LIKE THAT ..."

Everyone seemed to understand but they wanted to know when Mommy could come home and Grandpa too. Grandpa would be home in a few days; Mommy would be gone a long time. She would call and talk to them on the phone everyday, but she could only see them two hours a day three times a week. That lady that was here earlier would be with her.

Starting to cry Anna burst with the emotions of the child she was... "I HATE ANGEL ... IF SHE WOULD DO WHAT SHE IS TOLD EVERYTHING WOULD STILL BE THE SAME ... EVERYBODY WOULD BE HERE ... TOGETHER."

As she started to run to her room, Ray yelled after her ... "THIS WAS NOT ANGEL'S FAULT.... NEVER SAY THAT AGAIN." Ray couldn't believe her attitude. His family was getting so hateful; it was like a disease spreading to every member of the once loving family.

It was like Suzanne's family when her mother was alive. If there was such a thing as demon possession it was Suzanne's mother returning in Suzanne's head to make her evil. Suzanne wasn't near the monster her mother was; this was all his mother-in-law's fault.

Suzanne was given a room at work. She was a live-in supervisor, and traded off working on call twenty-four hours a day for room and board. She didn't tell them any details she simply said she had left Ray because they were fighting.

They were quick to believe it with the spectacle Ray made of himself when he had shown up. No one was real surprised after seeing what a hick farmer he was. It was obvious to everyone she was above him ... or so they thought without knowing all the details.

When she got to her room the first thing she did was call the girls to say goodnight. She said a little prayer as the phone rang and was thankful when Anna answered. Finally she could talk to someone who loved and missed her. She couldn't deal with hearing the coldness in Ray's voice or the disappointment in his mother's voice.

Anna told her that Daddy said she was sick and had to get better before she could come home. How dare he tell her children that she is the one who was sick? What was he trying to do make all of her children hate her?

The entire situation is what's sick; turning a simple spanking into mass murder. Suzanne explained to Anna that her Daddy had lied to her that she wasn't sick she just had some things to sort out. She blew her a kiss over the phone and spoke to the other kids.

After she got off the phone, she ran a very hot bath and climbed into the tub soaking 'til she fell asleep. When she woke up she was freezing. The water was cold; it reminded her of her night in jail. She put on a warm nightgown and housecoat and lay on her bed to read her father's letter.

DEAR PRINCESS
I LOVE YOU VERY MUCH...

Tears welled in her eyes blinding her, so she couldn't read. She sobbed for a few moments trying to compose herself enough to read on...

THE DOCTORS TELL ME I WILL BE ALL-RIGHT AND I WILL BE HOME IN A COUPLE DAYS. I SHOULD HAVE TOLD YOU A LONG TIME AGO, THE DOCTORS TOLD ME I WAS A WALKING TIME BOMB AND COULD HAVE A HEART ATTACK AT ANY TIME. YOU AND RAY WERE HAVING SO MUCH TROUBLE I DIDN'T HAVE THE HEART TO ADD TO THEM.

I HAVE SOME THINGS TO SAY TO YOU THAT YOU ARE NOT GOING TO WANT TO HEAR. WHEN YOU CAME HOME FROM WORK AND STARTED GOING ON ABOUT RAY BEING A HICK FARMER AND HOW YOU WERE ASHAMED OF HIM, FOR THE FIRST TIME IN YOUR LIFE I WANTED TO TURN YOU OVER MY KNEE AND SPANK YOU.

WHEN YOU FIRST MET RAY, I WILL ADMIT YOUR MOTHER AND I THOUGHT HE WAS A LOWLIFE, AND THAT YOU WERE TOO GOOD FOR HIM...

I WAS WRONG HE WAS TOO GOOD FOR YOU. HE WAS ALWAYS BETTER THAN WE WERE AND SO WAS HIS FAMILY. I NEVER SAW RAY OR HIS PARENTS EVER BEAT A HELPLESS CHILD, OR SCREAM FOR THE SAKE OF MAKING PEOPLE'S LIVES MORE MISERABLE. SUZANNE YOU ARE WRONG. YOU ARE WRONG ABOUT RAY AND YOU ARE WRONG IN WHAT YOU DO TO ANGEL.

YOUR MOTHER WAS BEATEN ALL HER CHILDHOOD SO SHE BEAT YOU; AND NOW YOU BEAT ANGEL. MAYBE ANGEL WILL HAVE A CHILD SHE CAN BEAT. IT'S TIME TO BREAK THE CHAIN. I AM BEGGING YOU... GET SOME HELP BEFORE YOU KILL ANGEL. THIS IS MY FAULT, IF I HAD MORE SPINE THIRTY YEARS AGO AND STOOD UP TO YOUR MOTHER, MAYBE YOU WOULDN'T BE THIS WAY. PLEASE FORGIVE ME FOR NOT RESCUING YOU ALL THOSE YEARS AGO.

I DID WHAT I DID FOR YOU AS MUCH AS FOR ANGEL. I PROMISE FROM NOW ON I WILL ALWAYS BE THERE FOR YOU AND LOVE YOU. I ONLY ASK ONE THING OF YOU... PLEASE GET HELP. DEAL WITH ALL THAT ANGER FOR YOUR MOTHER. YOU NEED A PSYCHIATRIST AND I WILL PAY FOR IT FOR YOU.

PLEASE CALL ME WHENEVER YOU NEED TO TALK.

LOVE YOU FOREVER NO MATTER WHAT ...

DAD

Chapter Seven

Suzanne dropped off to sleep with the letter in her hand, tossing and turning in a fitful sleep. She still couldn't get her mother out of her head. What was she doing there? What was she trying to tell Suzanne?

Suzanne tried and tried to remember that night. Everyone can't be wrong? She wasn't a monster, she wasn't. She started to think maybe she was crazy, maybe she totally lost her mind and didn't know.

For the first time since all this started, she thought about Angel. All her bruises, cuts and breaks started flashing through her head in an unwanted inventory. She tried to stop herself from thinking about it, but couldn't stop the flashes. It was burning into her head and there was no escape. Unfortunately she could not walk away from her own head when it was telling her things she didn't want to hear.

When Suzanne thought she couldn't stand having Angel's bruised and battered body in her head, her mind gave her a new vision to concentrate on. She was standing over Angel kicking, punching and pulling her by the hair. Her father was pulling at her trying to get her off that poor child lying on the floor, trying to cover her face, to protect herself.

Each time she pulled her hands from her face, the face changed. First it was Angel, then herself and back and forth, until she forced herself to wake up. Suzanne could feel her face wet from tears she had shed.

Trapped in her panic, she couldn't breathe, she couldn't stop shaking. She ran to the bathroom still trying to catch her breath, putting her head under the cold water tap in an attempt to wake herself from her nightmare.

As she stood in front of the mirror with water and tears streaming down, all she could see was her mother's face. It was different this time, it wasn't her mother's cold, angry face; it was a scared face, a helpless face...

Blindly reaching for something, anything she threw it as hard as she could screaming at the top of her lungs ... " LEAVE ME ALONE ... YOU HATED ME ALL MY LIFE ... WHY CAN'T YOU LEAVE ME ALONE IN YOUR DEATH ... LET ME HAVE SOME PEACE " ...

It was close to five a.m. before she escaped, exhausted and drained into the depths of sleep.

The desk downstairs gave her a wake up call at seven thirty. She had to be up early enough to call the girls before they left for school. When she went into the bathroom and was forced to realize what she had done, she knew she was truly insane. Her father, her husband, and her lawyer won she did need help. Maybe that was the point of her mother's visits.

Talking to the girls seemed to help calm her shattered nerves. Anna and Alice always made her feel better. They were both so grown now; she could hardly hear the child in their voices. R.J. was a lot of fun to talk to, it didn't matter what was going on around him he was always full of cheer and excitement. He had always reminded her of a little leprechaun, there to entertain.

Ray was still asleep, Suzanne told the girls not to wake him. She was sure he didn't want to talk to her any more than she wanted to talk to him. It wasn't that she didn't want to talk to him she just wasn't ready to talk to him. She had to get her head on straight first. She wasn't strong enough for the disappointment that was sure to be in his voice.

The girls told her that Angel was coming home, that Daddy was picking her up at lunch. Anna told her mother she wasn't going to speak to Angel; it was her fault that everybody went away.

What had she done? Now her entire family was split down the middle. Anna had to understand none of this was Angel's fault; she was not to blame Angel in any way. She needed the girls to be extra nice to Angel when she came home. It was important that they help and befriend Angel.

Suzanne cleaned up her mess from the night before, made an attempt to fix her face and look as good as was possible after two hours of restless sleep. Not needing anyone asking her a bunch of questions about how bad she looked, she needed to be left alone. There was lots of work to catch up on and lots to think about.

As soon as the clock struck nine she was right on the phone to Paul, she was surprised how long he spoke to her. He had a way of making her feel like she was his only client. Suzanne told him about her dreams and nightmares. She now knew that she did need help, that it was all her fault. She was that monster that hurt her own child.

Paul told her how pleased he was and that he knew how hard it was for her to admit it. Now that she could face it, she could also fix it. He gave her the name of a good psychiatrist, a female. He felt Suzanne would feel safer relating to a woman.

Suzanne was relieved when he told her the manslaughter charges were dropped and that her Dad would be leaving the hospital soon. It was a huge weight off her shoulders knowing her Dad was safe.

Paul seemed to be so caring and helpful she wondered if he was like this with all his clients ... he laughed and told her he only worked this hard when someone was worth saving. Suzanne loved to hear the first compliment she had heard in a very long time.

"WORTH SAVING "she liked that expression, she wasn't sure she believed it. She had been a screw up all her life. The only thing she ever was good at was her career. She felt so confident and self assured at work, there was no problem she couldn't solve. At home she was the problem.

Suzanne decided that if she were to meet herself she too would hate the person she had become. She doubted she would ever be friends with someone even the tiniest bit like herself.

Only she knew just how rotten she truly was deep inside. She was good at concealing and hiding her dark sides from all even those closest to her. She doubted even Ray and her Dad knew just how dark and truly evil she was inside.

Hanging up the phone, Suzanne took a couple deep breaths before calling the number Paul had given her. It was time to set up an appointment; if she waited she was sure to talk herself out of it. Any excuse would do to convince her to put this off.

This was without a doubt one of the scariest things she ever had to do. What if the psychiatrist saw through her? What if she saw how evil she really was? Or worse what if there was no help for someone as bad as her?

They had a cancellation for the next day at two p.m. or she would have to wait two weeks for the next opening. Even though she was scared to death, she was glad to have the opportunity to get it over with quick. It would be pure torture to stew and think about it for the next two weeks.

She called her Dad to tell him she had an appointment, sure he would be pleased. She wondered for just a moment why Daddy's approval was more important than her husbands. Maybe that was something she could talk to the doctor about.

As Suzanne sat thinking about her appointment she wished she had asked more questions. Was she supposed to make a list of all the things she wanted to talk about and change about herself? Maybe the doctor would only want to deal with the relationship between her and Angel.

More than Angel what she wanted to deal with were the insomnia and nightmares. Maybe she could deal with Angel calmly if she weren't so tired all the time. There was so much she wanted to deal with, little of it having to do with Angel and her spoiled behavior.

All of it would have to wait 'til tomorrow for now she had to get to work before she was fired and thrown out on the street. The first thing she had to do was check the reservation list, a customer was arguing with the desk clerk.

They may be the hotel's best customers but they were also a real pain in the behind, which was exactly what they expected everyone to kiss. As she watched the potentially explosive situation she stepped in to rescue the poor desk clerk who was obviously over her head trying to deal with this conceited arrogance.

The exhausted clerk mouthed a thank-you as she busied herself out of the range of fire.... "YOU ARE RIGHT ... I KNOW HOW YOU FEEL ... THEY SHOULD BE MORE EFFICIENT ... YOU KNOW HOW HARD IT CAN BE KEEPING AFTER STAFF ... I WILL TAKE CARE OF IT RIGHT AWAY ..."

They were pleased and Suzanne walked away thinking what a bunch of self-righteous fools. The complaint didn't matter, they were always the same. Coming for three days every second week, they always had to exert their power over the staff.

There was a lot of money thrown around tipping well, but the humiliation and the abuse was barely worth the tip. The second day was always the worst day for complaints. Suzanne always figured they took care of all of their business the first day and broke their boredom the second by torturing her staff.

Next on the agenda, was to smooth the ruffled feathers of Shelby the head chef, he was so temperamental that he went insane every time a customer sent something back to the kitchen. She could see him waving a huge ladle over his head as he shouted out obscenities at the rest of his staff.

Kitchen staff was one of her biggest headaches; it seemed she was always replacing them. Everyone was scared of the chef. Shelby was well worth the headaches he was the best... people came from all across North America to feast on his delights.

The first thing she did was to give all the kitchen staff a fifteen minute break so she could calm his ruffled feathers in private ...

"SHELBY YOU HAVE GOT TO STOP SCARING THE STAFF ... MAYBE THEY WOULDN'T BE TOTAL IMBECILES IF YOU WOULD QUIT SCARING THEM ALL AWAY? ... THE ONLY REASON THEY DON'T KNOW THEIR JOB IS BECAUSE YOU CONSTANTLY HAVE TO TRAIN NEW STAFF...

Shelby was out of control and she had to get him to see just how out of control. He really was a nice guy she actually liked him and enjoyed him as a friend and as a friend she had to get him to control his temper...

"YOU WILL CALM DOWN AND TALK TO THEM LIKE THEY ARE HUMAN BEINGS WITH FEELINGS ... OTHERWISE I WILL PERSONALLY ESCORT YOU TO AN ANGER MANAGEMENT SEMINAR ... "After a short pause she looked at him and smiled ... "YOU KNOW THAT IS NOT A HALF BAD IDEA ... WE WILL GO TOGETHER...I WILL LOOK INTO IT ...??"

As she started to walk away she could hear him yell ... " I WILL NOT GO ..." She turned and smiled her best little girl smile ... " YOU WILL DO IT FOR ME ... "

Grinning right back at her he said ... " DON'T USE THOSE WOMANLY WAYS ON ME ... THEY WON'T WORK UNLESS YOU GROW HAIR ON YOUR CHEST ... " She laughed to herself, the crisis was over he wasn't angry anymore ... " OH YA! ... YOU AREN'T ANGRY ANY MORE ARE YOU? "

As she walked away she whispered to herself ... "DAMN I AM GOOD..." and she was. She could smooth out the biggest of egos. She wondered why she couldn't do it with Angel. Every one of these people were every bit as difficult as her Angel.

After all that she made herself a hot tea and went to her office to gratefully tackle a very large pile of quiet paper work that didn't talk back, complain or argue. She also needed a little time to think before she called Angel when she got home from the hospital.

When she called to speak to Angel, Ray had already left for work. Angel was very hard to talk to. She didn't converse; she merely answered her mother's questions with yes or no and gave the phone to her grandma.

When Ray's mom came on the phone she told Suzanne to be patient that it would take some time. She went on to say that Angel looked a bit better; she seemed to be healing nicely, although she still sat in silence most of the time staring off into space.

Ray's mother lied to Suzanne; she was horrified at how bad Angel looked. While helping her bathe she could hardly find a spot on her tiny body that wasn't bruised. The bruises were all different stages of healing and colors.

Ray's Mom knew what that meant; this was not the first time this child took a beating. She couldn't talk to Suzanne about any of this but she would certainly be discussing it with her son when he got home, there was a lot she wanted to talk to him about.

The other children didn't play with Angel, she was always alone and most of the time either staring out the window or in the back of that dark closet with her rag doll. That rag doll was her only friend in the world and probably had been for a long time.

She tried her hardest to talk the other kids into playing with Angel; they said they never did play with her. Angel liked playing alone; she was too weird to have any friends. They told their Grandma nobody played with Angel even at school everybody knew how strange she was. Rays mom could feel the tears well up in her eyes and the lump in her throat. She had a lot of trouble not crying in front of the kids.

Rays mother went up to Angel's room, without saying a word she crawled into the back of the closet and sat on the floor beside her, then she reached out her arms and held her. Neither of them said a word but Ray's mother couldn't help but cry gentle tears that she couldn't hold back.

She wished she had paid more attention, she knew Suzanne was hard on Angel but she didn't imagine in her worse nightmare that things were this bad. This child was not only physically abused, but emotionally starved ... "MY GOD ... MY GOD .... WHY WAS I SO BLIND ... WHY WAS EVERYONE SO BLIND? "

When Suzanne hung up the phone she held everything inside long enough to call the desk and tell them she was going on break and to not disturb her. She could hardly get the words out before the tears came running down her face out of control. Pulling her knees up tight to her chest with her arms wrapped around them, she buried her face as she sobbed, her Angel hated her.

It carried her back to a time when she feared and hated her own mother. She too spoke to her mother in one-word sentences. If she spoke as little as possible her mother would have trouble finding something that might anger her.

As she got older Suzanne realized her mother didn't need an excuse. Getting up in the morning or being in the same room was enough to set her off. Was this her? Is this what she did to Angel? Did Angel feel about her the way she had always felt about her mother? It all melted together into one big blur, her life, and Angel's life. She wasn't as bad as her mother, she wasn't!

They did things together it wasn't all bad. Suzanne remembered reading to her when she was little. Lately they hadn't done anything together because Angel was always bad. If Angel would listen to her, they could do more.

Why was it always Angel being sent to her room? Why couldn't they get through even one day without a fight? All Angel had to do was not be so head-strong and quit giving her dirty looks.

Suzanne couldn't torture herself about it anymore she had to get downstairs and deal with the supper rush and the happy hour gang. She still had some trouble dealing with the drunks, you couldn't rationalize with them, and they were capable of almost anything, especially if it's something destructive or vulgar.

It was almost midnight when she got back to her room, Ray would still be up, he was working a three to eleven shift. It was time to start dealing with their marriage. It would only get worse the longer she put it off. When she called, he cut her off short, not giving her a chance to talk.

"I NEED TO TALK TO MY MOTHER ABOUT PROBLEMS WITH THE KIDS, SHE WAS UPSET" ... Suzanne couldn't believe it ... "SHE'S UPSET? ... I AM UPSET! ... DOES HE CARE? ... I AM THEIR MOTHER, HE SHOULD BE TALKING TO ME IF THERE IS A PROBLEM WITH ... MY! ... CHILDREN. "

When the phone rang she dove for it thinking it might be Ray. It wasn't, it was the bar downstairs they had a problem with a drunk that wouldn't leave. He was getting abusive to the staff. Suzanne had zero tolerance for this kind of crap. She would not have her staff abused.

Deep down it stirred all the old scars of William. It wasn't going to happen to anyone under her employ. She went so far as to have security walk every girl to their car at the end of the night. It was worth it if it meant no one got hurt.

Just when she thought she was talking him out calmly, he lost it and started swinging. The security guards grabbed him and carried him out, three seconds too late. Suzanne's nose was bleeding a great ending for an otherwise lousy night. The waitress brought her a drink while she held ice on her nose.

She had a few more after that, actually she closed the place and then some, one way or another she was going to get some sleep. She picked up another drink and drank a toast to...

"NO GHOSTS"

It was three a.m. before Suzanne staggered her way to her room and collapsed on her bed fully clothed. She could hear the phone ringing but it seemed so far away. Even though her mind was willing her body wouldn't get up or was it couldn't. She wasn't sure which but the result was the same ... an unanswered phone. She hoped it wasn't a problem with work. If it were, someone else would have to handle it.

Suzanne tried her hardest to lift her head when she woke the next morning only to discover that all those rocks in her head were far too heavy. This would never happen again, she couldn't have the respect of her staff if she were falling down drunk. From now on if she had to drink she would do it alone in her suite.

When she was finished lecturing herself, she changed into a housecoat and put on a pot of coffee, she had a couple hours 'til she had to actually look good. Even while she was thinking this the phone was ringing. It was Ray.

He was really upset, Suzanne had not heard him yell this much since his drinking days.

"WHERE IN THE HELL HAVE YOU BEEN? ... I CALLED YOUR ROOM ALL NIGHT THERE WAS NO ANSWER..."

Suzanne couldn't believe his nerve; he had brushed her off as though she were not even part of her own family now he wanted to know where she was...." WHERE DID YOU SLEEP LAST NIGHT? ... TWO NIGHTS AWAY FROM HOME AND YOU ARE SCREWING AROUND ALREADY. "

She didn't need this today; she simply told him she was having nightmares so she took a couple sleeping pills. Most of the time with Ray it was easier to lie than to go into a long drawn out explanation ... besides how dare he, after the way he brushed her off.

Maybe if he had spoken to her then he wouldn't have gotten into such a panic.

" SUZANNE, I HAVE TO TALK TO YOU ABOUT THE KIDS ... I AM REALLY WORRIED ... ESPECIALLY WITH ANGEL ... DID YOU KNOW SHE SPENDS ALL HER TIME IN THE BACK OF THE CLOSET IN THE DARK AND ALONE ... THE OTHER KIDS WON'T PLAY WITH HER ... "

He was so excitable he talked without taking a breath or stopping to take a breath. First he had no time to talk to her and now that everything was a mess he expected her to fix it. Where was he when she was trying to raise the kids alone for all those months? What did he think she did when he was always drunk and passed out? All of a sudden he is the concerned Daddy....

"ANNA HATES HER AND IS MEAN TO HER BECAUSE SHE THINKS ITS ALL ANGELS FAULT THAT YOU WENT AWAY AND GRANDPA GOT SICK ... I TRIED AND TRIED TO EXPLAIN TO ANNA THAT IT WASN'T ANGELS FAULT

BUT SHE DOES NOT BELIEVE ME ... MAYBE IF YOU TOLD HER... "

She had already spoken to Anna. Now Suzanne was ready to say her piece ... " WHAT ARE YOU DOING TELLING THE KIDS I AM SICK OR CRAZY?... THAT WAS NOT FAIR ... MAYBE I GOT PUSHED OVER THE EDGE ... MAYBE I WENT TOO FAR ... THAT DIDN'T MAKE ME CRAZY ... YOU KNOW HOW STUBBORN AND IRRITATING ANGEL CAN BE ... SHE COULD PUSH ANYONE TO THE BRINK OF INSANITY. "

She doesn't push everyone or even anyone, only Suzanne. Suzanne had to accept and deal with that, Ray wanted her to get help. She told him she already did. She had to go at two p.m. so if he called and she wasn't there it didn't mean she was in bed with some man. She couldn't resist getting in the last dig he was deserving of.

She couldn't understand Ray sometimes, she was fifteen when she met him, they had been together for what seemed like all of her life and he still didn't know her or trust her. She decided not to worry about it, maybe he was crazy because their lives were so upside down right now.

She said she didn't know what to do about Angel when she went to the doctors this afternoon she would talk to her about whether or not Angel would need some kind of counseling. The way she saw it, Angel had always been on the weird side since birth.

She had eyes that could look through a person and dissect their brain like she was picking through their very soul. It really was kind of creepy. Suzanne found this quality especially unnerving; she didn't need this child seeing all her demons.

There was a silence in the air an uncomfortable heaviness in the conversation. They both had things to say but weren't saying anything. It was Suzanne that finally broke the silence...

"RAY? ... WHAT ABOUT US? ... WHERE DO WE STAND? ... WHERE DO WE GO FROM HERE? ... DO YOU STILL LOVE ME? ... I DON'T EVEN FEEL LIKE WE ARE A COUPLE

ANYMORE. "There was a very long silence before he could answer, a silence that sent fear and panic through her.

She instantly regretted asking the question. If he no longer loved her she would rather live in ignorance. She didn't want to hear the words ... "JUST GIVE ME A LITTLE TIME TO DIGEST EVERYTHING THAT HAS HAPPENED ... I AM SO WORRIED ABOUT RESCUING THE FAMILY ... I CAN NOT THINK ABOUT US RIGHT NOW ... I HAVE TO GO? ... CALL ME AFTER YOUR APPOINTMENT ... I DON'T HAVE TO WORK TODAY I TOOK THE DAY OFF SO I COULD PICK UP YOUR DAD... YOU CAN TALK TO HIM THEN AS WELL. "

As she hung up the phone she thought about how cool and detached he sounded, it was almost like she was talking to a stranger or business associate. She really wondered if things would ever be the same or if she even wanted things to be the same. She loved being at work, she felt good, she felt worthwhile.

Whenever she was at home she felt she had no control, no purpose, she was neither a part of their world nor was she needed. She was some crazy person they had put up with. She had become a stranger in her own home.

Suzanne felt the same way her mother had always made her feel. She always came short of being what they wanted her to be. It didn't matter how hard she tried she was a disappointment to them all.

At work it was the opposite, everything she did worked out; she could handle anything and anybody. Which she had to go do or she wouldn't get done on time to get away for her appointment.

Suzanne's stomach churned, her hands trembled as she sat in the small office waiting room. She wanted to leave, just run out the same door she came in. Why did she ever let them talk her into doing this? She sat very prim and ridged feeling like a little girl in the principles office.

Taken back to a time when she was ten years old, sitting in the office waiting for her mother to come talk to the principal... A boy kept pulling her hair, so she hit him up the side of the head with her lunch bucket ... when her mother finally came out of the office, she slapped Suzanne in the back of the head and pulled her up by her arm.

She practically had to run to keep up with her mother as she stomped with as much dignity as she could. Her mother attempted to hide the anger building inside of her, Suzanne knew it was all going to irrupt all over her. She knew this was nothing; she would be killed as soon as her mother could get her behind closed doors. The painful memory left her head as soon as her name was called to go in to the office.

This was nothing like a normal doctor's office; there were beautiful leather couches and matching wing chairs. Suzanne asked if she was to lie down, she saw that on t.v. once. Doctor Anderson laughed and told her that was only for television. Suzanne was relieved, she was sure she would never relax lying down in front of a stranger.

"HAVE A SEAT AND RELAX, IT REALLY ISN'T AS SCARY AS IT SEEMS ... Suzanne really wasn't too sure what the doctor was saying she was overwhelmed. Paralyzed with fear, so many questions and all she could do was sit and stare as the doctor spoke....

FOR THE FIRST VISIT WE GET TO KNOW EACH OTHER ... SITTING AROUND TALKING LIKE OLD GIRL FRIENDS ... I WILL TELL YOU WHAT I KNOW, THEN YOU CAN TELL ME WHAT YOU THINK ABOUT IT ...

Suzanne was sure she would never be able to tell her anything, she was thankful that so far she was doing all the talking. Suzanne studied her face and expressions trying to determine what she thought of her. Did this Doctor hate her; surely she has had crazier patients. Suzanne hoped she would tell her the craziness was all temporary and she could just go home now, that wasn't about to happen.

"I GOT YOUR RECORDS AND TRANSCRIPTS FROM YOUR LAWYER... IT BASICALLY LAYS OUT ALL THE CHARGES AND GIVES A RUN DOWN OF WHAT THEY THINK HAPPENED THAT NIGHT ... YOUR LAWYER ALSO TOLD ME THAT YOU DON'T THINK YOU DID IT?... "

Suzanne explained to her how that had changed, that she now knew she had done it … "WHAT IS IT YOU KNOW YOU DID?"… Suzanne thought about it for a minute and realized this lady wasn't going to pull any punches … "I HURT MY DAUGHTER… "

Suzanne felt a slight relief that the words were finally spoken out loud; the doctor showed no sign of shock or emotion not even a slight flinch or gasp. Suzanne was expert at spotting the tiniest signs of mood change from watching her mother. The doctor was as cool as she could be … " HOW DID THAT MAKE YOU FEEL?… "

Suzanne needed to think about her answer, this lady was tricky. Suzanne didn't like that she couldn't read her … " IT TOOK ME A LONG TIME TO EVEN ADMIT I DID IT … YOU SEE, I KNOW I DID IT … WHEN ENOUGH PEOPLE TELL YOU SOMETHING YOU HAVE TO BELIEVE IT … IN MY MIND I SIMPLY SPANKED A CHILD THAT WAS BEING DISRESPECTFUL…"

"SO BY THAT DO YOU THINK YOUR HUSBAND AND THE POLICE ARE BEING UNFAIR TO YOU, TREATING YOU TOO HARSHLY? "

Suzanne did think they were being unfair, that all this was blown way out of proportion. She wasn't a criminal and she resented being treated like one. Things had simply gone too far, got out of control, she was pretty sure that wasn't the answer that this doctor wanted to hear. …

" I DON'T KNOW … I HAVE SEEN ANGEL AND ALL THE DAMAGE DONE TO HER … IF I DID THAT I WOULD HAVE TO BE A MONSTER … I DO NOT THINK I AM A MONSTER … I THINK OF MYSELF AS THE SAME AS ANYONE ELSE. "

Suzanne sat staring at the doctor waiting for some sign, perhaps confirmation she was that monster or maybe reassurance that she was just a normal person in a bad situation. Suzanne wasn't sure why but she needed acceptance from this total stranger she needed to hear she wasn't crazy… that she was alright after all.

"DO YOU THINK OTHER MOTHERS HIT THEIR DAUGHTERS?…"

"I THINK THEY DISCIPLINE THEM AND IF A SPANKING IS WHAT IT TAKES ... THEN... YES I DO BELIEVE EVERYONE DOES WHATEVER IT TAKES TO RAISE THEIR CHILD TO BE OBEDIENT AND RESPECTFUL... "

"WOULD IT SURPRISE YOU IF I TOLD YOU I HAVE THREE CHILDREN AND HAVE NEVER HIT THEM...?" No!... she wouldn't be surprised this was the coolest most in control person Suzanne had met since the judge, no it would not surprise her that this cool lady was never out of control.

What was this woman looking for? What reaction or answer did she want? Was this a trick or was she just trying to feel Suzanne out? Suzanne sat staring into the eyes of her attacker trying to see into her soul, trying to ascertain the game they were playing.

The doctor was stone faced no emotions, no hint of what she should say next. If she was going to do this then she might as well do it honestly.... "I WOULD BELIEVE YOU ARE THE EXCEPTION, NOT THE RULE... "

" WE ARE GETTING AHEAD OF OURSELVES, LETS GO BACK TO THAT NIGHT ... YOUR FATHER HAD A HEART ATTACK TRYING TO STOP YOU FROM HITTING YOUR DAUGHTER?..."

Suzanne wondered was that a statement or a question? She sat in silence listening, sure that the doctor was simply going over the facts not looking for an answer. Or maybe she was simply looking for a reaction to the statement? Suzanne's mind was still working overtime looking for the hooks if there were any.

"TELL ME HOW YOU FELT WHEN HE WAS TAKEN TO THE HOSPITAL... "

Slowly and with great apprehension she began her answer... "I WAS ANGRY ... I WAS WORRIED ... I WAS UPSET AND CONFUSED... "

Suzanne felt a swell of emotions that night none of which she could either control or understand. She spent much of her time since that night trying to forget those little details. They were details that could only stir up the heartache and pain of the moment. What did she feel?...BETRAYED... OUT OF CONTROL... Why couldn't her father have stayed out of it? Why couldn't he have saved her all those years ago?

"LET'S GO OVER THESE EMOTIONS ONE AT A TIME... WHY WERE YOU ANGRY? "

What a silly question, why did she think Suzanne was angry?... "THAT CHILD..."

"YOU MEAN YOUR DAUGHTER? ... ANGEL? "

Now feeling defensive like she was being attacked... "WHO ELSE WOULD I MEAN?... SHE'S SO DEFIANT... EVERYTHING IS A BATTLE... SHE STANDS LIKE A ROCK STARING YOU DOWN ... DARING ME TO DO SOMETHING..."

Suzanne was trying her hardest to maintain her composure, she was sure the point of this entire conversation was to make her loose it, to push her as far over the edge as she could. Suzanne was sure that the doctor was purposely trying to upset her to the point where she didn't know what she was saying.

Suzanne gazed down at her watch for about the twentieth time, surely this hour was almost up. She had to get out of there. Suzanne was sure she had stood all she could and couldn't take any more of this inquisition.

The good Doctor Anderson was still shooting questions at Suzanne, questions Suzanne didn't want to answer... "TELL ME HOW YOU FELT WHEN SHE STARTED CRYING ... A BROKEN ARM, A GASH TO HER FACE.... SHE MUST HAVE BEEN SCREAMING HER HEAD OFF?... DID IT MAKE YOU FEEL SORRY FOR HER OR DID IT MAKE YOU ANGRIER?... "

"ANGEL DOESN'T CRY ... SHE NEVER CRIES ... I ALREADY TOLD YOU SHE JUST STANDS THERE STARING IN DEFIANCE... SHE HAS EYES THAT CUT YOU RIGHT TO THE BONE ... I THINK THAT WAS WHY I DIDN'T STOP ... IT WAS LIKE I HAD TO BEAT THAT DEFIANCE OUT OF HER... THE MORE I HIT HER THE STRONGER AND MORE

DEFIANT SHE GOT ... SHE WAS DARING ME TO BREAK HER DOWN. "

The doctor sat silently watching her before she spoke, as though she were trying to digest what Suzanne had just said... "WHAT DO YOU MEAN SHE NEVER CRIES?... YOU MEAN JUST WHEN YOU ARE FIGHTING ... THERE MUST BE SOME POINT MAYBE LATER WHEN SHE IS ALONE... "

This was the first hint of any emotion or displeasure. The doctor's cool exterior cracked ever so slightly, Suzanne could feel her displeasure at what Suzanne was saying. This was the first sign that she thought Suzanne did something terrible, she was shocked.

Suzanne would have to pull back her answers a little obviously she was on the edge of this doctor judging her as everyone else did. "I WOULDN'T KNOW THAT ... SHE SPENDS A LOT OF TIME ALONE ... MOSTLY SHE LIKES TO PLAY IN HER CLOSET WITH HER RAG DOLL..."

"IS THERE SOME SOURCE OF LIGHT IN THIS CLOSET.. DO HER SIBLINGS PLAY IN THERE WITH HER? ... "

Finally the doctor was getting onto something. Now the Doctor could see it wasn't her that was weird, it was Angel. "NO... THE OTHER THREE PLAY WITH EACH OTHER ... THEY DO NOT PLAY WITH ANGEL ... BUT THEN ANGEL DOESN'T PLAY ... EVEN AT SCHOOL SHE STAYS ALONE ... ANNA TELLS ME SHE WON'T GO NEAR ANYONE AND THEY DON'T GO NEAR HER EITHER ... APPARENTLY THEY ALL THINK SHE IS TOO WEIRD..."

"ARE YOU NOT AT ALL CONCERNED ABOUT THIS? ... WHAT DO YOU SUPPOSE WEIRD IS TO KIDS AT SCHOOL? "

"IF YOU ARE TALKING ABOUT ANGEL... I THINK IT MUST MEAN TOTALLY ANTISOCIAL AND COMPLETELY CANTANKEROUS ... SHE REALLY CAN'T GET ALONG WITH ANYONE ... SHE GIVES NEW MEANING TO THE WORD STUBBORN..."

How could Suzanne possibly be responsible for what the kids at school do or think of Angel? What was she supposed to do, go to the school and order children to play with Angel?

..."SHE THINKS SHE KNOWS MORE THAN THE TEACHERS ... I WAS NOT TOO CONCERNED, SHE IS WEIRD ... I JUST FIGURED IT WAS ANGEL BEING ANGEL... "

Why was this woman trying to twist everything around, why was she going out of her way to make Suzanne feel she was a bad mother? It wasn't her fault that Angel was weird and no one could stand to be near her.

Did she expect Suzanne to force children to be friends with her? Suzanne really wasn't impressed with how this meeting was going; it was no where near what she expected. All she wanted to do was get through the hour and get out of there.

"I WOULD LIKE TO TRY SOMETHING WITH YOU BEFORE OUR TIME IS UP...

"Suzanne wasn't sure she liked the sounds of this, but she didn't seem to have a lot of control over any of this. All she could do was listen and hope whatever this was would take the subject away from Angel...

"I AM GOING TO GIVE YOU A NAME OF SOMEONE FROM YOUR FAMILY AND YOU AS QUICKLY AS YOU CAN GIVE ME A ONE OR TWO WORD RESPONSE THAT BEST DESCRIBES THEM IN YOUR MIND... TRY NOT TO GIVE IT A LOT OF THOUGHT... BLURT OUT THE FIRST THING THAT COMES INTO YOUR HEAD... "

MOTHER ... VISCOUS
FATHER ... QUIET, WELL BRED
HUSBAND ... STEADY, RELIABLE
ANNA ... MOTHERLY
ANGEL ... HEADSTRONG, OBSTINATE
ALICE ... SWEET, LOVING
RAY JUNIOR ... FULL OF LIFE, PRECOCIOUS

SUZANNE...

This one stopped Suzanne in her tracks; there were two Suzanne's, the professional hard working, efficient Suzanne and the mother and wife Suzanne. They were totally different people and personalities. Which one did this Doctor want to hear about?

"GIVE ME THE WORKING SUZANNE FIRST..." EFFICIENT, IN CONTROL.

" NOW TELL ME ABOUT THE AT HOME SUZANNE? " ... FRUSTRATED, OUT OF CONTROL, A SCREW UP.

Now without another word the doctor began to dismiss her. Wait a minute was there no discussion to this little exercise. Was she not going to tell Suzanne what she thought about her responses? The doctor was still babbling about the next session, about future sessions with the family and with Ray as she walked the baffled Suzanne to the door and guided her to the receptionist to set up other sessions.

Still numb and in shock she sighed a sigh of relief and confusion glad to be out of the hot seat. Once she was done and out of there she figured that maybe it wasn't too bad, she had survived it with minimal pain and embarrassment.

As she gave it some thought it occurred to her she actually felt good. This confused her; it was as though a weight had been lifted from her shoulders. Was she feeling good because she was out of there? Or was she feeling good because she finally said everything out loud?

Chapter Eight

Walking into the front doors of the grand hotel, she saw Paul standing by the desk. Was he checking in for a stay or looking for her, perhaps checking up on her? Smiling as soon as he saw her walk in, he told her he was always glad to see her. Remembering her appointment he thought she would need a friend to talk to or perhaps a shoulder to lean on.

They walked into the dimly lit bar and sat in one of the corners that the waitresses would teasingly say were for the wandering married. One of the girls pointed a finger at her and teased her with a tisk, tisk as she walked by... they ordered a drink as they sat down to talk.

It wasn't long before they ordered another drink and talked some more. They talked about the case, then about Ray, then they talked about Paul and his life. Small talk, big talk, just plain talk all flowed out of Suzanne as though she had been talking to this man all her life.

After quite a while she asked if he should be at home or work, it seemed to Suzanne someone somewhere must be missing this handsome man. He must have a family that needed him. He was far too good looking and charming to not be attached to someone.

He laughed as he asked if she was trying to get rid of him. On the contrary, she hadn't felt this good in a long time. She not only enjoyed his company but needed it. It was the first time in many years she didn't feel like an employee, a wife, daughter or mother. She felt like Suzanne.

She was enthralled as he talked, it was good to hear someone elses problems. She was sick of talking about hers. He told her, since his divorce, he was never in a hurry to go home. He hated that feeling of total silence and emptiness as he walked through the door.

It merely reminded him how empty his life was. A constant reminder of how he had no one in his life that cared if he was home or anywhere else. To him that had to be the worst feeling in the world.

Suzanne could think of a worse feeling. It was far worse to have someone there and know they didn't care. At least if he was alone, he had a chance of someday finding someone who would care. What her and Ray had was all so hopeless. She couldn't even lie to herself anymore that they could somehow get past all of this.

Paul knew exactly what she meant. He had been getting frostbite from his wife for years. It was nothing for them to be wandering around the same house and not speak for days.

When they did speak it was usually about money... her wanting some that is. The conversations were short and never very sweet.

Mr. and Mrs. Paul Andrews had not even slept in the same room together for years let alone make love. They were strangers, less than strangers at least strangers would have maintained a certain politeness. They were simply stuck in a cold tolerance of each other.

Suzanne wondered why he didn't leave sooner, and since he didn't what made him leave at all. He stayed because they still played the game for all the onlookers. His wife always worried about what people would think. He finally reached a point where the silence was unbearable; he didn't care who thought what.

He was lonely and he wanted to start looking for someone who would keep him company. It really wouldn't have been right to go out while still under the same roof as his wife. It was a situation where you are wrong no matter what you do, so you try to do what you can live with.

Suzanne thought it was a welcome relief to sit quietly and listen to his problems. Somehow it made her feel less insecure about the mess her and Ray had made of their life.

She continued to sit and listen for a couple hours that flew by as she enjoyed the moments of pleasant company. Anytime he got spooked from the loneliness he could call or come over.

Suzanne was the original insomniac and rarely asleep before the wee hours crept by. So even if he woke in the middle of the night a little lonely or bored, she could always use someone to talk to, to help her get through the night.

As long as he could remember that she was married and could never offer anything more than friendship. As he broke into uncontrolled laughter Suzanne's face flushed with embarrassment that this well-bred educated lawyer could ever be attracted to her. She blushed as she tried to stutter her way out of this. Now it was Paul who was in control, something she was sure he was used to.

Leaning forward, he took both her hands in his… "YOU DO UNDERSTAND MY DEAR AS AN ESTABLISHED LAWYER I CAN GET SEX ANYWHERE … YOU WOULD BE AMAZED AT THE BOLDNESS OF SOME WOMEN…"

She wouldn't be amazed or surprised it was all she could do to stay in her seat and not jump across the table and smother him with the passions that she was so desperate to restrain whenever he was within sight.

…" I FIND YOU EXTREMELY ATTRACTIVE…BUT I AM ALSO REFRESHED TO TALK WITH NO PRESSURE … I LIKE THAT YOU ARE NOT FLIRTING OR TRYING TO GET ME TO HIT ON YOU … I AM TRYING TO TELL YOU THAT FRIENDSHIP IS EXACTLY WHAT I NEED. YOU HAVE NO IDEA HOW MANY NIGHTS I LAY AWAKE WISHING I HAD SOMEONE TO TALK TO … NOT TO WORRY, I WILL NEVER CROSS THE LINE OR PUT PRESSURE ON YOU FOR MORE THAN THAT … JUST FRIENDSHIP WOULD BE JUST WHAT I NEED. "

As she watched him walk away she thought…. So good looking and such a pleasant guy to be with; he'll have no trouble finding someone. His biggest problem would be picking through the crowds of women that throw themselves at his feet. She wouldn't mind having him herself if it weren't for Ray and the kids.

Speaking of Ray, she would have to remember to call him at the end of the supper rush. He would be mad again. The thought of it almost brought her out of her good mood. Keeping in touch with Ray and her family was becoming more of a chore than a pleasure and that bothered her every time she took the time to think about it.

It was a long busy night. She didn't get back to her room 'til ten. Friday was always a long night; All the werewolves and vampires came out on Friday nights. As she kicked off her shoes and tried to relax she remembered Ray. She felt bad now it was too late to say goodnight to the girls; her Dad probably wouldn't be up either.

She wasn't in the mood to talk to Ray but if she waited for him to call her it would be a lot worse. She poured herself a mild drink and went to the phone to face the music. She started to dial the number then hung up so she could pour herself one more. Now she had a heavy enough dose of liquid courage, she could do what she had to do.

Ray was still yelling when she put the phone down on the couch so she could fix herself yet another drink. When she got back on the phone she could hear him yelling... "CAN YOU HEAR ME?..."

What a ridiculous question, the entire world could hear him. If there was life on another planet they could hear as well. She asked him to calm down, they could never discuss anything this way ... " WHAT IS YOUR PROBLEM ... " Ray screamed into the phone again ... " WHAT! ... ARE YOU DRUNK OR SOMETHING I JUST TOLD YOU WHAT MY PROBLEM IS...? LIKE YOU COULDN'T GUESS... "

Suzanne was getting very angry and had heard more than she cared to... "I AM WORKING ALMOST TWENTY HOURS A DAY... I AM EXHAUSTED... I STILL CALL YOU SO YOU DON'T WORRY AND ALL YOU CAN DO IS SCREAM MY FACE OFF ... DAMN YOU TO HELL! "She slammed down the phone hard enough it was a wonder it didn't break.

She no sooner hung it up when it was ringing again, she didn't even have time to pour herself yet another drink. She grabbed at the phone screaming before it even got to her ear ... "DAMN IT RAY! ... I SAID GO TO HELL ... I AM NOT TALKING TO YOU WHEN YOU ARE IN THIS KIND OF MOOD..."

When she stopped to get her breath she could hear a voice saying ... "I SURE AM GLAD MY NAME ISN'T RAY... "She was embarrassed but thankful for it to be anyone, but Ray.

"WELL IF YOUR NAME IS NOT RAY ... WHAT IS IT?" The voice on the other end said it was Paul with just a little indignance as she didn't recognize his voice. It seemed to Suzanne she was constantly in a state of embarrassment with this man. Now completely flustered she tried to regain a facade of professionalism.

Paul could feel her embarrassment and let her off the hook, moving on to the reason he had called. He had tried to get her earlier but she was hard to find. He needed her to call social services first thing in the morning, there were arrangements made for her to visit with her children tomorrow.

It was all she could do to not cry she hadn't fully realized how much she missed her children 'til he said she could see them. This was almost like a Christmas present on such an otherwise lousy night. This man could change his name to Santa Claus.

But for now he was content to be her rescuer, she asked him to stay on the phone and talk to her for a bit or at least 'til she was sure Ray wasn't likely to call back. She desperately needed a friendly voice.

Paul was pleased to be needed if he was talking to her he didn't have to deal with his empty apartment and even emptier life. He didn't care what she wanted to talk about as long as he could hear a voice.

After getting off the phone with her lawyer, she felt warm and relaxed, almost to the point of totally forgetting about Ray and the kids. She could deal with them tomorrow. It made her feel good to think of seeing the kids again. She really had missed them.

Suzanne was scared to death to face Angel, especially with someone else watching. She wished she could speak to her alone. Suzanne had to find a way to get Angel to understand, to know that it wasn't her fault. If Angel had only listened then it never would have happened.

Just one more drink to calm her nerves then she could sleep. She fell asleep with little effort that night and slept the entire night, something that rarely happened. Passed out in a deep stupor, she had deep dark sleep... no ghosts, no nightmares.

Nine a.m. on the phone to social services, today would be a double bonus as she could see her father as well as her children. Her Dad was also home, she missed him almost as much if not more than her children. There was so much she had to say to all of them, she just hoped she could get the words out.

The social worker was impatient and wanted to go as soon as possible. She wanted to get it over with so she could spend some of the day with her own family. She told Suzanne not to expect anymore Saturday visits.

They were making an exception since she had not been with them since the night she was taken away. Her lawyer had pulled some strings, and the social services seemed bitter about the entire thing. She neither appreciated nor approved of favoritism.

Suzanne was swamped with fear, it had been a long time what would she say? What if she froze and couldn't think of what to say? What if they didn't want to see her? How would she ever get them to understand why she couldn't be with them?

It didn't matter, she was going to see them and that was all that would matter. The rest would take care of itself as it all came up. She was a firm believer in not crossing bridges till you got to them. They were family and up until a week ago all loved each other surely that wouldn't change this quickly.

As the car pulled into the drive she could see the kids on the porch waiting for her. Seeing the big smiles and the excitement on their faces, she could relax they still loved her.

Before she was even out of the car the kids were on her, wrapping their arms around her trying to hug and kiss her all at the same time. All except Angel, who was nowhere to be seen?

Getting into the house was a welcome problem, with three kids hanging off her. Inside the door stood her Dad. Suzanne walked up to him with fear and hesitation, not sure if he even wanted to see her. He went to her with no uncertainty, embracing her long and hard. He whispered into her ear...

"I LOVE YOU PRINCESS. " That was enough for Suzanne; tears went streaming down her cheeks. Anna looked at her with great concern... "AREN'T YOU GLAD TO SEE US...?"

Suzanne looked at her father and her three children and said she was never ... "GLADDER "of anything in her life. Looking around there was still no sign of Angel ... where was she? Suzanne had to talk to her, to see her.

Ray came out of the kitchen and very coldly announced... "ANGEL REFUSES TO COME OUT OF THE CLOSET...SHE DOESN'T WANT TO SEE YOU AND I WILL NOT MAKE HER ... YOU ARE GOING TO HAVE TO BE PATIENT AND WAIT UNTIL SHE IS READY ... SHE IS SCARED OF YOU SUZANNE..."

Suzanne could not believe what she was hearing ... "SHE IS NOT SCARED OF ME ... SHE IS LOOKING FOR ATTENTION AGAIN." Ray looked at her with total disbelief ... "HOW MUCH ATTENTION IS SHE GETTING BEING ALONE IN THE BACK OF A CLOSET IN THE DARK ..."

Suzanne shook her head wondering why she was the only one who could see this...

"WHO ARE WE ALL STANDING HERE DISCUSSING? ... NO ONE BUT ANGEL!..." the social worker interrupted and said she agreed with Ray that the child had already been traumatized enough. She was not to be forced to come down.

If Angel wouldn't come to her then they should let her go upstairs to talk to her in the closet. They all said... "NO " ... Why were they all ganging up on her?

They didn't understand it wasn't good for Angel to keep thinking her mother hated her. She knew... she had spent her entire life that way and now it was too late. She would never know if her mother loved her.

Suzanne didn't want Angel going through all the doubt she had grown up with. They still said no. She looked at them ... "WHAT DO YOU THINK I AM GOING TO DO WITH ALL YOU PEOPLE HERE... I DO NOT HATE MY DAUGHTER ... I HAVE TROUBLE DEALING WITH HER ... PLEASE... SHE NEEDS TO KNOW I LOVE HER..."

Ray looked at her with hatred in his eyes; a look that nearly ripped Suzanne's heart right out of her chest. With tears running down her cheeks, she yelled as loud as she could ... "MOMMY LOVES YOU ANGEL... PLEASE DO NOT HATE ME ... I AM SORRY ... "by this time she was crying so hard she could hardly see.

Little arms wrapped around her waist and she heard the tiniest voice say ... "I LOVE YOU, MOMMY ... I AM SORRY I AM SO BAD ALL THE TIME..."

Suzanne picked Angel up into her arms and held her. They were both holding onto each other and crying, neither of them saying a word. It was the first time Angel had cried in almost two years. Now that the tap was turned on the waterworks weren't going to stop.

Ray took everyone else into the kitchen. The social worker went as far as the doorway; after all, rules were rules. Ray gave them about ten minutes alone together before he let the other kids go back in.

It was strange watching Suzanne and Angel together, they still had not spoken a word. They only needed to feel each other's love and forgiveness. Even if they weren't speaking they were still communicating. Angel cried, that was a major leap in itself.

Ray was scared to death that Angel was lost inside herself, now he knew she could be reached. Once they got through all the emotional ice, the rest of the visit went smoother. This visit was Angel's; the other kids would have to understand they'd had their turn for years.

She told them about work, and her new doctor; and how they would all have to go to an appointment together. Then they could all start working toward being a family again... A family that loved instead of hurt each other.

All the way back to the city Suzanne thought about her family and the mistakes she had made. She tried to think about the last time she'd hugged Angel, but couldn't remember. She had never really hugged her even when she was real little. She would put her on her knee and read stories. Anna was always on the other knee and it was always Anna's story. After all, Anna was the oldest.

Suddenly her mind was overrun with the unfairness of Angel's life. She didn't hug her or do things for or with her. There were times that she would do things for all the kids and Angel would be included...

That is except for this past while ... Angel was always grounded to her room. Was Angel that bad, or was it a convenient way to not have to deal with her? Did she look for reasons to punish Angel because she didn't want to be around her? Suddenly she felt drained and tired she couldn't think any more.

There was so much to deal with when she got to work as she had been letting things slide for a couple days. Hopefully she could work 'til she dropped. Then hopefully she wouldn't have time to think about any of it. Suzanne would keep her mind so full of work there would be no room for the dark, upsetting thoughts that her mind kept wandering back to.

She loved her job, and the more chaotic it was the more she loved it. She could work from sun up 'til the wee hours of the morning and never feel tired. Suzanne had her entire week planned out, it was important that she have every minute filled. Monday, Wednesday and Friday she saw the kids, and then on Tuesday and Thursday she would see the good doctor. Suzanne was looking forward to seeing her this time.

It was important to Suzanne to tell the Doctor about her visit home, her interactions with children and father. She wanted to talk to her about Angel ... her mind swam with a thousand things she was excited to tell her. For a fleeting moment Ray came into her head. They had not been together as a couple since this whole mess started.

There was no effort to even discuss it. Avoiding being with her, if he didn't bring it up neither would she. She hardly had time to get in the mood let alone do anything about it.

She wondered if Ray thought about making love when he was alone. Even when she was at the house today he said nothing, barely speaking to her. They really hadn't spent anytime alone, face to face, since the first day.

She thought she knew every thought and feeling he had, before he even had it. But this time she didn't know, or maybe she did know and didn't want to face it, or think about it. Suzanne was tired of trying to please Ray, tired of the way he always made her feel like she was a bad mother and a terrible person. She didn't want to be with him, so she hoped he never brought up the subject.

Suzanne headed up to her room. She had a ton of paperwork to take care of. She poured herself a drink and sat down to handle stacks of inventory, staffing and repairs that had to be ordered. She had four drinks in the two hours it took her to do the paperwork.

It was time to check on the dining room, to make sure everything was ready. They had a special reservation of twenty-four important people coming, and they were extremely persnickety; the tiniest of details had to be perfect.

She hated having to deal with these people, however they were regulars and they spent a fortune on a regular basis. Once she had checked and rechecked everything, she took the paperwork she had finished to her manager's office for his final stamp of approval ... knocking several times, there was no answer.

It wasn't like him to leave without giving her a list of duties for the day... she went to check if any messages were left at the desk. He hadn't left his suite in a couple weeks. Somebody had to have seen something or at least heard from him. The front desk was as confused and concerned as she was. He hadn't even called down to say he didn't want to be disturbed.

No one had seen or heard from him in at least twenty-four hours. Back at his door she paced in front of it for what seemed like several minutes, waiting for some kind of sign that would tell her what to do.

She held her pass-key in her hand as she prayed that something would happen, that she wouldn't have to cross his hallowed space of total privacy. He was always very clear about anyone invading his privacy. Hopefully she'd worked there long enough, and was good at her job enough... if he was in another of his many bizarre moods he would not fire her on the spot.

Suzanne slipped the key into the lock very slowly and quietly, still listening ... nothing. She turned it, slowly, quietly as though scared that it would actually unlock. If he was mad he was mad; but she had to know he was all right.

By this point her imagination was running wild. She had managed to get herself pretty spooked. As she walked into his office the hair on the back of her neck stood up, a chill had passed through her bones.

Only halfway into the room, her absolute worst fears came to light. Her manager was hanging by electrical wire from the ceiling light. She could hear a loud shrill scream, not realizing it was her. Running blindly toward the door, she tripped over a chair and knocked over a table.

She had never seen anything so horrifying in her life. Still shaking and trembling she tried to answer the many questions shot at her by the police. Suzanne had learned to dislike these authoritarian inquisitions the last time she was forced to deal with the police. What did they think she put him up there because she thought he was a nice decoration?

Suzanne had no idea what to tell them. No one knew him ... he was quiet, stuck to himself, obsessive about being left alone at all times, especially in the past couple weeks. She was used to his moods and handled everything. There were a few things like payroll that needed his signature. Other than that, the place ran well without him.

He didn't seem to have any friends or enemies, at least none that ever showed up. No one except hotel businessmen came to see him and most of them had been referred to his assistant...her. He didn't even seem to have family ... no one.

A note had been left on his desk, his attempt at an apology or perhaps one last chance to make peace for what his conscience couldn't live with. He had embezzled a large amount of money from the hotel to cover gambling debts. The police wanted to know if she had any clue that he was stealing money.

Suzanne felt like she had stepped into a bad soap opera. This kind of stuff only happened on television, never in real life. This was a person she had known, but obviously didn't know at all. Why hadn't she known? Why hadn't she seen or felt that something was wrong?

Word spread quickly through the hotel; people began to gather to see the show, trying to get a glimpse of the body. No one quite believed this could happen, but all wanting to see it if it had. Suzanne wondered about the aftermath of the hotel ... this mess had to be bad for business. Who would want to stay in a hotel where the manager hung himself?

Would he end up haunting the place? A tormented soul that couldn't cross over because he had broken God's laws and killed himself? ... Now he was to be damned forever, wandering the halls where he had imprisoned his soul.

It was time for Suzanne to get a grip on her wild imagination and get everyone back to work. Things had to be running as close to normal as possible. It would be days before people quit talking about it ... if ever.

Suzanne went up to her room and poured herself a double; her hands were still shaking. How could he let things get so far out of control? Once he lost a few times why didn't he give up, walk away, just quit gambling once his own money was gone. What was the fascination with gambling?

Trying it once, Suzanne had found it nerve wracking after losing only twenty dollars. She still scolded herself. She hated the feeling of having her money on the line and she hated even more walking away without her money and nothing to show for it.

It had been one hell of a day. No one should have to deal with so many emotional upsets in one day. She called the desk and told them she needed some time alone and not to call her unless the place was on fire or an otherwise equal emergency ... they fully understood.

Once in her room she poured herself the double shot of anything that she so needed. Lying on her bed she wasn't long drifting off to sleep. A deep dark sleep where she could hide from all the horrors locked in her head.

Waking up three hours later, she called the desk; all was peaceful. They told her to go ahead and relax the rest of the night. They could call her if anything serious came up.

As she climbed into the shower she couldn't help but think about the showers she used to take with Ray, how much she enjoyed being with him, being touched and caressed by him. She did miss his touch, she missed the intimacy of feeling wanted and needed as a woman.

After picking up the phone several times only to hang it up, she took another drink trying to get up some liquid courage. If she told Ray she needed him and he turned his back on her ... it would be more than she could stand right now.

Suzanne held her breath as she waited for someone to answer the phone, like a teenager calling the first boy she had a crush on. It was Ray who answered, she was thankful she wouldn't have the time to change her mind while someone went to get him. She started talking, not knowing what to say; she burst into sobs and could only manage to squeeze out ... "I NEED YOU, PLEASE COME ..."

By this time the tears were pouring out. She couldn't stop crying long enough to tell him what had happened. She needed him to hold her. She needed to feel loved ... she needed to feel something, something warm and safe.

Suzanne wanted to feel the way she did when Ray was her knight and would rescue her from her mother's beatings and abuse. Ray had always protected her and kept her safe from the world and its harshness.

She wanted to melt into his arms forgetting everything that had happened for the past year. What she really wanted was to forget there was even a world outside of them.

She didn't need to get the words out; he knew she needed him. Ray had been waiting a long time for Suzanne to simply need him. For a very long time he felt she not only didn't need him but she was ashamed of him. She wouldn't be ashamed this time.

Suzanne felt like a high-school kid getting ready for a first date as she put on her makeup and chose the appropriate outfit. She had to hurry to get down to the lobby to meet Ray. She wanted to make it as easy on him as possible. He hated coming to the hotel especially after the way she had treated him the last time.

The last time seemed so long ago another lifetime. She had a lot of regrets in her life, most of which came from hurting the people she loved the most. Suzanne thought about the old expression ... "YOU ONLY HURT THE ONES YOU LOVE ... "and wondered why that had to be so true. Was it her way of keeping people away from her? ... Hurt them before they hurt her.

Suzanne's breath was taken away the moment she saw Ray walk through the door. A tear came into her eyes as her hands trembled, he was wearing the suit they were married in. She had forgotten how handsome he was in it.

It's strange how a couple can spend so many years together and quit looking at each other. Ray moved toward her very slowly, or maybe it only seemed everything was in slow motion. He slipped his arm around her waist, pulled her in close, and kissed her with all the passion and anticipation of a first kiss.

Suzanne melted, her legs felt weak as they walked to her room without speaking a word. Sweeping her into his massive arms, he carried her through the door and into her room. With little effort he kicked the door closed and carried her to her bed.

Her shining prince was back to rescue her. She was in love all over again, reminded of all the reasons she had fallen in love in the first place....she had always been safe in his arms and she always would be.

They still hadn't spoken. They didn't need to; they could feel each others thoughts and emotions. She knew no matter what happened they would always love each other. It was the only true thing throughout their lives. They were together as they were always and would remain together. Nothing could stop their love. She should have known that and believed in it.

When they were both physically and emotionally drained Ray lay on his back and lit a cigarette as Suzanne poured herself a drink. Ray had things he needed to say he began blurting out his feelings. He had to get things said before the moment passed and they never got said.

He was sorry for being so cold to her. He felt confused and lost, needing time to make sense of it all. Never had he stopped loving her or needing her. Trying to convince himself he could; the more he tried to stop loving her the more he needed her.

Feeling the same way, she understood. She hated him for not being there when she needed him most, but couldn't stop loving or thinking of him. They held each other for the longest time, reminding each other of old memories and old feelings. They made a point of only talking about good times. They needed to only feel the good right now; there would be lots of other times for the rest of it.

It was about four a.m. when Ray left to go home. He didn't want the kids to wake up with him out of the house. Later when things settled down he could spend the night. The last thing he said to her as he was going through the door was ... "I REALLY DO LOVE YOU ... THAT WILL NEVER CHANGE." She fell into a deep peaceful sleep. For the first time in a long time she felt safe. She knew no matter what came their way they could survive it because they were a family.

Chapter Nine

Tuesday finally came, today Suzanne was to see Dr. Anderson. The Doctor was sure to be pleased this visit as, Suzanne's life had totally turned around. The entire staff commented on her energy and the grin she couldn't get off her face. The day flew by at a steady crawl, and it was finally time to go to her appointment.

As soon as she sat down the doctor picked up on her good mood. She would have to be deaf, dumb, and blind not to see the glow on Suzanne's face. This was going to be a good visit; there were so many good things to talk about.

"LET'S START OUR VISIT WITH WHAT EVER IT WAS THAT PUT THAT SMILE ON YOUR FACE..."

Suzanne could hardly hold it in, she began immediately telling her of the night she had spent with Ray and how he still loved her. "RAY STILL LOVES ME AND ANGEL FORGAVE ME... THAT IS A LOT FOR ONE TWENTY-FOUR HOUR PERIOD... THEY WERE, WITHOUT A DOUBT, MY BIGGEST WORRIES... "

Suzanne sat watching the woman sitting across from her watching for the mood of the moment, a trick she had learned while dealing with her mother's psychotic mood swings. Why was this woman not pleased at Suzanne's happiness?

"WHAT DO YOU MEAN...? ANGEL FORGAVE YOU? ... HOW DO YOU KNOW ... DID SHE SAY THE WORDS? "

Suzanne was puzzled by the turn this was taking. She would know if her daughter had forgiven her. It was the first time in a long time that she let her mother hold her. Or was it that it was the first time in a long time her mother bothered to hold her? ... "SHE LET ME HOLD HER, SHE CRIED AND SAID SHE LOVED ME!..."

"SO YOU THINK EVERYTHING IS ALRIGHT NOW, A FEW TEARS AND A HUG AND IT ALL GOES AWAY..."

"WELL NOT TOTALLY, BUT WE CERTAINLY ARE GOING IN THE RIGHT DIRECTION... "

By now the good doctor was taking a stern almost cold detachment..." YOU THINK BECAUSE PEOPLE TELL YOU THEY LOVE YOU THAT EVERYTHING IS GOOD AND ALL BAD THINGS ARE MAGICALLY ERASED?..."

This was really starting to make Suzanne angry, she had come in here in a good mood, now she wanted to deck someone she just wasn't sure whom? ... "WELL IT SURE HELPS... I CAN GET THROUGH ANYTHING AS LONG AS I KNOW SOMEONE LOVES ME!.. "

The doctor could see Suzanne was on edge, any push in the wrong direction and she would lose her trust. It was time to deal with her haunts and ghosts. It was time to change the subject and change it she did, straight to something Suzanne did not want to discuss.

She wanted to keep her good mood she wanted to feel good about herself and her life and she wasn't about to do that while discussing her mother. " .... I SAID DID YOUR MOTHER LOVE YOU? ...SUZANNE? ... "

There had to be a way of changing the subject of getting out of the hot seat... "YES ... I GUESS SO ... SHE LOVED ME ... SHE TOLD ME ALL THE TIME ... MOSTLY AFTER SHE HIT ME ... WHICH WAS ALL THE TIME ..."

"WHAT YOU ARE SAYING IS THAT YOU UNDERSTOOD AND FORGAVE HER FOR HITTING YOU AS LONG AS SHE SAID SHE LOVED YOU AFTERWARD... WHEN SHE WAS TELLING YOU SHE LOVED YOU DID YOU BELIEVE HER? "

Suzanne's cheery mood was passing all too quickly. Why couldn't this doctor let her feel good at least for a little while, wasn't that what shrinks were supposed to do help her feel good? All she wanted to do was dig up old ghosts. ...

"WHAT ARE YOU TRYING TO DO? ... I CAME HERE IN A GOOD MOOD AND HERE YOU ARE TRYING TO HURT ME ... TO UPSET ME AS MUCH AS YOU CAN... "

Suzanne was on the edge of tears, she had to get out of there to escape and now. She was on the verge of crumbling in front of this stranger. Suzanne would have to gain her composure any way she could. No matter what she was saying Suzanne would refuse to listen. She could let her mind drift to better thoughts.

She would lose herself in the memory of being safe in Ray's arms. That would be the only way to fight this. Safe in Ray's arms together they would get through this, if not in reality then in her heart and mind.

"CAN'T YOU SEE?... BY NOT DISCUSSING THESE THINGS AND FACING YOUR PAIN IT IS THE SAME AS ANGEL HIDING IN THE CLOSET ... YOU THINK THAT IF YOU DO NOT ACKNOWLEDGE SOMETHING IT WILL GO AWAY ... JUST AS ANGEL THINKS IF SHE HIDES IN THE DARK NO ONE CAN HURT HER.... WELL YOU ARE BOTH WRONG!!...

The Doctor took a moment for effect, a moment of silence to stair deep in Suzanne's eyes. A moment to see if there was any connection, were any lights going on? Was she getting through to this lady? What could she say to get Suzanne to look at the entire picture with truth and honesty?

"ALL THE THINGS YOU PUSH DOWN AND DO NOT DISCUSS, THEY ALL COME BACK TO HAUNT YOU ... I WILL BET MONEY YOU HAVE NIGHTMARES OR INSOMNIA OR BOTH.... HOW MUCH OF IT IS YOUR MOTHER COMING TO HAUNT YOU...? "

Suzanne could tell she was getting frustrated with the silence Suzanne was maintaining. This doctor wasn't going to win, she wasn't. Suzanne was safe in her hiding place. Why would she come out to face all the pain this stranger was trying to inflict on her.

"SUZANNE?... CAN'T YOU SEE IT IS TIME FOR YOU TO FACE THESE GHOSTS...? YOU CAN'T HIDE FROM THEM ANY MORE THAN ANGEL CAN... PLEASE!... I BEG YOU ... DEAL WITH YOUR PAIN BEFORE IT SWALLOWS YOU UP..."

It was too late, Suzanne couldn't hold it in any longer nor could she escape before the tears poured out..." MY MOTHER IS DEAD ... SHE CAN'T HURT ME ANY MORE ... I CAN'T CHANGE ANYTHING THAT HAPPENED IN THE PAST, NOR CAN I CHANGE WHAT SHE DID TO ME...

Why was this lady insisting on digging up old ghosts? Suzanne had put her mother and all her nastiness in the past where it belonged. She wasn't about to start digging up old wounds that healed a long time ago or so she hoped...

."I CAN NOT MAKE HER LOVE ME OR MAKE HER PROUD OF ME ... I COULDN'T DO IT WHEN SHE WAS ALIVE I AM CERTAINLY NOT GOING TO DO IT NOW SHE IS DEAD ... WHY ARE WE WASTING TIME DISCUSSING THINGS THAT CAN NOT BE CHANGED?"

Suddenly the mood changed, the doctor softened, Suzanne almost believed this person cared for her almost that is... there was a part of her knew it was a trick. She was doing a good cop, bad cop routine except that she was both.

Tricky, very tricky... but not too tricky for Suzanne she had spent her life dealing with the queen of game playing and this simple little game wasn't about to get past her. She had made her cry on purpose, the entire appointment was designed to hurt her as much as possible.

With a soft gentle caring in her voice the doctor continued to try to persuade Suzanne...." I AM TRYING TO KEEP YOU FROM SCARRING ANGEL IN THE SAME WAY YOUR MOTHER SCARRED YOU... "

Now the tears were gone and she had her back up. Now she knew the game they were playing she could harden herself. Keep herself from being hurt any further. Never again would she allow this woman to bring her to tears. Next time she would be ready, she would have her guard up.

"THAT'S NOT FAIR!... ANGEL AND I ARE NOT LIKE MY MOTHER AND I ... I LOVE ANGEL"

"DOES ANGEL KNOW THAT? "

"YES SHE KNOWS THAT... I TELL HER ALL THE TIME... HOW COULD SHE NOT KNOW I LOVE HER? ... I AM HER MOTHER! "

"LIKE YOUR MOTHER TOLD YOU AFTER SHE HURT YOU? ... I WILL ASK YOU AGAIN ... DID YOU EVER BELIEVE YOUR MOTHER LOVED YOU? "

Suzanne fought with all her might to hold back the tears. She wasn't going let herself cry, not again. Suzanne couldn't talk; she had a huge lump in her throat. She knew if she opened her mouth even a little, it would be sobbing that would come out. Instead of the words she so much wanted to defend herself with.

She took a deep breath then screamed through a river of tears... "MY MOTHER HATED ME ... SHE ALWAYS HATED ME ... SHE ONLY SAID THE WORDS ... I LOVE YOU, BECAUSE IT WAS A MOTHER'S DUTY TO LOVE HER DAUGHTER ... I COULD SEE THROUGH THAT ... JUST AS I CAN SEE THROUGH YOU NOW ... I TRIED TO MAKE HER LOVE ME, I REALLY TRIED ... THE MORE I TRIED THE MORE SHE HATED ME..."

By this time the crying was almost hysteria. She got up in a panic, frantic to get out of there. She couldn't sit and cry in front of this person who had worked so hard to see her cry. She wasn't going to give her the satisfaction. Suzanne wouldn't let her win, not now, not ever.

Suzanne hated this weakness that she couldn't control. It was this very weakness that made her mother hate her all her life. Her mother had always hated weakness, in everyone. It was one of the few things she agreed with her mother on. There was nothing worse than a whiner, a crybaby.

Suzanne had no idea where she was going as long as she was going. Barely seeing through the stream of tears covering her face she continued to run out the door and down the hall. She could hear the doctor yelling for her to return but she couldn't. She had to get out, she had to escape.

It was the only way she could save what little sanity she had left. It was all too painful, all too hard. It had been hard to live but now was inpossible to relive. "DAMN HER... DAMN HER TO HELL!!..."

She had come to her in a good mood, not just a good mood but a great mood. It had been a long time since she had felt that good. Why couldn't she just let her feel good? Was there some law somewhere that said Suzanne was never allowed to feel good not even for one day?

Now she was in the depths of despair, less than an hour ago she would have thought no one could spoil her mood. Was this woman possessed with her mother's soul, bent on hurting her as much as possible? Her mother was dead why couldn't she stop hurting her? ...

Now out in the lobby the doctor wasn't long catching her... "PLEASE DON'T LEAVE SUZANNE... SIT AND CRY IT OUT IF YOU HAVE TO, BUT DO NOT LEAVE... IF YOU DON'T GET THIS PAIN AND ANGER OUT OF YOU, YOU WILL CONTINUE TO UNLEASH IT ON THOSE YOU LOVE..."

"I HATE THIS! ... THERE IS NOTHING I HATE MORE THAN CRYING IN FRONT OF PEOPLE ... IT IS WEAK.... IF PEOPLE SEE YOU ARE WEAK THEY USE THAT WEAKNESS AGAINST YOU! "

"WHAT DO YOU MEAN THEY USE IT AGAINST YOU...? COME BACK AND TALK TO ME..." She was acting so concerned, so caring. Suzanne knew the truth...

"COME ON... ARE YOU GOING TO TRY TO TELL ME THAT WHEN YOU STARTED ASKING ME QUESTIONS ABOUT MY MOTHER YOU DID NOT KNOW I WOULD FALL APART ... THAT THE QUESTIONS WEREN'T SPECIFICALLY

DESIGNED TO CAUSE ME PAIN... TO MAKE ME CRACK... YOU WANTED ME WEAK SO YOU COULD GET INSIDE OF ME AND FIND OTHER WEAKNESSES TO USE AGAINST ME...

Suzanne was on a roll and it wasn't going to stop 'til she had it all out. The good doctor had hurt her and hurt her big, now it was Suzanne's turn to give some back. She had been getting kicked in the head all her life and this was the end.

DON'T YOU THINK MY MOTHER KNEW EXACTLY WHAT WOULD HURT ME MOST ... YOU THINK HER BEATINGS WERE BAD... THEY WEREN'T BAD ... I COULD HANDLE THEM... THE PAIN FROM THE BEATINGS WOULD GO AWAY EVENTUALLY

Suddenly Suzanne could see it all too clearly the Doctor had become her mother. Playing the same head games designed to do nothing but cause pain. It always seemed to sneak up on Suzanne she never saw it coming just as she didn't see this coming.

... IT WAS THE HEAD GAMES THAT HURT... THE EMOTIONAL BLACKMAIL ... SHE HAD TO ALWAYS KEEP YOU DOWN ... KEEP YOU FEELING WORTHLESS ... YOU DIDN'T JUST FEEL IT, YOU BELIEVED IT ... MY MOTHER WAS NO DIFFERENT THAN THE REST OF THE WORLD ... PEOPLE HURT EACH OTHER ... IT IS A FACT AND A WAY OF LIFE ... "

"WE CAN'T DISCUSS THIS IN THE HALL... TRUST ME ... "Suzanne didn't know much but in a few short visits she had learned she could not trust this person. How could she trust someone who goes out of her way to cause her as much pain as she could?

"IS THERE NO ONE YOU TRUST NOT TO HURT YOU ... HOW ABOUT RAY ... OR MAYBE.... YOUR DAD OR YOUR CHILDREN ... SUZANNE THERE MUST BE SOMEONE!? "

"NO ... NO ONE ... THEY WILL ALL HURT ME EVENTUALLY AND HAVE! ... MAYBE THEY DON'T MEAN TO ... BUT THEY STILL DO..."

Now she had her walls up, her strength back, the good doctor would never do that to her again. She was caught off guard but she would be ready for all the tricks next time. Suzanne could see what was going on.

This doctor was every bit as tricky as her mother and Suzanne would never forget that again. For a moment she thought she was her friend but now she knew better, she would never make that mistake again.

"SUZANNE WHAT POSSIBLE REASON WOULD I HAVE FOR HURTING YOU?"

"BECAUSE IN HURTING ME YOU GAIN CONTROL AND STRENGTH... MAKING YOU SUPERIOR AND ME WEAK ... THE WEAK ALWAYS LOSE ... IT IS A FACT OF NATURE, GOING BACK TO THE CAVEMEN... "

"OH SUZANNE... IT'S ANIMALS THAT PREY ON THE WEAK ... HUMANITY TAKES CARE OF AND PROTECTS THE WEAK ... I AM NOT TRYING TO HURT YOU ... I HAVE NO REASON TO HURT YOU ... I AM TRYING TO PROTECT YOU FROM YOURSELF AND YOUR MOTHER ... THAT PAIN HAS TO BE BROUGHT OUT OR IT WILL DEVOUR YOU ... YOU HAVE TO CRY ALL THE TEARS YOU HELD IN ALL THOSE YEARS AGO...

Suzanne had no idea what she was talking about how could something that happened many years ago change the fact that Angel was spoiled and out of control. Granted Suzanne had to find a new way to deal with Angel other than hitting but this had nothing to do with her dead mother.....

"YOU ARE DROWNING IN THOSE TEARS AND YOU DON'T EVEN KNOW IT ... I HAVE SOMETHING FOR YOU TO THINK ABOUT UNTIL YOU COME BACK ... IF YOUR MOTHER TOLD YOU SHE LOVED YOU AND YOU NEVER BELIEVED IT ... HOW MUCH LOVE DO YOU THINK ANGEL FEELS FROM YOU ...

Suzanne was making every attempt to ignore this doctor and all she had to say. Suzanne would sit there quietly and put in her time but she wasn't going to give her any more ammunition...."

WHEN YOU COME BACK I WANT YOU TO LIST EVERY PAINFUL THING YOUR MOTHER EVER DID TO YOU ... DO NOT STICK TO THE PHYSICAL BEATINGS, IF IT HURT PUT IT DOWN..."

When she comes back what makes her think she would ever go through this again? Suzanne would have to be really crazy to come back here. Why would she want to cause herself that much pain?

Suzanne had spent most of her life trying to forget every painful thing that her mother ever did to her, she wasn't about to spend even a moment trying to remember them all. Walking back to her car she was filled with a ton of conflicting emotions.

It was as though she were angry, sad, happy, confused and dazed all at the same time. She sat in her car for the longest time trying to grasp what she was feeling. Perhaps she wanted to swim in the emotions, feeling all of it, good and bad. She wanted someone, anyone to pity her to feel for her and her pain.

She felt so good when she went in, now she didn't know what to feel. One thing she did feel, that confused her even more, was that a weight had been lifted from her. Maybe in feeling her little girl pain she was able to also let go of that little girl.

Suzanne had a ton of work to distract her. She now had to keep her wits about her as she had to do both her job and the manager's. Taking a couple bellboys to his office she moved all the files to her own office. After seeing him hanging she wasn't about to work in his office.

As Suzanne walked through the door the chill of his dead presence ran through her as though his ghost had stepped through her body sending chills that froze her to the spot where she stood. The bellboy pushed past her loading boxes oblivious to the cold haunting presence only she could apparently feel.

She wished that all the people who felt the need to commit suicide would think about those who had to find them. She doubted she would ever get the image of him hanging out of her head. A memory she would be haunted with, forever rattling around her brain with the ghost of her mother. They would be good company for each other.

There was a difficult job ahead of her, searching all the files, the books, and the computer to find out where he stole the money from, and how he hid it. Even though Suzanne had excelled in accounting, her manager never allowed her to touch the books. Now she understood why. She thought it was because he didn't trust her. In reality he was afraid of how good she was. Afraid she would find his deception.

All the owners and share holders were gathering at the end of the month and she was expected to be able to explain what was going on, how much was missing and what kind of financial shape they were in. She found the losses fairly easily; he hadn't even bothered to hide them. He must have planned on putting it back.

It made her feel better that he wasn't a real thief, just a guy that screwed up, and didn't know how to get out of the mess he had made. A mess that still boggled her mind… Why?… why did it have to come to this? Why hadn't he gotten any help?

All the books and records were a mess; he hadn't handled anything for a long time. Everyone assumed that was why he spent so much of his time in his office not wanting to be disturbed. She wondered what he did with all that time. Did he just sit and stare at the wall? Why had no one put any of this together? Everyone thought he was weird, a loner.

She took a break from the paperwork to call Ray and the kids. She would have enough time to talk to him before he left for work. When she talked to him she told him every detail of her session with the doctor.

If they were ever going to be a family again she had to start letting Ray in. Not just into her life but deep into her soul. He had to know her fears, her thoughts and her secrets. Most of all she had to begin trusting not just Ray but everyone that touched her life with any importance.

Ray agreed with the doctor that she had to deal with her pain and anger. It hurt him that she said she didn't trust him not to hurt her. He had hurt her for many years while he loved the bottle more than her. He decided he would find some way of making her feel more secure, so she could trust him.

She really did love him; she had almost never put him first in her life. There was always one thing or another that had come before him. He was steady and reliable, he had always been there. Suzanne knew she could go off to other things, and he would still be there waiting for her, loving her.

It wasn't that she didn't love him. She took him for granted something she would never allow or tolerate from him. She had to be first always. As though someone flicked a switch, Suzanne could see all too clearly... clearer than she wanted to see... she was selfish like her mother had always told her, like Ray had tried to tell her. Now, she too, knew she was selfish and had always been selfish.

Ray attempted to tell Suzanne he wanted his Mom staying indefinitely, she had been a great help with both the kids and her Dad. He didn't want his father-in-law to have to do anything. Besides it was good for his mother to have people to take care of again.

He didn't have to work too hard to convince Suzanne, she couldn't think of anyone more loving and caring to be with her children. Suzanne felt good he at least pretended she was still part of the family and her opinion mattered. She knew there really was no other option.

Her mother-in-law was also good for Suzanne's Dad, who seemed to gain new life through her, filling a void in each other's lives. Suzanne's father had never known such sweet gentleness. She was a genuinely caring lady with no dark secrets.

Those were the traits Suzanne had always admired most in Ray's mother. It was the kind of gentle sweetness that can only come from inside. It can't be taught, developed, or faked. It comes only from good life experiences. You are what you live.

Suzanne asked to speak to the kids, starting with Angel. It was time for her to start convincing her daughter she had a mother that loved her. 'Til then she would make every effort to put Angel first.

Suzanne had to ask Angel question after question before she could get more than a one or two word answer out of her. There was no doubt it was going to take a lot of work. One brick at a time, she would eventually get that wall pulled down. Talk about not trusting Angel had a bigger problem with trust than she did, if that was possible.

Anna was filled with a thousand things to tell her. School was out for the summer and she had her report card. She wanted to surprise her Mom so she wasn't going to tell her until their next face to face visit.

Suzanne tried not to laugh so that Anna could hear her. The only thing that would surprise her was if she got all F's. Anna had always gotten all A's and B's. Suzanne would have to give her best interpretation of surprise.

It was Angel that had her worried. No matter what it was, she would support her. She asked Anna for a special favor. Would she make an extra effort to play with Angel, and to play nice, even if it meant playing in the closet? She told her to ask her Dad to put a light in the closet for them to play.

Suzanne loved talking to Alice and R.J.; they were fun and games, so full of life and happiness. Everything was so simple for them. She felt calmer; she let the pain pass out of her head.

She poured herself a drink, and sat grinning. Her mother would roll over in her grave knowing how much her husband liked Ray's mother. Actually it served her right to have Ray's illiterate white trash mother living in her home, caring for her husband.

She had treated Ray's entire family poorly as though they were all beneath her. She hoped that wherever her mother ended up she could see how happy her husband and her children were without her.

Suzanne sat down to get back into her books when the phone rang. It was Paul looking for a friend to talk to. She was glad to push the work and the thoughts of her family aside for almost any other distraction. Anytime she didn't have to think about her own life, that was a good time.

Paul had come from a meeting with his wife and needed a friend. Suzanne was thankful for Paul's friendship; it made her feel good that it was her he chose to call. Talking about the meeting in great detail Suzanne could tell it had been a particularly painful meeting.

Even though Paul and his ex-wife had no feelings for each other there were still memories of when they did. There wasn't too much of a fight over property, he made enough money that they could both live very comfortably. He gave her the house and all the furnishings.

It was only fair as it had been her home. For him it was merely a place he passed through on his way to and from the office, spending so much time at the office he barely knew what his home looked like. In many ways he figured he owed her at least that much, filled with guilt from the years of neglect he made her live through.

The best advice Suzanne had for him was that he get out his little black book and call a snuggle for the night. Find someone that would hold him all night long and take his mind off everything and everyone.

There was only one problem with that idea; he didn't have a black book. Lots of girls slipped him their phone numbers, but he was disinterested and pitched most of them. Suzanne couldn't help but laugh as she told him how silly he had been, and that the next time he should hang on to a couple.

She knew how lonely and scared she felt when Ray had left for a couple months. She couldn't even imagine not being held for years. He must have been unbearably lonely. He laughed and joked like it was no big deal. Suzanne couldn't imagine being alone with no one to love her. It would be a big deal.

Paul suggested she take an hour to have supper with him at her hotel. They could discuss her case to make it more ethical and sooth her conscience. That way they could both say it was a working supper... working at not being so lonely.

It didn't take much persuading for her to agree. She was dying to tell him about all the things that had happened to her in the past couple days. She wondered what she did before she had met Paul; his friendship had become such an important part of her life. She wanted to share everything with him.

She would meet him downstairs in two hours, and was there anything he particularly hated to eat. He liked everything, especially surprises. She thought that was a good response since surprise was exactly what they were going to have. She only hoped the chef knew how to make it. By this time she was not only feeling good, but cute.

Suzanne wondered why everyday had to be such a roller coaster ride of emotions. Constantly moving up and down, she could hardly keep up with what she was feeling. A small piece of her enjoyed Paul's attentions and if she were forced she would have to admit she was drawn to this man.

She was far too excited to concentrate on the books, so she climbed into the tub, turned on some music and fixed two drinks to take with her. She wanted to soak for a while and didn't need to be getting out of the tub to get a second drink.

The second one would be a stronger one to accommodate the ice melting and thinning it out. Soaking in the tub, she felt tiny pangs of disloyalty to Ray as she became over whelmed with the excitement of seeing Paul. She put the thought right out of her head.

There was nothing for Ray to be concerned about, there was nothing going on. They were only friends, a friendship that made her feel good. She enjoyed Paul's company and friendship; there was no more to it than that.

They were no more than two people trying to help each other past a hard time. Even as the thought whisked through her brain, she wasn't sure she even believed her own lies. She did feel an attraction to Paul, an attraction she chose to ignore.

She made it clear to Paul that they could only be friends. Suzanne was trying to convince herself as much as Paul. To reinforce the point, she would go out of her way to talk about how much she loved Ray, and how good he was for her. She would have to make sure she is never alone with Paul; it would be far too tempting.

It all felt strange to her, she didn't understand what she was feeling. Suzanne really wished she could have a better grip on her emotions. In a short twenty-four hours she was horrified, sensual, happy, depths of despair, in control, in love and now she was feeling like a schoolgirl with a crush.

It wasn't that she wanted to sleep with Paul, she loved the attention. He made her feel pretty and smart. She felt like a woman instead of a naughty child. Even when she was seeing William she had no desire to sleep with him, she liked being charmed by him. All those things he said may not have been true, but they made her feel good anyway.

He was good company for a while, that is until he turned into the monster in her worst nightmare. She wondered for a moment if it would turn out the same with Paul. Men weren't real good with friendships as a rule. Sex always got in the way sooner or later.

It didn't matter what his intentions were, she would see to it they were never alone. She would always keep what happened with William in her mind, and never make that mistake again.

Suzanne had laid out her prettiest, sexiest dress. Thinking of William was enough to make her put it back in the closet. Who did she think she was trying to impress anyway? If she didn't want his attention; she had better look like she didn't. She took her hair back down and took off some of the makeup, so she would look nicely professional, not sexy.

She met him downstairs with a cool handshake. He pulled her in close, and kissed her on the cheek. Her heart immediately jumped into her throat. She decided to ignore it, hoping he didn't feel her tremble, then melt.

They walked into the dining room and the chef came right over to them, telling them not to worry he had everything ready; all they had to do was sit and enjoy. They talked and talked through the most incredible servings of food imported straight from heaven. One thing about Shelby the chef, he did know his job.

The table talk ran smoothly as she told him about her appointment with the doctor, about Angel, about her Dad and her mother-in-law. What she didn't tell him about was Ray and the night they had spent together. She told herself that she didn't want to make him feel bad when he was alone, but that wasn't why. Somehow she felt they were on a date, and for one short evening she wanted to live the fantasy.

She kept telling herself this was all wrong, but she didn't want any of it to end. Suzanne was so confused. How could she feel this way after the night she and Ray spent together? Suzanne secretly berated herself for allowing these feelings for even a moment.

Paul ordered wine with dinner, not to mention the drinks she had while getting ready. She needed to go, she was starting to feel light-headed. The last thing she needed was to be out of control while with this man.

Suzanne stood up, intending to go to her room, she staggered, then stumbled. Paul came up and put his hands around her waist, to help her, to steady her. This would have been the right time to tell him to go home.

She could make it on her own, or get another staff to help her; but she didn't. Deep down where her passions were buried, she wanted to be alone with this man. As she leaned against the door, Paul put a hand on each side of her head, leaning into her. Her pulse raced, her entire body trembled, she wanted to tell him to go away but she couldn't speak. How could she with her heart stuck in her throat?

He stared deep into her eyes, knowing he was melting her into a trance. His lips touched hers and they kissed one long kiss that felt like it would never end or at least she hoped it would never end. She felt things inside her she had never felt before. Ray had always made her feel warm and safe, like she was protected.

This feeling was completely different, she thought he had somehow sucked all the breathe from her and she would never breath normally again. He whispered softly into her ear ... "I KNEW YOU WANTED ME!! ... YOU WERE ATTRACTED TO ME ... I COULD SEE IT

IN YOUR EYES, AND SOMEDAY YOU WILL COME TO YOUR SENSES ... I WILL BE WAITING.... 'TIL THEN..."

As he started to walk away, he turned and winked. He was so full of himself, so sure he was in control. Suzanne could not move or even openly react. She stood in total hypnotized paralysis, still trying to get her head and heart feeling the same thing. They were both lost in the fog of the moment.

... "TRY YOUR HARDEST TO FORGET THAT KISS ... TRY TO SLEEP TONIGHT AND NOT WONDER WHAT IT WOULD BE LIKE TO HAVE ME LYING BESIDE YOU ... "

With that he walked away, not even looking back. He knew exactly what he was doing. He had her, or at least he had her attention. Suzanne stood watching as he walked away. She was still trying to catch her breath, to put her feet back on the floor.

This man was dangerous and she was helpless against him. There had been chemistry from the start. She was kidding herself that they could be only friends. There was no doubt that they would have to stick to being phone pals and business acquaintances.

She knew she would never be able to deal with him face to face, not alone or otherwise. She wanted him more than she cared to admit and didn't dare think about. If he had picked her up and put her on the bed to make love to her, she would have made no effort to stop him. She wanted him and she wanted him more than she had ever wanted Ray.

Ray wasn't about passion; he was about comfort and security, he was about feeling safe. Paul on the other hand was pure, out-of-control, animal passion. A lust she felt deep inside her that couldn't be explained ... a passion that made her body betray her good sense.

She went into her room and took off all her clothes except a lace teddy. Suzanne lay on the bed feeling overwhelmed with sexiness. Paul was right; she had not stopped thinking about him since he left. That wasn't totally true; she had not stopped wanting him.

She reached over to answer the phone thinking it was Ray home from work. Instead it was Paul, wanting to know if she was still thinking of him. He apologized for leaving so abruptly, but he was running out of will power, and he didn't want to push anything she was not ready for.

She told him to promise her it would never happen again. If he couldn't promise her that, she couldn't continue to be friends with him. He had to promise his friendship was important to her. He was the best friend she had ever had and she wasn't ready to loose it.

He promised that he would never do anything she didn't want ... That kiss... she wanted it. All she had to do was say no he would have stopped. A little push, a word, a hint of any kind, that he wasn't wanted, that he was forcing himself on her, and he would have backed away instantly.

Suzanne tried her hardest to explain to him…It wasn't what she didn't want, but what she couldn't resist. With a huge confident, too self assured grin he said ... "SO YOU DID WANT ME!!" She couldn't lie to him, nor could she hide anything from him. She stuttered over the words as she explained to him that if he hadn't left, she would never have said no to him.

He tried to explain to her how he felt. It wasn't a matter of wanting sex and then having it ... he didn't want her to hate him or herself the next day. She may have been ready physically, but emotionally it would have hurt her. There could be no regrets in the morning.

She was adamant, sex could never happen between them. She had too much to lose; she really did love her husband. Paul needed to know if Ray had ever brought out the feelings that he had when he kissed her.

Paul promised her that the kiss would haunt her… Haunt her forever. She would never get the kiss or him out of her head. From this time on, every time Ray tried to touch her she would remember the passion she had shared with Paul.

Suzanne wasn't long figuring out that Paul was right, many times in the next couple weeks her mind had drifted off to that kiss ... How could one simple kiss stay on her lips for so long? There were times at night when she was drifting off; she could feel his lips pressed firmly against hers. She longed for more.

Suzanne held strong and kept the friendship by phone. She loved talking to Paul, and he kept his word. He never spoke to her of sex, intimacy, or anything else that crossed the line of friendship. The not speaking of it made her want it all the more.

The months came and went and it was finally time for her court date. She was more worried about having to be face to face with Paul, than what the verdict would be. What she really worried about was Ray seeing her reaction to seeing Paul.

Paul met them at the courthouse. Suzanne had Ray sitting on one side and Paul on the other. Her hands trembled, her voice shook from anxiousness. Her heart was beating hard, hard enough to jump out of her chest. She couldn't look at either of them.

She may be in love with Ray, but it was Paul she craved. Ray tried to hold her hand. She pulled it away, feeling like she was being disloyal to Paul. All her thoughts and emotions were so confused she didn't know what to feel, what to think, or even how to act toward either of them.

She couldn't follow her heart... it wanted Ray, or her mind that was being haunted by memories of a kiss she couldn't stop feeling. It was her conscience she had to listen to. The same conscience that reminded her of the father of her children, the conscience that spoke to her of the one person who had all her life been there to rescue her and keep her safe. Loyalty!.. That was what she had to have.

She didn't hear a word of what was being said. Her lawyer said everything was going to be all right and she believed in him. Both the psychiatrist and the social worker testified on her behalf. She was lucky she got a kind judge that believed in family, and understood making a mistake. He could see she was making every effort to correct that mistake.

She was to be allowed home on the condition that social workers check in twice a week for a period of six months, and she continued to see the psychiatrist twice a week. In six months she would reappear in front of him to reassess the situation.

If the worker reported any kind of abuse during this period Suzanne would go to jail, automatically with no bail ... the only thing she heard was that she could go home. Ray jumped up hugging Suzanne tight lifting her off the floor, as he kissed her all over her face.

As Ray thanked Paul a hundred times, Suzanne could see Paul's eyes fill with a kind of sadness, hers with apprehension ... she didn't know if she wanted to go home. As soon as the judge said the words she was filled with a sinking feeling, more like a drowning ... the hotel was her home and her life.

The house was a place where she visited, but it wasn't where she wanted to be. Even on visitation days she never felt like she was at home. Mostly she could hardly wait to get back to the hotel. She was no longer comfortable at the house. She was the outsider.

She told Ray she had to go back to work for the rest of the day. Now that she was full manager it was harder for her to get away. In reality, it was easier, but she wasn't about to tell Ray that.

She needed time to adjust to the idea. She had to change her thinking she belonged at home with her family. She needed to accept that, and live the life she had. The hotel was a fantasy world. It was time for her to wake up and go back to her own life.

Suzanne didn't want to loose Ray or her family ... but she didn't want to go home either. She liked things the way they were. It wasn't because of Paul; it wasn't even because she was unsure of how she felt about Ray.

She felt good about herself and her life while she was at the hotel. It was the only time she did feel good. When she was home with Ray and the kids she felt evil, like a screw up that could do nothing right. She was angry and depressed. How would she ever get Ray to understand she didn't want to come home? She wasn't ready.

The phone was already ringing as she stepped through the doors of the hotel room that she had called home for the past several months. It was Paul; he wanted to know what she was going to do. Was she going back to Ray?

Suzanne had great difficulty explaining to Paul it wasn't a matter of going back to Ray, she had never left him; they merely had different addresses. They were still a couple, they still slept with each other, and they still loved each other.

Paul didn't need to tell her she was kidding herself. He wasn't sure if she was lying to him or herself, but there was no doubt that she was lying. He had seen the look on her face when Ray hugged her. She didn't want him touching her.

Suzanne was flustered and confused. What she didn't want was to be having this conversation. Paul was right; she didn't want Ray touching her at least not in front of Paul. In her heart, she wanted it to be Paul hugging and kissing her.

What she didn't want was Paul knowing how much power he actually had over her. How could this man see what she was feeling before she even knew what she felt? How could a mere glance from his eyes pierce her soul and turn her head? She wasn't a teenager anymore; she could and would get control!

Everything would be fine once she went home. She had to go back, and right away, before she did something stupid that couldn't be taken back, something Ray could never forgive her for. This was not a time for burning bridges; it was a time to be a responsible adult making responsible decisions.

Paul wanted to know if that was what she really wanted. Would Ray be enough for her? Could she spend the rest of her life with a man she had out grown? A man that made her feel safe with no real passion... the passion of an adult man and woman instead of a little girl being protected by her Daddy?

He begged her to let him show her what love with passion felt like. What it felt like to be in bed with a man she really wanted deep into her groins. After reminding him of his promise she had to end the conversation as quickly as possible, before she crumbled under the truths that he spoke.

There was no doubt he knew what to say, he knew what buttons he was pushing. He was getting the reactions he wanted and he knew it.

He also knew she was defenseless against his charms. This slick, smooth talking lawyer knew exactly what he was doing and Suzanne had to keep this in mind. Making people think and feel what he wanted was what he did for a living.

Work kept her too busy to go home; at least that is what she told Ray the last three times he called. He sounded more intense with each call. She could tell he knew something was wrong.

She tried to force herself to start packing; with only a few things packed she stopped and sat on the side of the bed, unable to do it; even if she did go she would be totally miserable. She was miserable already just thinking about how her life would be.

What was she going back to? A life she had out grown, Paul was right about that. She wasn't that same helpless little girl that Ray had loved and protected. In her head she could already hear the prison doors slam.

That was where she was going back to a prison. All she could be was whatever Ray wanted her to be that imaginary wife that he thought he loved. She wasn't sure Ray ever loved the real Suzanne, she wasn't sure he even liked the real Suzanne.

Ray had always told her she was selfish and always put her own needs first. To her she had spent her life being what and who everyone else wanted and expected her to be. Was it selfish to be true to who you are? All she ever wanted was someone who could not only love her but love who she really was.

Suzanne wasn't leaving everyone; she wanted and needed time to think. If they loved her they would be patient and understand. When Ray answered the phone she could hear the fear in his voice. He knew she wasn't on her way home and probably wouldn't be.

She told him she didn't want to separate she needed more time. Suzanne wanted to see Doctor Anderson before she came home. She told him she would come tomorrow to talk to him and the kids, but for tonight, she would stay where she was.

He hung up the phone without saying goodbye, he said nothing, but then what was there to say. He knew it was over even if she didn't. Ray knew as soon as she got that job that she was lost to him.

Suzanne was no longer the person he fell in love with. He was in love with someone who no longer existed. They had grown in different directions and there was nothing could be done to take them back to what once was. They weren't even the same people. They had become strangers with similar memories, no more.

As Suzanne hung up the phone she felt like a piece of her had been amputated. She sat on the bed staring straight ahead wondering what tomorrow would bring and where she should go from here.

She poured herself a double and shot it back chased by another. She didn't want to think, she didn't want to feel, she wanted to sleep, a very deep sleep. Whatever it took to get her there was good enough. What she was hiding from were her feelings, all feelings, she was better off numb.

The phone was ringing again. Why couldn't everyone leave her alone? It had to be Ray he had let her off far too easy and now he wanted to let her have it. She had to answer the phone she deserved his hatred and whatever attack he had to give her. She was wrong it was Paul, why was it Paul? How could Ray let go so easily? Did he care so little, have no love for her that he could just let her walk away?

Paul was far too confident he knew she wouldn't be able to go back; she should only be going forward. Suzanne was emphatic about his not getting too excited; she didn't do it for him or even because of him. She did what she did for herself and her own peace of mind. It wasn't a matter of who she wanted to be with, but where she wanted to be.

It didn't matter how much she loved Ray or didn't love Ray, he would never adjust or accept the style of life she wanted to live. He could never love the person she had become, a piece of her wasn't sure she could love the person she had become or maybe it was the person she always was but hid from.

Paul fully understood everything she was saying. He had lived a lie disguised as a marriage for years. All those years wasted, being very unhappy, a stranger in his own home. His wife and him spent all those years chasing different lifestyles, in different worlds that neither could ever be comfortable in. What she needed from Ray when she was fifteen was not necessarily what she needed in her life now.

When she was young she needed Ray to be her knight, her rescuer, she needed to be saved and protected. She had now grown into a strong and vital woman who could stand on her own, because of her own strength and merits.

Suzanne felt differently with Paul than with Ray. Ray still saw her as the helpless little girl he had to save and protect. To him she was a helpless child. He hadn't figured out she was a woman of strength and accomplishments. The little girl Ray fell in love with and still loved had been gone for years.

Paul on the other hand saw her as an adult, competent woman and therefore treated her as a woman, and so that is how she felt when she was with him. She was a vital sexy woman who could not only stand on her own two feet but also hold up anyone who happened to come along.

That was why she didn't feel whole or complete while at home. The grown woman in her is left at work. There is even Grandma and Grandpa to substitute as a Mommy and Daddy to reinforce the feeling. She hated hearing every word of what Paul was saying, but he was right.

It scared her that he knew her so well after such a short time. Ray had lived with her, and loved her most of her life, and knew nothing about who she was inside. What she was outside of him. Paul was right she was a little girl to Ray.

The next day she dreaded having to face Ray and the kids. They would be full of questions for which she had no answers. She decided not to plan anything, but deal with whatever came up as honestly as she could?

The kids bombarded her with hugs and kisses at the door as soon as she walked in. Ray stood back cautiously waiting for the bad news that was sure to come. Once the greetings were over the kids were sent out of the room so the adults could talk.

Her father told her of his engagement to Ray's mother to break the ice. Suzanne was shocked and surprised, but pleased. She was sure they would be very good together. She had never seen her father look so peaceful and happy.

Anybody that could put a smile on his face after all these years was fine with her. He went on to say how nothing needed to change. They could all stay as one family. Ray interrupted and said he needed to talk to Suzanne alone.

The two of them went up to what was once their room to talk. Ray told her he was going to make it easy on her; he would do all the talking. He told her he loved her and always would.

He knew she had grown out and away from the family and didn't need them anymore. He wanted her to know, as much as he would miss her, he did understand why this was all happening.

From the time he had met her, he knew he was over his head and would never be able to hang onto her. When he hugged her for the last time she could feel him crying inside. He had far too much pride to let it out, but his body trembled with betrayal of the grief he was working so hard to hold in.

Suzanne gave him a gentle kiss on the cheek and thanked him. She thanked him for making it as easy as possible, for understanding, and most of all for keeping her safe all these years. He told her that would not change. In spite of everything, he would always be there for her no matter what.

They decided the best way to tell the kids was to take a trip to the park for the afternoon, maybe fill them in after ice-cream. They told them that everything would be the same as it had been for the last few months Mommy would continue to live at work.

Anna was the most upset, she was the homebody, and she wanted her family together. The other kids didn't seem to mind as long as Suzanne promised to call everyday. They spent the rest of the day together at the park, in a kind of limboed silence.

There was nothing left to say. Neither could help but get lost in the nostalgic memories floating through their mind and hearts, as they watched their children play on their last day as a family.

Chapter Ten

A weight had been lifted off Suzanne; she was leaving behind everything that she had been up to this point in her life. Including a man she once loved more than life ... why was she not filled with regrets and remorse? She wanted to stop the car and do a dance on the side of the road.

This revelation made her realize what a heartless, selfish bitch she must be. Suzanne didn't even feel the loss of her children or her father. As much as this puzzled her, she was in too good a mood to spend much time thinking about it.

She did have one small regret... things would be different now. She had always had Ray there to protect her, to keep her safe. If the world she had ventured into got too scary, she always knew she could run back to the security of Ray's arms. Her safety net would be gone.

Now she would have to deal with Paul in a real way. She no longer had Ray as an excuse. It was time for some truth, truth that Suzanne was afraid of. She was every bit as afraid of getting too close to Paul as she was leaving Ray behind.

She didn't want to jump from Ray's arms right into Paul's. She had to find out if she could be a whole person on her own, without being an extension of someone else. If he loved her, he would wait until she was ready.

There was one person Suzanne needed right now, her Dad. She called him from her room; she had to talk to him alone, no Ray, no children. She had to be sure he didn't hate her. She had to be sure she was still Daddy's girl, his princess. Did Daddy still love his little girl?

Suzanne wasn't at all prepared for her father's reaction. She thought Ray would be worse... if he could understand she assumed everyone else would. Her father tore into her, ripping her guts out.

He was ashamed of her; she was selfish and self-centered just like her mother. She had no right walking away. It wasn't fair to Ray or the kids. When you get married and have kids it's a commitment you make forever. Everything she had ever done in her life was to hurt not only him but anyone who got close.

Her mother had also hurt who ever loved her or got too close ... the apple didn't fall far from the tree ... and rotted when it hit the ground. That was his daughter, his princess...

"WROTTEN TO THE CORE ..."

Suzanne was crying so hard she could hardly speak, she needed him to understand, she wasn't trying to hurt anyone, she was trying to set things right, trying to stop hurting everyone in her path. Why couldn't he understand that everyone involved was as unhappy as she was? It was time to stop the pain!

If he had left his wife when he had the chance and taken the children, maybe they wouldn't all be such screwed up messes. Maybe she could have learned to love and trust. Maybe just maybe she would have had a chance at some kind of normal life where people could love and trust each other.

Slamming the phone down, it was the end of the conversation. She wasn't willing to give him the opportunity to hurt her more. If he loved her, he would not want her to spend the rest of her life making herself and her children miserable. It was not her father's place to sit in judgement. He didn't climb all over her brothers with their many divorces.

Suzanne poured herself a drink; she needed to wash away the pain and tears. The memory of her father's harsh words welled up inside of her, refusing to be washed away even by the alcohol she poured down her throat.

Still crying when Paul called, she couldn't talk to him, she was too confused, too hurt. He begged her to let him come over, he wouldn't try anything he simply wanted to be a friend and comfort her. He wouldn't even ask any questions if she didn't want to talk about it. He would be her shoulder to cry on, no strings attached. That was what friends did, support and comfort with no judgements or conditions.

Suzanne relented, he could come over, but she would have no hesitation in calling security if he tried anything cute. He told her to stay where she was. He would come up, there was no sense in her coming through the lobby as upset as she was.

Suzanne sat on the side of her bed wondering what she was doing. There had to be something wrong with her, she couldn't live her life unless she was filled with as much turmoil and confusion as possible. Her father was wrong it wasn't the people who got close that she was trying to hurt, it was herself.

A quick shower and change into a nightgown and housecoat, something comfortable she needed to relax. No sooner had she poured herself a drink than she could hear the door opening. She could see the grin on his face, and assured him she took a shower and changed in an attempt to calm down ... not to turn him on.

While telling him about her conversation with Ray she poured him a drink. Paul thought it was good for Ray to let go easily. She wasn't sure she agreed, in reality she was hurt that he could let her go so easily. At this point she wasn't sure of anything, least of all what she wanted.

Deep down there was a little piece of her that needed Ray to be hurt, to desperately try to get her back. How could he have loved her as much as he claimed and let her walk away without a fight or even a tear? How could all this not devastate him?

Because he was glad to get rid of her and she knew it now more than ever. Suddenly instead of being thankful Ray let her off easy she was filled with anger that he had dumped her without even looking back. It was all turned around now; she could now see it all clearly. He was looking for any excuse to get off the hook and here she handed him an easy out.

As she continued to stew in her own thoughts, she could hear Paul talking, reassuring but really had no idea what was being said. Suzanne was in her own world, a world she had created. Now she was in the middle of creating a new mess. Actually it was the same mess; the only thing new was the man.

Suzanne once again reminded him she did none of this for him. She wasn't ready to jump out of Ray's bed and into his. Somehow, she needed to say it out loud more to remind herself than him.

Being face to face with him, alone in her room, she had to keep saying the words to herself over and over again until she believed them. She needed to find herself. Be a single complete person before she could be any good to or for anyone. Now all she had to do was convince her hormones to stop jumping every time he came near.

Paul not only agreed, but also insisted, he didn't want her until she was sure she was ready. It confused Suzanne when Paul spoke this way. She thought all men wanted sex, anyway they could get it.

Paul needed to know if she was upset, when he called because she still loved Ray and wanted to be with him. She said no, and explained what her father had said to her. She could barely get the words out without being devastated in a pool of tears.

Paul moved over close to her and held her. She snuggled into him for needing to be held was what she needed most. Once they were close she broke down completely. There was no stopping the tears that were streaming down her face out of control. It seemed she would cry forever, or at least until she fell asleep in Paul's arms.

Paul picked her up and carried her to the bed, ever so gently, being careful not to wake her as he laid her on the bed. Pulling the throw blanket from the couch over her, he laid down beside her, watching her sleep. He didn't need sex with her. For now, anyway, being close to her would be enough.

He knew it was going to take a lot of time and patients to win her trust. He wasn't looking for a one-night stand he wanted more. To Paul it was worth waiting for. She was worth waiting for.

Panic ran through Suzanne as she woke, still half-drunk and dazed realizing she was in bed with Paul. As she took a deep breath and looked around she realized she was still fully dressed and so was Paul. It was fairly clear nothing could have happened.

He was such a gentleman even sleeping on top of the covers. She tried to figure out what his game was. He certainly wasn't like any man she had ever known. Deep in her gut, she knew there had to be a hook somewhere. She was too hung over to either find it or worry about it. As she looked over, Paul was watching her. She pushed him off the bed and hit him with a pillow.

He had no business being in bed with her. What did he think he was doing taking advantage of someone that was upset and extremely drunk? Is that the only way he could get close to a woman?

Suzanne's words were harsh cruel and completely unnecessary. She knew he had behaved as a gentleman, but she had to put him in his place for future advances. He was far too confident about what her desires were and where all this was going.

He tried his hardest to explain how he was fully dressed, and if he wanted to take advantage he could have, but didn't. She was upset and needed to be held, and that was all there was to it.

He was filled with indignance as he asked ... " YOU REALLY DO NOT TRUST ME DO YOU?.." He was not to take it too personally, she didn't trust anyone. He was on the edge of roughness as he pulled her into him and kissed her with all the strength and passion of a caveman.

She tried to punch him and push him away, but he was too powerful for her. In reality she didn't have the strength to fight because her heart wasn't in it. She wanted his advances, but he wasn't about to know that.

Paul let go of her and she fell back onto the bed. He walked over to the couch, put his shoes on and started to leave. Stopping halfway through the door, he turned and said ... " ONE DAY YOU WILL TRUST ME AND THAT IS WHEN WE WILL MAKE LOVE BUT NOT UNTIL ... 'TIL THAT TIME COMES CALL ME WHEN

YOU NEED A FRIEND ... I DON'T HAVE TO ALWAYS CALL YOU ... FRIENDSHIPS ARE TWO SIDED..."

Suzanne would never feel comfortable calling any man. She had never called Ray in all the time they had dated or been married for that matter. Paul smiled and said ... "DO YOU SEE WHAT I MEAN ABOUT TRUST? ... WHEN YOU TRUST ME YOU WILL BE COMFORTABLE TO CALL ... "With that he was gone.

Paul was certainly good at dramatic exits, probably a trick to make her think about him ... unfortunately it worked. She thought about him all day and all night. He certainly had her attention. He was without a doubt the most fascinating man she had ever met. She couldn't even begin to figure him out.

One thing was for sure he was going to keep life interesting; she hadn't been bored since she met him. Most of the time she felt like she was on an emotional roller coaster, and she was waiting for this particular ride to be over.

If his love making was anything like his kisses... she didn't dare finish the sentence even in her own thoughts. She had to stop this train of thought; it couldn't either be safe or healthy.

She had a lot of work to do and she would never get a thing done while she was thinking about being in bed with this man. It was only a few days before that she had been in bed with Ray, and had thought "HE" was all she would ever want.

How could she be totally attracted to Ray one day, then in the blink of an eye, turn around and be every bit as attracted to Paul. Suzanne had to find someway of sorting out what she felt for each of them. She had to go see Doctor Anderson; maybe she could help her work through the confusion.

Suzanne would be the first to deny it, but she was drinking pretty steadily. She called it socializing, but she drank more alone at night. Only to help her sleep, she told herself. A drink after supper would calm her down after a hard day, and keep her nerves in tact of course. There was always a ready excuse. She worked hard so she deserved it.

There was nothing wrong with it. After all, she was never drunk, and it never interfered with her work. Drunks were falling down, sleeping in the street. They were people that had no life outside of the bottle ... that wasn't her.

Suzanne didn't understand why everyone was on her so much about it. Ray was so self-righteous since he joined AA's. It was like one of those obsessive religions that people try to push down everybody's throat.

As soon as Suzanne walked into Dr. Anderson's office, she started blurting everything out before she even sat down. She had a million things to tell her and couldn't get them out fast enough. She babbled about the court, her Dad's engagement, Ray and the kids, all of their reactions.

She was slow to discuss Paul and all the strange, confusing feelings she was having for him. She wasn't sure if she should even mention him at all. They were friends; it was Paul that introduced her to the doctor. What if Doctor Anderson let something slip to Paul?

Unfortunately there was no one else she could discuss Paul with, at least not anyone with no emotional attachment. She had buried herself in work for a long time, leaving only enough room for family.

It was times like this she had wished she kept in touch with all her old friends from school. It was the first time she regretted putting Ray ahead of her friends and losing touch with all of them. At the time it seemed so important to put Ray first. They had a fresh new start when they went back together and she wanted to give it every chance.

Suzanne needed to take a deep breathe and slow down. They would deal with each issue one at a time. First issue was the court date and how Suzanne felt by what the judge had said.

How could Suzanne tell her she didn't hear a word of what the judge had said because she was too consumed with thoughts of Paul and Ray? Sad that her life was on the line and all she could think about were schoolgirl crushes. There had to be something seriously wrong with her.

... "I WAS VERY LUCKY AND VERY THANKFUL ... I HATE TO ADMIT IT, BUT I FELT WORRIED ABOUT IT BEING OVER WITH..."

Doctor Anderson thought that was a strange reaction and now she was hearing herself say the words she thought it was strange too... " IT WAS ALL VERY CONFUSING ... I LIKED LIVING AT THE HOTEL ... I FELT GOOD WHEN I WAS THERE ... I DID NOT WANT TO GO HOME ... I DID NOT WANT TO BE A WIFE AND MOTHER AGAIN ... I LIKED BEING SINGLE AND ONLY VISIT ONCE IN A WHILE ... WITH NO PRESSURE, NO DEMANDS..."

Now she did it. Suzanne opened a can of worms she didn't want to get into. She had no idea how this doctor always did this to her. She had a way of turning the conversation in a direction completely opposite to where Suzanne meant to go.

... "YOU WERE WITH RAY MOST OF YOUR LIFE, YOU HAVE NEVER BEEN WITH ANYONE ELSE? ... IT MUST HAVE HURT WHEN YOU HEARD HIM CUTTING YOU LOOSE...? "

... "NO!.. IT FELT GOOD... HE OPENED MY CAGE AND SET ME FREE ..."

... "YOU CONSIDERED YOUR MARRIAGE A CAGE?..."

Suzanne was trying to dig herself out of a hole that got deeper with every word. How could she get out of this? She hadn't sorted this out herself and was bound to feel like a fool or crazy person trying to explain it all. She had no idea what she felt or even why she felt it

" ... IT'S NOT THAT I THINK IT WAS A CAGE.... BUT I DID FEEL TRAPPED ... I HAVE SPENT MY LIFE BEING WHAT PEOPLE WANT ME TO BE ... I AM DADDY'S GIRL ... RAY'S WIFE ... THE KID'S MOTHER..."

Suddenly a light came on and she knew exactly what she wanted and it was all so simple. She wanted to be herself with her own life. She was tired of living everyone else's life.

...." THE ONE THING I NEVER WAS ABLE TO BE WAS MY OWN PERSON... I WAS NEVER ALLOWED TO BE ME ... UNTIL

ALL THIS HAPPENED AND I MOVED INTO THE HOTEL I
DIDN'T KNOW THERE WAS A ME OUTSIDE OF RAY AND
THE KIDS, OUTSIDE OF MY PARENTS ... I THOUGHT ALL
THOSE THINGS WERE ME ... I FINALLY FOUND MYSELF
AND I DIDN'T WANT TO BE LOST AGAIN... "

Suzanne had to be honest, she was on a roll. The truth might as
well come out. And the truth is that she had no regrets about leaving.
Not for one second did she miss any of it. It made her sad how little
she missed her life, her children, and her father.

... " I CALL AND STAY IN TOUCH BECAUSE I DON'T
WANT THE KIDS TO HURT, AND I DON'T WANT TO FEEL
GUILTY ... IF I COULD WALK AWAY AND FEEL NO GUILT
ABOUT HURTING THE KIDS, I WOULD IN A SECOND AND
NOT EVEN LOOK BACK ... I LOVE BEING SINGLE ... "

Suzanne could see the look of disappointment on the doctor's face
almost immediately... What did she say that upset her so much? She
was just trying to be honest, to tell her exactly how she felt.

..." LET ME GET THIS STRAIGHT... IN ESSENCE WHAT
YOU ARE SAYING IS, YOU DON'T WANT OR NEED A FAMILY?
... YOU HAVE NO PROBLEM STANDING ALONE?..."

What Suzanne wanted to say was that in her deepest of hearts she
had no family love or loyalty. She was part of a family because it was
expected of her not because she feels she is part of that family.

If the truth were to be said out loud it would be that she wasn't
part of the family. She was and had always been outside of all of them.
Outside looking in, that was how she had felt her entire life. Suzanne
did not understand nor could she control those feelings. She had
fought against them for years but they were always there reminding her
that she just didn't belong.

After a long pause, trying to choose her words very carefully Suzanne
suspected the doctor was trying her hardest to decide if Suzanne were
serious or simply trying to shock her. Slowly and choosing her words
carefully the Doctor began to talk breaking the awkward silence that
was between them...

"ONE OF THESE DAYS YOU ARE GOING TO HAVE TO DEAL WITH TRUST ... THE REASON YOU DO NOT FEEL LOVE IS BECAUSE YOU DO NOT TRUST ... WHEN YOU START TO TRUST YOU WILL ALSO LOVE ... THEY GO TOGETHER, YOU CAN NOT HAVE ONE WITHOUT THE OTHER ..."

Well, now Suzanne had heard it all. She wasted no time telling the doctor she was wrong. Maybe the reason that Suzanne didn't trust was because no one loved her enough to make her belong. It wasn't what she was doing. People went out of their way to keep her outside of the family.

Suzanne was sick of all this love trust talk. One had nothing to do with the other and she knew it. This doctor was trying to play with her head. Just another trick to put her off guard....

... " I CAN'T MAKE MYSELF FEEL WHAT I DO NOT FEEL ... LOVE AND TRUST HAVE NOTHING TO DO WITH EACH OTHER ... I LOVED RAY FOR MANY YEARS ... IN MANY WAYS I STILL LOVE RAY.... I HAVE NEVER TRUSTED ANYONE ..."

... "DID YOU LOVE RAY OR DID YOU NEED RAY TO RESCUE YOU FROM A BAD SITUATION ... WHAT IF YOU NEVER LOVED RAY? ... WHAT IF YOU MERELY CONVINCED YOURSELF YOU LOVED RAY BECAUSE YOU SO DESPERATELY NEEDED HIM? ..."

Suzanne didn't want to continue this conversation. The doctor had it all twisted around. Of course she loved Ray!...She married him didn't she? She had children for him didn't she? ...

Most of her youth was given to him through some very hard times. If that wasn't love then there is no such thing as love.

... "I AM NOT SURE EXACTLY WHAT LOVE IS ... BUT THERE WAS A TIME WHEN I HAD TO BE WITH HIM AT ALL TIMES, I HATED IT WHEN WE WERE APART... "

... "WHAT DID YOU FEEL WHEN YOU WERE WITH RAY IN THOSE DAYS?.."

Suzanne loved to take a moment and think about those days. For a moment she was lost in those feelings again. She had felt safe. She had felt loved. She had felt special. Suzanne only wished she could feel any of it again. She missed the way Ray could make her feel in those days.

..." SO YOU TRUSTED RAY TO KEEP YOU SAFE? ..."

..." OH, YES!... HE WAS MY KNIGHT, MY RESCUER... HE FOUGHT OFF ALL THE DRAGONS IN MY LIFE..."

"SO ... YOU CAN TRUST ...THEN IS IT FAIR TO SAY YOU ALSO LOVED RAY?..." They had done a full circle, Suzanne had no idea how they got there but the light came on none the less. She had trusted Ray and until this moment she had forgotten.

..." WE HAVE DISCOVERED TWO THINGS TODAY, WETHER YOU KNOW IT OR NOT... YOU ARE CAPABLE OF LOVE AND YOU ARE CAPABLE OF TRUST ... NOW ALL WE HAVE TO DO IS FIGURE OUT HOW TO GET YOU TO FEEL AGAIN, BEFORE IT IS TOO LATE FOR YOUR CHILDREN ..."

Driving back to work Suzanne couldn't help but think about her children. She wondered if they could tell she couldn't feel love. It wasn't that she hated them and resented them. She was proud of them and respected them as individuals.

She had feelings for them as she did for many other people; she simply had no feelings of family. It all seemed so confusing, it was no wonder Ray had told her so many times he couldn't understand her. How could he understand her, she couldn't understand herself.

She dreaded having to do a family chart for the doctor. It was bad enough she was forced to think about it. Now because of her big mouth she was forced to do two separate ones. The first one had to be her childhood family; the second was her adult family.

Bad enough she had to list them, but to write what she thought of them meant she had to really think about them. Suzanne had tried her hardest not to think of any of them for years and hated when destiny forced her to face both them and her feelings for them.

Once back at the hotel she called Rays Mom, she needed to spend time with her children. She needed to tell them she loved them and was still their mother. Perhaps she could bring them to the hotel, she wanted them to see and be part of her world. She hoped that if they came into her world she could love them. If she couldn't feel a part of their lives she would make them a part of hers.

Suzanne instructed Ray's mom to dress them in their best clothes, they could spend the evening with her and stay for supper. That would give them some family time alone, outside of Ray's world. She could help them to understand what was happening and why.

When she got to the house they came walking toward the car, she was filled with pride as she saw how well behaved and dignified they all looked. That is except Angel, where was Angel? Suzanne didn't have time for this.

Suzanne climbed out of the car to find out what was holding Angel up; she didn't want to hear that she was refusing to come. She would come and that was all there was to it. The door opened and Angel appeared on a full run to catch up to the rest of the kids.

BOOM! ... Down she went face first in the only mud puddle within a hundred-mile radius. Only Angel could do this. Why was it always her? Couldn't things go right just once?

Suzanne started toward her screaming at the top of her lungs ... "HOW COULD SHE DO THIS? ... WHY WASN'T SHE MORE CAREFUL? ... TODAY OF ALL DAYS "....

The closer Suzanne got to Angel the faster Angel crawled on her hands and knees, back to the house where her grandma would protect her... keep her safe from the monster she had lost battles to all too many times. Suzanne froze in her tracks as she saw the terror on Angel's face.

Suzanne was soaked with tears that streamed down her face as she realized just how scared Angel really was ... "I SWEAR... BABY, I WON'T HURT YOU ... I WILL NEVER HURT YOU AGAIN ... PLEASE TRUST ME ... PLEASE ... I MIGHT YELL ONCE IN A WHILE, BUT I SWEAR TO YOU, I WILL NEVER HIT ... NOT EVER AGAIN ... "

With that Angel rose very slowly, hesitantly to her feet. Once she was completely to her feet, she ran as fast as she could. Running into the house and up the stairs, to a hiding place that had always kept her safe. To the only friend that ever cared about her, her rag doll would know why she was so scared. She had to be in her safe place.

Suzanne's father and mother-in-law stood in the doorway keeping Suzanne from going after Angel. Her father looked at her with total disgust, telling her she would have to earn Angel's trust. Screaming at her for a simple accident wasn't how she was going to do it.

Angel refused to come. There was no changing her mind after that. There was nothing Suzanne could do. Once again, she had no control, no say about anything. Once again she was the monster and Angel won all the sympathy.

The only thing Suzanne could do was take the others, try to make them understand. Maybe they could explain it all to Angel, maybe she could get closer to Angel by phone. There had to be a way of getting through to her.

Most of supper was eaten in a tense heavy kind of uncomfortable silence. She had such good intentions wanting so much for this to work and now Angel had ruined it all for all of them. How could she or any of them relax or be comfortable with all this hanging over them.

When she drove the kids' home, Angel still refused to come down from her room and speak to her mother. When she got back to her office she made a handful of attempts to call Angel, only for her father to tell her to quit calling for now. Angel not only refused to come to the phone but refused to leave her closet.

What was she supposed to do? She had made every effort. If Angel wasn't going to meet her half way she couldn't do anything about it. It wasn't her fault; she had done all she could. No one understood, it wasn't her it was Angel who refused to give her another chance.

Suzanne's father had lost patience with her forcing her to talk with her mother-in-law.

Suzanne tried to explain how important it was for Angel to start being part of the family. She had to start letting people into her world.

Ray's mom coldly explained to Suzanne, Angel was more than willing to let her into her world. She had spent the entire day running around nervously trying to make everything perfect for her trip with her mother.

No one ever saw a child try so hard to please ... "YOU HAVE NO IDEA WHAT YOU DO TO THAT CHILD ... NO MATTER HOW HARD SHE TRIES TO PLEASE YOU ... YOU ARE STILL ANGRY WITH HER ... SHE CAN'T DO ANYTHING RIGHT! ..."

By this time Suzanne could hear the trembling in her mother in law's voice, she was on the verge of crying as she attempted to get Suzanne to see what she was doing to this poor helpless child...."WHEN SHE FELL IT WASN'T HER FAULT ... YOU COULD HAVE BEEN SYMPATHETIC OR AT THE VERY LEAST UNDERSTANDING... "

Suzanne wanted to hang up. She didn't want to hear any of this. Once again it was all her fault she was the monster. Suzanne forced herself to hold her tongue and listen. She needed Ray's mom on her side if she were ever to get through to her kids.

She would listen to all of it, no matter how much it hurt, no matter how much she was tempted to hang up on her. Suzanne listened to every word as her mother-in-law went on to tell Suzanne how Angel crawled back into her closet and it was all Suzanne's fault, everything was Suzanne's fault. Angel was not the problem Suzanne was.

How would Suzanne ever get through to Angel? There had to be a way. She had to spend time with Angel without alienating her even further. Why was she like that with Angel? Why Angel and not the other kids?

Anna could do the exact same thing as Angel, but when it was Anna it was all right, it was understandable. If it was Angel it induced rage, whatever it was. Simply walking into a room was enough for Suzanne to be angry with Angel... but why?

Suddenly Suzanne was swimming in truth. The truth was that she was a monster and she was unreasonable with Angel. Suddenly

Suzanne knew it wasn't Angel it was her. A truth she had never wanted to see but now was forced to. She had turned into her mother.

That evening Suzanne didn't pour herself that drink before she went downstairs to check on everything. She didn't even pour a drink when she got back. There was no drink to help her unwind, to help her stay calm and not even a drink to chase the ghosts away so she could sleep.

She wanted to think tonight.... clearly. For the first time in a long time she had the opportunity to think about what a total mess her life was in. A mess she had made herself. It wasn't Angel. It wasn't her mother. There was no one left to blame. It was her and it was time she faced it. There would be no more hiding, because there was no place left to hide.

It was time for her to forget about Paul, Ray, her Dad, and even her mother. The only important thing to concentrate on was her children especially Angel. There had to be a way of breaking through the wall she was building between them all, a wall that was getting higher and stronger with each confrontation.

Even Anna was a concern for Suzanne; her eldest daughter was far too grown up. She had thrown away her childhood doing the job that Suzanne should have been doing. She was the mother in that house and had been since she was big enough to walk and bark out orders.

As for Alice and R.J. they were friendly strangers that she hardly knew except for short visits. She didn't know them as a mother should know her children; they were a social event, pleasant company.

It was three a.m. when Suzanne got out of bed to do her family charts for Dr. Anderson. Suzanne had told herself she was too busy, but in her heart she knew she was avoiding in hopes the good doctor would forget. She decided to start with her adult chart only because she had the kids' fresh on her mind.

ADULT CHART

FATHER: (I am adding my Dad to this list because he lives with us so this is what I think about him now, later I will put him on the other list for what I thought of him as I was growing up.)

Tired, worn-out, trying to find peace in his life after years of guilt and pain... he has fought battles all his life and has no fight left.

MOTHER-IN-LAW: very gentle, caring lady willing to do anything for anybody esp. family... self educated, country girl yet wise ... I wish I could be like her, so peaceful and content within herself.

RAY: hard working, feet on the ground, steady-Freddie type, loves his children, a very devoted father and husband...once loved me very much, has gone through the entire marriage looking at me through rose colored glasses... has no idea what or who I am ... thinks he is a reformed alcoholic but I doubt he really is an alcoholic.

ANNA: seven going on twenty... far too grown up, takes after Ray's side of the family ... steady level-headed, reliable.... she holds everyone together, much like Ray's mom.

As Suzanne sat thinking about what to put under Angel's name she was swamped with memories. A few were good but most pretty scary. There were memories of fights with Angel, of lost moments when she could have been a good mother to her daughter.

Suzanne had to force herself to go on. To do this whether she wanted to or not. First she had to have a good cry. What she really wanted was a stiff drink... or perhaps a few. As many as it took to drown the pain she was forcing herself to see.

ANGEL: Strong, frustrating to deal with, stubborn yet scared of the world and everything in it ... six years old and has had more of life's scars than most adults ... she has the eyes of an old woman carrying the weight of

the world.... she has the ability to see through people
... likely why people are so uncomfortable around her
and why she has no friends.

Suzanne thought about Angel and her eyes, how uncomfortable
she always made her feel. How they pierced through Suzanne every
time she had tried to discipline her. It was those eyes that always
enraged Suzanne. It was those eyes that always made her feel her shame
and guilt. The same eyes that made her face her own weaknesses. She
was a little girl who had the power to take all control from her adult
mother, turning that mother into the little girl.

Suzanne could not fool Angel. Angel saw through her, saw her dark
sides. She even saw the monster that Suzanne tried to keep deep in the
darkest corners of her soul. The same monster that wanted to hit Angel
every time she forced Suzanne to see what she really had become.

ALICE: sweet Alice, a warm wonderful child, a
pleasure to be with, no scars or intensity, she is content
with whatever she can get in herlife ... everyone likes
her ... everyone loves her ... one of the easiest children
to love, you don't have to work at it, the love comes
naturally...
RAY JUNIOR: an energetic three-year-old ... very
happy, very funny, can't handle conflict wants everyone
to be happy and get along, does whatever he can to
keep people laughing ... Ray seniors pride for the future
generations of Briars .... my little leprechaun.
MOTHER: even though my mother is dead she still
haunts every day of my life, so I am adding a little blurb
about her.... to me she is not dead till I get her out of
my head ... unresolved pains, nightmares

Suzanne now had to do a list about her siblings. She hated having
to think about her childhood for even a moment. She hated that this

doctor was forcing her to feel the pain of those years again. It had taken her most of her adult life to forget all of it and all of them.

Her hands began to tremble as she started to write. She wasn't sure if they shook from the tears and pain she tried so hard to hold in or from the lack of a drink she wanted more than she cared to admit.

As much as she wanted to be done with this she had to sleep. Her eyes burned, her head hurt. She couldn't sit up for even another moment. Just a short nap then she could do it. Then she could face them all with a clear head.

Suzanne sat thinking about her siblings as she drifted into a deep sleep. She wondered why they had never been a family. It was more logical for them to be closer, if not for the sake of all the pain they had shared.

It was five a.m. before she was able to drift off to sleep. The desk woke her at nine; she had an appointment at ten with the owners. She picked a good night to quit drinking and stay up all night. These were not easy men to deal with and she found herself wishing she were rested and fresh.

After what happened with the last manager, they decided to have monthly updates on how the hotel was doing, and to go over the books personally. There would be no more blind faith. The past manager made it harder for everyone. Suzanne couldn't help but feel she was being punished for what he had done.

There were five owners, three were pleasant enough, and as long as she could account for all finances they didn't bother her much. There was one who was a pain in the butt always wanting to know the simplest of details, very pesky and picky. The last one was hard, bordering on cruelty.

Suzanne felt this man hated her or possibly all women in men's fields. She couldn't for the life of her figure out why, except for pure chauvinism. He almost reminded her of dealing with her mother. His name was Aaron and he was the stereotypical Jewish accountant.

The meeting went well, everything was in order. Suzanne was very good at what she did. Everyone was pleased and left that is except for

Aaron Weinstein who had to go over all the books one more time. He poured over them like he was sure there was something hidden or missed.

Finding nothing out of order no matter how many times he went over the books. Suzanne couldn't help but wonder if he had a problem dealing with women. Maybe he was one of those old-fashioned guys who believed women should be barefoot and pregnant in the kitchen.

Finally he was gone and Suzanne could relax. Now, she could get back to work, and not worry for another month, which was too soon for her. She wondered why or how people could dislike someone before they even took the time to know them.

Her mother had been like that. She would dislike someone for where they lived, how they lived, how they dressed or even who their associates were. If those weren't reason enough then she would dislike someone simply because she did.

Suzanne had often thought people like that must have very sad lives. Her mother was in total disapproval of Ray's mother, and for the sake of snobbishness, missed knowing one of the truly great women of the world.

It did Suzanne's heart good to think of her father marrying someone her mother considered a lower class citizen. Suzanne went to the kitchen grabbed some lunch and a glass of apple juice, she loved eating in the kitchen. Shelby had become best friend, she even liked his boyfriend.

She enjoyed being with a guy she didn't have to worry about hitting on her. It was like having a best girlfriend only better, he would never steal her man. That is, if she had a man, or maybe he would. They laughed as she teased him.

After lunch she took the time to call the girls and R.J., she was starting to get to know them so much better now. It was so much easier by phone, she was even beginning to gain some ground with Angel, bit by bit.

Although Angel still didn't trust her enough to go anywhere with her, Suzanne was sure that would come eventually. She simply had to hang in there 'til all the bricks were removed from her wall.

Dr. Anderson still wanted a family session. Suzanne talked to each of her children, trying to explain to them, so they wouldn't be nervous or scared. She wasn't at all worried about the three kids, but she was nervous about Ray and Angel, and what they would have to say.

The day finally came, Suzanne couldn't have been more anxious. Ray and the kids would meet her in front of the doctor's office so they could all walk in together. There was a long uncomfortable silence as they were all waiting for the doctor to come into the room. It was the first time Suzanne had been with them as a family since they told the kids about the separation.

The doctor introduced herself, and then she explained the point of the visit. It was to simply get to know each other better. In order to accomplish that the kids would go with the doctor's friend and play some games.

Turning to address Ray, she told him she understood they were separated, and so if he didn't want to participate with any of this it was understandable. She wanted him to understand that whatever pains Suzanne went through would affect the kids. He should have an understanding of what was happening to his family. He agreed and decided to stay.

" LET US START WITH THE NIGHT SUZANNE WAS ARRESTED FOR HITTING ANGEL ... HOW DID YOU FEEL WHEN YOU GOT THAT PHONE CALL? "...

At first he didn't believe a word of it. He didn't marry a monster; she would never have hurt anyone. All that quickly changed as he was forced to face the truth. He quickly became consumed with an angry confusion. He expressed controlled feelings he was angry, confused and worried but mostly he was frustrated in his helplessness.

He was upset with Suzanne, he had ordered her not to deal with Angel, and he would do all the disciplining when he got home from work. She had gone too far before and that was the only way he could think of to deal with it. There was something about Angel that set Suzanne off. It had always been that way even when Angel was a baby.

Doctor Anderson asked Ray to explain how anyone could not like a baby? She wanted to know the first time he noticed a problem. He began telling her about the time with the pillow. Angel had been crying for what seemed like days, he came home from work to find Suzanne standing over their baby with a pillow.

Suzanne's nerves were raw and on edge before she got there, it didn't take more than a comment to devastate her into tears. Ray acted like he was all right with their separation but he must have been after revenge for his pain to throw this in her face.

Suzanne tried to talk through the flood of tears she could no longer hold back..." I WOULD NOT HAVE KILLED HER ... I DID NOT WANT TO HURT HER, I ONLY WANTED HER TO STOP ... I WAS SO TIRED, SHE WOULDN'T LET ME SLEEP... WE WERE LIVING OUT AT THAT DAMN FARM, I WAS LONELY...I WAS SCARED ALL THE TIME..."

The doctor asked Ray for his next clear memory of a time between Suzanne and Angel ... he told her about how he thought if he could take Suzanne away for a break everything would be all right.

While they were away Angel wouldn't eat or sleep. Suzanne's mother didn't know what to do. Suzanne was angry with both her mother and Angel for ruining her vacation, her time to be special, to be first.

Angel was only about six months old at the time. Suzanne looked at her with hatred in her eyes.

"THAT'S RIGHT RAY... JUST GO OUT OF YOUR WAY TO MAKE ME LOOK AS BAD AS POSSIBLE... IT'S THAT JUDGMENTAL ATTITUDE THAT MADE ME HATE TO COME HOME ... YOU ALWAYS TREATED ME LIKE I WAS THE WORST MOTHER AND WIFE ON THE PLANET..."

Ray told Suzanne he never thought she was a bad mother or wife ... only to Angel. Why couldn't she have treated Angel like the other kids? She was the best mother in the world to the rest of the kids, why not to Angel?

Why couldn't you just try to understand Angel just a little, read her stories, rock her on your knee? Why couldn't you just love her a little? Children deserve to be loved by their mother. You can't pick, you can't love this one and hate that one. It doesn't work that way, why couldn't you just love her?

This time it was Ray on the edge of tears. He had held these questions in for all these years. Never able to say what he really felt, never able to even understand let alone fix it. Ray had his own guilt. The guilt of the head of a household he could neither fix nor hold together.

"THE LAST TIME YOU TOOK THE OTHER KIDS TO YOUR WORK, ANGEL COULDN'T GO!... WHY COULDN'T ANGEL GO SUZANNE?... TELL THE DOCTOR WHY ANGEL DIDN'T GO!... "

Suzanne was feeling cornered, she wished she could get out of this. She preferred to have her guts ripped out in private. This way everyone ever in her life could tell her how rotten she was, confirming how much she was despised and unloved how could she feel anything but trapped and cornered... " SHE REFUSED TO GO!... ALL OF YOU STOOD AGAINST ME AND LET HER REFUSE..."

Ray had to make her see, to make her understand. He had held his tongue far too long. There were things that needed to be cleared up, things Suzanne had to face. He wasn't about to back down now it all had to come out and now! ..." ANGEL REFUSED TO GO BECAUSE SUZANNE STARTED SCREAMING AND SCARED HER..."

"... I TOLD HER I WAS SORRY ... I BEGGED HER TO COME..." All the sorry's in the world meant nothing if Suzanne was going to keep scaring her. Suzanne needed to understand that.

" SAYING YOU ARE SORRY IS NOT GOING TO TAKE THE FEAR OUT OF THAT LITTLE GIRLS EYES OR HER HEART ... YOU DON'T EVEN KNOW ... SHE CRIES FOR YOU ALMOST

EVERY NIGHT, ALL NIGHT... SOMETIMES IN HER SLEEP SHE CALLS OUT FOR YOU..."

Suzanne didn't know about his sleepless nights; How he had to keep getting up in the middle of the night because Angel would be screaming, so loud and hard he had to wake her so she could go back to sleep in peace. Even in her sleep Angel would cry out..."MOMMY" ...over and over with tears running down her cheeks.

By this time Suzanne was crying so hard she couldn't talk, she couldn't breath, why was he being so cruel. Had he only come here to hurt her, to get revenge because she had hurt him? Ray leaned over to her and held her as she sobbed in his arms, as he had done so many times in the past.

He spoke to her with a gentle sympathy in his voice, a tone that showed his concern and caring. He didn't hate Suzanne, he could never hate her. He pitied her; his pity was the only thing he had left to give her.

Angel was so much like her; Suzanne spent the first year of their marriage crying in her sleep with nightmares and terrors. He couldn't count how many nights he had sat up, holding Suzanne as he now held Angel.

The only reason he even came was to put a stop to all of it. He didn't want to someday have to hold his granddaughter in the night because of what Angel did to her. This all has to stop right now, right here. This generation had to be the last to be raised on pain and hatefulness.

He looked at Dr. Anderson and begged her to please help Angel. It was too late for Suzanne and him, but Angel had a chance, or at least deserved a shot at a chance. This child was already filled with more problems and fear than most adults... "PLEASE BRING OUR ANGEL OUT OF THE CLOSET AND BACK INTO THE WORLD "...

Dr. Anderson was filled with a sadness and pity for what this family had endured. She finally had some hint of what she had to deal with. She told them she wanted to keep seeing Suzanne twice a week.

Angel would need sessions on her own for separate visits twice a week during the summer, and then once a month, see all of them together. She looked down at Ray and told him it would be up to him if he should choose to come.

Chapter Eleven

Still pretty shaken up when she got back to work, Suzanne had to pour herself a drink. Nothing else was about to calm her nerves or chase away the horror of the last few hours. She then sat down to call Paul's office. She needed a friend and Paul seemed to be the only one she could think of. Paul was pleased to hear from her, it was the first time she had called him on her own, simply because she needed him.

The tears streamed out with the first word she spoke. Amid all the tears, she tried to tell him she was sorry she called she couldn't talk after all. Suzanne felt she was wasting his time.

The last thing he needed was to hear some girl crying uncontrolled on the phone. Paul was wonderful as a friend, he told her that if she needed him it was never a waste of time. He would rearrange the rest of his day and be there as soon as he could.

When he arrived the door was unlocked, he entered slowly not sure what he would find. Suzanne was lying on the bed still crying. He had never seen her like this. It broke his heart as he had no idea where to start comforting her.

Paul lay on the bed beside her and held her in his arms feeling helpless to take away her pain. He tried to ask her questions, she put her finger to his lips and said..." SHSHSH.... HOLD ME ... DON'T TALK..."

After a few moments, she looked deep into his eyes and kissed him. It was the sweet, gentle kiss of a little girl in pain. There was a gentle hesitancy in her kiss as Paul could feel her tremble just a little. Suzanne needed to feel loved, she needed to feel wanted.

The kisses built in a passion that Paul could not resist. Was she sure? He didn't want to do it if it was only because she was hurting. She called him because she was hurting ... she was making love because there was no one else she wanted to be with.

Paul's touches were ever so slow and gentle... touching her cheek so slightly, as he kissed her lips, letting the kisses and the touch very slowly and subtly work their way down. Suzanne closed her eyes and drew a deep uncontrolled breath with each new spot. He worked his way to her breasts, first a gentle touch, caressing one while kissing the other.

As Suzanne started to touch and kiss him in response, he held her by both her wrists and put her hands up over her head, returning to her lips with a harder more passionate kiss. A kiss that seemed to go on forever, or at least she wished it would.

He had kissed and caressed every inch of her body, leaving each new area trembling and begging for more. She had never experienced such feelings, or even dreamt her body could be filled with such incredible passions.

She tried to let him continue it felt so good. Her breathing was out of control. Her body filled with electricity; she couldn't lie still any longer. Every touch seemed to be exaggerated. It was like trails of energy shooting through her. He wasn't making love to her; he was making love to her entire body.

Suzanne didn't know that making love could feel this way. Making love to Ray had actually become boring to her. She didn't know it could be different. She was doing things that surprised even her ... with a passion that she didn't know existed.

Her heart pumped out of control, her entire body shook. As her breathing raced, she had no idea what he was doing, but she didn't want him or the feelings to stop. She couldn't stand it any longer. She had to have him on top of her. She had to feel him inside of her. Her body had never wanted a man so completely.

Suzanne had no idea what Ray and her had been doing all those years, but it was nowhere near this. She pulled at Paul begging him to get on her. He told her to be patient he wasn't quite ready. He had to make her crazy first. She thought she was already as crazy as she could stand.

Her entire body went into a kind of a strange spasm; she had reached a peak and jumped off. She still hadn't caught her breath when he reached down to gently caress her again. It was mere seconds until she was out on the cliff again, waiting to jump off.

At the moment she was ready to go over she felt the weight of his body against her. She could feel him slide into her, filling her from the inside out. As his power and breathing increased she could feel their passions build together as one.

Soon there was no distinguishing her breathing from his. She had to hold onto him tight or she wouldn't be able to stand it. Suddenly they both took one long deep breath together and fell into a heap, intertwined with each other. Totally unable to move or talk, they held each other saying nothing.

What could she say? She had never experienced anything like this. She thought Ray and her had a good sex life, but it was barely sex. She felt like she had never experienced sex before this moment. Paul smiled as he looked down at her and asked if that was her first orgasm.

There was no lying to him, he already knew. It was pretty obvious he made her feel things she had never felt before, or even heard of. She had no idea what an orgasm was or that it even existed before that very moment.

She asked him how he had learned to be so skillful. He laughed, and told her it was a natural talent, that was a lot easier when you were with someone you wanted to please. When it comes to sexuality a person can only be as good as their partner and he had an incredible partner.

Paul had thought about, and planned a long time, what he wanted to do to her. She smiled an uncontrolled smile and told him he planned it well. She wanted to know if a shower together was part of that plan. Anything that had her naked was in his plans.

It was without a doubt the longest shower she had ever taken. She was absolutely fascinated with all this. Never had her entire body been touched. He even played with her toes. She had no idea a bar of soap could be so sensuous.

As they got dressed and went to supper it seemed so natural for Suzanne to be with Paul. They belonged together. Although Suzanne was scared by how comfortable she was with him, she didn't want to fall right back into the same trap she worked so hard to climb out of.

All the way through supper she tried to think of how to tell Paul she enjoyed the sex, but didn't want anything more than sex. She reached deep down into her soul and said ...

"PAUL... YOU KNOW WE ARE TWO FRIENDS MAKING EACH OTHER FEEL GOOD ... HELPING EACH OTHER THROUGH A TIME OF LONELINESS AND PAIN ... I CAN'T GIVE YOU MORE THAN THAT RIGHT NOW ... "

Paul looked deep into her eyes, reached across the table and held her hand with a light gentle touch. He understood and was willing to settle for anything she could give him. He knew what a mess her life and emotions were in and he could wait until she sorted it all out.

Good friendship, with some even better sex thrown in, was enough, for now. He had every intention of staying the entire night, but if she wanted he had no problem with leaving, so she could be alone to think. Suzanne had no problem with an evening of incredible sex as long as he knew the ground rules. His friendship was important to her and she didn't want to hurt him.

She still had more work to do around the hotel, so he could go, and come back later, or hang around the bar or her room. He had brought his brief case from the office, so he would go back to her room to work on some contracts and make some phone calls.

It was pretty late when she finally got back to her room. She hoped Paul wasn't mad at her. When she walked into the room, the lights were all off except a small lamp in the corner. She was sure Paul must have gotten bored and left.

Suzanne sighed with relief as she poured herself a drink and slipped out of her clothes making her way to the bed. She wanted to be with Paul but he scared her. Maybe a little breathing space would be good just to slow things down a little.

No such luck or maybe she was lucky... he hadn't left he had gone to bed and waited in the peaceful silence of sleep. Suzanne stood over Paul watching him sleep, he looked so peaceful and content like a little boy.

She let her slip drop from her shoulders allowing it to slide gently to the floor. Slowly she took off her bra then her panties. She knew he was sleeping but she still went through the sexy routine of a slow sensual strip tease.

Suzanne wanted to feel sexy as she slid slowly and carefully under the sheet. Gently she made her way close to him, close enough she could feel his breathes but careful not to quite touch or wake him.

Suzanne positioned herself as close to him as she could without actually touching him, slowly and gently kissing his neck, his shoulders, and his back. As she worked her way toward his belly button he woke up and rolled over very slowly. She hesitated for only a moment.

He opened his eyes ... "PLEASE DON'T STOP, IT FEELS WONDERFUL ... " She continued working her way up his belly toward his chest. She could feel his skin responding to the lightest of touches, the gentlest of kisses.

In slow motion she worked her way around his chest, her lips found his nipples. She felt very sensual as her tongue teased and fondled the tiny nipple in her mouth. He took her head in both of his strong large hands and pulled her head up to his, as they melted into a passionate kiss.

The beginning of a night of intense passion that didn't stop until either of them had the strength or desire to move. He looked at her, still half out of breath, and told her she was a fast learner. She said, only with a good teacher ... she would never again be bored with sex.

215

For the next several months her life seemed to be falling into place, everything was the way she wanted it to be. Work was going well, even Aaron Weinstein lightened up a little. He still treated her as though he didn't like her much, he couldn't complain though she did have the hotel running very smoothly and at a decent profit. As hard as he tried, and he did try, he couldn't find anything to criticize.

Her friendship with Paul was not only what she wanted, but what she needed. They talked on the phone nearly every day like old girl friends. A couple times a week they got together for incredible sex. Each time they slept together, he found new ways to heighten the passion.

Suzanne liked that they could lay in bed afterwards and laugh together. He made her feel so young and full of life. Best of all he never made demands or put pressure on her for more than she was willing to give.

Her only regret was that she and the kids were drifting further apart. She didn't call as often as she should there never seemed to be enough time. Suzanne would get distracted easily, and then it would be past bed time and too late to call.

Getting away for an afternoon to see them was even harder. Aaron was there so often to check on her, she had to stay on top of everything ... there were lots of reasons and lots of excuses.

To Suzanne they were all legitimate, Anna wasn't buying any of it. If her mother wanted to be there she would find a way. Anna was the most JUDGMENTAL. Angel was the coolest, and the other two rolled with the punches living their lives.

It was less than a week until Suzanne's father and Ray's mother were to wed. Suzanne made arrangements for a small reception at her hotel, as a wedding gift. This was to be the first fight her and Paul were to have.

Suzanne asked him to stay away for the weekend of the wedding. She didn't want to hurt Ray... she didn't mind hurting Paul. She reminded Paul of their original agreement, no strings, no ties just friends who happened to sleep together.

Paul wondered if it was really necessary to remind him he was no more than a behind closed doors piece of tail ... a good jump ... someone to keep the boredom down. He was wrong, he was everything to her. He was the best friend she ever had, and that friendship was important. He pointed out to her that he had not met any of her family or children.

She had totally kept him outside of her life. He was good enough for her bed, but nothing else. They hadn't even spent time together outside of the hotel. She had never even been to his office or apartment.

She couldn't deal with this. What was his problem? She had told him from the beginning where he stood. Why did he have to rock the boat when everything was so good? Why couldn't he enjoy what they had? Why did men always have to own women?

The one thing she didn't want to deal with were her feelings for Ray. She may enjoy sex with Paul, but the emotions came from Ray. She missed the way he looked at her with such love in his eyes. She liked that he was out there somewhere pinning away for her.

Maybe it was the memories she was in love with, but she needed to find out. He had told her he would always be there for her. She wanted to know if he meant it ... if he missed her at all. What she really needed to know was, did he still love her?

Suzanne left for the church early she was too excited to wait. When she saw her father he looked wonderful. He was wearing his dress uniform with all the ribbons and medals. She felt like a little girl again. She hadn't seen him in his uniform since he retired.

A tear welled up in her eyes as she went over to hug him. She told him to be happy, begging him to forgive her and not hate her. He held her tight and whispered ... "I COULD NEVER STOP LOVING YOU PRINCESS ..."

Suzanne's father not only loved her but more important understood. He was sorry he said all those hurtful things to her. Ray had explained things, he now knew in his heart that she did what was best for everyone. He was afraid his entire family was falling apart. Ray and her were the last, of what was left, of any sign of a family and he didn't want to lose her.

He had other news he had to talk to her about before the wedding, and he wasn't sure how she would take it. Ray had been seeing someone. They were very happy and very much in love. The girls all love her and she has even coaxed Angel out of her shell. She's a natural mother.

There was something he wasn't telling her. She had seen this look of fear on her father's face before. What was it that he wasn't telling her that kept him from looking her in the eyes?

The woman Ray was seeing was "THE NEIGHBOR "... the one that watched the kids while she was at the hospital. It was that same "NEIGHBOR" that called the police. Suzanne's mouth dropped as she stood in silent shock staring at her father.

..." YOU MEAN HE IS IN LOVE WITH THE WOMAN THAT STARTED MY NIGHTMARE! "   He had to remind Suzanne that she made her choices. She was the one who walked out on them. Bev was the one that was there for the kids when Suzanne had no time....

"I LOVE YOU AND I DO UNDERSTAND, NOW IT IS YOUR TURN TO UNDERSTAND WHAT RAY DID ... IF YOU CAN NOT UNDERSTAND ... THEN YOU BETTER AT LEAST ACCEPT IT ... "

He would expect her to leave if she couldn't handle it as he didn't want a scene at his wedding. She gave him a smile and told him she was fine, at least outwardly she was fine. He knew her well enough to know that she would keep face no matter what. No one especially Ray would ever know how much pain she felt. All her pain would be pushed down deep where no one would ever find it.

Pasting on her mother's best phony smile, to put up a false front, she was thankful for inheriting a trait of her mother's she had always hated as a small child. Paste on the smile, hold head high, walk with your best uppity posture and at all costs ... "SAVE FACE!"

He wanted "HER "to leave if she couldn't handle it. She was his family, not Ray. Maybe he forgot that. She smiled like she fully understood and everything was great. But it wasn't great. It hurt, and it hurt bad.

That little girl inside her, Daddy's little girl, wanted to lie on the floor and take a tantrum. She wanted to hold her breath, kick her feet and scream blue murder. Instead, she would paste on the smile, hold her head up high and walk with her best uppity posture. She would even shake hands with Bev when the time came.

Entering the church she slid into the back pew. She wanted to watch Ray and Bev and her kids. They were the family now. The way her family should have been with her. She fought back the tears that threatened to betray her cool facade.

Thoughts of all she had left and walked away from flashed through her memory. She watched the closeness and love of a family that should have been hers. Why could "SHE " be part of the family when there was no room for Suzanne? Why was Suzanne always left on the outside?

Her father was right, they belonged together, anyone and everyone could see that...

"DAMN YOU MOTHER!... DAMN YOU FOR MAKING ME SO I CAN'T LOVE OR EVER BE PART OF A FAMILY ... DAMN YOU FOR CURSING ALL YOUR CHILDREN TO A LIFE OF LONELINESS AND MISTRUST ..."

Suzanne couldn't hold back the tears anymore. She got up quietly and slipped out the back. She couldn't stand all this love and happiness. She went out to her car and sat crying, trying to figure out what to do. She couldn't leave, so that meant she would have to compose herself.

She stayed in the car until people started coming out, then she went over and joined them. She went over to talk to the kids, reaching over to straighten Anna's bow ... Anna pulled away, saying that Bev knew how she liked it.

Walking away Suzanne couldn't help but notice she never even looked back at her. Suzanne felt like she was with strangers. She didn't know anyone anymore. She didn't belong in their world.

Suzanne smiled politely and greeted everyone with grace and warmth. Just the way her mother had taught her. She thought ... just hold your breath and get through it, the day will be done soon enough.

She was relieved when they got to the hotel for the reception. There were a lot more distractions there. She could keep herself busy and out of sight. If she kept moving, she would be all right.

Suzanne could see Ray coming, out of the corner of her eye, with Bev in tow. Suzanne wasn't ready for this she maybe never would be ready for this. She pretended that she didn't see them coming, and slipped into the kitchen to talk to the chef.

Shelby looked at her with a big grin on his face and asked her if she was hiding. He was joking as he said it, but knew immediately that it was true. She tried to tell herself and Shelby that she wasn't hiding just procrastinating. She just needed a little time to get used to the idea.

Shelby was a great philosopher telling her that things didn't go away just because she was hiding from them. He was right, and she knew it. She bit the bullet and went back out to face the music...

Remembering how Ray had let her off the hook, and made leaving easy on her. It was time to return the favor. Suzanne walked up to Ray and reached out her hand to Bev, thanking her for doing such a wonderful job with the kids.

Suzanne gave them both a kiss on the cheek and wished them well ... "BOY THIS PHONY SMILE SHIT WAS EASIER THAN SHE THOUGHT ... NO WONDER HER MOTHER WAS SO GOOD AT IT."

Suzanne should have learned to play this game with her mother. Maybe if she had learned to smile and appease people when she was younger, she could have used it to get along with her mother, who would have been proud at how well Suzanne pulled it all off.

She ate dinner at a table with the kids, which she enjoyed. No matter what else she did in her life, she had to start making room for her children. She had to make more of an effort to have them in her life and love them, as they deserved to be loved.

It was all too easy to let them drift away. She hardly knew them any more. What were they going to be like in a couple years, total strangers or non-existent? They were already total strangers or at least shadows of a past she hated to remember.

Ray had a sitter take the kids home right after dinner so they could stay and enjoy the reception. Once the kids were gone Suzanne had no reason to be there. It wasn't only the kids that had become strangers.

They were all strangers; she hadn't been close to her brothers and sister since her mother's funeral and even long before that. Suzanne made her excuses, told everyone to stay and enjoy themselves then quietly slipped away to her room to be alone.

Once in her room, it was time to mend fences with Paul. She needed to say she was sorry and was thinking of him. For some reason it was important to her to let him know she had left early. He was surprised, and wondered what went wrong.

Suzanne kept it simple explaining how she felt like she was with strangers; once the kids were gone she had no one she wanted to talk to. Paul was more than willing to come over and keep her company, give her some moral support.

Suzanne needed to be alone, she hoped he understood. She had a lot on her mind and needed to think without distractions. She would call him later if she changed her mind. Even as she spoke the words she knew she wouldn't.

Suzanne ran a hot bath and soaked in it a long time, trying to sort out what she was feeling. The strangest part being... she felt nothing. She was numb. It bothered her that she wasn't sad or upset, she wasn't happy either. She was nothing, and felt nothing, simply empty, an emptiness that threatened to consume her.

Putting on her housecoat, she poured herself a drink and lay on the bed staring into emptiness, no thoughts, and no feelings. There was nothing left of her past except the emptiness of that very past that somehow refused to stay either in the past or the present.

She could hear a very light knock at the door. She hoped it wasn't Paul; she was not in the mood. Suzanne could hear Ray's voice asking to come in. Suzanne hesitated for only a moment to take a deep breath before she opened the door.

As she opened the door Ray stood alone, looking very sheepish and shy. She asked where Bev was. He told her she was still down at the reception. He needed to talk to Suzanne alone and Bev understood that.

He asked if he could come in for a few minutes. He wanted to explain about Bev. There was nothing to explain he owed her nothing. Suzanne asked him if he loved her and was happy. She needed to know if he had gotten over her completely.

He said he did love Bev, but not the instant chemistry kind of love they had together. This was more of a steady, comfortable, reliable love. He never expected to find the kind of love he had felt for Suzanne, but he was happy and very content in the life he and Bev had made together.

Bev has been so good for the kids. He hadn't seen them so happy and well adjusted in a very long time. Bev was so much like his mother, filled with the patients of a saint. Just because Bev was a good mother didn't mean the kids didn't need their real mother; they would always need Suzanne in their lives. He had talked it over with Bev and they agreed it was important for Suzanne to stay in the kid's lives.

Ray gave Suzanne a long fatherly hug before he turned to leave. Suzanne stood in silence not sure what to say or even how to react. She did the only thing she could do, she watched him walk away.

As Suzanne stood thinking, she knew that Ray closed more than one door that night. There was no going back now. The past was where it belonged in the past. Never again would she question or think about what she was feeling for Ray.

Those were little girl feelings. Now she was a woman, and there was no room for being a little girl or for little girl feelings. That was the empty numbness she felt, those little girl feelings from the past leaving her.

Standing very still she could hear her mother's voice as clear as if she were in the room saying to her ... "HERE IS YOUR BED NOW

LIE IN IT ... "even dead she had a nasty tone in her voice. Suzanne looked up at the ceiling and said… "GO AWAY MOTHER, I AM TIRED..." as if her mother could actually hear her.

Suzanne had no difficulty getting to sleep that night however it would be a short sleep. Every time she allowed herself to drift off she would drift into the same nightmare. No matter how many times she woke herself up, it would come back, over and over.

There was a pretty little girl, dressed in a pretty little dress, standing all alone in the darkness. There was nothing else in the dream except a tiny little light in the distance. The girl turned and started to run toward the light...

She ran and she ran the more she ran, the further away the light would be. The girl was frantic and scared to death. Suzanne could feel the little girl's loneliness overwhelm her. When Suzanne forced herself to wake up, she wondered who the little girl was. Was it her? Was it her mother? Was it Angel? Suzanne figured she could have been any one of them or all of them.

They were all lost little girls. For that moment, Suzanne could feel all the fear, the loneliness and the despair of all three of them. For the first time, she could feel empathy for her mother, pity for her daughter and heartache for herself.

This time when she went back to sleep, the dream changed ...The little girl was now her mother, as she was when she died. She had a warmth and friendly peacefulness about her. She looked so caring, Suzanne could hardly recognize her.

She whispered in that same gentle softness words Suzanne had wanted to hear all her life... "I ALWAYS LOVED YOU PRINCESS ... "turning away and slowly walked into the light, and then was gone.

Suzanne woke up with tears still in her eyes, mumbling the words ... "I LOVE YOU MOTHER ... I FORGIVE YOU ... "This time when she sobbed it was a warm and healing cry.

A healing was taking place, the big knot that was always in her stomach was gone. For the first time in her life she could relax and feel safe. Nothing could hurt her anymore. She felt complete. A small tear trickled down her cheek, but this time there was no crying, just one last lonely tear.

Chapter Twelve

Now all she had to worry about was saving her children from herself. Was she doing to her children what her mother did to her? Would they grow up not knowing how to love or be part of a relationship?

The one difference between her children and herself was that they had Ray and their grandparents to teach them how to love and be a part of a true loving family. Now, they would also have Bev to teach them how to be better mothers. They could be the kind of mothers who would love their children instead of torturing them.

She wasn't sure how she felt about Bev with Ray, or if she was ready to let go of him; but there was no doubt that her children were ready for a real full time mother. For that she would always be thankful to Bev.

At her next visit with Doctor Anderson she was different. She could discuss her mother without crying. Not only was she not crying, but she wasn't hurting either. All the pain and knots were gone.

The good doctor tried her best to bring up painful subjects, but there wasn't any pain to find. Suzanne didn't even feel like she was the same person. She had no reason to avoid or hide anything. Everything was out in the open now.

The one thing she did have regrets about was her children. She wanted the doctor to help her find a way to reach them, to get through to them. Angel was still scared to death of her, and Anna straight out hated her wanting nothing to do with her. The other kids ... they could forgive anything and love anyone.

The doctor told her as far as Anna went it would take a long time and a lot of persistence. She simply needed to know that if she lets you back in, you wouldn't hurt her again. Hang in there, and no matter what Anna says or doesn't say, keep going back.

She needs to know you will always be there, not just when it is convenient to you. Suzanne had to know that if she continued the way she was she would lose Alice and R.J. as well.

A silence filled the room as the doctor hesitated; she had something to talk to her about, but couldn't find a way to start. Suzanne needed to know what was going on; they might as well get it over with and simply blurt it out. The doctor needed to talk about Angel, and the findings from all her visits.

Suzanne told the doctor that she had hurt Angel a lot, and that she was the cause of all Angel's emotional scars. The doctor told her that what she did to Angel may have added to things and made them worse.

However, Angel had scars outside of what Suzanne had done to her. The doctor was trying to explain but she wasn't sure what had happened only that something had. It was as though Angel had a dark secret she kept deep inside. It was a secret that scared her so much that she wouldn't discuss it or even face it.

There were hints, little things that Angel divulged without actually talking about. Whatever it was that had happened to her. Suzanne was confused what could have happened to her, she was only ever with family.

Suzanne dismissed whatever this doctor was trying to tell her. It made no sense; she didn't know what she was talking about. Nothing could have happened to Angel. She was the only one that hurt Angel; everyone else protected her and loved her.

The doctor told Suzanne they might never get to the bottom of it. It is as though she were living in fear. The doctor was fairly sure it wasn't just the fear of her mother but something more, something she wasn't so far willing to discuss except for small hints here and there.

Suzanne walked out of the office stunned, trying to remember every moment of Angel's life hoping to find a clue. Hoping she can find the spot where this all started. What could she have meant? Suzanne was fairly sure she was the only evil in Angel's life.

Her mind kept going back to the time when Ray and her went away. A time when Angel went into an emotional shut down, refusing to eat or sleep or even cry. Did something happen to her while they were gone? Could her mother have done something to her? She beat them all as children but what could she do to a baby?

Suzanne was sure, well almost sure. Her mother wouldn't, she couldn't. That was the question what could she have done if she did anything at all? She was capable of anything mean or cruel but she wasn't sick enough to harm a baby?

Suzanne had to talk to her father she had to find out what happened that weekend. If she hurried she could catch Ray before he left for work at four. She had to talk to the adults in the household without any children. That meant getting there before school let out.

She tried her hardest to explain what the doctor had said to her, but it was all so vague, simply a suggestion. There was no real fact to any of it. She asked what both Ray and her father could remember especially about that weekend. It seemed to Suzanne that was when the weird silent spells started.

She looked at her father, his head was down he didn't speak. "DAD ... I HAVE TO KNOW... WOULD MOTHER HAVE DONE SOMETHING TO A BABY? ... WOULD SHE HAVE HURT ANGEL? "

He still had his head hung when he started to talk as if he were addressing the table. He told Suzanne her mother would do this thing to Suzanne and Barb when they were babies. She had told him girls needed to be washed from the inside out. Girls were dirty and had to be cleansed even on the inside, she would use warm water and vinegar. He knew nothing about babies he had to trust that she did.

It was after that Angel quit eating, sleeping or making a sound of any kind. It was scary the way she would just lay still as though she were a porcelain doll. He had begged her to call Suzanne, to come home. She didn't want to call she was sure she could handle Angel; he had to order her to make the call.

He had tears streaming down his face as he looked up ... "I DIDN'T KNOW THIS WASN'T RIGHT ... WHAT DID I KNOW ABOUT GIRL BABIES ... IN THOSE DAYS NO ONE DISCUSSED THOSE THINGS... "

It was at that time that he told them that she hated Angel every bit as much as she hated Suzanne all her life. He lied to himself for years telling himself it wasn't true that she wasn't hurting any of them. He could no longer tell himself the lies he couldn't believe.

Ray, his mother and Bev, sat in shock and disbelief. They couldn't talk. They didn't even know how to react. People didn't do these things, not in real life. They couldn't even figure out who was the bad guy. Who was to blame?

Suzanne's Dad went to her and held her this time it was her turn to forgive. Forgive him for his lack of knowledge and strength; forgive him for not protecting all of them from the evil of the wife he had chosen. Will the heartache from her mother never heal; she stays even beyond the grave to haunt them all. As though Suzanne wasn't a big enough mess, she had to scar the next generation as well.

There was a silence that hung over the room for a long time. It was Suzanne who finally broke it. She wanted to know why her father had never done anything. Why didn't he leave or at least stop her? She wanted to let him off the hook easy, she wanted to tell him it was all right. She couldn't, she simply couldn't she needed answers and if it hurt her father to get them then he would have to be hurt.

He sat back in silence and watched as her mother destroyed not only her own children but Suzanne's as well.... "WHY DIDN'T YOU SAVE US...? WHY DIDN'T YOU EVER STEP IN AND STOP HER? "

How could he answer her, she could never understand. He didn't understand himself. It was a different time. The men worked, the women took care of the children and the house. No one left ever no matter how bad it got. His wife made it so easy for him to lie to himself.

He didn't know, he was an army man, discipline was everything. How was he to know it was different at home, different for small children? He had to trust in her judgements. She was the wife and mother how was he to know that all mothers weren't born to be caring and loving?

His wife always seemed to have everything under control, everything perfect. How was he to know it wasn't like that when he wasn't home...? He could feel the tension in the home but it was always over with by the time he walked through the door.

He was gone so much of the time ... always moving around. He had to trust that she knew what she was doing. It wasn't until he retired, and the kids were older that he started to suspect. By that time it was too late.

Her father looked totally devastated when Suzanne finally left. She told him it wasn't his fault that she held no blame for him. She said whatever she had to say to try to undo some of the unbearable heartache she had just dumped on him. Why did she feel the need to hurt everyone, to cause as much pain as she possibly could?

Suzanne lied, she didn't understand any of it, she never understood how he could stand by and do nothing, see nothing. Most of the beatings and abuse happened when he wasn't home. When he was home everything had to be perfect, they had to be perfect.

He must have known or suspected something. Where did he think all those black eyes came from, all the bruises, the cuts? There were many times Suzanne or her siblings could not go to school because the bruises showed. He had to have known there was no way he couldn't have?

Suzanne stopped her car at a corner store to use a pay phone. She had to talk to Paul. She called his office first, but they said he was working at home on contracts. That's what he gets for switching to corporate law. If he had stuck to criminal law like he had been doing when she first met him, he wouldn't be breaking his brain on paperwork.

Paul was both pleased and surprised to hear from her. He was also surprised when she told him she wanted to come over, so he should put the coffee on. She had a lot to tell him. It occurred to Suzanne that Paul had told her everything about himself; she took care to what she had told him especially about her childhood. Deep down she believed everything her mother had ever told her about what a terrible person and a screw up she was.

She was afraid if he knew who and what she was, he would hate her to. He was a well-educated man from a normal world. How could he like her after all the things she had done to everyone that ever got close to her? She was like her mother who hurt everyone in her path, especially those that dared to love her.

When she got there they did a few minutes of small talk. Your house is beautiful ... how was your day...the weather is fine, all that kind of stuff. Paul poured her a coffee then he went to the bar and added a shot of rum. He told her she looked like she could use it.

Suzanne was slow to start talking hoping she could ease her way into it. She had a lot to tell him and she had no idea where to start. It was all bad and he wasn't likely to approve of any of it. Suzanne knew all too well how screwed up her life had been all her life but it wasn't 'til she started blurting it all out that she really knew it.

Somehow saying it all out loud seemed so much worse than when she was actually living it. Each incident was horrific in of itself but put it all together and she had a lifelong nightmare that she was more than ready to wake up from.

If he wanted to quit seeing her after she told him, she would understand and quietly walk away. There would be no questioning his decision nor would she blame him for even a moment. If their friendship was going to continue he needed to know what he was getting himself into.

Paul couldn't imagine her doing anything bad enough for him to walk away from the friendship that had become so important to him. She was the best thing that had ever happened to him. It was because of her that he could look forward to every day again. There was nothing short of murder that he couldn't forgive her for.

Once Suzanne started talking, it all came out. She talked and talked; then she talked some more. Leaving nothing out, she told him about her mother, her childhood, her father, her children ... Then, hardest of all, she told him about William and her fears about R.J.

Taking a deep breath, she ended with her conversations with Doctor Anderson, suspicious about Angels possible abuse. There was no doubt her family and all who came near it was a mess and she was the messiest.

After more than an hour of one-sided conversation, she sat silently watching Paul, trying to see his reaction. He said nothing, just sat looking at her. Suzanne felt he must have thought he was looking at a total stranger.

She took a deep breath, held back the tears and the lump building in her throat, and got up to leave. She understood how he felt, and didn't blame him one bit. She could hardly stand to look at herself. How could she expect more from him?

Paul ran to get between her and the door. Telling her that it took him a long time to get her there, he wasn't going to let her out that easy. He asked her why she would think that, he or anyone could hate her for any of what happened.

Suzanne needed to understand she hadn't done any of this. It was all done to her, not by her. She was the victim not the criminal. Paul couldn't believe that she would blame herself all these years for her mother hating her, or a brutal animal raping her.

He held her tight as she cried into his shoulder. As he held her he declared... "I COULD NEVER HATE YOU ... I LOVE YOU ... I HAVE LOVED YOU SINCE I FIRST SAW YOU, BUT NEVER MORE THAN THIS VERY MOMENT ..."

Suzanne cried all the harder. She didn't want him to love her; she always hurt the people who loved her. Trying her hardest to pull away, to push him away, she had to get away from him before he got hurt too.

If she left now, ended this right now, he could find someone he deserved, someone to love him, a good person ... Someone as good as he was who would deserve his love. That person could and would never be her. She would never be a good and loving person. The only thing in the future of anyone who loved her was pain and heartache.

Suzanne punched and kicked, she even tried to bite him. No matter what she did, he hung onto her with a death grip. She was frantic to get out, to get away from him. They were wrestling on the floor like schoolyard brawlers.

Finally he had her pinned she was going nowhere. She stopped fighting and crumbled into a pile of emotions. Her body shook as thirty years of pain started pouring out of her. Suzanne cried so hard that she couldn't stand the pain of her heartache.

Paul sat on the floor still holding her, not saying a word. Neither of them spoke even after Suzanne finally ran out of tears. She laid still and quiet, being the wet dish rag she had become. Paul finally picked her up and carried her to the bedroom. She was still staring as he undressed her, handed her a pill, and told her to swallow it.

She obeyed as if she were a wind up toy he was playing with. He laid her down, covered her up then left the room pulling the door closed behind him. Leaving it cracked just enough he could hear her if she needed him. Admit it or not there was no doubt she did need him.

Paul prayed she would forgive him when he took it upon himself to call the hotel and tell them she would not be in for at least two days. He knew Doctor Anderson couldn't tell him anything when he called her, but she did give him an appointment to see Suzanne the next day.

He tried to talk to her, to get some direction, some further truth to where Suzanne's pain was coming from and how to deal with it.

Doctor Anderson was strict on the rules of confidentiality, whatever information he got he had to get from Suzanne.

She did tell him he should feel privileged that Suzanne had trusted in him. She had told him things she had likely never told another living soul. The doctor had to stop talking to him; she had already walked the edge of breaking confidences. Suzanne was to call the office first thing in the morning to find out the time of her appointment. The only advice she would give to Paul was to let Suzanne sleep for tonight.

Paul tried his hardest to concentrate on work while Suzanne slept, it was impossible he couldn't think of work when the only thing on his mind was Suzanne. He sat on the side of the bed, watching her sleep as he had done so many times in the past.

The difference this time was that when she tossed, turned and moaned in a light restless sleep, he now understood what haunted her. Even on the nights when she woke him screaming, she offered him no explanation or understanding, becoming agitated if he grilled her with too many questions.

Suzanne never liked him getting too close, now he knew why. He didn't even want to think about how angry she was going to be that he called her work. She would have to understand that he did it as a friend who cared.

It was after midnight when Suzanne woke up, still pretty groggy, it took her a few minutes to figure out where she was. As she looked around she saw Paul slumped down in a chair, sound asleep. His neck was bent over on a weird angle. She knew if she didn't wake this poor baby, he was going to hurt real bad by morning.

Suzanne leaned over and kissed his forehead, and his cheek, then his lips. He kissed her back as he pulled her down toward him until she was sitting on his knee. He brushed the hair out of her face and asked her if she was all right.

Suzanne smiled a half smile, very hesitantly, waiting for his response. They snuggled and held each other. That was all the response she needed. She felt safe and she felt loved, for now that was enough.

Suzanne finally pulled away a little and said they had better get some sleep they both had to work tomorrow. Paul told her that he called her in sick, and if she didn't like it that was too bad, because she was staying with him for a couple days. It was time someone took care of her. It was time he took care of her.

She had spent far too much time caring for him. It was his turn to return the favor. It made him feel good to pamper her. She thought that was good since she loved to be pampered. It had been such a long time since anyone bothered to care about her needs.

He made her an appointment with Doctor Anderson, he hoped she wouldn't be too mad, had he crossed a line? She told him it was good, that she realized she needed to see her. Paul took a deep breath; he never knew what would set her off.

Suzanne walked into Doctor Anderson's office in silence. Yesterday she had been desperate to talk to her, but today she felt empty and numb. The Doctor did manage to pry out of her what her mother had done, or what they suspected she had done. Who knows what else she could have done when no one was around. Most of Suzanne's worst beatings were when there were no witnesses.

The problem was how could she discuss her feelings when she didn't know what she felt? How many shocks could one person endure in a lifetime? Suzanne spent most of her life scared, in pain, or numb.

There were only a handful of moments when she had felt happiness, and never feelings of joy. Mostly because, when she did start to feel happiness, she clouded it with fears of what may be coming around the corner. There was always a nightmare to follow the dreams.

There was always pain in the shadows, waiting to jump out at her. Happiness was all an illusion, a magic trick. Now you feel it, now you don't. Real life hurt. That fact had been proven to Suzanne many times over. Not only was it proven, but constantly reinforced.

The next two days were like heaven. She felt like she had run away from home and joined the circus. They went everywhere together; long walks in the park, to the theater, and to dinner.

They even went skinny-dipping, something she secretly loved. It was scary and exciting all at the same time. She was scared to death someone would come and catch them, yet exhilarated by the fear of getting caught.

It was the coolness of the water, Suzanne felt so free and fresh with the water moving around her body, caressing it every time she moved even the slightest. She couldn't help but think about how shy she once was, how she had been embarrassed for Ray to see her naked for the first time.

On their second day together, they picked up the kids and took them to the beach for the day. It seemed strange watching Paul run on the beach with her children. Suzanne had never pictured Paul as a father type. She had trouble imagining him out of his suit.

The kids took to him instantly, well most of them. Even Angel went right to him. It was Anna that gave him the freeze. She stood back coolly, studying him. Every time he tried to get her to join in she would give him a cold shoulder. Even when he grabbed her and threw her in the lake, she yelled at him, and stomped off mumbling how she was going to tell her Dad on him.

All this was too perfect, too wonderful. It was all going too smoothly. Suzanne was waiting for the other shoe to drop. When was this bubble going to burst? She decided to enjoy the moment.

Tomorrow it was back to the real world, and she would have to back Paul up a little or a lot. This was all too fast for her, feeling too much like a relationship... a commitment.

Suzanne still had no idea what she wanted, especially from Paul. It was wonderful for now, but it wasn't real and could never last. It wasn't good for her or the kids to get too attached. Perhaps Anna had the right approach; go slow and watch with caution.

Suzanne was amazed at how fast Angel accepted Paul. She had tried for years to get through to her, and here he is a virtual stranger, and she goes to him with no hesitation. Maybe Angel only felt safe with men.

Men had always protected her, where women had always hurt her. To Suzanne this was a small blessing. When she got older, she would be able to get into a relationship with a man and trust him.

The fantasy was over. It was time to get back to the real world, and real problems, putting Paul on a back burner. He was a lot of fun, and good company when she needed someone to lean on, but he had nothing to do with her real life.

He was a mighty fine distraction, well maybe more than a distraction, but she wasn't in a position for more than that. Suzanne didn't need another man hanging on her, counting on her for more than she could give. Suzanne wasn't ready to be put back on a leash; to ask permission and get approval for everything.

Alone, no matter what she wanted to do, she could do it. She didn't have to go to anyone and tell them where she was going, what she was doing, or who she was doing it with. No drawn out explanations on why she wasn't there, why she was late ... why she just didn't feel like it.

Suzanne wasn't doing anything with anyone but Paul, she couldn't even imagine wanting anyone but Paul, but if she did want to she could. She didn't need Paul thinking all this was real, that it changed anything. They were friends, free agents individual people with individual lives.

When he called her on the first night she was back at the hotel she told him she was pretty busy and needed to catch up on all the work she missed while she was off playing with him. He almost got frostbite from the coolness in her voice. He figured she was either tired or thinking about work. Maybe she had Aaron within hearing distance. He had called before when Aaron was there and she was equally as cool.

It was three days before she allowed him to come and see her. He was excited to be with her, but she was quiet through dinner. A feeling of formality making him feel he was with a business acquaintance.

They went to her room and she immediately took him to bed for sex. It was different this time. It was sex, not love making; there was something missing. He thought he had broken through all the walls and here she had built them back up stronger and higher than ever.

Paul was thoroughly confused. What could possibly have happened in three short days? The other day they were crazy in love, she even let him meet her kids. The days she spent with him were perfect, what could have happened between then and now.

Suzanne couldn't figure out what his problem was. Everything was still the same; they were still only friends, no more. She couldn't give him more than that. He knew going in how things had to be, that hadn't changed and would never change.

He told her that it was over a year ago, relationships change and grow, people learn to love and trust, to lean on each other. They should have been getting closer until the two lovers are as one, one couple. He wanted all of her not just little scraps she threw him when she was lonely.

Suzanne didn't work that way. She didn't want things to grow, to change ... she liked things the way they were, and didn't want more. It was lonely her way it wasn't enough. He wanted to share all he had and be a part of her life, her entire life. He wanted the good and the bad to share in everything.

He didn't want an occasional playmate. He wanted a partner, a better half, someone he could come home to. He wanted to be greeted at the door with a big kiss and a smile. He was tired of coming home to an empty house.

Suzanne never asked for any of this. He knew going in what she had to offer. He had no right putting all this on her. He knew what she would give. If he wanted more he should have gotten someone else. That is the way things had to be, he could either accept it, live with it or walk away.

He looked at her as if he had never seen her before, or maybe he hadn't... "YOU REALLY ARE A COLD HEARTED BITCH ... SO YOU WILL LET ME JUST WALK OUT THE DOOR ... YOUR WAY OR THE HIGHWAY ... I KNOW YOU LOVE ME ... I FEEL IT EVERY TIME WE ARE TOGETHER ..."

Suzanne looked at her lover with the coolness of a judge handing down a sentencing and said ... " YOU ARE WRONG ... I DO NOT LOVE YOU, I CARE ABOUT YOU AND ALWAYS HAVE ... IF YOU NEVER WALKED THROUGH THAT DOOR AGAIN I WOULD MISS YOU AND HOPE YOU ARE HAPPY ... BUT, I PROMISE YOU ... I WILL GO ON WITH MY LIFE AND NOT LOOK BACK ..."

Paul saw the cool emotionless expression on her face and knew she meant every word of what she had said. There was no sense in discussing it. She was firm; he could not only see it but feel it. There was nothing left for him to do, he got up, got dressed and walked out the door hoping she would call him back, but knowing she wouldn't. He kept going, forcing himself to not look back no matter how much he wanted to.

Once the door was closed and she knew he was gone, Suzanne whispered to herself ... "IT IS BETTER THIS WAY ... I DID YOU A FAVOR ... YOU JUST DON'T KNOW IT YET."

As she lay still trying to drift off to sleep, she wondered who wrote the law that said she wasn't allowed to be happy. She did love Paul, but then she had also loved Ray. Loving them didn't keep her from destroying them; or was it herself she was trying to hurt and punish?

From here she could only see two choices... she could either stay alone like her sister Barb, or she could try to find a jerk that was as cold hearted as she was ... Someone who would never fall in love, or get hurt by her.

Chapter Thirteen

There was only one guy she could think of that filled that description ... that would be Aaron. Wouldn't that be a strange turn of events? He couldn't stand the sight of her. Besides, how would anyone ever have sex with him with his suit glued on?

He was so cold and rigid, he was probably a virgin. The thought of him waltzing around in his boxer shorts with a party hat on seemed hilariously ridiculous to her. It suddenly occurred to her that within one hour she had sex, dumped her boyfriend and was now thinking about her next victim. She truly was a sick woman.

It took a couple of drinks to get her to sleep that night. From now on she would have only her kids and work in her life, although she would always miss the sex with Paul. He could get her body to do things she had never before heard of or felt.

For the next couple years Suzanne merely put in time, getting through each day anyway she could. There was the occasional fling but Suzanne never let them hang around more than three dates. She wasn't going to walk into the same trap. If they didn't hang around they wouldn't get attached strangers never expected anything.

Her visits to Doctor Anderson were cut down to twice a month. Her life actually seemed to be on an even keel. Even the kids were doing well, especially since Ray and Bev's wedding. Bev was a Godsend for the children. They were growing into such wonderful people.

Anna maintained an air of coolness between them; she never forgave her mother for leaving them all. She would understand once she had a family of her own, but then on second thought, maybe not. Anna had a different kind of personality than Suzanne. She always put her family first.

It was Angel that was more likely to understand. They had the same personality. This was why they could never get close, always keeping a wall between them. If a person couldn't like themselves how could they like someone just like themselves.

Suzanne wondered if that was what happened with her and her mother. Suzanne's father had always said her mother was jealous of Suzanne but maybe she was trying to beat out of her what she saw in Suzanne that she hated in herself. It was simply a case of self-loathing.

Maybe she wasn't beating up Suzanne but herself. Suzanne couldn't believe it after all these years. Her mother had been dead forever and yet Suzanne still worried about why her mother didn't love her.

Would she ever get that scared little girl out of her? Would she ever find the answers? Maybe there were no answers to find. Maybe she should simply live her life instead of sweating over someone who had thrown her own away. Why was she still so concerned about her mother and whether or not she loved her?

Suzanne and Aaron had actually become tolerable friends over the years. Not as close as she and Paul, but then no one could have the closeness she felt for Paul. They had a special bond. There was hardly a day since he walked out that she hadn't thought of him.

Paul put a serious crimp in her sex life. Every time she went to bed with someone, she thought of Paul. Her partner, whichever stranger it was, could never come close to the passion and desire Paul brought out in her.

Suzanne missed having someone in her life that cared about her. There was no one to share anything with. There was no one to give her a hug when she was down, or celebrate with her when something wonderful happened. She didn't even go to weddings because that was a couple's occasion.

What she really missed most was lying in bed after great sex, with naked bodies touching, and casually discussing the day or sharing a laugh. Suzanne thought about the pillow fights she once had with Paul. She missed laughing and playing she hadn't laughed or even felt good since she forced him to leave.

Suzanne had to stop, thinking this way; Paul was gone because he was chased away. She chased him away because she needed him to be away, or so she thought at that time. She wished she had taken some time to think before she so coldly brushed him off. Who was she trying to punish herself or him? Had she pushed him away because she didn't believe she deserved happiness?

One day, coming out of Doctor Anderson's office she saw Paul across the street. As she was about to call to him, she saw him kiss a very young beautiful lady on the cheek and help her into a cab.

Suzanne stood watching the biggest mistake of her life unfold before her very eyes. He saw her and waved a shy apprehensive wave. Suzanne returned a sheepish smile and a nod as she watched him join the beautiful young lady in the cab. All the while wishing it were her he was joining.

He still had it; he could still put her heart in her throat at a glance. Her heart was still racing, her hands trembling, even when she got back to the hotel. It was too late; he looked so content, so comfortable with that other woman.

Suzanne wondered if anyone would ever make her feel the way Paul had. She may have chased him away, but he could have kept trying. If he had loved her he would not have walked away so easily. He would not have let her push him away. He would have made some effort to convince her how wrong she was.

Nothing could be done now; all she could do was get on with her life as she told Paul she would do when he was gone. She couldn't help but wonder if he had thought about her over the years. The only thing she could do now was keep herself busy. The secret was to work until she dropped.

With Aaron cracking the whip, it wasn't hard to keep busy. That man was such a persnickety, perfectionist. Suzanne thought she was hard on her staff, but she was actually laid back at least compared to Aaron.

He must have retired from his accounting firm. Suddenly he had to come everyday, and everyday there was something new that had to be changed. Once he made his mind up, there was no talking him out of it.

Even compromise was out of the question. He would get on missions and not let up until he accomplished them. She often thought he needed a good piece of tail, something to vent all his energy and frustration. Shelby and her often joked about it.

They even laughed about Aaron figuring he could go either way, since he seemed disinterested either way. They laughed as they compared him to a neutered puppy that had lost interest.

For a man that she didn't particularly like much, Suzanne was surprised how often she actually thought about having sex with him. If he were anyone but her boss she probably would have done it and gotten it over with.

She was sure he was the kind of guy who would fire her if anything went wrong in a relationship. That would be a complication she didn't need in her life ... bad idea, real bad idea.

She needed to keep that thought out of her head. She couldn't afford to even play with the idea. It was not only her job at stake, but her home, her life. A life she liked just as it was.

It was late when she finally got back to her room. She was so tired she was ready to drop. As she stepped off the elevator and looked down the hall, she thought she was hallucinating. Paul was sitting on the floor his back against her door. He was attempting to juggle his briefcase on his knee as he passed the time with paperwork.

She stood frozen in her tracks as she tried to decide what to do how to react. Part of her wanted to turn and run. The rest of her wanted to run to him as fast as she could, and make mad passionate love to him where he sat.

It was too late to run as he was already staring up at her. Once eye contact was made there was no going back. He knew she could never resist those eyes; he could always melt her with a glance.

She walked up to her door very slowly, feeling more sensuous with every step. Suzanne unlocked her door without saying a word. Paul followed her in, pressing her up against the door as he pushed it closed. They didn't need to talk; their bodies were doing all the talking for them.

Paul wasted no time picking her up into his strong arms. Pressing her up against the door he kissed her passionately over and over stealing away every breath she fought to catch. He went at her with the hunger of a starving animal, which couldn't get enough or get it fast enough.

Lowering her to the floor, he started to pull at her clothes, nearly as fast as she was pulling at his. On the floor in front of the door she had the most powerful sex she had ever had. When he was done he rolled onto his back, his chest heaving, still out of breath.

He smiled and mumbled ... "I KNEW YOU WOULD MISS ME... GET ON WITH YOUR LIFE... JUST TRY TO FIND SOMETHING LIKE THAT ANYWHERE ELSE... I DARE YOU ..."

Suzanne punched him in the shoulder as hard as she could ... " I HATE YOU...DO YOU ALWAYS HAVE TO BE RIGHT?..." He was right! She had missed him, she had thought of him often. There was no one she felt so passionate with. No one even came close to what she felt while making love to Paul.

They fell back into each other's arms and rolled on the floor laughing and embracing each other. She gave him about fifteen little kisses all over his face ... "I MISSED YOU SO MUCH... I DID!.."

That was all Paul needed to hear, but Suzanne needed to hear more..." WHAT DID YOU DO WITH YOUR LITTLE HONEY FROM THIS AFTERNOON? ..." He tried to keep himself from laughing as he explained how she was just a little girl. The daughter of a business associate that he had known since she was a baby her name was Cassy.

That didn't answer the question nagging at her the most... was there a woman in his life? There was no one steady or important. He had tried being with many women, but none of them were her. None of them could even come close.

Suzanne had the same problem. She had tried to move on, but she couldn't go a day without thinking of him. Suzanne missed his phone calls. What she really missed was the snuggling. No one could touch or hold her the way he could.

He got to his feet, picked her up, swung her around, and carried her to the bed saying that if that was what she missed most then he had better get busy pleasing her. That was now his sole purpose in life.

They laid in each other's arms touching and caressing each other, not in a sensual way, not to turn each other on, but to reacquaint themselves to each other's bodies. To reclaim what was now theirs again.

They had so much to catch up on and yet they melted together as though they had never been apart. Neither of them noticed the time passing until the sun came shining in to wish them a good morning and a very good morning it was. It was the best of mornings.

With the light shining in all the dark corners bringing brightness once again to her life she could now be honest with Paul, or at least as honest as she was capable of. How could she tell him the entire truth when she herself didn't understand the truth?

Suzanne did the best she could to attempt to tell Paul her feelings, her true feelings. She had to make him understand she was afraid of him. There were too many emotions and strings attached to him. He wanted more than she could give.

Suzanne did love him and had right from the start, that love didn't change the fact that she was no good at the little woman routine. Paul hugged her as he laughed, he was no good at the little man thing so they would be a good match.

Paul continued holding her tight as he told her he wanted a life with her. It didn't have to be everyone else's life; they could make a life that would work for both of them. They were both independent adults there was no reason they couldn't reach a workable compromise.

That was all well and good, however, it didn't allow for the fact that she was a big screw up when it came to a personal life. She never learned how to love or be loved. It was simply something she was not good at.

Paul had heard enough; surely she knew that he had been around long enough to already know her shortcomings. He kissed her on the forehead as he put on his fatherly face telling her to go to sleep. There was no reason it all had to be settled in one night.

A relationship took time. It was something that had to be built one day at a time. All he was asking was that they start working on it, that they quit pulling away from each other and pull toward something.

No one could scare her like he could, but he was right. It felt so good falling asleep in his arms that night. For the first time in a long time she felt like she had come home. Home was where she was whenever she was in Paul's arms.

If anyone could teach her how to love, how to feel he could. All she had to do was stop running and let what was already there happen. She could now admit to something she had spent years denying, she needed him.

She couldn't just walk away and not look back. She had looked back many times. From the time Paul walked out she hadn't stopped looking back. There was barely a day passed that she didn't regret him being gone from her life. She wanted to take it all back.

She made an appointment with Aaron to discuss her position and employment contract. She wanted a clause put into the contract for every second weekend off, along with two weeks a year vacation time.

Until recently the hotel had become her entire existence all she wanted or needed in her life. Now, she wanted a little time outside of the hotel, a life that would include Paul. She owed Aaron no explanation but she felt obligated to let him know what was going on.

If she was going to go back with Paul she owed him the best shot and Aaron would have to know she would not be available twenty four, seven any more.

There was even a possibility that at some point in the future she would want to move out of the hotel and hold down a normal nine-to-five job. As soon as she said the words she pushed the thought out of her head. If she had to think about it, panic would set in and she would want to run again.

Aaron didn't have to panic just yet, the latter was probably over a year away if ever, but it was a tentative goal. With the same straight and sober face he always had, without even cracking a smile he told her to reconsider going back to Paul. He loved her and had for a long time. They could be a great couple, running the hotel together as partners.

He was standing in front of her... straight, stiff and rigid, without even the tiniest hint of emotion. He had shown more emotion going over the books for the month... "WHERE DID THIS COME FROM!?..."

Suzanne didn't know whether to laugh or feel sorry for him. This was all puzzling to her ... how could he love her? Most of the time she doubted whether or not he even liked her. He never showed a hint of emotion, or even interest toward her.

Suzanne was still lost in shock and disbelief when she questioned his not so funny joke. Aaron assured her he never joked about anything. He was quite serious. The seriousness she could see... the entire world could see. He had no emotions, never cracked the slightest smile ... how could he love her or anyone, he seemed so totally emotionless.

Suzanne knew she was blabbering trying to find the right words. He was a special friend and she would always cherish his friendship, but she had been in love with Paul for many years.

She hoped that this would not interfere with business. He reassured her that he had total control of his emotions at all times, and there would be no problem with them working together as they always had.

He was a professional, and would keep everything on that level. He then got up and walked out as he had at every other business meeting.

She was still puzzled long after he had left. She wondered if this was a strange dream or something.

It couldn't be real. He showed no emotions, none ... who tells someone they love them, proposes and walks out, never once blinking? This was a moment for the memory book. She truly had seen it all now.

Suzanne walked out of her office still lost in the fog of confusion, she had to discuss this one with Shelby, the chef couldn't believe it either. At first he thought this was another of Suzanne's many jokes about Mr. Aaron Weinstein.

Shelby was half-hoping Aaron was gay and would want him. Suzanne laughed as she dared him to take his best shot, she wouldn't stand in his way. That would be as equally unbelievable as what she had just gone through.

After she left the kitchen, she felt guilty for not taking Aaron's proposal more seriously. She shouldn't be making a joke out of all of it... IT WAS JUST THAT IT WAS STILL SO TOTALLY UNBELIEVABLE!

Suzanne went to her room, poured a drink, and called Paul to tell him about the meeting with Aaron. She told him how she was taking every second weekend off to spend with him at his apartment. That is if he could stand her for three days and two nights.

He could certainly stand the nights, but he thought he might have to lock her in the closet during the day. What she didn't tell him about was the proposal, she wasn't sure how he would take it and she certainly didn't need him to order her to quit her job.

Paul wanted her to call Ray as soon as possible to ask him if the kids could stay with them on those weekends. She asked him if he was sure. He loved her kids, and thought it was great having someone of his own mentality to play with.

Suzanne loved to hear the playfulness in his voice. She wondered if all that cuteness meant he was coming to spend the night with her. She hoped it meant he was in the mood for some serious adult playing.

It was a dirty job, but if she insisted, he would have to come and take care of business. Suzanne was sure that if he could get his butt over then she would try to put up with whatever he had in mind. After all that was her womanly duty.

Since Suzanne still had a lot of work to do, he could either bring work with him, or wait and come later. He would bring some work with him and still come later ... boy he really was in a cute mood. He should be a lot of fun, if he could hold that thought.

She started down at the bar, where she had a couple drinks while she checked the receipts of the week. While she was there, Aaron came in and had a drink with her. This was another first; Aaron was filled with all kinds of surprises!

Aaron Weinstein never even socially pretended to sip on drinks. She told Aaron she still hoped that they could be friends, and she was sorry if she made light of the entire situation. It was simply that she had never even suspected he looked at her in that light.

Suzanne had to confess that most of the time she felt like he didn't even like her. He wasted no time in telling her that she was wrong. How could she feel this way? It was obvious how much he admired her, why did she think he spent so much time there? He didn't care that much about the hotel, he knew she could do her job; he just wanted excuses to be near her.

Suzanne was uncomfortable with all this she wished she had not gotten back on the subject. She had to get out of this; she excused herself awkwardly saying her boss would fire her if she didn't get back to work. He assured her that her position was secure.

He almost laughed as he said he had heard her boss was a slave driver. For a split second, she thought she might have seen the slightest crack of a smile as he attempted jocularity. He was still straight and rigid and completely buttoned up there was no sign that he was flirting or even joking although the words he spoke sounded like he meant them as jokes.

On her way to the desk to check on the next day's reservations, she stepped outside to see if there was a full moon. Sure enough it was as full as a dinner plate at thanksgiving. That certainly would explain Aaron and Paul's lunacy. She hated the full moon in the bar business. There was almost always some fool who had to howl at it.

On to the kitchen needing to pick up receipts for the day, Shelby was still there doing a specialty dessert for a banquet the next day. He was the only person in the place that worked almost as many hours as her. Suzanne sat and had a drink with him while he worked; it gave her an excuse to be off her feet for a moment.

The conversation was light, mostly about Shelby's new boyfriend. Suzanne loved talking to him about the men he was dating, it seemed so strange that he had the same problem with men that she did. There were times it even felt like they dated the same type of guy. Suzanne thought about that for a moment then decided not to tell Paul, even if she did find it just a little funny.

Shelby and her always found the funniest of things to talk about. He was one of the few people who could make her laugh. It never failed any time she was really down she could count on Shelby to put it all back into perspective and put the smile back on her face.

Heading to her room to get ready for Paul, she heard her name being paged to go to the bar. Not another drunk to be diplomatic with, she hated loud obnoxious people. It was a good thing she had given Paul the key.

As soon as she entered the bar she was hustled in to the back room. The girls were giggling as they tried to tell her what the problem was. This really was a full moon night, everyone was insane ... Aaron was their problem.

Staggering all over the bar he had to tell everyone who would listen and some who wouldn't, how much he loved Suzanne. Now this was truly embarrassing, but she wasn't sure who should be most embarrassed. Her cheeks were the ones that were red.

Suzanne would never have believed this of Aaron. It was all she could do not to laugh. What a strange day it has been! She had known him for years and never did he break his image, never did he show any emotions.

She called the desk and asked for any available room. She walked up to Aaron Weinstein and asked him to come with her. He followed her like a puppy, telling her he would follow her anywhere. She thought ... "HOW HOAKIE" ... at least he came. Suzanne leaned Aaron against the door as she struggled to unlock it.

Once inside she attempted to get his jacket and tie off while avoiding his advances. The shoes had to be taken off, the rest he could sleep in. There was no way she was attempting to undress him. If he was passed out he would never know how uncomfortable he was.

Somehow in all the confusion she managed to get in the way of his lips as he planted a big wet kiss on her. Flustered and confused she wasn't sure what to do or what she felt about it.

It was at that moment he passed out cold. It was a good thing as she was ready to plant her hand across his face, instead she could only laugh quietly to herself and leave him to sleep it off.

At last she could get to her room and Paul. Wrestling with Aaron somehow heightened her mood for Paul. Suzanne dove on him the minute she got in the door drowning in passion. Suddenly feeling very playful she got up and wouldn't let him touch her.

Paul chased her around the room and finally caught her at the bar where she stopped to make a drink. He was nibbling at her neck and fondling her breasts as she dropped ice in her glass. Of course one of the cubes was saved to cool Paul off ever so slightly.

Suzanne pretended to be undressing him, turning him on; this allowed her to drop ice in his pants. She could see by the look in his eyes there would be retaliation. Paul grabbed her kicking and screaming ... While holding her down with one hand he used the other to rub her body down with the same ice. Screaming, yelling and pretending to fight as hard as she could while secretly she loved the feel of the ice melting on her hot skin.

It reminded her of when they went skinny-dipping. She loved the cold water caressing her body. She felt so free, so sensual. She had never wanted nor enjoyed sex more than in the water. The coolness of the ice melting made Paul's body up against hers feel all the hotter.

Suzanne had been sleeping with Paul a long time and yet each time was as fresh and exciting as the first.

It wasn't till they were done playing and laying in each other's arms to catch their breath that she finally had the opportunity to tell Paul about Aaron. They laughed at his drunkenness, once again she omitted both the proposal and the kiss.

Paul had a good laugh trying to picture Aaron staggering with dignity down the hall. Suzanne thought she would die laughing as Paul tried to impersonate him. Suddenly deep inside her she felt a pang of guilt laughing at Aaron. There was the tiniest bit of her way down deep that was secretly attracted to Aaron.

Suzanne couldn't help but wonder if sleeping with Paul would stay this incredible. Could it possibly be this exciting if they slept together every night? Would they fall into the same traps and ruts that all married couples fell into, that her and Ray had fallen into? But then sex with Ray was never this incredible.

Suzanne was lucky enough to be working at the front desk when Aaron came down to turn in his key. Using every bit of strength and will power she had Suzanne restrained the laughter building inside of her.

She had to keep a serious professional face for Aaron's sake. There was no sense in embarrassing him more than he had already embarrassed himself. It was important for him to hang onto some pride and dignity.

He told her not to bother trying to lie to him. He could remember every embarrassing moment of the night before. For most of which he was sorry, all except for that kiss. Now it was Suzanne's turn to be embarrassed, she wasn't sure why but she was flustered. She stumbled over her words as she tried to brush it all off lightly.

She told him everyone had to let loose once in awhile, that it was good for him. Perhaps he should consider doing it more often. Aaron had enough embarrassment to last a lifetime.

Suzanne started to move away as Aaron moved in close to her ear, part of her was afraid yet wanted another kiss. He whispered very softly that the proposal was very real and if she ever reconsidered he would be there.

It was nice to know she would have something to fall back on if she had to, but she doubted she would have to. She hoped that this wouldn't affect their working relationship; she loved and needed her job. Her job was her entire life.

She wasn't ready to be completely dependent on Paul. He would surely use this as a way of getting her to move in, to hang on to her tighter. She was definitely not ready; she could feel the noose tighten just thinking about being with Paul full time.

Her first weekend with Paul and the kids was pretty scary. She hadn't spent more than a couple hours at a time with her children in years. The last time she was a full time mother she was caring for babies, now in the blink of an eye, she was dealing with teenagers.

Anna had turned thirteen on her last birthday, Angel was eleven almost twelve, while Alice was ten, and R.J. was now eight. It almost felt like she had borrowed the neighbors' children for a weekend sleep over.

Paul was a natural father. The kids loved him. But as warm as they were to Paul, they were equally as cold to their mother. Anna spent the entire weekend complaining how she was forced to be there and was much too big to be ordered around.

The best they could do was to try to keep everyone busy. They took the kids to a petting farm. Anna wasted no time in telling them she was not a BABY! She spent the entire day bored and full of attitude. Angel stayed glued to Paul, her protector, Alice and R.J. loved being there. They were in heaven and didn't want to leave.

It was late by the time they got home and Suzanne began sending them one by one for their bath, then into pajamas. Everyone finished except Angel who for some reason went into the bathroom sat for half an hour then came out fully dressed and as filthy as when she went in.

Suzanne could feel the anger and frustration building in her, this time she would handle things differently, this time she would keep her head. Ray had always told her if she would listen to Angel that she would be easier to handle.

Taking Angel into the kitchen so they could talk quietly, Suzanne explained that she was trying to be patient, but she didn't understand why Angel couldn't do it. The other kids had all taken baths.

Every time Suzanne tried to talk to her daughter, Angel would get a look of terror on her face making it impossible for Suzanne to keep her composure. This time was no different. Suzanne's anger was growing, growing bigger than she could contain... "WHY DO YOU HAVE TO LOOK AT ME THAT WAY ... I HAVE NOT LAID A HAND ON YOU IN YEARS AND I NEVER WILL AGAIN...?"

She looked around and saw Paul standing in the doorway as she realized she was yelling. Paul calmly walked to her and kissed her sweetly on the cheek. The other kids were waiting for her to say goodnight. He could deal with Angel while she did that.

She looked at the terror on Angel's face and knew she wasn't going to get anywhere. It was the same as with Ray, the same dance she had done since Angel's birth. Open defiance of her mother then sucker the men in her life to rescue her, making Suzanne the monster.

Talking to Angel, he explained to her that eventually she would have to start talking to her mother so they could gain an understanding of each other, and thus get along and learn to trust in each other. Until then maybe she could trust him enough to tell him the problem. Big alligator tears started to well up in her eyes as she put her head down so low that Paul could see her chin on her chest.

Angel began whispering in a tiny little voice that he could hardly hear... she was scared, but of what? What could a tiny little child be so scared of? Paul couldn't begin to imagine what could be so scary in his bathroom. Angel didn't know. All she knew was that she was real scared. The fear was real if not warranted; he could see every bit of that fear piercing his heart from the helplessness in her eyes.

He offered to check the bathroom and leave the door open, but that wasn't going to be enough for Angel. He asked her about one of the other girls going in with her. Angel finally agreed but only if it was

Alice. After the way Anna had behaved all day, he didn't want to be around her either.

Calling Alice he began to explain that he wanted her to sit in the bathroom with Angel while she had her bath. Alice wasn't one bit impressed; she was tired of keeping Angel company in the bath. It took Paul a minute to catch up and realize this was a common occurrence. According to the kids Angel never took a bath alone.

Alice didn't object for long, it broke her heart to see Angel cry, and had to go with her so she would stop. As Paul strolled past the bathroom door he could hear Alice, telling one silly joke after another, trying to get Angel to laugh or at least smile.

Paul was lost. He had never spent a lot of time with children, and even if he had it would never have prepared him for Angel. He wanted to save her, to protect her, but how? How could he protect her from her own head? How could he chase ghosts and fears that only Angel could see and feel? He felt every bit as helpless as he did when Suzanne woke in the night screaming and trembling with unspoken haunts.

All the children were finally tucked in and asleep. Suzanne and Paul could finally have some quiet time, alone. Suzanne asked him if he was ready to run yet. He pulled her over to him on the couch, until she was sitting on his knee.

Even though he was scared to death of this whole fatherhood thing, he had always liked the idea of kids. He wanted to find a way to talk to her about the kids but he worried she would resent his interfering. He decided to wait 'til he had a better idea of how things were going in the future. Maybe things looked worse because he was so new to this responsible for children thing.

Suzanne gave him a big hug and kiss and told him she loved him, it was good that if he had to be around the children that he share in dealing with them and their problems. It was already pretty obvious that he was better at it than her, especially with Angel. Suzanne was forced to come to the painful realization that she had become a stranger to her children, they had grown up without her. She couldn't believe how much she didn't know about them ... Angel never took a bath alone.

It made her wonder what else she didn't know about her children. As she gave it thought, it wasn't a matter of what she didn't know, but what she did know which was very little. What else was Angel so scared of and how did she get so scared of so many things? Suzanne knew Angel had always been different. She had always felt things stronger than anyone else.

Suzanne asked Paul if he noticed Angel's eyes. He wondered if Suzanne was referring to the way Angel could crawl inside of you with her eyes, analyzing and dissecting every bit of a person's soul.

Breathing a sigh of relief, Suzanne was thankful that someone else felt it. She had wondered if it was only her that Angel did it to. She was glad to hear a stranger's description of something she could feel but not quite describe or even put her finger on.

There was a chilled laughter as she asked him if he thought she really could see through people and into their souls. Maybe that was the problem. Angel could see the evil and the anger coming before Suzanne could feel it.

She wanted to change the subject. The entire idea gave her the creeps, was far too weird for her liking. It made her feel like Angel was bewitched or perhaps possessed with something that wasn't human.

She gave her lover another hug and kiss. Paul asked her what it was for... Her answer was...simply because... "YOU ARE YOU ... "She offered to make the hot chocolate and popcorn while he found an old movie to watch; something schmaltzy, a tearjerker. He told her they already had all the romance cornered. That was why she loved him so much; he always knew the right thing to say and when to say it.

Paul sat at one end of the couch; Suzanne put her head on his knee stretching out across the rest of it. She drifted off about ten minutes into the movie. He eased out from under her slipping a pillow under her head so he could go and do some paper work.

It was a little past midnight when he could hear some muffled noises coming out of the bedroom. He thought maybe a couple of the kids had woken up and were talking. As he made his way quietly into the room to check on them, a sudden panic came over him. Angel wasn't anywhere to be seen.

He looked around finally spotting her in the corner of the room. She had her knees pulled up tight to her chest and her face buried tight into a pillow, crying her heart out. When she saw him standing over her she nearly jumped out of her skin, scurrying even tighter into the corner.

When he saw how scared she was he moved very slowly talking to her, trying to tell her he wouldn't hurt her. She looked at him like she didn't see him. He was sure she was still sleeping and in the middle of some terrifying nightmare.

Sitting on the floor, he put his arms around her trying to wake her gently. He knew nothing about nightmares and wasn't sure if he should wake her or not. Whatever was happening in her head she needed rescuing from it.

When she finally woke and realized he was there she wrapped her arms around his neck and hung on for dear life. He rocked her in his arms and told her not to worry that he would keep her safe. Picking her up he carried her into the kitchen where he made her a hot chocolate. Then he made her a little bed in the big armchair by his desk where she could watch him work.

Paul could not help but watch her; he could see a gentle helplessness in her. He could also see so much more of life in her eyes. Angel was hard to understand and even harder to explain. It was as though everything inside of her was old. Yet outwardly, she was this tiny little girl even for her age, very tiny. Alice had towered over her for a long time.

It was impossible for Paul to get any more work done. All he could think about were the two girls sleeping; one on the couch, the other in the chair. Both of them were helpless against the haunts and fears that they fought daily.

They were fears that no one could ever know or understand. How could this have happened? What was it that caused them to yell out in their sleep? To make them so hard nosed by day and so weak and helpless by night?

Paul left Angel sleeping in the chair and woke Suzanne to go to bed. He told her about Angel's nightmare; Suzanne wondered if she was still haunted by the rats or if it was one of her many rages that scared Angel.

Suzanne tossed and turned most of the night haunted by the guilt of what she had done to Angel. She hadn't fully realized just how screwed up Angel was till that night. Somehow in her mind she thought Angel had outgrown it all.

Paul could only shake his head in disbelief at all this helpless child had endured in such a short life. Rats, beatings, being the outcast, feeling that she had a mother that didn't love her, always being the screw up... the list was long and endless it was no wonder this child cried in her sleep. Paul could not help but shed the tiniest tear for her and her pain.

Chapter Fourteen

The next morning Anna got up with the kids and had them all at the table eating breakfast when Paul and Suzanne finally crawled out of bed. Paul sat at the table as three little princesses jumped up to wait on him hand and foot.

Suzanne was filled with jealousy and envy as she watched how hard her children tried to please him. It all seemed so easy for him. They took to him like they had known him all their lives. Why couldn't she have that kind of connection? Why couldn't they work that hard to please her?

Suzanne stood at the counter drinking her coffee, watching them laugh and play. She wished she could be a part of it. They looked and sounded like a family, a family she didn't belong to. Even Paul, who had been a bachelor for years, knew how to be part of a family.

Suzanne was so tired of being outside of everything and everyone. She couldn't stand to watch them anymore. The more they laughed the more she felt like crying. She had to get out of there she took her coffee into the front room, to the bar where she poured a very liberal shot of rum into her coffee ... a little something to clear her throat she told herself.

Suzanne didn't realize that Paul had followed her out. As he kissed her, he could taste the rum a familiar taste of late. One he didn't plan on getting used to. There was sarcasm in his voice as he asked her if it wasn't just a tad early.

She fumbled over a list of feeble excuses, she had a tickle in her throat, and she thought she was coming down with something... She wasn't sure if she was lying to him or herself. In his eyes she could clearly see the same look of disappointment her father always had. Now she was getting both angry and defensive, how dare he? He had no right sitting in judgement on her, who did he think he was?

As she remembered it, he was the one who developed her taste for rum in her coffee in the first place. Anyone that had a bar as well stocked, as his had no right. Her claws were out and she was ready to attack if she was forced to.

Paul did all he could to get her to calm down, trying to take back the criticism, he wasn't trying to sit in judgement. He was concerned and had been for some time. He never felt secure enough to mention it, but now the kids were here it wasn't a time to be drinking before breakfast.

Couldn't she wait till they were gone? Now he was going to tell her what was best for her kids. Talking to her as though she were one. As though he were her father. She took that for years from Ray

Suzanne wasn't one of them, she was all grown up. She didn't need his patronizing or his concern. She would decide what was good for both her children and herself. It wasn't like he had seen her drunk more than a couple times since they had met.

Suzanne had to change the subject, she wanted to get out of this fast, before she said something she was sure to regret. She did all she could to lighten things. They had better things to do today than talk about her drinking.

Next time she would be more careful. The next time she wouldn't get caught putting a shot in her coffee. She wasn't being sneaky about her drinking she was simply avoiding confrontation. There was nothing wrong with her having an occasional drink; she just didn't want to do battle every time she wanted one.

First thing bright and early Monday morning, Suzanne went back to work and home; where she could relax and be herself. The first thing she did was to go to her room, pour herself a cup of coffee and put in

a large shot of dark rum. At least there was one place where it was nobody's business if she wanted a shot in her coffee.

Now that she had both her caffeine and alcohol levels back in tact she could go do her rounds and checks of the hotel. While at the lobby desk Suzanne spotted a peculiar sight wandering through the front lobby.

She worked very hard to hold back the laughter that permeated from behind her. The entire staff had come to stare; they hadn't had a good laugh in a long time. Suzanne restrained her own laughter as she turned and shot her best silent reprimand to silence them. Aaron was a boss and owner and they would show respect, even if that owner and boss did look pretty silly in rolled jeans and the white shirt and tie he was born to wear.

Suzanne could attempt to control and restrain her laughter but she had no control over the stare she was lost in. How could she not stare, she had not seen this man in anything but a suit since she met him? Dressing down to Aaron Weinstein was taking off the jacket and hanging it over a chair.

Trying to be as dignified as a man his age dressed like a teenager could be, Aaron asked if he had a wart on his nose. As though he had no idea why everyone was staring, how could he not know?

Aaron explained to Suzanne that it was time for him to lighten up, to get a new image and style. He was tired of being so staunch and ridged. He had been discontented with his life a long time but was having trouble finding a way of changing, not only himself but also his life.

This had to be some sort of MIDLIFE CRISES ... or straight out insanity. That was it Mr. Weinstein had stepped into insanity. As strange as it was Suzanne was slowly getting used to the new Aaron. Somehow she found it an interesting look.

Suzanne liked her Mondays; it was her time to be alone. Paul knew Suzanne well enough to know she needed her space and had come to respect her Mondays away from him. She mostly hung around her room having a few drinks and generally pretending to be a vegetable.

Occasionally she would go and have a drink or two with Aaron but only if he agreed there would be no business. Aaron and Suzanne had become great friends. Suzanne found herself enjoying his company and friendship, much like she once enjoyed Paul's friendship. It made her miss and crave what her and Paul once had and was now not only gone but strained.

The entire hotel staff understood that Mondays were to be considered her time off. They were not to bother her unless the hotel was on fire. That is why when the phone began to ring on one of her quiet Mondays she felt instant anger.

On the other end of the phone she heard Ray's voice. A voice she rarely heard anymore. Usually he simply sent messages through the kids. Suzanne was sure that was his way of being respectful to Bev his new wife.

He spoke very softly but hesitantly, Suzanne knew him well enough that instant panic came over her. "MY CHILDREN.!?..WHAT HAS HAPPENED TO...?" Ray cut her off, it wasn't the kids. She had to get to the hospital immediately.

Her father had another HEART ATTACK a bad one this time, he didn't know how much time there was but he was asking for Suzanne, he had something to tell her before he could go to his grave...

"GO TO THE GRAVE?!..." He couldn't, she still needed him. She rarely talked to him any more but she still needed to know he was there if she did want to talk to him. Suzanne dropped the phone and ran out the door blind with hysteria.

As she drove to the hospital she was overwhelmed with feelings of guilt and regret. How could she be such a bad daughter? She had done nothing but disappoint him her entire life. Why was she always so selfish, why did she always put herself first?

A prayer began to pass her lips. She hadn't prayed in years but she needed help and there seemed no one else to turn to. Promises of a better Suzanne, a better daughter and mother, blindly she made all the promises she was sure God wanted to hear followed by... "JUST LET HIM LIVE... I WILL DO ANYTHING..."

Suzanne could hardly see through the tears that filled her eyes. She wiped the tears from her eyes and took a deep breath before walking into the hospital that scared her to death. She didn't want her father to see how scared she was. She had to act as though everything were fine. He would be all right; it was nothing more serious than a head cold.

"PLEASE, PLEASE, PLEASE... LET HIM BE ALIVE...!" He had to still be alive. She had to tell him she loved him. He couldn't die till she made things right and said all the things she should have been saying right along. There were so many regrets, how could she put them all right in a short visit in emergency.

Her entire body trembled uncontrolled as she walked through the door, she could see Ray's mom sitting by his side holding his hand, eyes red from the tears she refused to shed. She would be strong; she promised... he didn't need her falling apart. She was his wife and she would be as strong as he needed her to be.

Suzanne wrapped her arms around the tiny woman and held her tight trying to give her strength and reassurance. Or perhaps she was trying to get strength and reassurance. Either way they needed each other, they both loved the same man and hated the idea of loosing him.

Ray's mom whispered into Suzanne's ear that it would all be fine, she wasn't too late. Her father needed her now and it was good she came. With that she gave Suzanne a kiss on the cheek and left the room. She understood they needed to be alone.

They both had things that needed to be said and it wasn't her place to interfere with her husbands final wishes. Her father opened his eyes, he looked so weak, it was as though half of him were already gone.

Suzanne leaned down and gave him a gentle kiss on the cheek telling him she loved him. At least she got that out that was the important part. He struggled to speak in a voice so weak it barely made it past his lips. She tried several times to shush him telling him he could tell her when he was stronger.

Now as though he gained a sudden burst of strength he told her to shut up and listen for once..." I KNOW I AM GOING TO DIE..."

he said it so calmly, so matter-of-factly, it was as though he had made peace with the idea.

"BEFORE I DO I NEED YOU TO FORGIVE ME... PLEASE SUZANNE ... I AM SORRY, SORRY FOR ALL OF IT ... SORRY I NEVER DID ANYTHING ... I KNEW ... I KNEW ..." Suzanne couldn't listen to this. He had been a great father, she would never have traded him she loved that he was her father. It was her that should beg forgiveness.

Suzanne's eyes once again filled with tears but this time there was no holding them back. Her face drenched as she sobbed uncontrolled for the mistakes that they had both made and regretted.

Her father grabbed at her with desperation, he had to be sure she was listening that she heard every word he said ..." I DIDN'T KNOW WHAT TO DO ... I WOULD COME HOME FROM WORK YOU WOULD BE BANGED UP ... YOUR MOTHER ALWAYS SAID YOU WERE A CLUMSY CHILD OR YOU WERE ROUGHHOUSING WITH YOUR BROTHERS... "

Now it was his turn to cry from mistakes he could never correct. He had cried for her in private most of her life. She needed to know how much he loved her and regretted not saving her, not doing all things he had to do to keep her safe and secure.

If he had she would not have all the difficulties she now had to deal with. She would be able to love and be a mother and wife. He had robbed her of all of that. It was not her fault, it was never her fault and she needed to know that before he died.

Even weaker and barely able to draw a breath let alone speak he continued..." IT WAS EASIER NOT TO KNOW... TO LOOK THE OTHER WAY ... I CAN'T GO TO MY GRAVE WITH THIS HANGING OVER ME ... SUZANNE YOU NEVER HAD A CHANCE TO FORGIVE YOUR MOTHER OR MAKE PEACE OF THE MISTAKES SHE MADE... IF YOU ARE EVER GOING TO HAVE ANY PEACE IN YOUR LIFE, I BEG YOU ... PLEASE FORGIVE ME..."

Suzanne was almost hysterical, as she sobbed the words her father so desperately needed to hear. She would forgive her father anything. She loved him and had always loved him. He was the only one that made her childhood bearable in many ways he did save her.

He was still struggling to speak. Suzanne wanted him to save his energy, he was exhausting himself and none of this needed to be said.... forgive him, there was nothing to forgive, it was he who needed to forgive her.

There was no stopping him he had things to say and all she could do was listen..." I SHOULD HAVE TOLD YOU YEARS AGO ... I WAS A COWARD ... ALL THE SECRETS AND LIES... I WAS SO SCARED YOU WOULD HATE ME ... PLEASE DON'T HATE ME ..."

The collar of his shirt was soaked with the tears streaming down her face ... "I LOVE YOU DADDY... I KNOW YOU DID THE BEST YOU COULD ... IT WASN'T YOUR FAULT..."

He cut her short, it was his fault it was all his fault there was so much she didn't know, so much he had never told her. She could hear him gasp for a labored breath as he slumped into an exhausted still lump.

He was so tired it was his time. She was not to worry or feel bad because he would always be with her and watch over her, as he couldn't do during her life. He begged her not to cry for him. He was finally going to be out of his pain and able to relax in peace.

Suzanne wrapped her arms around his neck and told him she loved him over and over. She begged him not to die. She still needed him, as she held him in her arms she could feel the slightest of beats. It was weak and it was irregular but it was a beat.

She reached up calling for the nurse, it wasn't too late they could save him there was still time. Once again he tried to speak she had to put her ear tight to his face. She couldn't miss what was so important, what was it he was trying to say?

Suzanne screamed at the top of her lungs please hurry, save him. A code was called and within moments the room was filled with professionals and the life giving equipment they were so well trained to use.

Ray's mom came back into the room, one last goodbye to the man she had loved the man who had taken away her loneliness who had given her reason to go on each day. Suzanne couldn't help but envy her mother-in-law and the two men who loved her so completely. She had so many people in her life to love and be loved would Suzanne ever know that kind of love.

As Suzanne watched her she seemed so strong, so stoic. Suzanne wished she had her strength. But then she had a lot of people who loved her and would keep her strong. Suzanne wondered who would cry for her when her time came.

Suzanne breathed a sigh of temporary relief as the crash crew worked their magic and he was saved at least for the moment. She quietly made her way out of the room leaving her father alone with his wife.

There was no way of knowing how much more time they had together, Suzanne had her time now it was theirs she had made her peace, said all she needed to say. In her heart she wanted to stay 'til his last breath was drawn but she knew it wasn't right, they needed their time.

Refusing to allow herself to drop into self-pity at a time like this she left the room and walked to the pay phone. She saw two of her brothers and not far behind them were the rest. Even her sister Barb was there. Somehow Ray had found them all.

They all melted into a muddle of hugs and sobs. Suzanne couldn't believe they were all together; they hadn't been together in many years. They hadn't even all gotten together for their mother's funeral.

This was good it would please her father. Now he could make his peace with all of them. One by one they went in to say their good-byes, one last hug, one last tear. They all had so many regrets, so much guilt. Hopefully now they could all put it in the past.

Suzanne made her excuses and went to the pay phone to call Paul. She couldn't get hold of Paul he would be out of the office all day on business. Monday was his busiest day for court. She left a simple message for him to come to the hospital as soon as he could, she would be there all day and probably half the night.

A nurse came into the lounge to explain the strict policies of the hospital. Visits were to be kept short. His wife could stay by his side at all times, but no more than one other person for no more than a few minutes at a time.

They all spent the day sitting in the lounge waiting and worrying. Ray and Bev came to give moral support for Ray's mother. She wasn't that strong herself, Ray worried what this would do to her strength.

This poor woman had now taken care of and out lived two husbands. She was such a wonderful person she deserved more happiness in her life. She deserved to not spend her old age alone. It simply wasn't fair or right, she was a good person who only deserved good things out of life.

She hugged Suzanne and told her she had been very lucky in her life. She had not one, but two great men who loved her. Most women never find that one person that can make them feel loved and fulfilled.

Always being loved, she had enough memories to keep her happy all the rest of her days. She was not going to be alone, nor had she ever been alone. She had wonderful people in her life, people who loved and cherished her. She had family.

If family were not enough her memories would be her company. She had no regrets or sadness. Neither of her husbands were gone they were both still very much with her in her heart where they would always be.

A piece of Suzanne not only didn't feel sorry for her mother in law but envied her. She had found a love and peace that Suzanne still searched for and would probably never find. She was right she was lucky to be loved and love so many.

It was after five before Paul finally showed up. Suzanne was relieved to see him. After introducing him to the family, they went for a walk outside, as she needed to catch her breath. The two walked in silence, Paul finally interrupted the silence to ask her if she was all right. It surprised even her how well she was maintaining her composure.

She had made her peace with it all, said all she had to say. He didn't go suddenly leaving everything unsettled like when her mother died. There was so much that Suzanne wished she could have said. But not this time she said what she needed. He knew she loved him and he loved her that was enough.

Suzanne was however a little scared; she liked the idea of her Dad being there for her. Even if they didn't speak for long periods of time, she liked knowing he was there when she was ready to talk or when she needed him.

There was no other love in the world that was the same as a father's love. It didn't matter how much Paul loved her or her children loved her. It wasn't the same as being daddy's little girl. She would never feel that kind of fatherly love again.

This was all so final; there was nothing anyone could do to change it. Death was so permanent. Her father had told her never to be afraid of death. It was a time of peace and rest from all the turmoil on earth.

She asked Paul if he believed in God. Paul looked at her puzzled, he wasn't sure. There was a time he believed and had no doubt. The past several years he had built a wall of cynicism. There was little belief and a lot of doubt.

If there was a God, how could he let your mother hurt you all your life, not to mention the hardships that Angel had suffered? If there was a God why wasn't he protecting the children?

Adults were different they generally made their own heartache and hardships but children.... they were so helpless and innocent, they didn't deserve what came at them. That was why he had to give up criminal law.

There was a time he believed he was protecting the innocent, but somehow it all got turned around, it was the innocent that were being forgotten and the guilty that were being protected.

He had seen too many injustices, too much abuse. If there were a God then why didn't he just stop it all and protect the innocent. He could protect his children if he were really there and watching it all. Why doesn't he protect Angel and stop all the nightmares that they both are haunted by.

Helpless babies and old ladies abused nothing happens no one protects them. No one stops it. Maybe he didn't mean to say he didn't believe in God, maybe what he meant to say was that he didn't understand God. He had always believed there had to be a higher being. He believed that having a soul he could hang around and take care of loved ones after death.

What he believed in most was that each individual had to find their own truth and beliefs. Whatever there was after life, it had to be easier than life was now. She figured she was already living her HELL here on earth.

Suzanne's father passed away quietly in his sleep during the night. It seemed so strange to Suzanne that she shed no tears, no mourning process or sadness. She said a simple quiet good-bye at the coffin before they shut it.

It was her sister Barb who fell into a puddle of uncontrolled emotions. Suzanne felt so sorry for her, she was so alone. Her brothers had to carry her to the car after the funeral. Barb would never find peace from her ghosts; they were all so scarred in so many different ways.

Suzanne was glad she settled things between her and her father, it was the unfinished business that haunted. She quietly thanked her father under her breath for leaving her with peace. She wished she had a chance to settle things with her mother. There was so much she wished she had asked and answered.

Aaron insisted that Suzanne take a few days off for bereavement. Suzanne insisted she would be all right. She kept this to herself, not telling Paul so she could spend the time alone. He would expect her to spend it with him and would probably want her to bring the kids.

What she did do was get a couple of bottles of the best and hold up in her room, just her and her bottles. She was due, the way she saw it she was over due. Suzanne needed a good drunk. What she didn't need was anyone around to ruin her perfectly good time.

Suzanne ran herself a very hot bubble bath, poured herself a very large rum and coke, then climbed into the tub to begin her solitary drunkenness. No pressure, no demands, she could think and feel anything she wanted.

She thought about how she wished she could put things back the way they used to be with Paul. She didn't want to share him, especially with her kids. It seemed all he wanted anymore was the family stuff.

The worst part about all of it was that he wouldn't even have sex with her if the kids were over, and they were always over. Even when he came to her place he spent most of his time talking about the kids, which broke her mood completely. There was nothing like a long conversation about kids to really put a person in the mood.

If it was like this now what was it going to be like when they were living together full time; something else he was on her about all the time. Why did he always want too much? Did he have to own her...? All of her? Why couldn't he settle for feeling good when they were together?

Nobody in their right mind wants all that crap he keeps pushing for?! Suzanne tried so hard to make things nice for him, for them. When it's the two of them alone at the hotel, things were good, they were down right wonderful.

They could snuggle and make love all night long. There was no pressure, now there was nothing but pressure. Pressure and tension, and she was sick of it. If she had wanted all that family stuff then she would have stayed with Ray.

She was about halfway through her bottle of rum, and doing a good job of talking herself into backing Paul way up. There was only one problem, she really did love him, or at least she thought she did. At the moment she was expending a lot of energy trying to convince herself she was wrong.

Suzanne knew that if she tried to pull him away from the kids and go back to the way things were he would walk away. He loved being with the kids as much or even more than he liked being with her. She couldn't stand to lose him again. Nor could she stand keeping him the way things were.

She heard a knock at the door ... "DAMN…! HE FOUND ME" She would have some serious pleasing to do for him to forgive her for not telling him about her time off. She had it all figured out.

As soon as she opened the door, she would wrap her arms around him and make mad passionate love to him before he could open his mouth. At least that way he would be lost in how much she pretended to miss him.

She opened the door, dove into his arms and laid the biggest wettest kiss she could muster up. She was halfway through the kiss when she opened her eyes and found herself nose to nose with Aaron.

Falling and stumbling Aaron caught her in his arms, a place she felt safe. It felt good, a little too good. Suzanne's heart was lodged tight in her throat she couldn't speak; all she could do was melt into a lump of trembling confusion.

… "WHY DID YOU STOP...? I LIKED IT..." Suzanne was as embarrassed as she could be, not quite.... as she pushed out of Aaron's arms she fell on her butt. Now, she was as embarrassed as she could be. Aaron picked her up into his arms kicking and screaming all the way. He carried her into her apartment, dropping her on the couch.

He was enjoying this too much, teasing her and goading her on. He wanted to know why she was hitting him when she so obviously wanted him. Wasn't she the one attacking his body at the door? Suzanne fumbled to find the right words mixed with the right amount of indignance.

She wanted it all to disappear; she wanted it to have never happened. She continued to protest as loud as she could, she would never have greeted him that way if she knew it was him. She didn't want him nor had she ever wanted him. She was attempting to do her best lying. What she didn't know was who she was lying to him or herself.

Aaron assured her he would be sure to wear a disguise next time, if it would get him a greeting like that. He could sure stand to have more of those greetings, especially from Suzanne. Suzanne managed to get to her feet and staggered to the bar, telling him she would pour him a drink if he could behave himself.

He reminded her once again, he was not the one misbehaving. Was she going to have to hear about this forever? She might as well hear about it, he wasn't likely to forget it. She needed to change the subject, this all made her extremely uncomfortable.

It was cutting into her alone drinking time. All she wanted to hear was if he was going to shut up and join her or was he going to take all this conversation elsewhere. The only thing she was interested in was getting herself into a stupor as quickly as possible.

Aaron stayed and watched her kill the bottle. They talked about everything and nothing. Everything, that is, except her kids and Paul. Mostly she talked about her Dad and men in general. How generally lame most of them were.

How could they fall in love all the time when they don't know the first thing about the girl outside of how pretty she may be? How every time they got into a relationship that worked they had to own, to change, to ruin all the good things. Why couldn't men just appreciate what was good and go with it as it was? Why did they always want more, ruining what could have been a very nice uncomplicated time together?

Aaron had no idea what she was trying to tell him, he believed all women were out to get married to some rich guy. Any woman on the face of the earth would have wanted Aaron or Paul and here she was turning them both away.

Didn't all women want a commitment? It seemed to Aaron that she was reacting with a man's attitude. Thoroughly confused, Aaron couldn't begin to count how many women wanted him and he didn't even have to be nice to them.

It always amazed him how much garbage a woman would take to get their claws into a rich man; that is 'til Suzanne crossed his path. What he loved most about Suzanne was that she didn't want him.

It didn't take Suzanne long to pass out cold on the couch. Aaron picked her up into his arms and carried her to bed. It was the least he could do after she tucked him in on his last bender. It took all the strength he had to leave her sleeping peacefully. It would be so easy to just climb in beside her. With that much booze she would never remember, but then he would know even if she wouldn't.

He grabbed a spare blanket from the foot of the bed and crashed on the couch. The mood he was in he should have left but something held him back. He told himself he had too much to drink but it was more.

He couldn't stop himself from watching her sleep. She was so peaceful, so beautiful. For now watching her was enough, it would have to be. Surely she wouldn't object to him quietly lying on the couch.

When she woke in the morning her head was pounding just as hard as it pounded almost every morning. Well maybe just a little harder than usual. She needed caffeine or maybe hair of the dog would be more effective.

Not too worried about what she had on, half-dressed and half-undressed she walked to the small kitchenette. The nice thing about living alone nobody cared how many clothes she had on. Still running around in a state of undress Suzanne finally noticed Aaron sitting quietly on the couch grinning from ear to ear.

Screaming loud enough to pierce ears, she ran into the bedroom. Returning in a housecoat she wasted no time getting up in his face..." WHAT ARE YOU DOING HERE?!! "

Aaron clasped his hands behind his head, placing his feet on the coffee table he was filled with mischief..." JUST CATCHING THE

SIGHTS PRETTY LADY ... AND MIGHTY FINE SIGHTS THEY ARE..."

Suzanne hoped he got a real good look because it wasn't anything he would ever see again. If he were any kind of gentleman he would have let a lady know he was there. He had never claimed to be a gentleman, besides her great beauty left him speechless.

She had enough of his crap; it was time for coffee ... and a shot of course. It was a hair of the dog kinda day. If she ignored him maybe he would just go away. Luckily he was the kind of guy who could take a hint. With only a small amount of rubbing it in he left.

Once rid of Aaron, Suzanne could call Paul; she would let him know she had a couple days off. She was now strong enough to take his company for the night if he wanted to spend it with her.

Just as she thought he told her to grab the kids and meet him at his place for supper, he would be home by six at the latest. Barely speaking above a whisper she tried to explain to him she wanted to be alone with him. Suzanne could hear the disappointment in his voice but he didn't object.

It was time for them to talk, and talk honestly. She couldn't keep going the way they were. It was making her crazy and putting a wall up between them. They were almost never sweethearts any more. They were settling in like an old married couple. Suzanne was far too young to be an old married lady.

She loved being a sweetheart. She needed all that highschool sweetheart stuff. It was time to go shopping; she needed something to put the slinky back into their nights. Five shops later she had the sexiest, slinkiest nightgown she could find and expensive perfume to go with it.

Ambiance was the key to romance, candles wine glasses and last was a very special meal, the best Shelby could put together. When the dinner was brought to the room it was accompanied by two yellow roses with sprigs of baby's breath, perfect.

She had to show Paul how perfect things could be. She wanted things back the way they once were. She wanted to; no she needed to be lovers again. Suzanne refused to even think for a moment about what she would do if he didn't see things her way.

How could she marry him and move into his apartment? She hated every moment she spent there. He had to see they would both be happier this way. Surely he could see her tension and unhappiness away from the hotel. All the times she slept at his apartment and she still didn't feel comfortable or at home while there.

A small voice began whispering to her in the darkest corners of her conscience. Was she being selfish? Suzanne worried she wasn't capable of real love. The kind of love that put someone else first, the kind of self-sacrificing love that lasted a life time.

Maybe she was selfish and self indulged her father had told her and Ray had reinforced it. Were they right? Was this proof of it? Was she merely in lust with Paul? Suzanne thought long and hard wondering what love was, maybe she had never felt it.

She thought she was in love with Ray but she only needed him to rescue her. If she loved her children she would want to be with them. Mostly she put up with them because it was her duty, it was expected.

As for Paul the more she thought about it, the more she realized she never thought about him in any way other than sexual. Every time they had a problem with their relationship, it was when he tried to move it to a higher level; when he was pushing family hour, and happily ever after down her throat.

She didn't want to lose him, but they didn't want the same things out of life. She tried, she really did try. If she couldn't stand alternating weekends, how could she stand day to day?

The other problem was the kids; the longer they were together the more he wanted the kids around. She left Ray because she didn't want to be a full time mom and that had never changed over the years. If anything, she felt stronger about it, all the years on her own merely confirmed how she felt.

Nightgown, perfume, makeup, candles lit, champagne chilling; everything was ready, everything was perfect. That is except for herself, after making a drink, a little liquid courage she would need it.

Suzanne thought about what to say and how to say it. She was most likely to totally chicken out. Everything was so perfect why ruin the evening she could talk to him in the morning. Then if he walked out she would have one last final spectacular memory.

Paul used his key to let himself in; he was immediately dumbfounded and stood waiting for the mood to freeze in time. All the lights were off except for the candlelight, Suzanne stood by the table, she truly was a striking beauty that left Paul frozen in his tracks. He told her he had forgotten how beautiful she was.

Paul's movements all seemed to be in slow motion. Every kiss and every touch seemed to linger in the air, adding to the intensity of their passion. Suzanne was lost in Paul's passion, in his touch.

She loved being with him so much, how was she ever going to talk to him, get him to understand how she felt? As hard as she tried to be tough and cold-hearted he would warm her heart and there was nothing she could do to stop him.

After making love and drinking champagne they laid in each other's arms. This was her favorite place to be, in Paul's arms in her apartment. She loved the feel of their naked bodies against each other.

They did talk and she tried her hardest to drop hints without actually saying it out loud. She missed the way they once were. She needed to be his sweetheart again. The weekends they were spending together were making her tense, they were pulling them apart. Paul simply wasn't getting it. She had never stopped being his sweetheart; he loved her as much or more now than he had ever. He never believed he could love anyone as much as Suzanne that he could be so close to having an entire family.

As for the weekends they were spending together they were great, even the kids were wonderful. The entire family bent over backwards to please Suzanne and make everything perfect for her. He had never seen kids that tried so hard.

Maybe it was the loss of her father, maybe it was the funeral and all the confusion making her crazy. She was so caught up in the emotion of losing her father that she didn't know what she was saying. She obviously wasn't seeing things clearly.

Suzanne couldn't talk to him with their bodies pressed so close together. How could she feel his arms holding her so passionately and tell him he was crowding. She needed him to back off a little.

He wanted what she couldn't give and perhaps would never be able to give. She knew exactly what she wanted, she just didn't know how to convince Paul it was the right thing.

Paul drifted off to sleep still blind to what she was trying to say. Suzanne lay awake watching him; she loved the way he slept. He was always so relaxed, so totally asleep and at ease. Suzanne wondered if he would sleep so peacefully if he fully understood how close they were to breaking up.

He looked like such a peaceful little boy when he was asleep. Suzanne was envious of anyone who could sleep so deeply and soundly. She sat on the couch finishing off the champagne, trying to figure out where to go from here.

She felt trapped. She couldn't stay and she couldn't go either. Why did Paul have to make it so hard? Why couldn't he see they would be happier...? Their time together could be so much better.

The morning was tense. Paul could feel it, Suzanne could feel it but neither of them spoke of it. They walked to the door together to say their good-byes. Paul was hesitant as he walked out the door and down the hall. Something wasn't right, he wasn't sure what, but something felt different.

Suzanne ran out calling to him, diving into the arms of a very confused Paul. Why did she have a tear in her eyes and desperation in her hug? What was going on? There were many times he had wished he could crawl into her head; Paul always found it hard understanding her but never as hard as at this moment.

Nearly squeezing the life out of him she began to cry, the only words she got out were… "I LOVE YOU "…

To Paul it sounded like she was saying good bye and not just for now, he was overwhelmed by that uneasy feeling that he knew all too well. Was she running again, he could feel her pushing him away? Suddenly it all became clear. He could finally see what she was trying to say.

It was goodbye, but it was Paul that was saying it. He decided to get away from her and not give her a chance to say anything they would both regret, sure she needed time to think. He had to go, he had an early appointment and he couldn't hang around. Hugging her again, he held her face between his large hands. Looking deep into her eyes he said he loved her. He didn't want her to ever lose sight of that.

Running back to her room she closed the door as she devastated into a flood of tears. Completely confused, why was she crying...? She had everything any normal girl would want. She had the whole world at her feet. But she didn't want Paul's world or what was in it.

Suzanne poured a liberal shot into her morning coffee, she dreaded the day ahead of her. What she feared most was being with her family without her father there to smooth the waters.

It was amazing how incredibly tense she was, thinking about it all. She hated the idea of Daddy's Will being read. To her it was ghoulish her father was gone. Suzanne had her memories and that was all she wanted.

She would have liked to have her Dad's uniform; but in her heart she believed that was the kind of thing that should go to his first son, her brother. He was a brother who had not been in any of their lives for years.

In her mind she decided to hold her breath and say nothing. She also decided she would need more courage for that. Liquid courage, that is. If ever anyone needed a drink to get through anything it was this meeting. No one would argue her right to a drink at such an emotional time in her life.

They all sat in the lawyer's office waiting. Suzanne couldn't help but wonder how this bunch of strangers could be her family. A stranger walking into the room would think they were all totally unrelated as they sat in silence neither speaking nor looking at each other.

Why didn't she simply get up and leave, she didn't want any of her father's estate. It belonged to Ray's Mom. It was Ray's mom who gave her Dad the only happiness and love he had ever known. He had told that to Suzanne many times.

There were no surprises; the house was left to Ray's Mom, as it should have been. Suzanne wanted to get out of there not really knowing what she was doing there in the first place. She needed a drink. She needed breathing space. In the same room with her entire family of strangers the air seemed so thin, the room so closed.

Suzanne continued to sit politely as the lawyer talked about the trust set up for each of the twelve grandchildren. Everything else was to go to Ray's Mom. Suzanne was relieved. She knew her father would do the right thing by her. The house was not to be sold and divided among her brother's and sister. Suzanne hated to think where Ray and the kids would have gone.

Suzanne's sister Barb sat in pained silence; it was hard to know what she was feeling behind the cold silence in her eyes. Her brother's on the other hand were yelling at the lawyer, Ray's Mom and even each other. There had never been anything silent about them.

It was awful. Ray's mom stood in shock, trembling with grief, trying hard to make sense of everything they were saying. She cried as she told them she didn't marry him for the money or the house. She didn't care about the money.

Suzanne's heart broke as she put her arms around her mother in law and escorted her out the door and down the hall to the washroom. Once inside she took a Kleenex out of her purse and dabbed at the tears streaming down her mother in laws face. Ray's mother hung on to Suzanne still trembling and crying. She told Suzanne she loved her father...." I WASN'T AFTER THE MONEY...I WASN'T...!"

Suzanne didn't know what to do or what to say to comfort her... "HE GAVE YOU THE HOUSE AND THE MONEY BECAUSE HE LOVED YOU AND WANTED TO MAKE SURE YOU WERE TAKEN CARE OF ..."

Suzanne pointed out to her that the entire family was a mess and not to worry too much about what any of them had to say. She had belonged to the family long enough to know what total screw ups they were. They had all been angry and bitter long before their father took her as a wife. There was nothing she could do to change that.

Even if Dad had left the money to his children they would have blown it all on booze, drugs, gambling or who knows what. Her Dad was well aware of the shortcomings of his children. He could do nothing to help or change the life his children had, but maybe with the trust money he could help his grandchildren.

Paul was a great corporate lawyer and investment councilor, leaving Suzanne pretty secure financially. She didn't need the money and neither did her brothers... with the exception of her oldest brother who paid alimony to three ex wives.

Suzanne told her to go back in the office and accept the gift that was intended for her. If any of those ungrateful children have anything to say about it you remind them it was their father's final wish.

Suzanne felt good that she could be there for her mother in law. She was the closest thing to a mother she had ever known. She was the only one around to show Suzanne's girls what a real mother should be like. Suzanne would owe her a debt that couldn't be repaid.

When she got back to work she went looking for Aaron. She told him she'd already had more R&R than she could stand. She was going back to work. The sooner the better, she couldn't stand rattling around in her personal life. Work was her escape, her rescue from herself.

Aaron had never been more relieved, he was sick to death of soothing the ruffled feathers of the pompous, the arrogant and the straight out idiots that had nothing better to do than make everyone miserable. He wondered how she could stand it. She had more than enough practice dealing with her mother all her life. Her mother was the Queen of the pack, the snob of all snobs.

Aaron wanted to be sympathetic to the death of Suzanne's father but he still couldn't help but crack a half smile at Suzanne's comments.

Aaron was always content to simply stand and listen to Suzanne; she could always put a smile on Aaron's otherwise stone expressions.

Since she was back to work she better start with Shelby and smooth the waters before he killed his entire staff. Once again he had no idea how she kept Shelby so calm all the time. This time it was Suzanne's turn to smile ... " IT IS GOOD TO BE APPRECIATED!..." Suzanne was home and this truly was where she not only wanted to be but where she belonged.

Suzanne was tense while at Paul's because it wasn't where she belonged. She was trying to be what Paul wanted her to be, not what or who she really was. Paul was wonderful and it was hard to not want or love him as the truly perfect guy he was.

However, if it wasn't right, it wasn't right and nothing could make it right. For the first time in a long time, she felt good. She felt good about her life and where she was. Everyone in her life, including Paul, took great pains to turn her into something she wasn't, making her feel guilty for not being who they wanted her to be.

There was nothing wrong with whom or what she was. Just because she wasn't what everyone else wanted her to be, didn't mean she was bad. Why couldn't anyone ever love her for the person that she was?

Barely through the doors of the kitchen, she could hear the war blazing. Shelby ranted and raved with the force of a dragon slaying the knight. Distraction was always the best weapon. Whatever was wrong he would have to calm down, she had something important to discuss with him. More important than who burned his delicate sauce or who forgot to order the eggs.

Stopping immediately he was a sucker for a piece of juicy gossip. Smiling from ear to ear he was glad to see her back. Trying to be sympathetic he gave her his biggest bear hug, while asking if she was all right... she was never righter.

Suzanne poured two cups of coffee and directed Shelby to follow, she needed him as a friend, and she needed to talk. Whatever had him in such a tizzy would take care of itself, she was more important.

Shelby sat and listened as Suzanne told him what she decided to do with Paul. She would never be what Paul wanted and Shelby was enough of a friend that he fully understood with little explanation. Although he wasn't sure he agreed with her theory that great sex was no reason to hang onto a guy, to Shelby that was the only reason to hang onto a guy.

Shelby wouldn't be much of a friend if he didn't help her to see all sides and one of those sides was that Paul was more than great sex... he was good looks, pleasant company, lots of money, lots of security, and intelligence, not to mention good for her kids.

Paul loved her more than life itself; Shelby wasn't real sure what more Suzanne wanted. He and every woman on the planet had searched for those very things most of their lives. There was no doubt Suzanne was different, she was special and she did deserve happiness even if she didn't believe it herself.

Shelby had witnessed first hand the transformation in her temperament when she returned from the weekends at Paul's. He never fully understood what was wrong but something was absolutely not right. She always looked exhausted and drained. Shelby never felt it was his place to ask so he waited for her to come to him.

Suzanne did have to admit that sitting down and making two lists.... One list would consist of good sides, the other of his bad. The only thing she could think of to put on his bad list was that he clipped his toenails in bed. She wanted to put a need to be with her children on that list but the rest of the world would have considered that a good thing so she relented and added it to the good list.

Suzanne tore the lists into bits and threw them both in the garbage. It didn't matter how great or wonderful he was the problem was that they didn't match. It wasn't about who he was but who she wasn't.

If she tried to force herself to be what he wanted her to be then she would be miserable and eventually destroy them both. No matter how perfect he was they didn't fit and never would if anything looking at the good list merely convinced her of that.

281

Suzanne knew all too well that if she pushed him away this time he would stay away. There would be no changing his mind; he almost didn't come back the last time she pulled this same thing. Shelby still wasn't fully convinced Suzanne understood how much she had to lose.

How could she begin to explain to Shelby that even though she had a lot to lose she was gaining herself? If she couldn't convince Shelby how could she ever convince Paul? She had to find herself again. She was drowning in Paul's dreams and unable to hold onto her own.

Suzanne knew she was doing the right thing because she had no feelings of regret or doubt. There was nothing inside of her trying to talk her out of it. It must be the right thing to do if she wasn't wrestling with herself about it.

A slight smile crossed her lips as she realized her mother would be rolling over in her grave. Paul was everything her mother wanted for her daughter... power, status, money all rolled into a nice looking respectable son-in-law.

An evil voice inside her wished her mother was alive to see her break up with Paul, if she weren't already in the grave it would have surely put her there. Was she doing this as her own secret rebellion against her mother? Was there still a little girl in her that needed to hurt her mother even if she wasn't there to hurt?

Suzanne would have to do this by phone she could never look Paul in the eye and tell him she never wanted to see him again, never wanted to sleep in the same bed again, to have him touch her and hold her. She would never be able to tell him anything face to face.

Paul had the power to talk her into anything simply by looking her in the eyes. It wouldn't be right to call him at the office; she would have to wait to catch him at home, before he came to the hotel to see her. Her mind was working overtime trying to figure a way out, a way that would keep it as simple and as painless as possible. Keep it simple that was the key simply that it wasn't working and she wanted out.

Surely he already suspected that it wasn't right. Surely he could see how miserable she was every weekend that they spent at his house. He had to feel that she could hardly wait for their weekends to be over.

The more Suzanne thought about it the more she realized a phone call wasn't going to work. He would ask her too many questions, there would be no discussion. She didn't want to find a way to work it out. It would only postpone the inevitable.

There was only one way, she would have to write him a letter and slip it into his mail box.

MY DEAREST PAUL

I WANT YOU TO KNOW I LOVE YOU VERY MUCH AND CHERISH EVERY MOMENT WE HAVE SPENT TOGETHER. IF IT WERE NOT FOR YOU I WOULD NEVER HAVE KNOWN WHAT IT IS LIKE TO BE TRULY LOVED. I WANT YOU TO UNDERSTAND THAT I AM NOT DOING THIS TO HURT YOU. IT IS TO HELP YOU, TO SET YOU FREE.

IF I AM HANGING ON, YOU WILL NEVER FIND SOMEONE WHO WILL LOVE YOU THE WAY YOU DESERVE. I CAN NEVER BE THAT PERSON, THE KIND OF PERSON YOU WANT ME TO BE. I WILL NEVER BE ABLE TO MARRY YOU OR MOVE IN WITH YOU.

I DO NOT BELIEVE YOU WILL EVER BE CONTENT WITH THE KIND OF PART TIME RELATIONSHIP I AM MOST COMFORTABLE WITH. I TOO COULD NEVER BE COMFORTABLE WITH THE FULL TIME RELATIONSHIP YOU ARE MOST COMFORTABLE WITH.

EVEN THOUGH I ALWAYS TOLD YOU I COULD NEVER BE THE LITTLE WOMAN, THERE WAS SO MUCH MORE I NEVER TOLD YOU. I HOPED I WOULD GROW UP, THAT I WOULD LEARN TO COMMIT. I HOPED THAT YOU WERE SO PERFECT THAT I WOULD GET OVER MY PROBLEMS.

I TRIED I REALLY HAVE, BUT I HATE IT AT YOUR APARTMENT, I HATE ALL THAT FAMILY TOGETHERNESS STUFF. I REALIZE THE KIND OF PERSON THAT MAKES ME AND I HAVE TRIED TO FIGHT IT TO BE SOMEONE ELSE BUT I CAN ONLY BE MYSELF.

I AM NOT THAT NICE SWEET WONDERFUL PERSON YOU THINK I AM. YOU NEED TO TAKE OFF THE ROSE COLORED GLASSES AND SEE ME CLEARLY I AM THAT SELFISH BITCH THAT RAY ALWAYS SAID I WAS. YOU ARE BETTER OFF KNOWING AND ACCEPTING THAT.

THE HARDER I TRY TO BE SOMETHING I AM NOT THE MORE I AM FILLED WITH GUILT AND RESENTMENT IN OUR RELATIONSHIP. A PIECE OF ME WILL ALWAYS LOVE YOU BUT IT IS STILL GOODBY, IT HAS TO BE

SUZANNE

Suzanne would have to hurry to get it to his house before he came home. If she had to face him she would melt the first time she saw his hurt puppy imitation. She still wasn't sure this was what she wanted to do but want to or not it was what she had to do.

Suzanne stood staring at the mail box still filled with apprehension; she knew this was it there would be no going back once she put it there. Taking a deep breath she dropped it from her trembling fingers forcing herself to let go of it.

Crying her heart out all the way back to the hotel, she told the desk she didn't want to be disturbed she wanted to be alone. She would take no call that way he wouldn't be able to call and talk her out of it. She had to be strong; she had to stand her ground.

It would be so much easier if he simply accepted this as a good thing. He must be able to see it wasn't working and never would. Surely he isn't happy either how could he be? If he thought about it for a moment he would realize how much better off he was without her.

Suzanne tried to force herself to work on the books and the accounts as she sipped on a drink trying to enjoy the solitude and convince herself this was good. If it wasn't, there was no going back. It was done, good or bad.

Paul walked through the door, just as he had many times before, no explosion, no tears. As soon as Suzanne saw the briefcase he sat beside the door she knew he hadn't been home yet, he came straight from the office.

She sat in silence as she watched him walk across the room. She stayed in silence as he walked around her desk and leaned to kiss her. Paul had been worried all day after that strange behavior when he left.

He laughed nervously as he told her he felt like she would break up with him before the end of the day. Every time the phone rang his heart sank thinking it was her with the bad news. He could clearly feel that ...YOU ARE GETTING TOO CLOSE MOOD ... that she always pushed him away with.

Suzanne stood up and slowly turned toward him trying to force herself to cut it off clean right now. She kissed him long and hard. A kiss filled with longing and a passion she would have to hang onto forever. Paul responded to her passion immediately taking it as a sign that all was well and he only imagined her discontent.

Moving into the bedroom they began to make love, never once letting each other go. Paul barely noticed the sadness in Suzanne's love making. Suzanne was saying goodbye even if Paul didn't know it.... It was a fond farewell.

She knew she should have told him as soon as he walked through the door, but something stopped her. She wanted to feel his lovemaking one last time fixing and freezing it in her heart and mind forever.

Once they finished Suzanne was overwhelmed with feelings of guilt. She felt dirty, she felt low as low as any human with a conscience could feel. She had to get out of there; she wanted to take it all back. It wasn't worth the way it made her feel.

With her head down trying to avoid eye contact with the lover she just used like a piece of meat she slipped into her housecoat. Never before had she felt so naked nor was she so self-conscious of that nakedness.

She needed a drink she was filled with distaste that she had to get out of her mouth and her head. How could she be so low? She couldn't stand it if Paul touched her even for another second. She had to get away, to find a way to erase this entire night.

Paul knew immediately that something was wrong; there was something she wasn't saying. The same feeling of doom that he felt all day had come back. He thought since they just made love all was well, but it wasn't. He had no idea what was wrong but something was. If he knew nothing else about her he knew she loved to snuggle, to be held after sex.

Paul watched her with impatience wondering when she was going to feel fit to fill him in on whatever was going on. He couldn't stand it any longer, he began screaming at her. He wasted no time getting right up in her face...

"JUST SAY IT STRAIGHT OUT...WHATEVER IT IS, JUST SAY IT OUT LOUD ..." He liked to take his Band-Aid off quick, get it over with whatever it was. It couldn't be more painful than the silent heaviness that stood between them now.

Tears streamed down her face as she told him about the letter sitting in his mailbox. The letter explained everything all he had to do was go home and read it. She couldn't talk; she couldn't get words past the lump in her throat. All he had to do was leave. Simply go home and read the letter.

Still sobbing all she could do was yell at him. It was the only way she could get the words out. Why hadn't he gone home first like he always did. Why did this have to be so hard? She wanted to escape; she couldn't stand to look at him. Looking at him merely forced her to face what a terrible person she really was, what a selfish Bitch she really was.

Paul was in total shock, she had caught him off guard, they had just finished making love. If she didn't want to be with him then why was she just with him? Why didn't she tell him as soon as he walked through the door?

Suzanne hung her head unable to hide her guilt as she explained how she just wanted to make love with him one last time. She hated the idea of never making love to him again. She liked everything about him but she had to break up with him anyway. Paul was sure her only problem was that being happy and having the perfect life made her miserable.

By this time his anger built, he was red in the face and nearly out of control. She told him it was all in the letter all he had to do was go home and read it. Paul would have none of it; if this was going to happen then it would happen now face to face.

He wasn't about to let her off easy the way Ray had. This time she would have to face her own mess. People had all her life let her off easy, never forcing her to face the repercussions of her actions.

Suzanne owed him more than a stupid letter in a mailbox. He had her by the arms and was shaking her with all his might hoping he might be able to shake the truth that she wasn't speaking right out of her.

When he finally let go she flew across the room and into a wall, knocking the wind out of her. He left her lying there in a puddle of degradation and tears. She needed to feel what she had done. She deserved this pain, he wasn't about to go pick her up apologize or even console her. It was her turn to be hurt; he was tired of being the one to be hurt.

Getting dressed he continued to rant and rave saying all the hurtful words he had held in for a very long time. He swept things onto the floor, threw other things. He was in a rage and there was no stopping or controlling it.

Suzanne could not believe he was acting this way. She had never seen the tiniest hint of violence or anger in him before. But now as she lay on the floor still frozen in the spot where he had thrown her she feared him.

As he pulled his pants on he looked at her with hatred... "SO WHAT YOU ARE SAYING IS THAT I AM NO MORE THAN A GOOD PIECE OF ASS TO YOU...? YOU ONLY HUNG AROUND FOR THE SEX...? WELL YOU KNOW I HATE TO DISAPPOINT YOU ... YOU WANT SEX, I WILL GIVE YOU SEX... NEVER LET IT BE SAID THAT PAUL ANDREWS DOESN'T GIVE A WOMAN WHAT SHE WANTS... WHAT SHE DESERVES "...

Picking her up, he threw her onto the bed. She tried to get away, but the harder she fought, the harder he hung on to her. Every touch, kiss and caress had pain and anger in it. He wanted to hurt her, and hurt her bad. He wanted her to feel the pain she had inflicted on him. He wasn't making love to her he was punishing her for all the times she had hurt him.

After it was all over he fell to the floor by the bed and cried. Curled up in a ball he looked helpless it broke her heart. She knelt down beside him to hug him, to somehow make all the pain go away. Pushing her away, he didn't want her touching him, he didn't need her pity.

Paul needed to compose himself; he went to the bar and poured them both double shots straight up. He was past all the emotions he had gained control and could now talk to her calmly. As he handed her the drink there was a new calmness in his voice.... "THIS ISN'T ABOUT ME OR EVEN US ... IT IS ABOUT YOU AND YOUR NEED TO RUN WHEN PEOPLE GET TOO CLOSE."

Paul believed in his heart if he just loved her enough if he gave her enough room that she would get over it. That she would learn to trust him and allow herself to let him get close. What he never understood was that it was the loving of her that always made her run.

" IT IS THE LOVE THAT IS SCARING YOU ... IF I WAS THE KIND OF GUY TO USE YOU FOR SEX ALONE AND NEVER WANT ANYTHING ELSE WE WOULD NEVER BREAK UP..."

Paul wasn't that kind of guy and could never pretend he was. He needed the whole package not just the sex. It wasn't enough for Paul and it never would be. Suddenly he could see what Suzanne had been trying to tell him it would never work, she wasn't about to change her needs and neither could he...

"FORGIVE ME FOR TRYING TO LOVE YOU... YOU KNOW IF I WALK THROUGH THAT DOOR IT WILL BE DONE, THERE WILL BE NO COMING BACK AFTER AWHILE ... THIS WILL BE IT... "

Suzanne looked at him with coolness as she said ... "THIS IS HOW IT HAS TO BE ... I WILL MISS YOU ... "with that he walked out of her life forever. She knew he meant it just as he knew she meant it.

Chapter Fifteen

It took several drinks to get Suzanne to sleep that night. It wasn't breaking up with Paul that upset her; it was all the cruel but true things he said. Suzanne needed someone to talk to about it all. Unfortunately Paul was the only one she could think of to talk to.

That was the downside to all this she wasn't breaking up with her lover she was breaking up with her best friend. She had hoped there was some way of breaking up with Paul and still maintaining the friendship that she cherished so much.

Logically there was no way but she had hoped. She knew Paul loved her too much to simply be friends, he would never be able to handle things on that level.

It wasn't 'til early the next day that Suzanne realized the damage Paul had inflicted on her. She was covered with bruises, bites, hickeys and welts. Everything ached including her head. She hadn't realized how rough Paul had been; no matter how rough he had been it wasn't anything she hadn't deserved. Paul had every right to feel the way he had. She'd handled things badly.

Suzanne needed a shot of Rum for her coffee but she had finished it off the night before, she would have to settle for Gin. It seemed a reasonable substitute; it was more for the ache than the taste anyway.

The phone ringing startled her; she could not imagine who could be calling. It was even too early for emergency calls from the desk.

Paul spoke softly as though he were afraid she would hear him. He was sorry, he didn't mean to hurt her, he was embarrassed.

He had gotten her letter and had all night to think about what she was saying and how much he had missed while he was caught up in his own happiness. He had been completely blind to her needs. He had assumed that if he was happy she must be.

Deep down he knew it wasn't working but every time the thought crept up from his subconscious he pushed it back down. He knew he was trying to make her into what he wanted instead of loving who she was.

He had a quiet fear in his voice as he asked her to remain friends with him. There would be no strings or demands, she was his best friend and he didn't want to lose that. Paul was content to be a big brother, best friend or uncle what ever she wanted or needed he would be. Suzanne was relieved, friendship she was good at. They would meet for dinner at the hotel and discuss it further.

She would meet him in the dining room it wasn't right to have him in her room at this point. Suzanne wasn't sure if it was him or her she didn't trust alone. But she wasn't going to test it to find out.

As she hung up the phone she was feeling good, it was a relief to know that he was alright and that the friendship would survive. This way she could hang onto all the things about Paul she liked the best.

Sex wasn't important from Paul, she could get that anywhere, it was always around. Suzanne had thought for a long time that one nightstands would be better. She would never go out with any one guy more than twice. That would help her avoid all the traps of love and commitment.

Suzanne was feeling guilty; she had hurt first Ray and now Paul. She had to start being more careful of people's feelings of their attachments. She hated feeling this way; she hated the pain these men got in their eyes every time she had to leave.

If a guy showed even the slightest sign of attraction then she would steer clear, including the attentive Aaron Weinstein. It was clear he was a man she would have to stay away from. A tiny little voice way deep in the back of her mind wondered if her fascination with Aaron was why she had to suddenly cut Paul loose.

There was no doubt that she had thought about it. She was more than curious how he was in bed. This was not healthy thinking; this is what got her in trouble all the time. She had to quit thinking in this direction. Aaron had to be off the menu, she couldn't afford another disaster like the one she just had with Paul.

As Suzanne stood in front of the mirror she decided it was a turtleneck day. Middle of the summer and she was going to wear a turtleneck! Better to be too hot than to have anyone see what kind of shape she was in.

She had a sleeveless dress that had a turtleneck but it didn't cover the bruises on her arms. It took a lot of digging to finally find something respectable that covered most of the damage. As she got dressed she had to get to the kitchen to talk to Shelby, he would tell her the truth. She needed to talk to a friend that would not sit in judgement that would understand.

Suzanne spun a slow circle as she enquired if he could see any bruises, hickeys or marks of any kind. Shelby was puzzled as he told her he had to really look to see them. How could she have hickeys if she broke up with Paul? He was full of questions, how could he not be? He was completely puzzled and extremely concerned.

Suzanne dragged him into a back room where she took off her shirt. Shelby was horrified there was barely a speck of skin that wasn't marked. His advice to her was to throw someone in jail. Shelby sat in silence as she told him the entire story, every grizzly detail, every embarrassing moment. Shelby would normally never condone a beating to anyone however he could see why Paul would explode into a violent rage of frustration.

Suzanne fully understood Paul's reaction and believed she deserved it, it was time she got punished for all the pain and heartache she brought to so many especially Paul. If anything she felt better, somehow in her way of thinking it evened the score.

Shelby had heard it all, did he hear it right? Was she really meeting this man for dinner after the story she just told him? Suzanne knew she was playing with fire but her friendship to Paul was important and it would be important to her children.

Right up in her face, he had to tell her what he thought. SHE WAS TOTALLY NUTS!!... Paul was in love with her, friendship was not going to work. When there is enough passion to explode into rage that passion can't be simply set aside and left on a shelf.

Suzanne believed he was wrong, it was the love that would keep them friends. She had talked to Paul in length and she believed what he said to her. It was Aaron she was having trouble keeping on a friend level.

Shelby laughed out loud as he wished he had Suzanne's man problems. He would settle for her overflow. Suzanne was sick of it all he could have every one of them and welcome to them. She could easily live with no men in her life.

All Shelby would have to do was convince them to change their sexual orientation. As they laughed together Suzanne felt rejuvenated, it felt good to laugh, it had been far too long. She had almost forgotten how to turn her mouth upward.

Suzanne loved this guy and his silly jokes; no matter how down she was he could always put a smile on her face. Too bad all men weren't more like Shelby, the chef. But then, she would never have a date if they were. There were things about men she liked; she simply wanted those things in small short doses.

Suzanne swore Shelby to silence, he couldn't tell anyone she had broken up with Paul. She was worried about the pressure Aaron would put on her. What she worried about the most was if she could resist that pressure.

Paul would continue being around as a friend so no one would guess they were no longer sleeping together. It really was no one's business anyway. What Aaron didn't know wouldn't hurt her.

Suzanne was worried that Paul would notice she was dressed completely inappropriately for evening. She worried for nothing he didn't seem to notice or care what she was wearing, they were consumed in conversation. Her best friend was back.

Maybe they were meant to be friends in the first place; maybe they should have never had sex. Then she hated the idea of not having the great memories they shared and they did have great memories. Memories she was fond of recounting as she drifted off to sleep.

Paul's biggest concern was staying close to the kids, he didn't want them hurt. A tiny twinge of jealousy shot through her heart. She tried to convince herself she was wrong, he didn't only agree to remain friends to stay close to the kids.

He did care about her; it was more than the kids? She couldn't have been that wrong about him. Why did she always have to revert back to that little girl trying to get Daddy's attention?

Was Paul now the daddy that she didn't want to share? Did she break up with him because she didn't want to share him with the kids? Was that why she left Ray…because he loved the kids more? So much insecurity, so many questions, Suzanne hated when she was forced to face her eviler side.

She smiled politely, nodding as though everything was fine as she silently wrestled with her guilt and petty jealousies. There was no reason you couldn't stay close to the kids… there was no reason we couldn't all still get together for occasional weekends…

She could hear herself saying the words but even she didn't believe what she said. She hated that Paul was closer to the kids than she was. He loved the kids more than her; they loved him more than her. Couldn't someone love HER more? Was that selfish to want to be loved by someone, was that too much to want?

While Suzanne sat smiling politely and carrying on in polite conversation the spoiled child inside her was taking a tantrum, jumping up and down, yelling her head off, Suzanne used all her polite strength to ignore that child that she was sick of being controlled by.

Suzanne knew now, as she had never known before, something was wrong with her. She had the nicest guys in her life and she always treated them like crap. The nicer they were the worst she treated them.

What was it that kept them around? Why did they put up with her crap...? And she was full of crap. She would never have taken this kind of treatment from any of them, but then they were nice guys and she was the BITCH.

Paul kept his word; he never crossed the line of friendship. Once in a while she would catch him looking at her wishfully, but he never spoke the words or made the moves. She too found herself looking at him and thinking about what they were like in bed, the warmth, and the passion. What she missed most was the talking and laughing after sex.

Suzanne wasn't about to reopen that can of worms no matter how good the sex once was. It was important, she had to stay focused, and she had to continually remind herself why she broke up with him. Sometimes it took several reminders.

He was her best friend. Next to Shelby, he was her only friend. There were more acquaintances than she could count, but only two she came close to trusting and confiding in. That was more important than the best sex in the world and there was no doubt Paul was the best.

Suzanne had pretty much resigned herself to celibacy. She tried a few times, but somehow they all left her feeling cheap, like a piece of meat. It was the caring and respect that she missed. Without that, sex alone really wasn't satisfying.

Not only was it not satisfying, but it was degrading. Content to fill her life with friends, family and work. That would be enough; not forever but for now. The next time she climbed in bed with a man he would not only have to be in love with her, but she would have to know what she wanted and where she was going.

She still had an incredible allergy to commitment. It seemed to her she had become even colder about men since she began seeing Paul. There was a bad attitude about commitment and no respect for men at all. That fact was confirmed to her daily.

It amazed her how many rich powerful men were nothing more than fools and idiots. This fact was especially clear when it came to women. Everything was physical, about appearances. Ladies had to have tiny little bodies, blonde hair, and blue eyes and be as dumb as possible, before they would even look at them. Somehow a man couldn't feel like a man unless some lady batted her eyes and pretended to be helpless.

That was all it took for men to fall all over themselves trying to get close to them. Even Paul was guilty of this convenient blindness. This was a man that Suzanne once idolized for his intelligence and character. Yet he melted with the slightest of flirting. Men really hadn't evolved beyond cavemen and their animal passions.

It was the evening of Anna's sweet sixteen, and arrangements had been made for a small formal dinner for her, and a few of her best friends, including boys; not including sisters, brothers or family of any kind.

Suzanne was not completely senile. She hooked Paul into escorting and Shelby into chaperoning. Ray was upset with his ex wife, his little girl was far too young for such a grown up party, especially a grown up party in a hotel where drinking was all around them.

Suzanne flashed back to memories of their dating when she was a mere fifteen in the back seat of his car. She wondered how he planned to explain that she was pregnant at the same age. Ray sure hadn't thought sixteen was too young when he was getting what he wanted. Maybe that was Ray's problem.

Suzanne won the argument and the party was on, but then she always won. It wasn't worth fighting if it wasn't worth winning. Both Paul and Ray were infuriated at the way Suzanne had to always win. She didn't feel she necessarily won them all, they would get tired and give in. She always knew how to get her own way with men. Too bad she had never learned that with her mother.

She went down long enough to give Anna her birthday present. It was an antique locket and a charm bracelet, both engraved. Anna seemed both pleased and very grown up to Suzanne she had seen her little girl to maturity.

Anna blushed as she shyly pointed to the boy she had a crush on. Ray had forbidden her to date as long as she was in school but Suzanne thought that ruling a tad excessive and overboard. What he didn't know wouldn't hurt him. Suzanne saw no problem with them talking and stepping out together as long as they weren't alone in a car. Anna smiled and hugged her mother.

Suzanne loved being on the side of the good guy for a change. After giving her daughter a sweet kiss on the forehead, she bowed out gracefully and left her little girl in the hands of her two best friends. It almost killed her not to go back to the party and spy from some hiding place, but a deal is a deal.

Aaron came to her room to keep her company and have a few drinks with her. It amazed Suzanne that Aaron was still hanging in there after all the rejection she had given him. Every few months he would restate his offer, simply a reminder that it's still there. If she were to be honest she would have to admit to playing with the idea of sleeping with him.

If he didn't keep insisting on telling her he loved her, she would never have held out this long. Unfortunately she had the same problem with Aaron that she had with Paul... he wanted more than she was willing to give.

The next day after the party Paul took Anna to get her beginner's driving license. His birthday present to her would be driving lessons. It seemed beyond belief that she had a daughter old enough to drive a car. Once Anna got her license she could drive the kids to see her whenever they wanted.

Angel began highschool that year. It was a big change for her. She finally had friends and appeared to find a pack of friends that she fit in with. They went everywhere together. Suzanne was convinced they were the strangest bunch of misfits anyone had ever met.

The boys had hair down the middle of their backs, while some of the girls had their heads shaved in weird patterns. Many dyed their hair in bizarre colors redying every couple of days. And all of them wore baggy raggedy clothes making it difficult to tell the girls from the boys.

Suzanne forbid her daughter to come to the hotel unless she could dress with some sense of respectability and neatness. It wasn't that she didn't want to see her, or didn't love her. It wasn't even that she was ashamed of her daughter.

Angel had to understand it was not only her mother's home but also her career. Her image was vital, how Angel looked affected that image. Angel would just have to understand and if she couldn't then she would have to comply regardless.

Angel could dress the way she wanted when she was anywhere else, but at the hotel she would have to dress respectably. Every time Angel showed up it was a battle. Why couldn't she comb her hair and change her clothes before she came?

To Suzanne it didn't seem to be an unreasonable request? To Angel it was a declaration of war. A war she didn't intend to lose. Angel went out of her way to set Suzanne off and embarrass her at every opportunity.

Angel was turning sixteen and to celebrate it Suzanne agreed to a weekend at Paul's with the kids. It would be a weekend from Hell. It started out fairly normal, well as normal as Suzanne and the kids together at Paul's could be.

It started with a joint of marijuana found on the floor in the girl's room. It took Suzanne a blink of an eye to turn to Angel. It had to be Angel's no one else was capable of that sort of misbehavior. She was the only one that had the kind of friends that would be able to get that sort of thing.

Paul jumped immediately to Angel's defense; weird friends didn't necessarily mean drug use. There had to be some other explanation. Suzanne was right though, he couldn't imagine any of the other children being involved.

He couldn't think of any other explanation that Suzanne would buy. How could he help poor Angel when he too believed there was no other explanation? It was completely out of character for the other kids. It was Angel that was always making bad choices, trying to shock everyone.

Suzanne tried her hardest to be as calm as she could, they sat all the kids down, the plan was to not directly accuse Angel right off. The plan was to give her a chance to explain. That was how it all started out, at least for the first second or so.

As Paul requested Suzanne tried to give Angel every opportunity to explain, a full confession would be better... " YOU KNOW YOU BROUGHT THIS INTO THE HOUSE ... YOU AND YOUR LOWLIFE FRIENDS ARE ALL A BUNCH OF DOPERS ... I TOLD YOUR FATHER NOT TO LET YOU HANG OUT WITH THAT CROWD..."

Suzanne and Ray fought many times about Angel's choice of friends he never did stand up to her, whatever Angel wanted Angel got in Ray's eyes. She had been right out of control ever since she started hanging out with these kids. Suzanne didn't care what the other kids were doing she wouldn't tolerate this behavior from her daughter.

This wasn't fair to Paul, he had been good to children that weren't even his and now Angel brings drugs into his home showing no respect for him or his home. It was bad enough she had no respect for her mother but she was going to show Paul respect in his own home.

The first thing they had to do was stop all the bad influences. Now Ray would have to listen when she tells him Angel's friends are bad for her, all of them are likely to land in jail or worse someday soon. As far as Suzanne was concerned the sooner the better.

..."ALL THOSE ROTTEN FRIENDS YOU HANG OUT WITH... I DON'T CARE IF I HAVE TO HAVE THEM ALL ARRESTED...." Suzanne was on a roll and there was no stopping her. Even Paul couldn't get her under control. She was heading for disaster and had already said more than Angel would be able to forgive her for. There was no sharper tongue in the heat of anger; even Paul dreaded having to argue with her.

Suzanne was uncontrolled with her accusations and irrational attacks. Angel sat in silence through all of Suzanne's rantings, not saying a word. Dirty looks and evil glares shot from her eyes, but not a word was uttered not even in her own defense.

Angel had perfected the "DREADED" evil glare at a very young age. She was well aware of how far this glare would push Suzanne over the edge as it always pushed her over the edge of rational behavior.

Finally Angel spoke in a voice that was calm and cool enough to send chills through the strongest of hearts..." FOR YOUR INFORMATION, MOTHER!!... IT IS MY WEED ... I HAVE BEEN SMOKING FOR YEARS ... LONG BEFORE I MET ANY OF MY FRIENDS ... MOTHER! ...

Each word she spoke cut deeper, Suzanne could both hear and feel the venomous hatred that was designed to do nothing but hurt as much as possible..." AS A MATTER OF FACT I TAUGHT THEM HOW TO SMOKE ... NONE OF THEM DID DRUGS BEFORE ME ... THEY ARE NOT THE BAD INFLUENCE ... I AM!... YOUR LOVING LITTLE ANGEL IS THE BAD SEED ... BUT THEN YOU HAVE ALWAYS KNOWN THAT… HAVEN'T YOU MOTHER...? "

Suzanne was so red in the face angry that she forgot what happened when she lost control, she forgot the consequences of hitting in a fit of rage. For the first time since "THAT DAY! " She raised a hand in anger toward her daughter. Paul wasted no time grabbing her wrist, with a grip so tight it hurt. Angel was ready for battle she had been waiting for this her entire life...." GO AHEAD MOTHER HIT ME…! I WANT YOU TO... I WON'T EVEN HIT YOU BACK... YOU CAN PRETEND I AM A HELPLESS BABY...

This time she wasn't that helpless little girl that would run and hide. If her mother wanted to do battle then she would have one HELL of a battle...."THAT WILL MAKE IT BETTER FOR YOU... WON'T IT MOTHER...? WON'T IT GIVE YOU MORE PLEASURE?!... DO IT ... YOU HAVE WAITED FOR YEARS FOR A RESPECTABLE EXCUSE TO HIT ME AGAIN...NOW I GIVE IT TO YOU... DO IT... WHAT ARE YOU WAITING FOR!!?..."

Paul pushed his way in between them, telling Suzanne to go home. He couldn't defuse this unbearable situation until she left. He could drive the girl's home and talk to Ray. He would call her and fill her in, but he really needed her to just leave.

Suzanne was putting on her coat as she instructed Paul in a hysteria of fast forward instructions. Angel wasn't about to back down now. It had taken her a lifetime to stand up to her mother and now she had started she wasn't about to let her mother get off the hook.

..." GO AHEAD MOTHER, RUN ... WHEN YOU DON'T HIT YOU RUN ... WHY DON'T YOU JUST GO BACK TO SOME BAR AND POUR YOURSELF BACK INTO A BOTTLE?!..."

How was Paul ever going to put an end to this war? There had to be a way of making peace, of these two headstrong females forgiving each other. One thing was for sure Suzanne was an adult and Angel right or wrong would show her mother respect as long as she was in his home. Angel knew exactly how to fix this problem and fast. She bolted as fast as she could, out the door. Everyone yelling and begging for her to come back didn't slow her down.

Anna grabbed one set of keys and Paul grabbed another. Anna had to find her sister before she told anyone WHOSE drugs they really were. Angel had already taken the blame there would be no sense in both of them being in trouble. Besides who would believe her anyway?

Suzanne had no choice but to stay and be there if Angel came back on her own. Suzanne would have to call Ray and explain why the kids were so late. It was no surprise to Suzanne that Ray took Angel's side before he even heard what had happened. He didn't need to hear what had happened it was always Suzanne's fault.

Suzanne wasn't doing this. Why she had to explain anything to him he was going to believe what he wanted no matter what she said. Suzanne had to get off the phone; one of them may have been trying to call.

Suzanne knew it was wishful thinking, Angel wasn't about to call and if she did and heard Suzanne's voice she was likely to hang up. Suzanne was the last person Angel would call willingly. The lines were drawn; Angel hated her more than ever now.

It was just like Angel to be as dramatic as possible. She always did know how to get all the attention, how to make all the men in her life jump through hoops. Once again Suzanne was the bad guy, the monster, and everyone had to run to rescue Angel from the big bad monster.

Angel had been cruel, abusive and using drugs, yet somehow all that spun into Suzanne's fault. Where is the fairness in all this? Suzanne wasn't letting her get away with her dramatics this time. When they got Angel back, Suzanne was going to tell her about herself. She was due for at least a verbal lashing.

It seemed like only moments when Suzanne could hear Ray pounding on the door with the rage of a father protecting his poor helpless little girl. He was going to find her and when he did Suzanne would never get close enough to harm her ever again. Angel was more likely to come to her father, her protector.

All the anger that she couldn't vent on Angel she now vented on Ray. This wasn't her fault, it was his fault, he had always been too lenient. If he had supervised her choice of friends this would never have happened.

Suzanne wasn't stopping 'til she had said all she had to say. She had held a lot in over the years now was the time to get it all out. How dare he call himself a good father when he let his daughter wander around so slovenly, so completely ill mannered?

Angel had no respect for adults especially her mother and that was all Ray's fault, after all he was the one raising her why wasn't he doing it properly? If he didn't constantly criticize Suzanne in front of the kids they would have more respect for her.

Ray wasn't playing this game he had a daughter to find. He had no time for her tantrums. If the kids didn't respect her it was because she hadn't earned respect. Ray found it difficult to understand how Suzanne could expect to come first when it was Angel who was out on the street alone and probably scared.

Anna was the first to come back, no Angel ... she needed gas money if she was going to keep looking. Paul stopped at a payphone to see if

Angel was back. He was getting worried maybe it was time to call the police. They would wait a little longer to see if Ray found her.

Suzanne was sure she was simply attention getting and there was no sense giving her that attention. She was sick of Angel's dramatic prima donna act. What would they ever do to stop this pattern, Angel gets the attention and Suzanne is the bad guy every time.

Paul drove toward his building as he had an idea where she may be. He drove to the back of the building and parked, then he got out to walk, needing to look more closely. He needed to check all the dark little corners someone as helpless and tiny as Angel could crawl into. Dark corners were Angel's specialty. Somehow they provided her with a feeling of safety, hidden and protected as only dark corners can do.

Curled up in a tight ball she trembled with helplessness. Angel's body shook as she tried to hold back the sobs that could only spill out into a flood of heartache. Paul, good suit and all got down on the ground beside her and attempted to comfort her by holding her in his arms.

As he held her he began to cry with her, his heart broke with the pain this child had to live all her life. He continued to rock and hold her amidst the dirt and the darkness. He had promised to protect her and keep her safe. He had failed both her and himself.

He had many clients on drugs, but never anyone he loved or cared about. He was filled with feelings of guilt and helplessness as she told him to give up on her. She wasn't worth his effort she had been bad all her life, only ever caused trouble everywhere she went. He was too blind to see that she was nothing but trouble as he had always been blind to Suzanne.

She was her mother's daughter; they were two of a kind. Angel was sure to disappoint him and break his heart just as her mother had. It was clear to Angel he just wasn't capable of seeing the true evil that hid deep in a person's soul.

Paul tried his hardest to hold back the lump of tears welling in his throat as he spoke. She was wrong. Angel may be a lot like her mother, but like her mother she was special. She had always been special.

As she looked up at him and stared into his eyes she broke his heart. He had a close up view of the pain she both felt and lived. Her eyes were a mirror to her soul a tortured and tormented soul. The soul of a little girl lost in pain and heartache.

Paul could not take his eyes away from the trance that held them... "IF I AM SO SPECIAL THEN WHY DOES MY OWN MOTHER HATE ME?... SHE HAS ALWAYS HATED ME AND YOU KNOW IT ... I CAN FEEL IT EVERY TIME SHE LOOKS AT ME..."

That was all she could say for the sobs choked any other words that might have been spoken. By this time she cried so hard she began to dry heave, if she couldn't cry the pain out she would wrench it out.

Paul was completely helpless, he didn't know what to do other than hold her and be there for her. Angel lay in his arms in an exhausted silence as he picked her up and carried her home.

Both of them had tear stained faces as they went through the door. Ray and Suzanne ran to the door to meet them in a whirlwind of chaos, yelling and crying. Angel buried her face in Paul's chest; she'd had enough and couldn't deal with any more.

Paul pushed past both of them laying Angel on the couch. He gently covered her and then kissed her on the forehead as he whispered that he would take care of her. Angel looked so tiny and helpless, how could he not feel the need to protect her.

Paul grabbed Suzanne by the arm firm enough she had no choice but to follow him to the kitchen. Ray wasted no time following along, Paul was right Suzanne had caused all this and she needed to be put in her place.

Paul had no intentions of discussing who's fault it may or may not have been, as far as he was concerned they were both equally responsible for this mess. There was only one answer; he called Dr. Anderson who suggested a psych ward at the hospital specializing in teens with problems.

Suzanne was the first to open her mouth. Her daughter wasn't going, Angel wasn't crazy she was simply spoiled and they could deal with that alone. There was no reason to put her in a nut house. Angel was doing what Angel always does...ATTENTION SEEKING!...

Suzanne taking her stand instantly made Ray Paul's ally. They both turned and looked at Suzanne like she was the one that was crazy. Paul grabbed her by the shoulders, Suzanne had about enough of his man handling her and he could stop instantly. She wasn't his property to push around.

Looking Suzanne square in the eyes Paul asked her where she had been for Angel's entire life. Not only was she stuck at the emotional level of a five-year-old, but she was filled with more scars and fears than any adult should have to carry around.

Suzanne had her head in the sand long enough and it was time she took a good hard look at her daughter and start facing the real world that she lives in. The longer they make excuses and hide from what is really going on the harder it would be to help Angel.

Paul could not believe how much they had forgotten or chose not to remember at all. It was as though Angel had become invisible or perhaps an unwanted dream. Paul stared Ray straight in the eyes as he asked him how many nights he had sat up holding Angel, trying to comfort her past some nightmare. Why does she at sixteen years old still need a sister to sit in the bathroom and talk to her while she takes her bath?... "SHE DOES NEED HELP!... SHE NEEDS IT NOW...."

Suzanne had to dig deep past her stubborn pride to the reality that only her heart could accept. The truth was that Angel was unstable and needed help. More help than a few sessions in an office. More help than either her or Ray could give even if they knew how. It was pretty obvious that no one within the family was going to save her.

In accepting the truth, she then had to accept blame and responsibility. She had to face the guilt she had hidden from for years. She "WAS "the reason for her daughter's nightmares as her mother was the cause of hers. She had become her mother, made the same mistakes. It was a truth that hurt Suzanne more than any beating her mother had ever given her. It was a sharp edged truth that cut deep into her heart.

As much as she hated Angel talking to her the way she had everything Angel said was true. It was a harsh truth maybe, but truth none the less. Angel always could see through her mother. Remind her of every short coming and every mistake.

Suzanne was forced to face the realities she was an expert at avoiding. One more thing Angel was right about, Suzanne did always run when things got uncomfortable. Suzanne never forced herself to deal with anything; not her mother, her husband, lovers, life, marriage or even children, none of it, nothing that took emotions to handle. Suzanne did not like to feel.

That's why she hid from her life at work. At work she could be an efficient robot, no feelings, no emotions ... just get the job done. That was why she dated only strangers and kept Paul as far away as he would allow.

Paul described to them how he found Angel, where she was, what she looked like and everything she said. Suzanne looked at Paul in pain and disbelief. She didn't understand why Angel hated her so much. Why did Angel insist on continuing to punish her for one mistake so many years ago?

Suzanne hadn't hit Angel since she was little. She'd stopped, so why did she still hate and fear her. In Suzanne's eyes she had always been there for her; had given her everything she ever wanted... or was it everything she wanted for Angel.

Ray interrupted her, he had to tell her she gave her daughter nothing except the pain and heartache of being raised by a mother that couldn't stand her. Suzanne never gave she only took. She took from Ray and she took from Paul.

As for the kids, the only time she was ever with them was when it was convenient, when she needed to pretend to be a family. Even then she didn't give; she took all their love and sent them back till she needed them again.

Suzanne couldn't talk, she couldn't think..." IT WASN'T TRUE...
IT WASN'T! "She gave all the time, there were lots of times she was
with the kids when she didn't want to be. In her heart she believed
every word she said.

Now it was Paul's turn to take a strip off Suzanne's already pealing
veneer, he agreed with Ray completely. When things didn't go Suzanne's
way or there was the tiniest bit of tension, any demands on Suzanne
and that would be it.

There would be Suzanne running back to her safe secure hotel
where she could bury her head in the sand and hide from the rest of
the world. Suzanne needed to know people loved her but never felt the
need to give any love back.

Why were they talking about her it was Angel with the problem.
The subject needed to be changed and now. Ray and Paul were both
shocked that Suzanne couldn't see it was the same subject.

Why did she think Angel was such a wreck? Maybe because no
matter what Angel did her mother still pushed her away, pushed
everyone away. The only reason it was easy for her to love Alice and
R.J. was because they never asked or expected love back never made
demands.

Paul was on a roll. Since he had opened this can of worms he was
not going to stop until he said it all. He told her she pushed everyone
away. As soon as someone loved her and expected to be loved back, she
ran as far and as fast as she could.

Suzanne had no problem with people loving her, as long as they
didn't want love back... " THAT IS ANGEL'S PROBLEM, SHE
EXPECTS YOU TO LOVE HER BACK, SUZANNE YOU NEVER
DO ... THE TWO OF YOU ARE THE SAME, YOU BOTH CAN
TAKE ALL THE LOVE YOU CAN GET ... UNFORTUNATELY
SOMEONE HAS TO STOP AND GIVE BACK ... YOU CAN'T
ONLY TAKE, YOU HAVE TO LOVE BACK..."

Paul couldn't stop this was all too important, he had held it in far
too long. He went on to say that he thought that perhaps Angel could

have survived everything, the abuse the hitting even the rats... if only Suzanne could have shown the tiniest bit of love.

Suzanne couldn't stand it, she had to get out, she needed a drink, she needed to get away, she didn't want to think, it wasn't true, none of it. Paul was bitter because she broke up with him. She didn't understand why was he doing this? Was it revenge, was he bitter because she wouldn't commit to him and now he had to hurt her.

What did he know? He didn't have any kids. He didn't know how much they can break a heart or disappoint a parent. They didn't know how heart broken she was inside. She loved; if she didn't, how could she be so broken hearted right now?

Out the door and gone, there was no way Suzanne was going to hang around for this abuse. She wasn't more than a block down the road when she pulled the car over to the shoulder of the road. She had a bottle of gin in the glove box. She needed it and she needed it now. She couldn't wait until she got home. Her hands were shaking so hard she could hardly grip the cap firm enough to get it open.

As she felt it warm her throat, she thought she deserved this drink after what they put her through. Suzanne felt, the whole world was against her. She looked down to see her hands were still trembling.

She had to get home. Everything would be all right once she got home. One thing Paul was right about, she was safe at the hotel. People liked her there; no one felt the need to attack her every time she turned around.

It only made sense that anyone would want to be where they felt safe and secure. She was no different than anyone else. Even Paul and Ray had their own hiding places, hadn't Ray spent years in a bottle and Paul in a loveless marriage?

Back at her room, totally drained and exhausted, Suzanne wanted to sleep. She could think about all this tomorrow. Tomorrow she would go and talk to Angel when she was fresh and calm.

She poured herself a drink and used it to wash down a sleeping pill. She had to clear her head. If she could get to sleep everything would work out. She simply wanted to drift into empty darkness where time could pass without her.

Sleep wasn't coming, so she poured another drink and took another pill, surely two would work. Finally she drifted off, not a deep dark sleep but a fretful sleep. It wasn't long before she was in middle of one of her night terrors.

In total blackness, one by one, the people in her life were walking up to her and telling her they hated her. First her mother, then her father, the kids, and Paul, then Ray and Bev were there. As each one came they stood around her screaming at her that they hated her. She tried to run but they followed.

No matter how fast she ran they were still there screaming at her. It got louder and louder until she thought her head was going to explode. Forcing herself awake, her nightgown was soaked with perspiration causing her to fall into uncontrolled shakes. As she shook she couldn't catch her breath.

Suzanne flew out of bed still half-asleep; she had to escape the nightmare she was trapped in. She went to the bar and with trembling hands poured herself a needed drink. As she poured it down her throat she didn't even take the time to taste it.

She knew what she needed; she needed to fall into a deep dark sleep. Deep enough and dark enough she could hide from the nightmares. Sleeping pills, they had been slipped to her from a friend that thought she looked over worked. The big bags that had now permanently taken up residence under her eyes were likely the first clue.

If one didn't work alone then she should take at least two together. She had to sleep she was so tired. She had to find a way of getting past the fear of her nightmares. She simply couldn't stand another.

Suzanne could hear a distant ring of the phone, it seemed so far away. Was it part of her dreams, everything was so fuzzy? All she wanted was to let herself drift into the now safer darkness of sleep.

Paul drove to Suzanne's as quick as he could, why wasn't she answering the phone. The receptionist told him she was there she had gone to her room as soon as she arrived back at the hotel. Why wasn't she answering the phone?! Everyone knew she was a light sleeper.

It was a little past midnight when Paul entered Suzanne's room. He expected to find her very drunk and had prepared himself for her drunken wrath. He had to tell her about Angel. Drunk or not she needed to know her daughter had been checked into a psychiatric ward at the hospital.

The room reeked of booze; there was an empty bottle in the living-room and another in the bedroom. How could she have gotten so drunk so fast? He went to the bed where she was passed out, determined to shake her out of her stupor.

She wasn't hiding from this; there was no escape from this not even in a bottle. It was rare these days for her to get to sleep with out the assistance of her best friend the bottle or sometimes she had several friends to keep her from her nightmares.

Something was wrong; this wasn't the same drunken stupor he had found her in many times in the past. Her skin was cold and clammy and she was scarcely breathing. It only took moments for Paul to see the almost empty bottle of pills by the empty bottle of rum.

..." DAMN YOU SUZANNE!... Paul continued to shake her as he screamed at her...."WHY DON'T YOU KNOW PEOPLE LOVE YOU...? IF YOU DIE, ANGEL WILL NEVER HAVE ANY PEACE ... HOW CAN YOU DO TO YOUR CHILDREN WHAT YOUR MOTHER DID TO YOU? ... HOW MANY TIMES HAVE YOU CRIED OVER YOUR MOTHER'S SUICIDE?...DAMN YOU!... DAMN YOU TO HELL!..."

Paul picked her up into his arms and carried her as though she were his baby. Tears streamed down his face as he gently kissed her cheek and forehead begging her not to die. She was leaving too much unfinished and Paul was not allowing it.

Paul broke every record trying to get Suzanne to the hospital. By this time her breathing was so shallow he couldn't see her chest move even the slightest. He whispered prayers as he tried to wipe away his tears to see.

Hysterical by the time he reached the emergency room he scooped her once again into his arms and screamed his way through the doors. It was only moments before the staff surrounded him and took her out of his arms.

They worked frantically with Paul screaming his story out over their shouts of orders he could never understand. He could hear a voice screaming...what did she take?!... We have to know what we are dealing with... What did she take?...

Paul reached into his pocket and pulled out the remains of the bottle by Suzanne's bed, thankful he had the sense to grab it. He had no idea how many pills were taken but he had no doubt there was a lot of booze involved. She had a long history of unstable addictive behavior.

Paul stood frozen as they rushed her off still working on her as they ran down the hall. Paul slumped into a chair unable to believe the last few moments. Still unable to understand how she could do this to all of them. To Paul suicide was the most selfish of all acts.

Paul stared at his watch if he hurried he could still catch Ray and Doctor Anderson in the psychiatric ward with Angel. It wasn't that long since he left there. He dreaded having to tell them this. They all have been through enough for one night, for one lifetime.

As he walked down the hall he could see them talking at the nursing station, he could tell right off they had read the worry on his face before he even got to them. Falling completely apart, he couldn't get the words out. Trying to tell them he brought Suzanne in without having to actually say the words. He couldn't say them; the words wouldn't cross his lips.

Doctor Anderson could read his pain; a gentle smile was enough to show him she understood. Ray walked away not saying a word, he didn't care and didn't want to hear. This was just another example of Suzanne turning things around to be about her, so she was the center of attention once again. He had enough of Suzanne and her selfish dramatics. The panic wasn't about any of his kids that was all he needed to hear.

Doctor Anderson led Paul into a private room where they could talk. Where he could calm down and get the entire story out. Things weren't as bad as they seemed, after checking with the doctors at emerge she could reassure him Suzanne would be fine.

Suzanne needed extensive detox and counseling. Maybe it would be good she was here now Angel and Suzanne could be counseled together. Doctor Anderson would now have a better chance at bringing them together, helping them get past their pain.

Arrangements were made for Suzanne to be admitted to the psychiatric ward. She would be on a different wing from Angel. Suzanne argued this was not what she needed right now, she was not suicidal. She was simply trying to get to sleep and lost track of how many pills she had taken.

Doctor Anderson was trying to smooth the waters trying to get Suzanne to accept this with as little fight as possible. The fact that she had to take booze and pills to sleep should have been enough to convince her she needed help.

It didn't matter if she accepted this or not she was brought in as a possible suicide and that was illegal. She would have to submit to a period of assessment, while Doctor Anderson ascertained how unstable she was. Suzanne needed to understand that if Paul hadn't come, there was no doubt she would be dead.

The next day Suzanne sat in Doctor Anderson's office consumed with a combination of resentment and shame. She was embarrassed but she was also angry. She wasn't a crazy person that needed to be locked up.

She felt like a naughty schoolgirl waiting for the principle to chastise her. How was she going to convince everyone she was not suicidal, she had simply screwed up how many pills she had taken while under a lot of stress. It was perfectly understandable, to her anyway.

The good Doctor was masked in cool professionalism as she greeted Suzanne. Not even blinking there was no doubt she was the queen of poker faces. Suzanne might as well have told her about the weather. Suzanne continued telling the story of that night and where it all began.

..." WE CONFRONTED ANGEL WITH IT ... ALL HELL BROKE LOOSE ... ANGEL RAN OUT THE DOOR ... PAUL AND ANNA WENT TO FIND HER ... I CALLED RAY AND WAITED IN CASE SHE CAME BACK OR CALLED..."

Why wasn't the doctor interacting? Why was she just sitting there stone faced? Suzanne silently ran everything she had just said through her mind in a fast forward reassessment. She was sure there was nothing wrong with anything she was saying so why did she feel like the Doctor was sitting in judgement of her?

Suzanne went on with the rest of the story trying hard not to elaborate or add any more than she had to. Trying to make it all seem lighter than and not as dramatic as it was at the time. She was trying her hardest to take all the emotions out of the night.

..." I WAS EXTREMELY TIRED AFTER ALL THE FIGHTING WITH RAY, PAUL AND ANGEL ... IT WAS A HUGE EMOTIONAL DRAIN ... I NEEDED TO SLEEP, A DEEP SLEEP WITH NO NIGHTMARES, SO I TOOK A SLEEPING PILL THEN HAD A DRINK WAITING FOR IT TO WORK ... WHEN IT DIDN'T WORK I TOOK ANOTHER...

Everything started to blur after that but she wasn't about to admit that to the good doctor, she was already looking at her as though she were completely crazy. Suzanne had to be careful what she said and how she said it or she would never get out and back to the nice safe world she had built for herself. The only thing she knew for sure was that she had to get out. She cursed Paul over and over again for getting her into this mess.

"...I FINALLY GOT TO SLEEP BUT I HAD A NIGHT TERROR SO I HAD TO FORCE MYSELF AWAKE ... I THOUGHT IF I TOOK ENOUGH PILLS I COULD GET INTO A DEEPER SLEEP... DEEP ENOUGH THAT I WOULDN'T HAVE THE NIGHTMARES ... I JUST WANTED TO SLEEP...THERE WAS

NO THOUGHTS OF ENDING MY LIFE...WHY WOULD I DO THAT I LOVE MY LIFE..."

There was a long endless silence as Suzanne waited for the doctor to speak. She was done her story why was there no comment? Suzanne had decided the silence this Doctor was making her endure was specifically to unhinge her.

Another of the doctors tricks to push her as far over the emotional edge as possible. It wasn't going to work, Suzanne's emotions were private and they were staying private. This full of herself doctor wasn't seeing any of them.

..." SUZANNE YOU SOUND SO CASUAL ABOUT THE ENTIRE NIGHT. AS THOUGH IT WERE A NORMAL DAY ON THE HOME FRONT. YET YOU ENDED UP ALMOST DYING AND YOUR DAUGHTER WAS CHECKED INTO A PSYCHIATRIC WARD ... DO YOU THINK MAYBE IT IS TIME YOU STARTED DEALING WITH YOUR LIFE AND ALL THE ISSUES THAT GOT YOU HERE..."

It was yet another long pause to reflect, no doubt. Suzanne was tired of these long pauses designed only to make her squirm. As with her mother while saying what she didn't want to hear, she drifted her mind off into another place.

She vaguely caught pieces of the unwanted lecture... She was a snowball, her life was an avalanche ready to crush her...ya ya ya. Does she really think Suzanne doesn't know what a mess her life is in? How could she not know she was living it?

Suzanne drifted back to catch the tail end of the conversation... What is that?.. Wait a minute?... " ... SUZANNE YOU MAY HAVE A DIFFERENT HIDING PLACE BUT YOU AND ANGEL ARE BOTH HIDERS...ANGEL HIDES IN THE CLOSET AND YOU HIDE IN THE HOTEL OR IN A BOTTLE... HIDE FROM THE WORLD, KEEP EVERYONE OUT... THEN YOU CAN'T BE HURT...."

Suzanne sat dumbfounded how she could make such a wild judgement. Who was she to think she knew Suzanne well enough to analyze her entire life. No one knew her well enough to crawl into her head that way.

..." THAT IS NOT TRUE, I HAVE A LOT OF PEOPLE IN MY LIFE, MORE THAN MOST ... I AM SURROUNDED BY PEOPLE AT ALL TIMES, I RARELY GET TIME ALONE... BETWEEN PAUL, AARON AND THE KIDS, NOT TO MENTION RAY ... I AM SURROUNDED AND SMOTHERED AT EVERY TURN... I CAN'T GET RID OF THEM EVEN WHEN I TRY..."

Why was she harping on this, none of it was her business. None of it had anything to do with what was going on. Suzanne was sick of all this, sick of playing her games; sick of being talked to like she was a child out of control. She was not the child out of control, Angel was.

All she wanted to know was when she could get out of there. Suzanne had decided she would let her ramble on just a little longer then she would convince her all was well and she would be a good girl from now on.

..." THIRTY DAYS!... I CAN'T STAY THIRTY DAYS ... I HAVE A JOB AND A LIFE TO GET ON WITH..." It didn't matter what Suzanne said the doctor had already made her mind up. Suzanne protested as stern and controlled as she could but it wasn't making a bit of difference. It was law a thirty day assessment for suicides..." BUT I AM NOT A SUICIDE..."

Suzanne got up to leave, and not soon enough when the doctor called her back. One last jab of the knife no doubt...." AREN'T YOU EVEN THE TINIEST BIT CURIOUS ABOUT ANGEL?..."

Chapter Sixteen

Suzanne walked back to her room still feeling the dazed effect from the night before, or perhaps they gave her something to keep her calm. That would explain why she didn't hit the doctor in the head after that last jab.

It was true though she hadn't given Angel a moments thought. Why was that? She should have been worried? It should have been the first question out of her mouth.

Suzanne lied to herself. She always lied to herself, consoling that she was still fuzzy from all the drugs. If they hadn't drugged her, she would have asked about Angel. This Doctor had her so distraught how could she possibly be expected to think straight? Of course she was worried about Angel even if she didn't say the words.

She really wasn't that selfish bitch they all claim. She is a good mother and she does love all her children, including Angel. Just because they can't see it, doesn't mean she doesn't feel it. Suzanne began having trouble focusing, everything was so fuzzy. That was it, she was sure they must have given her something.

One thing she would have to do was call Paul or Aaron to bring her proper clothes, slippers a robe perhaps a little makeup. She hated those paper slippers the hospital was making her shuffle around in. Maybe she would have a little sleep first.

She had to clear the cobwebs out of her head. It wouldn't do for her to sound fuzzy and out of control to the rest of the world. She had to convince them all that it was Paul and the Doctor who blew a simple situation into something far bigger than it needed to be. Her friends would believe her as soon as she told them all the truth.

Her room was plain and boring. Everything was either gray or white. There were no extras, not even a mirror or a clock. The only thing in her room was a small white dresser, a small bed made with starched white sheets and a white too thin thing doing an impersonation of a blanket.

Beside the bed there was a hard uncomfortable wooden chair. There weren't even curtains to open or close. The morning sun was going to kill her; she was used to sleeping away the morning hours.

It seemed sleeping would be the only thing to do in this place. That is except for her daily sessions with the brilliant doctor Anderson who would do all she could to keep Suzanne on edge as much as possible. How she did like to make Suzanne cry.

The only thing she wanted was deep dark sleep and that would be impossible in this bright sterile environment. Suzanne lay on the bed praying for sleep to overtake her. What she really prayed for was for it to overtake her minus the nightmares.

When she woke she saw Shelby grinning down at her, a face she was very happy to see. She flew into his arms needing a strong hug from someone who would care about her. He commented on what a mess she had gotten herself into. He wanted to comfort her, to tell her it was all right. He couldn't, for the first time since he had met her he was very upset, suicide was never the answer. She should know better.

He had tried suicide many times himself, when he was younger before he accepted his homosexuality. It always made things worse, causing no end of grief and heartache to everyone in his life.

Once again she said the words..." I WASN'T TRYING TO COMMIT SUICIDE!.." She thought that if anyone, Shelby wouldn't believe she was capable of committing such a weak act. Did she seem like the hopeless type? She simply lost track of how many pills she had taken because she was too distraught over how cruel everyone had been to her.

He near hugged the life out of her, relieved that she wasn't going to depart from the earth none too soon. She was the only one who understood him. She was more than that, she was his best friend.

Shelby explained how Aaron was on his way; however he's so homophobic that he didn't want to be seen in the same car as Shelby. Certainly couldn't have the world thinking they were out on a date.

Suzanne joined Shelby in a good laugh as they made jokes about the uptight Aaron. Suzanne needed a laugh; it helped to lift the tension. Shelby suggested Suzanne should jump his bones so Aaron would not have to be so insecure about his manhood.

That was all Suzanne needed, like she didn't already make enough man trouble in her life. Besides she was sure Aaron had no problem getting anything he wanted anytime he wanted. It wasn't likely he was a virgin, that revelation put them into stitches once again.

Suzanne enjoyed laughing with Shelby, so much so that she almost forgot where she was and why. They were still laughing as Aaron walked through the door. His walking in the room made them laugh even harder, confusing Aaron who expected to find them lost in sadness.

Yet again Suzanne found herself explaining..." I AM NOT SUICIDAL!.." It was strange but she was fine, it was as though the storm had hit hard and now it passed or maybe she was in the eye of the hurricane. Whatever it was, she was at peace for this moment and this was the moment she was living and the only moment that counted.

He was relieved she was all right but near fell off his chair that she had to stay thirty days. That meant he would have to run things himself, he hated the two days she had off for her father's funeral.

Suzanne told him to lean on Glenda, she couldn't do the accounting or bookkeeping but she had good people skills and could smooth the roughest of waters. Shelby promised to do his share...no meltdowns till after Suzanne got back.

It would work Glenda could handle the politics while Aaron did all the paperwork. She reminded him that she would be back and he had better not do such a good job that he didn't need her anymore.

In her mind she felt safe. She purposely picked Glenda, knowing she could do only half the job. She may be in a nut house but she wasn't crazy. One of her morals in life, besides keep everyone at a safe distance was..." WATCH YOUR BACK!.."

It wouldn't be the first time some conniving female tried to take her job. There were even a few who tried to hit on Aaron, he mostly seemed disgusted by girls who were obviously climbing to the top with a mattress strapped to their back.

A fling was all right if it was behind closed doors and he was making all the advances but he had no use for deals or tramps. He believed there was no excitement without chase that was why he was so excited about Suzanne she was all chase.

Suzanne couldn't help but wonder if she ever gave in to his advances, would he loose interest and respect along with it. She always said no, it would make things very uncomfortable at work when she felt crowded and was ready to end it.

The hotel was her home and she didn't want to be in a position of being uncomfortable at work, or even worse, fired. Besides she was enjoying the friendship a friendship she didn't want to loose. She was not making the same mistake she made with Paul. Suzanne couldn't afford to lose anymore friends.

Alone at last, finally they left. She enjoyed the visit but she needed time alone. She was feeling guilty for not being more concerned about Angel. She wanted to go down to her wing and see if she could see her.

Angel was sound asleep Suzanne sat by her bed watching her, she seemed so peaceful. Suzanne had never seen Angel sleeping so still and peaceful. She wondered if it were a natural sleep or the deep sleep of the sedated.

She looked so little and helpless, Paul was right; she was still like a five-year-old. Curled up and sucking her thumb, for the first time in a long time Suzanne was seeing Angel, really seeing her. She cursed herself for not looking at her before. Why had she never seen this little girl before?

Suzanne sat quietly watching her baby sleep. Angel wasn't peaceful for long, she began thrashing and turning first ever so slightly. Before Suzanne could think of what to do Angel sat up sound asleep and screamed. It was a scream that cut her through to her heart; it was the scream of absolute terror.

Laying back down she began swinging her arms wildly as though she was fighting the fight of her life. Suzanne crawled into the bed beside her and held onto her. It was now her job to comfort her little Angel. None of her knights were there to save her. How ironic that it was likely Suzanne who gave her the nightmares and now she had to be the one to save her daughter from them.

Suzanne had always known of Angel's night terrors but it was Paul and Ray who actually dealt with them. Angel felt safer with men, at least that was what she told herself, in reality she never believed she really had any. Suzanne had always thought she was attention seeking.

Suzanne wrapped herself around Angel holding even tighter quietly whispering begs for forgiveness. Tears streamed down Suzanne's face as she held and rocked the baby she had turned her back to years before. How could she have been such a rotten mother?

They were right, they were all right. Everything they had said rang through her head like a broken record... she was the most selfish person on the planet...she was a terrible person and an even worse mother.

While holding and rocking her baby, Suzanne for the first time since she gave birth to her daughter felt connected. It was a connection she liked. Angel began snuggling in close, holding onto her mother so tight that Suzanne thought she would squeeze the life out of her.

Suzanne whispered into her ear words of comfort and reassurance... "SHSHSH... IT'S O.K. BABY, MOMMY IS HERE ... I'LL HELP YOU THROUGH THIS ... I DO LOVE YOU ANGEL ... I ALWAYS HAVE ... I JUST NEVER KNEW HOW TO SHOW YOU... I DO NOT KNOW HOW TO HELP YOU...PLEASE BABY...PLEASE BELIEVE ME..."

As fast as Angel began waking out of her sleep, she was jumping out of bed and slapping at her mother. It broke Suzanne's heart as

Angel screamed at her..." NEVER TOUCH ME LIKE THAT AGAIN, NEVER!!..."

She had no right to pretend she was a loving mother. Suzanne hadn't held or loved Angel her entire life and she didn't need to start now, sure her mother was simply trying to put on a good show for the staff...

"DO YOU REALLY THINK THEY WILL LET YOU OUT EARLY IF YOU PRETEND TO BE A LOVING CONCERNED MOTHER...I KNOW YOU... YOU CAN'T TRICK ME... I KNOW WHAT KIND OF MOTHER YOU ARE!..."

Suzanne ran from the room crying, running right into Ray and Bev as they came to the door. Ray demanded to know what was going on. He ordered Suzanne to stay away from his daughter she had hurt their family enough. He was putting his foot down and Suzanne would obey.

..." SHE IS MY DAUGHTER TOO... YOU WON'T KEEP ME FROM HER ...I AM LEAVING NOW BUT I WILL BE BACK AS MANY TIMES AS IT TAKES FOR ANGEL TO BELIEVE I LOVE HER..."

As Suzanne marched off she could hear Ray still yelling at her. He wasn't saying anything she didn't already know in her heart. She had never been a mother to Angel. But it wasn't too late, she could still be her mother all she needed was a chance to make things right.

When she returned to her room someone had left a huge stack of paper and a pen. Well... Dr. Anderson wasn't wasting any time, the question wasn't when to start but where to start. The instructions on the sheet were to make lists and comments about men that touched her life. Suzanne was pretty sure the doctor had no life of her own so she could only get excitement by peaking into Suzanne's. The next question was whether to shock or be puritanical.

She was fairly sure the doctor wouldn't buy puritanical, maybe split the difference... made mistakes but not a total tramp, which would work. Besides it wasn't too far from the truth. The first on the list was Ray... no lies so far, he was the first.

What could she say about Ray? They were very young; she thought she was in love. Ray was everything, her protector, her knight. He saved her from her childhood. He did everything he could to keep her from growing up but they out grew each other anyway.

Suzanne wanted to leave William off the list in her mind he didn't exist and never did. Besides he was none of the doctors business it had nothing to do with what was going on now. She was already far too aware of the mistake she made in allowing him to get too close. She didn't need the doctor to tell her what she already told herself many times over the years.

Paul... she had to be very careful what she said about Paul. The doctor preached confidentiality however Paul had been friends with the doctor for years. Suzanne could not convince herself that the doctor wouldn't let things slip.

Suzanne began to write, she wrote what she thought the doctor would want to hear. She wrote what she thought the doctor would buy. I WILL ALWAYS LOVE PAUL IN MANY WAYS. HE BROUGHT ME FROM BEING A LITTLE GIRL TO A WOMAN... HE HAS LOVED ME AND TAKEN ALL MY CRAP FOR MANY YEARS I HAVE MANY TIMES TRIED TO TELL HIM TO MOVE ON AND FIND SOMEONE WHO WILL BE THE WOMAN HE WANTS. WE ALWAYS BROKE UP FOR THE SAME REASON ... HE WANTS WHAT I CAN'T GIVE... HE WANTS TO MAKE ME INTO SOMETHING AND SOMEONE I AM NOT...

Suzanne read the instructions again...THE MEN IN MY LIFE?... What did that mean? Did it include friends, bosses, and casual acquaintances? What did it include? She decided she would add Shelby as her best friend and Aaron as her boss. It would impress Doctor Anderson that she was capable of having a platonic relationship; she did have people in her life who cared about her as she cared about them.

That brought her to guys like Steve, Dave, Dan, Rob and one or two that she could barely remember after her drunken stupor. Did she really need to hear about every one-night stand? Maybe if she cut it down to two that would be reasonable.

When she finally finished her version of the list, she reread it several times trying to see it through the doctor's eyes. Good or bad it was done and hopefully it does more good than harm.

Suzanne went into the washroom to freshen up; when she came back into the room Paul was holding her papers. She ripped them out of his hand as she screamed at him. How dare he, it was none of his business.

He laughed at her as though she could have any secrets from him. He did however find it interesting why they broke up. He was sure that Doctor Anderson was never going to buy any of the crap Suzanne was trying to feed her.

Suzanne wasn't taking any of this, with all the indignance she could muster up she demanded to know what he was talking about. Paul told her he knew the truth and Dr. Anderson wasn't about to believe in fairy tales either.

Paul could see she was getting extremely irritated. He knew her well enough to know he had better change the subject and fast. It was never a good idea to make Suzanne face things. It was a hard lesson he had learned their first year together. She will run before she will admit to the truth in her life.

Paul placed the clothing and personal items he brought for her on the bed, hoping to distract her to another subject. It put an instant smile on her face. She hugged him big and told him how wonderful he was, followed by a cute I love you... Paul knew she thought she meant what she was saying. Either way it didn't do much good.

At that moment Paul put a massive hand around her throat in a gentle but firm grip..." IF YOU EVER SCARE ME LIKE YOU DID LAST NIGHT AGAIN ... I WILL HAVE TO STRANGLE YOU AND PUT US BOTH OUT OF OUR MISERY..."

..." REALLY PAUL I AM NOT, NOR HAVE I EVER BEEN SUICIDAL... NEVER ONCE HAVE I THOUGHT I WANTED TO BE DEAD ... I HIDE FROM LIFE, I DO NOT STOP IT ...

BESIDES I AM HAVING TOO MUCH FUN TORTURING YOU..."

Paul loosened his grip on her throat only long enough to pull her into himself and squeeze the life out of her. A single tear left his eye as he held her declaring he wouldn't be able to stand life without her in it.

Suzanne hated this, she never wanted to deal with how much Paul loved her, or how much she did not love him. She told him he had better take off his rose colored glasses and take a good look at both her and their non relationship.

He would be much happier and better off without her. Paul grabbed her head into his hands and pulled her close enough their noses almost touched. Suzanne was suddenly filled with a fear. A fear of a man she had played with for far too long.

Paul spoke, slow and clear the words left his lips he wanted her to hear clearly without mistake, every word. He could see, all too clearly, it was her that should put on glasses and take another look at the way things really were.

He stared down at the list, even though they hadn't slept together for many years, he hadn't thought about her being with other men. She dared a smile not wanting to show the fear she felt for him...

"WHAT DID YOU THINK I WAS DOING FOR GRATIFICATION ALL THESE YEARS... DID YOU REALLY THINK YOU WERE THE ONLY ONE THAT COULD BRING ME PLEASURE...? BUT THEN YOU ALWAYS WERE NAIVE... OR IS THE WORD VANE...!?"

He was naive; he did think he was the only one that could bring her pleasure. He also thought when she discovered this she'd come begging. It was all Suzanne could do not to laugh as the proud was humbled. Suddenly Paul appeared a child to her a child that didn't understand the first thing about life.

Suzanne had to redirect, get the light off her and on to Paul. He must have slept with other girls, it had been three years. Paul was a very sensual man and Suzanne wasn't about to believe he didn't even give into a one-night stand.

He assured her he hadn't been with anyone; he had gone five years without sex before her. When they were first separated he had tried to date but it never felt right to be in bed with a person when all he could think of was Suzanne.

He didn't believe in making love unless the love part was there. Since he had never stopped loving Suzanne it couldn't come for anyone else. All he could think about while with other women was how they were strangers and not Suzanne.

Suzanne was fairly sure he was only telling her these things to make her feel bad, and it worked. This new revelation confused her. She felt both flattered and guilty. A piece of her liked that she couldn't be replaced.

Suzanne loved having sex with Paul, but she couldn't do the whole commitment thing. She didn't want the cottage and picket fence, she didn't want to be married or even live together. NO STRINGS sex would be great with her.

Paul gave her a gentle kiss on the forehead and smiled. He said he wasn't that kind of guy. He tried to say it like he was joking, but there was a sadness in his voice that she couldn't miss. She knew all too well they had this conversation before he wanted all of her or none of her.

There was a heavy silence between them as they walked down the hall to see Angel. Suzanne had grabbed some of the flowers out of her arrangement from Aaron to take to her.

When they got there Ray and Bev were leaving. Ray nearly knocked Suzanne off her feet as he pushed past her without a word.

Angel's face lit up as soon as she saw Paul, just as she scowled at her mother's presence. There had always been a magical connection between Paul and Angel. flying into his arms, she gave him a big hug that nearly knocked him over.

She thanked him over and over for rescuing her he was her knight. It was his pleasure and he would be more than happy to rescue her anytime she needed him. This was all starting to turn into a bad soap opera. One she wanted to escape from.

Suzanne was invisible, even when she tried to converse or interrupt, Angel would give one of her killer dirty looks and continue cooing over Paul. Suzanne wondered what she was doing there. It was very obvious Angel neither wanted nor needed her. Suzanne quietly slipped out of the room and went back to her own, feeling very dejected and unwanted. No one could do that to her better than Angel.

As Suzanne lay on her bed tears began streaming down her face. She made no attempt to stop or control them. It was time for a good cry she needed it, she deserved it. Paul came into her room, one last goodbye. He told her she was wrong that Angel not only needed her but wanted her; all that hostility was her defense from getting hurt.

She too believes her mother doesn't want, need or even love her. He held her in his arms as he tried to explain that they were both the same, afraid of not being loved back. He gave her a gentle yet sad kiss on the forehead as he once again said his goodbye.

As he walked away he turned, one last look, he couldn't help but whisper under his breath.... "MY TWO PRINCESSES, SAFE IN THEIR CASTLE..." He took a deep breath and a silent prayer. Pray was all he could do now.

Suzanne lay back on her bed still filled with a sad despair as she stared at the blankness of the walls. Feeling herself begin to tremble inside her entire body was shaking out of control, and then came nausea, followed by dry heaves.

They weren't stopping, even long after her stomach was empty. Suzanne lay on the floor in front of the toilet weak and trembling. She was consumed with hot flashes followed by cold sweats.

What was happening? She used all the strength she could to reach up and grab at the call bell; sure she was dying or at least wishing she was. A nurse came and helped her into bed, she seemed so calm and yet complacent. Suzanne almost felt like she was being patronized. Why wasn't this nurse taking this more seriously?..." HELP ME!.."

The nurse was filled with words like...PERFECTLY NORMAL... and THIS IS TO BE EXPECTED ... Suzanne had no idea what she was talking about but she wanted it to stop. She couldn't stand this.

Suzanne wanted something that would make her feel better. If that couldn't be done then put her to sleep, anything that kept her from feeling this way. Dr. Anderson came in to examine her and explain what withdrawals to expect. Suzanne couldn't believe what she was hearing. How could she have withdrawals? She wasn't a drug addict; she had never done drugs her entire life.

Alcohol withdrawals...how could that be she wasn't a drunk?... It was rotten hospital food or maybe a flu bug. It was not alcohol; it couldn't be she drank often but no more than anyone else.

An alcoholic couldn't work and maintain a real life. The only reason she got as drunk as she did was because Angel had upset her so much. If her family didn't put so much pressure on her she wouldn't drink at all.

Dr. Anderson wasn't about to argue with her or even discuss it, they had time for that after she was through her sickness. With that she walked out of the room. Suzanne couldn't believe she was simply walking away. Why didn't she do something?... give her some medicine, fix her..." DO SOMETHING!..." She was supposed to be a Doctor, so why wasn't she doctoring.

The nurse placed a cold cloth on her forehead and quietly explained that there was nothing to do but wait it out. Suzanne was far too weak and sick to argue. Even the flu would pass eventually she would have to just get through this and get out as quick as she could.

That first week was one that would be engraved in Suzanne's memory for the rest of her life. There was only about a thousand times she wanted to walk out the front door. She had no use for any of it.

It was bad enough that she was sick and in constant pain. She had to also endure... "ATTACK SUZANNE " sessions with Angel in Dr. Anderson's office. These sessions were designed specifically to hurt Suzanne as much as possible. There were times Suzanne was sure Dr.

Anderson and Angel had bets on to see who could make her cry the hardest.

She was thankful when she finally got through her flu bug. At last she could get through a day without shaking and trembling into dry heaves and cold chills. Withdrawal indeed that was one thing the doctor was wrong about. Suzanne drank because it made her feel better not because she had to.

All she could do was try to appease everyone and get out. That was her upper most thought. All she could think about was when she got out. She missed her friends, her job, and her home. What she missed most was her freedom to do what she wanted when she wanted.

If she wanted a drink she could have one. If she wanted to sleep all-day she could. All those interviews with the doctor and Angel were getting on her nerves. To think she once liked and admired that doctor. That is before she decided to make a career of hurting Suzanne.

Suzanne didn't dare say what she thought out loud or the doctor would never release her. Suzanne survived it as she had survived for her entire life. Finally the day came for her release and there was nothing the doctor could do about it.

Doctor Anderson wanted her to sign herself in for a longer stay. She felt Suzanne hadn't dealt with anything. She still had a lot to face and accept especially with Angel and her lack of committed relationships. Suzanne still had not learned to either accept the truth or trust in anything or anyone.

Suzanne was not in any danger nor was she a danger to anyone else so she had to be released. Angel talked her father into signing her in longer, she felt safe there. Her initial stay was for an extra thirty days then thirty changed to sixty, then on to six months.

Suzanne begged Ray to get her daughter out of there; it couldn't be good for her to hide from the world. Besides Suzanne was filled with the guilt, she couldn't go back into that place, yet she knew she would be criticized for not visiting her daughter.

She was free and she was home. She couldn't imagine Angel wanting to stay longer. Suzanne couldn't get out fast enough. Her first night home, it was party time. She was due; she had been a good girl long enough. Now it was time to do something for herself. She had been waiting for a very long month for a drink and a laugh and she intended to have both. She wanted it all and she didn't want to wait.

Aaron and Shelby threw her the coming home party of all coming home parties. Everyone was there, everyone that is except her disapproving family and Paul of course. Paul was completely disgusted that she had to go out and get drunk her first night out, while still claiming she didn't have a drinking problem.

Opening her eyes as slow as she could so her head didn't cave in from the hangover there was no avoiding, Suzanne froze instantly. Who belonged to that body in the bed next to her and why couldn't she remember bringing anyone home?

Suzanne attempted to slide off the bed but fell on the floor instead. Not only was her head ready to explode but her legs had turned to rubber. She had to move very quietly or she would have to deal with the question of morning sex.

It was one thing to have drunken sex with a total stranger but she could never do it with a sobering hang-over. She only made it half way to the bathroom as she heard a voice that was all too familiar. It was Aaron.

She knew instantly that she had screwed up and screwed up big. Suzanne fumbled with the words that just wouldn't cross her lips, the words she needed to speak to make this all right. How would she ever convince him that things had to stay the way they had always been?

This was all a big mistake, a mistake she couldn't even remember. She tried as hard as she could to remember the night. So much of it was a fog and the rest was completely blank. There had been many sleepless nights fantasizing about going to bed with Aaron. Now she finally had and she didn't even have the memory as reward. She had no idea if it was pleasurable; it was obvious it wasn't memorable.

Aaron lay quietly on the bed staring up at her discomfort. He was taking great pleasure in how uncomfortable this all made her. Unable to talk she would deal with whatever was going on later. This was a good time for retreat. Still flustered and blushing she ran into the bathroom.

She was lucky she had left her clothes on the floor the night before. Suzanne stepped into the shower and dressed, taking a long time to put on makeup and arrange her hair. She was thankful that Aaron hadn't made a sound while she was in there.

She half expected him to be pounding at the door, but then he had always been a gentleman. What she really hoped was that he was gone when she came out or better yet had never been there and it was all a disastrous dream.

Quietly and slowly she crept the door open hoping he wouldn't see her come out. Finally a small piece of luck, he had fallen back to sleep. She slipped out of the room as quietly as she slipped out of the bathroom, she needed to see Shelby.

Suzanne had to find out how she got herself in this mess and Shelby was the only one she could think of that could even possibly bring light to her vague confusion right now. Maybe she could get a better idea of what to say if she knew what had happened. But then, maybe it wasn't such a good idea to know how big a fool she had made of herself.

Shelby had a huge grin from ear to ear as she walked into the room a grin that could not be held by the laughter that spilled out as she got closer. It was worse than she thought, she had no idea what, but it was.

Still immersed in uncontrolled laughter, he hugged her and asked how the honeymoon was going. Suzanne punched and pushed him away at the same time. She was not impressed and it wasn't a funny joke...not one bit funny.

It didn't take Shelby long to figure out that she could remember nothing of the night before. She did have a vague memory of Aaron picking her up and carrying her around the room everything beyond that was pretty much forgotten. Shelby told her she had better start remembering fast because they were a newlywed couple. Not only did she get married but she insisted on it, begging Aaron to marry her.

It certainly didn't take her long to talk him into it. Everyone there tried to talk her out of it, joke her out of it, Shelby even tried ordering her out of doing it. He figured it was the ordering that made her so determined she never did obey orders.

... "VERY FUNNY..." Suzanne was still not buying any of it. What she couldn't figure out was how the two of them pulled this joke off. It really wasn't funny or believable. Suzanne was hung over and tired and not in the mood for Shelby's cuteness.

..." VERY FUNNY... VERY FUNNY ... HAHAHA... NOW TELL ME WHAT REALLY HAPPENED...." Grinning from ear to ear, he handed her a stack of pictures. With each picture her mouth dropped open wider.

Shelby couldn't stand it a moment longer. He held his belly as he laughed hard enough he fell against the counter. Suzanne threw the pile of wedding photos at him. Stomping out of the kitchen, she was consumed with frustrated anger. She wasn't angry with Shelby or even at Aaron. Suzanne was angry with herself. How could she have done this even drunk?

Maybe Paul was right, she did have a problem. This was all crazy and if she did this she must be crazy. Shelby was still roaring with laughter as he fell against the swinging doors yelling the wedding march.

Suzanne ran as she always ran, she wanted to hide; she wanted to set the clocks back. What she didn't want was to go back to her room and deal with Aaron her new husband. Now she did it, now she managed to even screw up and put her job and everything she liked in her life at risk.

Surely Aaron could see this was all done in fun. He couldn't possibly be serious about this marriage. They knew nothing about each other. They hadn't even had a date yet. How could she marry someone she had never seriously kissed?

If he knew how hard she was to live with he would be glad to be rid of her. Where was his head? What was he thinking? Surely he could

331

figure out that she had just come from the nut house and wasn't in full charge of her faculties, she could use the insanity plea.

There had to be at least a hundred people at that party that could testify that she wasn't of right mind and neither was Aaron. Suzanne tried her hardest to bring up memories of the night before especially the bedroom part. She had no idea if they even consummated this farce of a marriage. And if they did ... did she enjoy it?

Suzanne slipped into her room as quietly as she could. She needed some time to get some coffee into her and collect her thoughts. The words she spoke to Aaron had to be perfect. She couldn't just let herself ramble on and hope that he got it.

A couple of aspirin were probably a better idea than her usual shot of rum in a cup of coffee. Suzanne needed a clear head more than ever now. She was sitting on the couch drinking coffee and trying to sort it all out when Aaron finally crawled out of bed.

A big smile could be seen on his face as he entered the room. Suzanne wondered how anyone who drank all night could wake up looking and feeling so good. Straight and tall, with the pride of a peacock, he leaned over to kiss his new bride.... "GOOD MORNING... MRS. WEINSTEIN..."

Suzanne was not impressed. Whatever Shelby and he had planned it wasn't going to work. They might as well let her in on the joke and be done with it. They've both had a good laugh at her expense, but now it was time to get serious. It was morning, a new day, the joke was over.

Acting indignant, a smirk crossed his lips ever so slightly, how dare she act this way when it was all her idea. Everyone including himself tried to talk her out of the entire wedding idea. It was her and only her that kept not only insisting but demanding.

He pointed out to her that she was the one who dragged the Justice of the Peace over. He also insisted they were all too drunk to do this. Now she knew it was all a joke, he was Jewish was there not some sort of law about Rabbi's doing the service.

Aaron laughed as he put his arm around her shoulder, he was only half Jewish his mother was a gentile. He was raised non-denominational. One of the few facts he would expect a wife of his to learn.

Suzanne needed to think. There had to be a way of convincing Aaron the mistake they had both made. Aaron took both of Suzanne's hands into his and as serious as he could he began to speak..." SUZANNE... I KNOW YOU ARE SCARED OF COMMITMENT... IT IS EVEN WORSE BECAUSE YOU DO NOT REMEMBER ANY OF IT. THERE HAD TO BE SOMETHING IN YOU THAT REALLY WANTED TO GET MARRIED.... "

Suzanne sat in silence as she listened; she loved the soft caring tones in his voice. She had thought it was her that had to do all the talking but somehow she was entranced by what he had to say.

... "THERE HAD TO BE SOMETHING IN YOU THAT REALLY WANTED TO GET MARRIED OR YOU WOULDN'T HAVE GONE TO SUCH LENGTHS TO TALK ME INTO IT...I WISH YOU COULD REMEMBER THE NIGHT AND I REALLY WISH I DIDN'T SEE SUCH REGRET ALL OVER YOUR FACE..."

She couldn't believe he could read her so well she hadn't even started to talk and he could feel what she was thinking. She had spent most of her life feeling invisible but now this almost stranger could see her. What else could he see?

If he could really see her then he would know she wasn't the kind of person anyone would want to be married to. His voice continued to ring through her head; he was saying all the words she wanted to hear...

"I HAVE GIVEN THIS A LOT OF THOUGHT... I LAID AWAKE ALL NIGHT THINKING THIS THROUGH AFTER YOU FELL ASLEEP... UNLIKE YOU I WASN'T DRUNK LAST NIGHT... I KNEW WHAT I WAS DOING... THAT'S WHY WE DIDN'T HAVE SEX LAST NIGHT ... I WANT YOU TO ALSO KNOW WHAT YOU ARE DOING..."

They didn't have sex! Suzanne knew she had a man of character and now she knew he was a man of strength and fortitude. For a second she was disappointed. She should be relieved, why wasn't she?

All her emotions were so confused she was off balance and therefore unable to defend or protect herself. All she could do was sit and listen with her mouth open unable to speak words.

..." LET'S DO THIS MARRIAGE ON A TRIAL BASIS... WE CAN WRITE A CONTRACT FOR SIX MONTHS... IF YOU STILL HATE IT, EVERYTHING WILL GO BACK EXACTLY AS IT WAS BEFORE THE MARRIAGE... INCLUDING YOUR JOB AND INVESTMENTS... MY PROPERTY AND MONEY ... NO ALIMONY ... EVERYBODY CONTINUES AS ALWAYS ... ALL I AM ASKING IS A FAIR CHANCE ..."

Suzanne sat staring at him for long seconds before she could speak..." YOU DON'T UNDERSTAND... I AM NOT GOOD AT THIS MARRIAGE STUFF ... I AM NOT EVEN GOOD AT GOING STEADY ... I HAVE BIG PROBLEMS WITH COMMITMENT ... WHY DO YOU THINK PAUL AND I HAVE BROKEN UP AND GONE BACK TOGETHER SO MANY TIMES?... BECAUSE I AM A SELFISH SELF-CENTRED BITCH!..."

Aaron was serious and not about to take any excuses, he told her to get a grip. She had broken up with Paul so many times because he wasn't right for her. They weren't meant to be together.

..." CAN'T YOU SEE I AM NOT LIKE ALL THOSE OTHER MEN...? I DO NOT EXPECT YOU TO GIVE UP THE HOTEL OR CHANGE YOUR LIFE OR EVEN WHO YOU ARE ... WHY CAN YOU NOT SEE HOW PERFECT WE COULD BE FOR EACH OTHER...

Aaron was talking fast, trying his hardest to convince her he was worth the chance and she should grab at it. If she could jump straight in with both feet then she should at least see if she could get used to the water before getting out. He was willing to meet whatever terms she laid out if she would simply give them a chance.

...."THE ONLY THING I EXPECT FROM YOU IS LOYALTY AND FOR YOU TO BE IN MY BED AT NIGHT ... I DON'T EVEN EXPECT YOU TO LOVE ME BACK... ONLY RESPECT ME AS YOUR HUSBAND..."

Suzanne wanted to believe all he was saying, she wanted to do this she wanted to say...

"WHAT THE HELL..." How was this going to work they had such different lives where would they live. She didn't even know where he lived when he wasn't at the hotel. She knew nothing about him outside of the hotel. He was virtually a stranger. She was weakening, but wanted to stay strong.

..." WE COULD LIVE HERE IN YOUR APARTMENT DURING THE WEEK THEN GO TO MY HOUSE DURING THE WEEKENDS ... IF YOU HATE THAT IDEA WE'LL CLOSE UP THE HOUSE AND LIVE THE SIX MONTHS OR EVEN FOREVER HERE AT THE HOTEL.... SAY YOU WILL WAIT THE SIX MONTHS BEFORE YOU DECIDE..."

Did he want an answer right now, this minute? Suzanne had to think and she couldn't think with him sitting beside her half-naked. She needed some time, and Aaron would wait patiently 'til the end of the day. Suzanne couldn't believe how persuasive Aaron could be.

Instead of her talking him out of this marriage he had nearly talked her into it. Maybe he wasn't persuasive; maybe she really deep in her heart wanted this. Maybe there was something to what he said.

That is if he meant what he said, men were so good at wanting one thing, then when they think everything is comfortable, they throw in a lot of changes a girl can't live with. She needed someone to talk to Shelby wasn't serious enough. Unfortunately Paul was whom she would talk to normally but she was pretty sure he wouldn't want to discuss or even hear about this.

She remembered his lecture at her need to party her first night out. She remembered all his lectures about her drinking, did he have to be so self-righteous? He had been over critical of her bad choices for a long time, how could she ever tell him this story?

Unfortunately he was her lawyer and she would need legal advice before she went into this. She needed to know about the contract Aaron suggested and wanted to know not only how legal it would be but also any possible future pitfalls.

One thing for sure she had to face him straight up no cowardly letters or phone calls he could hang up from. She learned her lesson the last time she was cowardly, in her heart she knew he deserved better and she deserved whatever rage he would inflict on her.

She had no choice she would have to go to his office, being a married lady it wouldn't do for her to go to his apartment. At his office she could get help or witnesses if he went insane with rage. There was a small piece of her that was scared of him. He had spent years trying to get her to commit and now she had committed to a virtual stranger while drunk.

Suzanne wondered if her husband boss would give her the day off, if ever there was a good time to ask him it was now. She was fairly sure he would refuse her nothing ... at least until she gave him an answer.

As she walked into Paul's office a wave of panic shot through her. She could see the same disapproving scowl he had when she invited him to the party. Wouldn't he kick himself for not coming when he heard her news?

If Paul had come she would never have gotten herself into this mess. Maybe she could spin this somehow so it was all his fault. Judging by the scowl she didn't dare. She had better play it humble.

Paul wasted no time lecturing her about her drinking and her choice of friends that cared so little they had to get her drunk her first night out. How could she be so selfish with her daughter still in the same institution? He started in on her immaturity and her need to grow up.

Suddenly like a flash of brilliance, she knew exactly why she had a problem with committing to him. He thought he was the father. How could she ever see him as a husband when he insisted on acting like her father?

She looked up to the heavens and thanked God that she had never married this judgmental jerk. For the first time in years she had no feelings for this man, no regrets about their relationship. She simply felt free.

Suzanne began to wonder how she could have even thought of him as a friend. A friend would accept her as she was and understand her short comings instead of trying to mold her into what he wanted her to be.

Just like that, no feelings, with a flick of a switch; on one minute off the next. Everything seemed so clear. She was in a big flood of awareness remembering all that Paul had said and what Aaron had said. Why had she not seen this sooner?

Suzanne sat in silence letting him run on, untouched by the harshness of his words. She didn't argue, she didn't interrupt or even defend herself. She let him give his speech. When he finally finished she stood up very straight and proud as she announced... "I MARRIED AARON WEINSTEIN LAST NIGHT ... END OF DISCUSSION..."

Now he could take his fatherly lecture and shove it, she didn't care what he thought. Holding her pride and dignity she turned and walked out of his office. He was in shock, speechless and Suzanne loved it. She had done many things over the years that had surprised him, but she had never managed to shock him like this.

Where did this come from? Why? He was yelling at her..." STOP WALKING AWAY FROM ME AND DISCUSS THIS..." There was nothing to discuss it was done and she was glad. She didn't discuss with him her doubts or her regrets and at this moment she had none.

As she stepped onto the elevator she could still hear Paul ranting... "WHAT ABOUT LOVE...?!" If only he knew that it was the lack of love that would probably make this work. She always hurt the people she loved. Maybe the lack of it was going to save Aaron from her nastier side.

When she went to Paul's office she had been filled with so much doubt, so much regret. Regret about Paul, about Aaron, her marriage, her drinking, and where she wanted to go in her life. Every aspect of her life and what she had done was in question.

Now as she walked away from Paul for the last time she was filled with clarity, she knew exactly what she wanted. She would make every effort to make her new marriage work. Not only was it going to work, but also it was ideal.

Suzanne had always been at her best while dealing with business and friendship. Aaron was right it was the perfect arrangement for her. That is if he stuck to the arrangement and didn't spring any surprises on her.

It was all that Love stuff that confused her. With the pressure off maybe she wouldn't feel the panic that made her run. He was even willing to let her live at the hotel if she wanted. That was all she needed she had made her mind up. Strangely it was Paul that convinced her.

Before she went back to the hotel to tell Aaron she would give it her best shot she had to go to the hospital and tell Angel. Paul was sure to visit her and give his version. The news had come from her mother even if she wasn't likely to take it well.

Angel was very close to Paul and would hate Suzanne even more than she already did for hurting him. A piece of Suzanne was jealous of the closeness the two of them had, she wished Angel could love her so unconditionally.

Suzanne hated walking down those halls again. She hated the smell, even the feel of the place. Unlike Angel, it made her feel anything but safe. She hoped she wouldn't run into." THE GOOD DOCTOR ANDERSON."

Suzanne no longer trusted or respected her. She had no intention of ever setting foot in hers or any other psychiatrist's office ever again... Suzanne never did figure out what the game was; only that she couldn't win so she wasn't going to play.

What purpose was there in keeping her in as much pain as possible as long as possible? Suzanne was sure the doctor got some sort of demented pleasure from her pain.... Suzanne would call it the..." PAIN GAME "... a game she would never play again.

Angel was finally found in the lounge playing solitaire. It was a place that brought back all too many memories. Suzanne wished Angel would have checked out when she did. Suzanne hated that she had to come back to her personal hell, just so she could visit with her daughter.

Angel was in a particularly cooperative mood, she even followed Suzanne back to her room so they could talk in private. Suzanne held out her left hand and dazzled her new ring. Angel was puzzled her mother had a look of fear and apprehension on her face. Why would her mother not know that she wanted her mother to marry Paul from the moment they all met him?

For the first time in many years Angel smiled the biggest smile Suzanne had ever seen... "YOU ARE MARRIED... YOU FINALLY PUT PAUL OUT OF HIS MISERY... THANK-YOU MOTHER... THANK-YOU SO MUCH... YOU WILL SEE... HE REALLY IS THE BEST..."

Suzanne took a deep breath to prepare her for the wrath that Angel was sure to put upon her. She had to tell Angel straight out, no hedging, no show of fear or weakness. ...." ANGEL... IT WASN'T PAUL I MARRIED... I MARRIED AARON WEINSTEIN..."

There was no need to tell her that she married him by accident, while she was in a drunken stupor. Suzanne could see the rage that instantly fell on Angel's face. It was anger and disappointment like Suzanne had never seen before. It was an anger that held Angel in silence only for a moment.

Once Angel found her tongue, every word was designed to cut like a knife. Angel was not surprised at her mother's choice. Everything she had ever done was designed to be hurtful and this did hurt, even if Angel's rage hid that pain.

If there was ever a wrong thing to do, her mother always did it, and if someone could get hurt in the process then it was all the better. What her mother did best was cause as much pain in as many directions as possible.

Angel pointed out as complacent as she could be that this was no different than what Suzanne had been doing her entire life... cause pain was her mother's only goal...." YOU CAN'T HURT ME ANY MORE... MOTHER... A PERSON HAS TO CARE TO BE HURT AND I JUST DON'T CARE ANYMORE... FIND SOMEONE NEW TO HURT IT DOESN'T WORK ON ME ANYMORE...."

For dramatic affect, she walked out of the room. Not in anger or even with attitude, but as though Suzanne were not there. To Angel she wasn't. To Angel Suzanne was invisible, simply no longer existed?

Leave it to Angel to turn this whole thing around like it was about her. Like Suzanne had married a complete stranger to cause her daughter pain. It wasn't to hurt Angel it wasn't to hurt anyone. Suzanne couldn't help but search her brain...

Why did she marry Aaron, being drunk certainly wasn't an excuse? Everyone always says that a drunk only does what he is not brave enough to do sober. There must have been something in her that wanted this.

Suzanne had enough to worry about today without getting into this further with Angel. Suzanne let her walk away, a small piece of her wanted to go after her, wanted to make her understand and beg her forgiveness... what was the point. It would only give Angel one last chance at attacking her.

She had to convince her other children that this was a good thing. That things would have never worked out with Paul. She simply wasn't happy with him. Suzanne couldn't stay with Paul simply because her children liked him. It wasn't enough for Suzanne.

Suzanne knew Paul well enough to know that he would likely never talk to her again but he would always be there for her children. Paul had always thought of them as his own, it was Paul not Ray or Suzanne that the kids went to for advice and moral support.

Angel was likely never to accept Aaron but he had a chance with the other kids. They would learn to care about him once they got to know him. Aaron was a good man and Suzanne should have realized it sooner.

Suzanne began walking toward the exit when she was stopped by Angel one last attack was necessary. It wouldn't do for Suzanne to escape unscathed. They weren't allowed to be in each others presence without Suzanne being devastated to tears.

... Angel shot her mother the coldest nastiest look she could conjure up as she screamed at the top of her lungs... "JUST LIKE YOU MOTHER TO DO THE MOST IRRESPONSIBLE SELFISH THING YOU POSSIBLY COULD ... WHY DO YOU HAVE TO BE SO HURTFUL?... DOES AARON WEINSTEIN KNOW WHAT A COLD HURTFUL BITCH YOU ARE?..."

Suzanne ran down the hall wanting to escape Angel. Tears streamed down her face blinding her. She bumped into a few people and kept moving not wanting to look back. She had to get out of there.

Suddenly she was revisited by all the pain she felt her entire stay in this house of pain and heartache. Suzanne could hear Angel screaming after her... "THAT'S RIGHT... RUN MOTHER RUN...AND KEEP RUNNING..."

Once she got into her car she sat still shaking and crying, trying to compose herself. Tears were still streaming down her face. She would never be able to see to drive ... all she could do was sit and let the pain consume her.

Suzanne drifted into a light sleep her only escape at the moment. Someone tapped lightly on the window, asking her if she was all right. It was Doctor Anderson, signaling for her to roll down the window. Not today Doc., we're not playing your pain game today. Suzanne had just finished a round of that game with Angel and she wasn't up for another.

As she drove away she stared at the doctor with contempt, bordering on hatred. After all it was all her fault. Dr. Anderson was always there to remind Angel of all the pain, of how much she hated her mother. If it weren't for the great doctor Angel would have forgotten years ago and they could have gotten on with their lives as mother and daughter.

Suzanne's anger and hatred for the doctor helped compose her enough that she could now drive. Suzanne could put aside the pain she felt from Angel and concentrate on blame.

Emotionally drained and physically exhausted Suzanne went back to the hotel. She would have her other children come there for supper she could break it to them without Ray's input. If they took it well perhaps they could begin getting to know Aaron.

Anna was going to be the force to reckon with. She had for years been making Suzanne feel like she was the child. Now that Anna was eighteen, she believed herself to have all the answers as the full-grown adult she thought she was.

Dealing with Anna would be no easier than it had been with Paul and Angel. The difference was that Anna was indifferent toward Paul. It was likely to be worse since with both Paul and Angel she could walk away that wouldn't be so easy with Anna.

Her confrontation with Anna was as she expected it would likely be a year before she was forgiven by her eldest daughter. That is unless she meant it when she said she would never speak to her again.

Alice and R.J. took a wait and see attitude sitting the fence nicely. Amazing how everyone has pity for poor Paul. Not one person showed happiness or congratulations for Suzanne.

Chapter Seventeen

Suzanne was never so thankful to be home. At last she could have a drink alone and think. How strange it all seemed to Suzanne. She was having her first day of marriage and she hadn't even seen her husband all day.

It felt the same as any other day. Hopefully the rest of her married life would feel the same ... just another day... every day... A piece of her wished her husband were more demanding and smothering. Maybe he didn't love her; maybe he just wanted a trophy wife.

Suzanne could not believe how self-defeating she was. All along the one reason she had to let Paul go was because he was too smothering and now she thinks Aaron her new husband isn't smothering enough.

Maybe she was wishing he were more smothering so she would have a reason to walk away. It was harder to leave a guy who was giving all she ever wanted and asked for nothing in return. Maybe Aaron was the only truly selfless person on the planet.

Suzanne seemed to be having a lot of trouble thinking about spending the night with her new husband. What was even harder was thinking about spending every night with her Aaron Weinstein. Mostly she had spent the last several years sleeping with men who would disappear the next day, or better that night.

Still trying to figure what she was feeling, Aaron walked through the door. Suzanne laughed as he uttered some old cliche like ... "HI HONEY, I'M HOME ..."

Actually it was the right thing to say at just the right moment, breaking the ice. It took Suzanne a long time to get used to Aaron's dry humor. Once she found the subtleties of his humor, she could like and understand him so much better.

Suzanne had spent years discovering that liking was so much more important than loving. Loving was so totally irrational. It made no sense at all, but if you could get someone to like you that was a much bigger feat in life. Anyone can be loved; you have to be someone special to be liked.

Aaron poured himself a drink as though he had lived there forever. There wasn't even the tiniest of hints that he was not at home. He was perfectly natural as he sat down beside her and kissed her on the cheek. He seemed so proud of himself.

Having accomplished his life's mission, he didn't ask her any questions, no discussion, not even a doubt. He simply made himself at home. Why wasn't he scared or worried?…perhaps because Suzanne was scared enough for both of them.

Aaron sat beside her and explained he was neither scared nor worried because this is what was meant to be. To him it all just felt right, and he was comfortable. The only thing he figured left to do was to christen the union. To make it official so to speak, if she knew what he meant.

Suzanne knew exactly what he meant, how could she not the grin on his face said it all. Somehow she had not thought about that part of their marriage. The thought of sex spun her into another panic attack.

She wasn't sure why, it wasn't like she was a virgin bride. She didn't understand anything she was feeling; everything was so strange... she had spent so much of her time saying no to him. This was so different; she wasn't going to bed with a stranger that would go away afterward. This was someone she would have to face not only the next morning but every morning.

Suzanne would need another drink to get through this night. That was her problem she hadn't had sex sober in years. Aaron told her he would appreciate it if it were her last drink of the night. He would never ask her again, or tell her what to do, tonight he had to have her sober.

She was falling over drunk when they got married; he wanted her sober to consummate it. He needed to know that she was clear headed and knew whom she was with. It seemed a perfectly reasonable request to her.

The only problem she had about it all was how nervous she was. She hadn't had sex sober or otherwise, even one nightstands had become unappealing to her for a long time before she had been committed. She hoped Aaron was a take charge kinda guy. She was in no shape to take the lead. Suzanne couldn't even seem to take charge of her own emotions.

Suzanne sat on the couch in silence waiting to see what was going to happen; not knowing what to say or do. She was a lot more nervous than she had been the first time she slept with either Ray or Paul.

Aaron meandered over to the stereo and put in a tape of soft gentle tunes that Suzanne thought would lull her into an equally gentle sleep. As Aaron slowly walked over to her he put out his hand for her to take it. She stood, a little apprehensive, not knowing if he wanted to dance or go straight to bed.

Taking her in his arms he waltzed her around the room, floating in the slow motion of the music, like magic. It was a wonderful dream, a sweet fantasy, which she loved being lost in.

Her new husband was right; they blended together as though they had been dancing together forever. It felt right, it felt good; maybe it felt too good. It certainly didn't feel like a business arrangement. For a guy that never seemed to have a girl in his life, he sure did know exactly what it would take to make one feel good.

Long after the music was over she could still feel the tune. Aaron stared deep into her eyes, putting her into a trance. He told her she didn't have to be so afraid of him, he was very nice to be with. Women told him that all the time.

Suzanne wanted to ask him..." HOW MANY WOMEN TOLD YOU THIS?..." When he smiled and gently kissed her the question left her head which was now swimming. At first it was a lot of tiny kisses all over her lips, then he built it into a stronger passionate kiss.

It was a kiss like no other kiss, building in passion as though it had a life of its own. As she tried to kiss him back he stopped her and told her he was in control for tonight, and she should lay back and let him be in charge.

He took her in his arms, and continued dancing. The music was long since over but it was locked in her head, as this night would be forever. Suzanne could not believe what an incredible dancer he was. It was as if she were dancing in a different time. The period was old world, an old movie she was lost in.

There was a knock at the door; Suzanne resented the break in a perfect moment. Aaron stopped and told her to go into the bathroom and grab a shower and change; he had left her something to slip into on the bed.

Suzanne was impressed he had thought of everything. Suzanne went into the bathroom as Aaron made his way to the door; hesitating just long enough to be sure Suzanne was out of sight before he answered it. He was so cute, she couldn't help but like every moment that he had so carefully arranged.

She could hear Shelby's voice but couldn't make out the whispers. Suzanne was getting very frustrated trying to figure out what the two of them were up to. Suzanne made the shower an extra long one; it would be good for Aaron to wait. He was much too confident tonight.

As soon as she got out of the shower she went over to open the beautifully wrapped box sitting on the bed. It was the most incredible white sheer lace peignoir she had ever seen. The man certainly had good taste.

She walked toward the livingroom, only to stand paralyzed in the doorway... yellow roses all over the room, candle light dinner, champagne chilling and the sweetest little wedding cake. It was all so perfect.

He hadn't forgotten a single detail, maybe she could learn to love Aaron after all. There had to be something wrong with a woman that couldn't love a man that could do all this.

They sat in silence through dinner, absorbing the atmosphere. Aaron hadn't lost eye contact, since she emerged like an angel from the bathroom. Suzanne was fascinated watching him use a knife and fork never once looking down at his plate.

Once finished the meal, he poured them each a glass of champagne, which was held up for a toast... "HERE'S TO A NIGHT THAT WILL NEVER END OR BE FORGOTTEN..."

She smiled a shy little girl smile for that was how she felt, like a shy little girl. Suzanne thought she would never forget the feel of this magical evening. She wasn't sure about love, but there was romance in the air.

Aaron put down his glass and walked to her side of the table everything seemed to be in slow motion. Leaning down with what Suzanne thought was going to be another kiss. He picked her up in his arms and carried her to bed, kissing her a long and passionate kiss.

Then he kissed her a few shorter kisses. She was already addicted to his kisses and couldn't get enough of them. He got up off the bed and told her not to move, he would be right back.

As she heard the shower, she thought about joining him as a surprise, but this was his night and everything would be done exactly as he planned. There was also a spot deep inside of her that was still pretty nervous; all this brought shyness out in her. She couldn't stop trembling as she awaited his return.

When he came out of the shower wearing nothing but a smile and a few water drops, he walked to the bed and told her he loved a girl that knew how to take orders. She told him he better enjoy it, this would be the only night he would give orders that she would be likely to follow.

He laughed out loud as he knew he was in total control, just as he knew she was loving every moment of it. He figured that was the mistake that every man in her life had made. They let her have too much control.

All women liked being controlled; they just refused to admit it. Tonight it was his job to show Suzanne that he was in control and she would like it that way. Suzanne wasn't so sure, but she was willing to play his game, at least for tonight.

As he lowered himself on top of her in an embrace that she would not soon forget, she wondered if she had finally met her match with this man. They made love a few times that night, but it was the first time that was the most memorable.

It was memorable because he took no pleasure or satisfaction himself. His goal was to see how many times she could orgasm, to see just how much pleasure she could stand. Even she had no idea the extent of pleasure he was capable of showing her.

About the time she thought her body could stand no more, he got up and poured each of them another glass of champagne. He told her this was only a breather, he wasn't done until she had used every bit of energy. He was letting her catch her breath, then he would finish the job.

Suzanne secretly hoped that sex wasn't like this every night, as good as it felt, a week of this and she would be old and gray in no time. Damn! It did feel good. Mr. Weinstein's lovemaking was much like his personality, methodical and perfect.

Mr. and Mrs. Weinstein slept 'til noon, and then made love again. This time the lovemaking was different. It was sweet and gentle, little kisses and gentle touches. This was one of Suzanne's favorite times.

She loved sex when she was still half-asleep, especially slow and gentle. She felt good, better than she deserved. She didn't have a clue when she married Aaron, but if this was any indication, she had made a good choice.

He told her that he had cleared the entire day for both of them. He wanted to show her his world. It occurred to him that they knew nothing about each other outside of the hotel. The first stop was the Weinstein family home.

It was a massive home, built on the side of a hill. The back was totally glass overlooking an exquisite view of a hill that blended naturally with the calming vision of a lake. There was a long boardwalk down the face of the hill and out onto the water. They held hands as they walked out to the end of it.

Suzanne took the opportunity to talk to him about the kids. They had never discussed them in any way, even as friends the subject never came up. He told her that he had no problem with the kids being in their lives.

He would never expect to marry her and not have her children in their life. This was her home and it would be her children's home as well. The door would always be open to them.

He held her tight and told her that he loved her and wanted things to be anyway she wanted them to be. If she found she wasn't comfortable in his home he had no problem living at the hotel with her. He only wanted for her to be happy. He hoped they would eventually take some honeymoon time. Suzanne thought a honeymoon would be incredible especially with the memory of her new husband's talents still haunting her.

They had to wait at least a couple of months. She needed time for both herself and her children to get used to the idea of the marriage before she could leave. With both of them gone there was no one left to run the hotel? She would need the time to train an assistant. She hadn't even begun to straighten everything out from when she was in lock-up.

Aaron was happy to spend the week at the hotel getting used to the idea in familiar surroundings. Then they would spend the weekend at the house alone. If it all went well then they could try it with the kids the following weekend. She needed time to see if she could get Angel out of the hospital, at least for a weekend visit.

Angel would be the test; if he could endure Angel he could endure anything. That is if Angel ever forgave her mother enough to ever step foot in their home. Maybe she would come simply to let them both know how much she hated them and their marriage.

Suzanne loved the smell of the lake and the coolness of the breeze. She loved the solitude feeling so free of worry and pressure. For the first time in her entire life she was home.

She had found herself a new safe haven. There was no doubt in her mind or her heart; this was where she wanted to be. Aaron was right they were meant to be together. She had finally found her place.

The only thing she wondered about was why she hadn't given Aaron a chance sooner. Everything was falling into place. Only something that was destined to be could be this easy, this comfortable. Her and Paul had struggled from the beginning. The only thing that was ever right was the sex and even that had pressures and strings attached.

Angel refused to come, and Anna wanted nothing to do with her mother or her new husband. Anna wouldn't even talk to Suzanne on the phone. It broke Suzanne's heart that they couldn't even give this new marriage a chance. They jumped right into Ray's marriage, why couldn't she have the same kind of support?

If she could just get them to come and see for themselves, they would know this was the best thing that ever happened. Suzanne hadn't had even one nightmare since she had married Aaron. Why didn't they want her to be happy, to be at peace?

Suzanne had never felt so safe and secure. Aaron was strong and could take care of her. He didn't feel the need to smother or own her, like Paul and Ray and every other man she had ever known. He loved her enough and was strong enough to let her be her.

She had no panic so there was no need to run or hide. He was perfect and she was home. Someday her children would know and accept the life she now had. Someday she would find a way for them to be a part of that life.

Suzanne and Aaron had been married two years. The time flew by in what seemed like a blink of an eye. It was at their second anniversary dinner that Alice and R.J. told Suzanne that Anna had gotten married. Suzanne was crushed, how did they get so far apart? There was a time when she was closer to Anna than any of the children. There had to be a way of getting that back.

Suzanne wasn't invited. After all Anna wasn't invited to Suzanne's wedding. Anna was married and Suzanne had no idea how long they even dated. She had never even met the man that now filled her lost daughter's life.

From everything the other kids had told her he was a farm boy much like Ray in personality. Apparently they had their own home already. Dan, Anna's husband and his father had built it together before the wedding day.

The family owned a lot of land and now the young couple would live on and work that land. Suzanne remembered back to a time when Anna was very little she had always loved the farm they lived on when she was so little.

Enough was enough. It was time for Suzanne to put an end to this foolishness. Anna was so stubborn, and would never come to her mother first. There was only one way to deal with this once and for all. Suzanne would have to get in her face and stay in her face 'til she accepted her mother back in her life.

They were close once and they would be close again. Two years was long enough to be in a snit. It was time to go visiting. Suzanne gathered a couple of baskets, filling them with everything that a new household might need. It could be a wedding present or perhaps a peace offering whatever Anna wanted to accept it as.

As Suzanne pulled into the long drive it took her back twenty-years; a handful of good memories and many bad, lonely ones. A nightmare for Suzanne was heaven to her eldest daughter. Suzanne was filled with the memories of the nights Anna cried to go back to the farm.

The tiny house was kind of cute. Anna had planted flowers along the front. There was a beautiful wrap around porch with a swing at one end and two rockers at the other. It was all very quaint exactly what Suzanne would expect from her eldest daughter.

There was no answer at the door, so Suzanne wandered back to the barn, where she could faintly hear voices. Anna was wearing an old flannel shirt, about six sizes too big, baggy jeans, and rubber boots. She looked happier than Suzanne had seen her in a long time.

It warmed Suzanne's heart to see Anna in a life where she was so content ... that is, until she looked up and saw her mother. Her content face was instantly consumed with contempt. Contempt for a mother that made far too many mistakes far too many times.

Anna wanted to know how she found her, and why she bothered. In an attempt to lighten the moment Suzanne joked about bribing her brother. Anna wasn't in the mood for jokes. Anna had a lot of work to do and wanted to get back to it. There would be no time for her mother for socializing or anything else.

Anna's husband had to step in and introduce himself, Daniel Ellis... he stated as he shook her hand. He insisted he could manage and Anna should take her mother to the house for a cup of coffee and a talk. Anna still in the honeymoon stage didn't argue but glared evil looks as she had to show how unimpressed she was.

Anna walked to the house in silence; Suzanne could feel the anger that surrounded her every movement. As soon as they reached the house Anna turned to her mother with impatience..." WHAT DO YOU WANT...MOTHER?!... "

Anna made extra effort to be sure there was a sting in the word. "MOTHER" ... Suzanne wondered how a word that was supposed to represent loving, always sounded like a swear word crossing her children's lips.

Anna was getting colder and harder, no emotions, not the tiniest glimmer of warmth or family love. Anna might as well have been talking to a vacuum cleaner salesman that was irritating her... "TELL ME WHAT YOU ARE HERE FOR SO I CAN GET BACK TO WORK..."

Suzanne begged her not to be so heartless. Anna told Suzanne she had learned it from a good teacher. In the heartless department her..." MOTHER "was the best. The only one that beat her at hurting those that loved her was Angel who had both inherited then improved the trait.

Suzanne was determined not to cry or show weakness. Anna was sure to pounce if she knew Suzanne was weaker. As hard as she tried she couldn't hold back the flood of tears that welled up on the edges of her eyes determined to fall off.

Why did Anna have to be so cruel, and hateful? Was Suzanne so evil that she couldn't be forgiven? Hadn't Anna ever made a mistake that she needed someone to forgive her for.

Couldn't she understand that her mother was human and in being human she was capable of mistakes like every other human. Like every other human she begged and needed forgiveness. She deserved that much.

Suzanne had to hit her where she was most vulnerable, she had to find a common ground that Anna could relate to. Suzanne asked her daughter if she felt safe and secure in her marriage and with her husband.

When Anna answered that she had found everything she had ever wanted, that she was finally home. It was time for honesty, it was all that was about to be accepted by Anna.

Suzanne explained to Anna that she had married Aaron by accident, while in a drunken stupor. Despite that it was the best thing she had ever done. She too had quite by accident found everything she had ever wanted she too had finally found her home, her safe haven.

For once her children were more important than her pride if she had to crawl to get her daughter back, then crawl she would. Suzanne begged Anna to forgive her or at least listen to her explanation. Anna had to let her mother prove that she meant every word she spoke.

Suzanne wanted a chance to spoil her grandchildren. She had been a lousy excuse of a mother but given a chance she could be a great grandmother. That is when grandchildren started coming. She wanted and needed a chance to prove she could be a better person to everyone in her life. She not only wanted but needed a chance.

Anna crumbled into a swell of emotions, Suzanne was taken by surprise it was so unlike Anna to crumble or show any emotional weakness. Anna hugged her mother for the first time in more years than Suzanne was willing to admit to.

As she wiped the tears from her face she confessed that she was already five months pregnant. She did want her mother by her side. She was scared and didn't want to do this alone. She had wanted to forgive her mother for a long time but pride kept getting in her way.

Crying in each other's arms they couldn't help but forgive each other. There had been far too many years between them and they had a lot to catch up on. They talked for hours, that is 'til Anna's husband finally came in wanting his supper.

Suzanne and Anna fixed supper together. It was late before Suzanne finally made it home; she was feeling both triumphant and loved. Now if she could do this with Angel then her family and her heart would be fixed, all would be perfect in her life for the first time ever.

Suzanne started calling Anna every couple days, then Anna started calling on her own. Suzanne looked forward to their daily talks, sometimes before work, sometimes after, but a day didn't pass without discussing its events.

Suzanne needed to know if anyone in the family had heard from Angel since she ran away. Anna told her about Paul hiring detectives, but they didn't have any luck, no one heard anything since she ran about ten months prior.

Anna told Suzanne when Angel ran she was doing a lot of drugs and with a real bad crowd. Ray and Bev had washed their hands of her and didn't even ask about her. The only one who hadn't given up on her was Paul.

Suzanne couldn't go to Paul. He hadn't spoken to her since she married Aaron. But then, it was for Angel, she could swallow her pride, and he could get over it. She was filled with so many mixed emotions making her afraid to see him again.

She once had a lot of feelings for him and she had no idea what she would feel seeing him again or worse how he felt about her. He hated her after their last visit. Had he gotten over it, would he be willing to put it aside and help her with Angel?

There was no way of presuming or even guessing what would happen if she just appeared at his office. She couldn't call ahead for an appointment he was sure to refuse to see her. She had to make him see that it was for Angel that Angel needed to make peace with her mother and all her childhood ghosts.

When she walked into Paul's office as though years hadn't passed and she had every right to be there, his secretary tried to intervene, to stop her and make her wait for an appointment. Suzanne refused she wasn't waiting; she had to speak with him and now.

As she pushed her way through the door, Paul dismissed his secretary telling her he had a few minutes and would speak with Suzanne. He greeted her with the cool professionalism of any other client, all business.

He showed her no emotions as he told her that Angel had called every couple months. Every time she did he tried to talk her into coming home. He offered to send a ticket anywhere she was if she would just come home.

He had offered for her to come live with him if she couldn't bare going to either of her parent's homes. He would take care of her and keep her safe. He would be the parent that Ray and Suzanne refused to be.

Suzanne ignored the insult, as though it were not aimed directly at her. She would let him away with it and let him talk. Angel was more important than the battle of the moment. Suzanne needed information that only Paul could give her.

The last time she had called Paul she was getting close to being ready to come home. She sounded so scared and so tired all the time, but the last call she sounded beaten down. The world had beaten her, Paul could hear it in her whisper of a voice.

She was lost and unable to find her way back. He knew all too well Angel couldn't be pressed into anything. She wasn't about to come back until she was good and ready. She was like her mother, right or wrong, she had to do what she had to do. It would never make any sense to anyone except her, and probably not even to her.

As Suzanne started to get up to leave Paul asked her if she was happy. She almost felt guilty as she told him she had never been happier. She was more than happy she was content. She had finally found the place where she belonged. There were no more ghosts or nightmares.

As much as she thought she was in love with Paul, Aaron was the best thing that ever happened to her. She said Aaron didn't let her push him around like he always had. They gave balance to each other, because of who they were not whom they could change each other into.

Suzanne finally found someone to stand up to her, which was exactly what she needed. Paul smiled and agreed that he was too much of a puppy. He was always afraid that if he stood up to her she would leave him. His biggest problem was that he was too much in love with her.

Before leaving she had to make it clear to Paul that she did love Angel, and that if she were to call again she would appreciate it if he would try his hardest to get her to call her mother, collect... any time day or night.

Suzanne needed Paul to tell Angel that her mother thinks about her every day, that her mother loves her. He must find a way of convincing her that her mother loves her and will be there for her anytime she calls.... but she has to call.

On the drive home she thought about Anna and her first grandchild. She was going to be a better grandmother than she had been a mother. Then she thought about her poor lost Angel and what a mess they had all made of her.

Would Angel ever know what it was to be happy or to find her place in the world? Would she ever get through a day straight or a night without screaming? It took Suzanne forty years to find her place. Hopefully it wouldn't take Angel that long.

It was only a few days before Paul got back to Suzanne at the hotel. Angel had called; she was ready to come home. He sent her a ticket, Angel should be at his house within the next forty- eight hours. He had already talked to Ray and Bev and they wanted nothing to do with her.

Paul was taking full responsibility for her. There was no way of knowing how much help she would need or what kind of shape she was in. Paul didn't want to ask her too many questions afraid it would make her change her mind about coming.

Angel appeared at Paul's with the tiniest little newborn he had ever seen. She had run away because she was pregnant. She couldn't bring herself to tell her parents, so she took off. The father of the baby was dead.

Angel was not willing to go into a lot of detail, even about how he had died or who he was. Paul didn't dare pry any deeper than she offered. It was all he could do to talk her into coming home and he wasn't about to push her out again.

Angel went from place to place, living like a gypsy putting her head where she could. Often she slept in alleyways, going days without eating. Once the baby came, she knew she had no place to go but home. The streets were too dangerous for a helpless baby.

Suzanne's heart broke as she looked at her once beautiful daughter; half starved obviously beaten recently. Suzanne didn't dare to ask questions she would never be able to hide the judgements in her voice.

Between Suzanne and Angel there had always been a fine line between question and answer or accusation and judgement. They had spent years of building their walls and they weren't going to come tumbling down because Suzanne was having a moment of motherliness.

Once again she found herself having to wait until Angel trusted her for answers; answers she may never hear. Angel looked so thin and tired. At the age of seventeen she looked like an old lady, filled with fear and desperation. There was no sign of the teenager she should be.

As much as her inner conscience tried to talk her out of it, she had to ask Angel if she was still on drugs and if the baby was alright. Angel still had little or no patience for her mother's accusations... "MOTHER

... YOU HAVEN'T LISTENED TO ANYTHING I HAVE TOLD YOU ... IF I HAD NO MONEY FOR FOOD... I SURE WASN'T GOING TO HAVE ANY FOR DRUGS ... BESIDES THE BABY HAS A NAME ... ELIZABETH MARIE BRIAR..."

Angel didn't bother to tell her mother that she had never been into drugs; her mother would believe what she wanted. She would make her own truth. She didn't deserve an explanation. If she were any kind of real mother she would know her daughter and what she was capable of.

It was time to change the subject Suzanne had to lighten things up, she thought Elizabeth Marie was a beautiful name. She apologized for sounding like she was attacking her. She was worried and nervous, but she wanted Angel to know she loved her and would be there for her. She didn't mean to always sound so JUDGEMENTAL.

Suzanne asked Angel what her plans were. Where did she think she was going from here? Angel had no plans; she and Beth were taking things one day at a time and would handle whatever came their way.

Paul walked Suzanne out to the car, where they talked a long time. Paul would call her in a few days after he had a chance to work things out with Angel. He assured her that Angel and the baby would have a home with him as long as they wanted it.

He gave Suzanne a fatherly hug and told her not to worry. The hardest part was getting her home at least that was what he believed at the time. He had no idea what was yet to come or where any of them would end up. He hadn't planned on a baby but he liked the idea.

Suzanne knew what she had to do... She had to get Ray to listen to her, to be more reasonable about Angel. This wasn't just a screwed up kid any more, it was the mother of his first grandchild.

Unfortunately he was as hateful to Suzanne as he was to Angel. They had both hurt him and he was not forgiving either of them. He wasn't about to open the doors that would set him up for more pain.

The last time Suzanne had tried to talk to him, he hung the phone up on her before she could even get a word out about why she called.

The kids were old enough she could deal with them directly. There was no reason for him to have to deal with her in any way.

Suzanne thought about going through Ray's mother but she had been so sick. The kids told her that she had cancer and only had a few months to live. Maybe that was why Ray was so miserable for the past year. To Suzanne it was all the more reason for Ray to listen. His mother had a right to see her first great grandchild before she passed away.

Suzanne decided to drive there instead of calling, that way he couldn't hang up on her. All he could do was slam the door in her face. Aaron went with her for moral support. It was Ray's mother that answered the door.

She looked awful; she was thin, weak and very pale. Her face was worn; it was obvious she was in a lot of pain. Suzanne told her she needed to talk to Ray about Angel, it was important.

Ray was yelling that his mother was supposed to be lying down. When he realized that Suzanne was at the door, he yelled he had nothing to say to her and for his mother to shut the door. Suzanne yelled for him to be a man and come to the door to fight his own battles. His mother was too sick to pass on his messages.

The least he could do was face her himself. Walking to the door, he shoved Suzanne back so hard she fell off the front stoop. He told her if she had been any kind of mother for the past fifteen years, maybe they wouldn't be going through all this mess.

Going back into the house he slammed the door as hard as he could, end of discussion. Aaron grabbed Suzanne by the arm, dragging her back to the car, while she was continuing to scream at the closed door...

"YOUR MOTHER HAS THE RIGHT TO SEE HER FIRST GREAT GRANDCHILD BEFORE SHE DIES... MAYBE NONE OF YOU CARE ABOUT ANGEL BUT AT LEAST YOU COULD CARE ABOUT LITTLE ELIZABETH..."

The front door began to open, Suzanne could see Ray's mother walk slowly onto the porch. Barely hearing her whisper of a voice she asked Suzanne to take her to Angel.

Aaron ran to scoop her up into his arms, as she was on the edge of passing out. It was obvious that every step brought her excruciating pain. Both Aaron and Suzanne worried if she would make the trip, debating if they should take her to hospital instead. She could barely get the words out; she had to see her Angel and her name sake.

When they got to Paul's, Aaron carried Ray's mother in. There was nothing to her; she couldn't have weighed more than eighty pounds. Aaron set her gently on the couch, Angel stood in shock almost scared she would break if she hugged her. Slowly almost animated she began hugging and kissing her gently, both of them had tears welling in their eyes.

Angel's grandmother loved and missed her. She never wanted to worry that way again. Angel ran to get the baby; she told her grandmother that she had named her Elizabeth after her.

This started the well of tears; Angel's grandmother started crying all over again... "YOU NAMED MY GREAT GRANDCHILD AFTER ME ... THANK-YOU ... THANK-YOU SO MUCH ... I LOVE YOU BOTH SO MUCH ..."

Suzanne stayed long enough for the two of them to have time to talk. Ray's mom told Angel she only had a few months to live and that now she could die in peace, knowing her favorite and most special grandchild was home and safe. She begged for Angel to be patient with her father and not give up on him.

Suzanne knew she did the right thing as soon as she saw the two of them together. Ray could be as angry as he wanted but those two had a special bond and needed to be brought together. This was the only female in the world that Angel was ever able to trust, especially now that Bev was forced to stand by her husband.

Aaron held the baby while everyone hugged goodbye. Angel even had a hug for her mother this time, as she whispered a hesitant thank-you. Maybe there was hope for them all yet.

Chapter Eighteen

..." GRAMMA!!..." Ray's mom began to swoon at the door as Aaron caught her in his arms. He carried her to the car still passed out. Laying her across the back seat, he covered her with a blanket that Paul had given them.

Suzanne screamed for Paul to call Ray to meet them at the hospital. She was thankful it was Paul calling, Ray would never give Paul the abuse he would vent on Suzanne. There was no doubt in Suzanne's mind that this too would be blamed on her.

Ray was filled with over flowing rage by the time he got to the hospital. How dare Suzanne try to murder his mother? Suzanne was about sick to death of his dumping all the guilt and blame for everything that went wrong in his life on her.

Alice and R.J. showed up behind their Dad, even they told him to calm down that he was out of line. Suzanne felt a little better it was the first time her children defended her against Ray. She had become so used to being the bad guy it took her by surprise.

It was only moments later that Anna and Dan ran down the hall desperate to see Grandma before she died. With Paul bringing Angel and the baby, Suzanne's family was together again. Granted the circumstances could be better but they were together and that was the start of bringing her family together...

As worried and upset as Suzanne was about her mother in law, she felt warm and thankful to have her family together again. It was the first time in many years that they all even pretended to be a family.

Anna watched as Angel held her baby, how could she be angry with anyone holding a baby. Staring at her first and so far only niece, Anna informed Angel that she too was going to be an aunt. Angel appeared to show no reaction but in her heart she wondered how anyone so cruel could ever be a good mother.

Angel stepped back from Anna as a statement of caution. She wasn't sure how to take Anna. They had never been friends; Anna mostly always had a hook to her kindness. It was with a soft, sympathetic voice that Anna spoke to her lost sister. Was this a trick?

Angel wanted to forgive her sister, to trust her. She wanted to be back in the family. Elizabeth would need family, even if Angel wasn't sure it should be this family. How could Elizabeth grow to need and lean on a family that her mother had spent a lifetime learning to mistrust?

Ray went into intensive care, making the obvious point of turning his back on Angel and her illegitimate child. He wanted nothing to do with her. Neither her nor her baby would ever cause him pain again. Angel was dead to him and the child would simply never exist in his world. He had been hurt enough and wasn't about to open doors that would only set him up to be hurt even more.

As Ray went to speak to his family, Suzanne and Bev went to a payphone to call the rest. Suzanne and Aaron took baby Elizabeth from Angel to take her home with them. It would give Angel a chance to spend time with her brothers and sisters.

And hopefully find some way to get back into Ray's heart. He had a heart that had grown far too cold. He once loved and protected her no matter what. He needed to see her, and realize how much she needed him to protect and love her again.

Everyone was surprised when Angel allowed her mother to take baby Elizabeth home. Angel was overwhelmed with emotions. Her grandmother was dying and she wasn't ready to let her go. With her father turning his back on her, her grandma was one of the very few people left to love her unconditionally.

Suzanne loved having a baby in her arms again. Elizabeth was so tiny and so delicate; she was the same china doll that Angel once was, so sweet and helpless. This little Angel wouldn't have the pain and torture her mother did. This little Angel would stay sweet and innocent; the line of abuse would end with this generation.

Suzanne could give her grandchildren what she could never give her own children. She would be the best grandmother ever. She could now give her grandchildren all the love and attention that her own children had been cheated out of.

Suzanne had finally grown up and she knew and wanted to make up for all her mistakes, starting with this little Angel. Suzanne sat up most of the night holding and rocking the tiny bundle as she had done years ago with Anna.

Aaron never had children of his own, and so, thought having grandchildren around to watch grow would be the next best thing. The two of them sat discussing plans of a guest nursery. Making plans for all the things they could do for and with their grandchildren. It all sounded so wonderful.

Suzanne had missed so much of her children's lives and planned on making up for it. She had so many fences to mend with her children especially with Angel. She only hoped and prayed that Angel would give her the chance.

She watched as Aaron held baby Elizabeth and drifted back to a time when Angel looked every bit as innocent and full of wonder for the world. Elizabeth had her mother's eyes. Suzanne could feel them following her, taking in every detail. Suzanne hoped that she would be easier to love than her mother had been.

While Aaron rocked the baby to sleep, Suzanne got on the phone to Paul. She wanted to talk to him without Angel around. They had to discuss what was to be done from here. It was so strange talking to Paul again as a friend. She had missed his friendship, their long talks on the phone, his advice.

Paul seemed a little hesitant on the phone. Suzanne was puzzled surely he could see something had to be worked out for their future. He was going to try to talk Angel into some kind of further education, perhaps a trade school of some kind. Perhaps secretarial, then she could get a job in his office. He was fairly sure that he would hire a housekeeper nanny type to give Angel the room she would need to figure out her future.

That was all well and good but none of these plans included her or any of the family. Suzanne wasn't sure it was Paul who should be sticking his neck out so far. She was her mother, Ray her father; they were the ones that should be taking care of Angel and Elizabeth.

Maybe instead of Angel being with Paul they should set her up in her own apartment. She could be Elizabeth's mother. It wasn't good to make things too easy for her. How could she be a responsible mother with a nanny doing all the mothering?

Angel had just come home. She had already spent far too much time on her own. She needed to know she had people she could count on. Besides he was tired of being alone. He needed company; he needed Angel and Elizabeth as much as they needed him.

Angel shouldn't be alone; she was still haunted by night terrors. If anything they were worse than they had ever been. Someone had to be there for her to keep her safe during these times of terror. She had seen enough hardship in her day and it was time for her to feel safe and cared for.

He was right and Suzanne knew it, but it was Angel's own family that should be keeping her safe. It was clear Angel wasn't about to let Suzanne help her. She was still totally defensive and guarded with her. They could never live under the same roof when they both brought the worst out in each other.

It was almost lunchtime when Suzanne took the baby back to Angel. She had hoped that Angel would let her keep her for the day. Angel had already called several times wanting her home with her.

As Suzanne arrived, she was filled with all kinds of ideas for both Angel and the baby and she wasted no time telling Angel all her plans for Elizabeth. She had it all worked out, they could spend the day shopping. Elizabeth would need so much.

Maybe afterward they could go out to lunch, perhaps hit the beauty parlor for a make over.... Angel looked at her mother with pure icy hatred as she snatched the baby out of her mother's arms.

..." NEITHER I NOR MY BABY ARE FOR SALE... QUIT THINKING YOU CAN BUY US... CHANGE US AND MOLD US INTO WHATEVER YOU WANT US TO BE...GO HOME MOTHER!.."

Angel wasted no time telling her mother all the years of neglect and abuse couldn't be wiped out by a day in the mall. A few bobbles would never make everything from the past disappear.

When was Suzanne going to figure out that people couldn't be molded? She had to either accept them as the people they are or walk away. Walk away was the choice Angel had in mind, since she had no intentions of spending a day with her mother, or even another minute.

As Angel spoke she pushed her mother closer to the door 'til she could finally push her out slamming the door in her face. Suzanne could not believe what Angel was saying to her. She may not have been the best mother in the world, but that was in the past, couldn't Angel ever forgive her?

Suzanne believed in her heart that she didn't deserve any of this abuse. She went out of her way to try not to sit in judgement of Angel. She did all she could to bury the past so they could start fresh with the present, leaving the past behind them.

Angel's dissension and arrogance was making Suzanne fume with anger. She wanted to slap the look off her face or better yet turn her over her knee. A good spanking was what that child needed..." HOW DARE SHE?..HOW DARE SHE?!.."

No one would argue that Angel needed a reality check. Who did she think she was? Did she really think she was going to be a better mother? She had no goals, even less future. Did Angel really think she could raise her child when she was filled with the same scars that Suzanne had raising her?

Suzanne wondered whom Angel would go crawling to when her child hated her as much as Angel hated Suzanne. Eventually Angel would need someone, and then it would be too late.

Suzanne certainly had no intentions of taking any more of her abuse. Angel had been punishing her mother for her entire life, hadn't she been punished enough for one night of madness.

Suzanne knew that even if Angel did find herself needing someone it would never be Suzanne she would come to. She was the most stubborn and ungrateful of all children everywhere. She would crawl through shit before she'd crawl to her mother.

If Angel didn't want her mother's help then she wouldn't get it. Angel had a lot of nerve acting like it was her mother's entire fault that her life was in a mess. Like she didn't create most of the mess herself and then wallow in it expecting everyone to pity her.

..." NO MORE...!!" never again was Suzanne going to feel guilty. Angel could not only take responsibility for her own mess but she could also clean it up.

If Angel wanted Suzanne in her life, she could call her. Never again would Suzanne crawl to her or beg her forgiveness. She had other children that loved her, she didn't need this abuse, nor did she deserve it.

Suzanne was still crying by the time she got home. Aaron had the good sense to not take any sides. He sat quietly as she ranted and raved through a flood of tears. He had known her long enough to know that he had to let her carry on until she wound down.

Secretly it broke his heart that there was a chance they would never be real grandparents to little Elizabeth. He knew both Suzanne and Angel were stubborn enough to never speak to each other again.

They had spent a lifetime stubbornly hurting each other. There was no peace in sight and little hope of it ever coming. Neither Suzanne nor Angel would ever be the first to break down the wall that rose ever higher between them. They both believed with all their heart they were justified. Unfortunately they were both right as they were both wrong.

It was days of agony and torture before Ray's mother finally passed. Suzanne believed that if anyone deserved a peaceful, painless death, her mother-in-law did. She did nothing her entire life except love and care for other people.

It was what happened after the funeral that left them all dumbfounded. The reading of the will. She had left the money and most of the estate to be divided evenly among her children and her husband's estate to be divided among Suzanne and her brother's and sister.

It was the house that shocked everyone. She left it to Angel, the same house that Ray had raised his family in and taken care of for their lifetime. No one expected anything except the house to go to Ray without question.

She left a note in the will explaining, how Angel more than all the other children would need to know she had a home no matter what. She had to know as she went to her grave that Angel was cared for.

Less than two weeks after the funeral Ray and Bev were served with an eviction notice. Suzanne was both shocked and surprised. She always knew Angel hated her but she thought Ray and Bev had a bond. Even with Ray not speaking to Angel at this time he had always been her hero and her protector. She had always worshiped him.

People thought of Suzanne as cold hearted and incapable of love but Angel was far colder and crueler than she had ever been. Angel didn't even want to live in the house; she simply wanted to hurt her father. She continued living with Paul.

This would clinch things; she had guaranteed that she would be outside of the family forever. No one in the family would ever forgive her now. She had made her bed but could she sleep in it?...

Suzanne couldn't help but think of her mother. It had been a long time since Suzanne even gave her a thought. Angel reminded her of all the pain her mother was capable of inflicting on all that crossed her path.

Three generations of cold-hearted bitch's and Angel was the Queen. The coldest and hardest of them all... "ME FIRST AND SCREW EVERYONE ELSE..." after all no one ever cared about her why should she care about anyone.

Anna had tried very hard to bridge the gap, to keep some semblance of family ties; but Angel was too cool and nasty. It seemed that Angel didn't need a backward farmer's wife in her life. She now traveled in more prestigious circles, Paul's country club set.

Angel now traveled in all the right circles with all the right crowds, going to all the right parties, dressed in all the right clothes. She was now basking in the light of society that Suzanne once gave her children up for.

It was a society that Angel once loathed. She hated her own mother for trying to cram it down her throat. Now they had all done a full circle and ended up in the same place. Three generations of women all craving society all unhappy after they got what they thought would bring them happiness.

No one was real surprised when Paul married Angel that year. No friends, no family, only justice of the peace with a stranger for a witness. He said he married her to give Elizabeth a more respectable standing in social settings, to give her a good name and a chance at life.

Suzanne knew he married her so he could have a piece of Suzanne. He had no idea what kind of monster Angel could be. She would eventually turn on him the same as she turned on everyone who got close.

He did love little Elizabeth and the company, not that Angel was much company. It didn't take her long to start running with the country club set that he had left his first wife to get away from. Paul could no more stand up to Angel than he could Suzanne.

Every once in a while Angel and her new uppity friends would come to the hotel to Lord over their staff, and snub Aaron and Suzanne. Mostly Angel would not acknowledge her mother's existence, while giving her a knife in the gut with a mere glance.

Her eyes always were her best weapon and her sharpest tool. Angel never had Paul with her, but then Paul would never allow her to play her nasty games. She needed someone to stand up to her, to tell her "NO" and that someone was going to be Suzanne.

Aaron and Suzanne were soul owners of the classiest hotel in the city. All the best people went there to put on heirs. Aaron was ready to ban Angel and her entire crowd from the hotel for life or at least until they grew up.

Suzanne would not hear of it. Deep down she felt she deserved every bit of the degradation Angel dished out to her. However Aaron and the rest of her staff did not. There was little doubt that Angel was their worst customer.

Aaron was a very prestigious man of breeding and background, not to mention money and he was not going to be snubbed by a full of herself spoiled brat nineteen year old. He didn't care whom she was married to or who her mother was. It wasn't going to happen.

Suzanne begged him to let her handle it. So the next time Angel and her pack of hoodlums showed up at the hotel Suzanne was ready. Suzanne quietly but firmly requested that Angel accompany her to her office.

It was no surprise when Angel refused; Suzanne was hoping she would refuse. She was looking for an opening, any opening. Suzanne started the show, right where they stood in front of her silver-spooned friends. No holds were barred, below the belt shots all of them.

Angel knew her mother well enough to know that the only way to shut her up was to follow her, they would do battle in private. As Suzanne marched her rebellious daughter down the hall to her office, she could hear the rumblings from her pack...

"DO YOU KNOW THESE PEOPLE?..DON'T LET A COMMON SERVANT PUSH YOU AROUND..." there was no mistaking the air that was filled with shock and disapproval. Suzanne had dealt with these people in adult form; they had learned their attitudes from their parents. They had many times reminded Suzanne just how far below them she was.

No sooner had the door closed when Angel attacked, how dare her mother embarrass her. She had no right, she was not her daughter she was a customer like every other customer. She wasn't like any other customer; she was the worst rudest customer they had to contend with but not any more.

Suzanne was relieved to hear she wasn't her daughter. She would hate to throw a relative out on her ear. She wasted no time telling the little snip how things were going to be from now on. Suzanne was on a roll and it felt good.

She had allowed Angel to both verbally and emotionally abuse her for years now she was ready to give some of it back. Suzanne had spent most of Angel's life feeling guilt. That was all over now, never again would she allow those viscous attacks.

From now on Suzanne, her husband and her staff would no longer take her abuse simply to entertain her friends. Suzanne didn't care if Angel never accepted Aaron as her stepfather, she would show him respect as the owner of this establishment.

Suzanne went on to say that the next time she came into the hotel with attitude, it would be Suzanne's pleasure to bring her down as many pegs as she could. There were many skeletons in Angel's closet; it would never do to rattle those bones.

The particular crowd that she ran with was unmerciful about proper breeding. Was Angel sure her full-of-themselves friends would understand?...It was the end of their discussion; Angel more than got the point.

Angel tried hard to retaliate against the seasoned fighter but Suzanne had out grown her need to impress people. She didn't care who Angel told what to. The only one she cared about she also had no secrets from. Suzanne laughed as she dared Angel to start the war and see who could cause the most damage. Suzanne was looking forward to this battle.

There was a smirk as she asked if maybe they should bring Paul into it. Perhaps he was the one who needed to clip Angel's wings. Suzanne knew it would kill Angel for Paul to be disgraced by his wife's bad behavior.

Angel looked at Suzanne with a loathing hatred, stronger than she had ever seen before ... "PAUL WOULD NEVER LISTEN TO YOU, HE HATES YOU AS MUCH AS I DO..." Suzanne smiled a sly smile to let Angel know she had the upper hand...

"HE DOESN'T HATE ME... HE LOVES ME AND ALWAYS HAS ... HE MARRIED YOU LOOKING FOR ME ... IN YOUR HEART YOU KNOW I AM RIGHT OR YOU WOULDN'T BE SO ANGRY..."

Angel wasn't listening to any more of this she was worn down and worn out. She couldn't get out of the door and the hotel fast enough. She knew it was true and always would be. There would never be a time when Paul didn't love Suzanne. He never married Angel for love, he married her for pity.

Poor pathetic Angel, charity case... the only people who really loved her were dead. Good thing they were because they would all hate what she had become. That is except for Suzanne's mother, who would not only like this behavior but also find it admirable.

Suzanne on the other hand was disgusted by it. She didn't have to deal with it again; Angel never came back to the hotel. That was enough to get a cheer of relief from the entire staff. Quietly Suzanne felt saddened by it.

As long as Angel was coming there was a slim chance of getting through to her. A very slim chance but a chance, that was better than the no chance she had with her not coming at all.

The entire family gathered at Anna's farm for her son's birthday, Daniel Raymond Ellis was two years old and adorable? That is of course excepting Angel. Ray and Bev had become good friends with Suzanne and Aaron.

It was such a pleasure to have everyone together and on good terms. Suzanne loved to watch them laugh and joke together. They had all grown to be such wonderful adults. A piece of her filled with guilt at not being a part of who they had become. At least she was given a second chance that she wasn't about to screw up.

The icing on the cake was when Anna announced her second pregnancy. Danny was a farm boy and wanted lots of sons to work with him. Suzanne hoped all the sons he planned for loved the farm as much as he and Anna.

Suzanne loved to see Anna and Danny together. They were such a wonderful couple, the way a couple should be; doing everything together, totally balancing each other, and totally loving each other. Something that took her a long time to figure out and would take Angel even longer, that is if she ever got it.

Suzanne felt life was going by so fast; Alice got married last year to a young boy in dentistry school. He was a quiet shy kind of boy that blushed far too easily. It actually worked well for both of them as a couple since Alice was friendly enough for both of them.

Suzanne was amazed at how boisterous Alice was, and how much her husband Stanley would not only be embarrassed by it but love her for it. After only a few months of marriage Alice was told she would never be able to conceive children.

She said she was all right with that and that eventually they could adopt. But every now and again Suzanne could see the hint of a tear as her youngest daughter held her sister's baby. It was such heartache of all Suzanne's children; it was Alice that had the most love to give a child.

Then there was Angel with a child she never had time or love for. Angel was in a very few short years going to feel from her own daughter, every stinging word she had said to Suzanne. Why did each generation have to pass the line of abuse on to the next? Why did none of them ever learn from their own childhood?

Why did the pain and heartache have to be passed on like an unwanted disease? Suzanne passed on her mother's heartache and now Angel was passing on her mother's. Which generation would stop the pain? Who would break this chain?

Suzanne was filled with a wide range of emotions, as she watched her baby walk down the aisle, everything from pride to regret. Regret she had not been there more for them all. Now her baby was flying out of the nest to build a new nest of his own. She was lucky that her family had grown to be such wonderful adults. She knew she had little to do with the pride she felt for the people they had become.

R.J. was marrying a wonderful girl; her father owned the grocery store where R.J. worked since he was fifteen. He was already a part of their family; it was only natural that these highschool sweethearts would tie the knot.

Suzanne had the reception at her hotel. It was what she did best and putting it all together for her only son made it all the more gratifying. It was a grand affair. Ray on the other hand was more interested in when his only son and name sake would become a father himself.

After the candle light service that took everyone's breath away, they all made their way to one of the most exquisite receptions ever. Everything was in its place, no detail was left undone, nothing forgotten, everything perfect. Nothing was too good for her son.

She had an incredible staff that always did an incredible job but this time they amazed even Suzanne. She could not have been prouder of the entire evening. There would be substantial bonus in each of their paychecks.

The meal was finished and coffee was being served, as the plates were being cleared away. Angel made her dramatic grand entrance, falling over drunk and stoned out of her mind. Angel staggered across the room, yelling obscenities at the entire family, which she couldn't seem to find.

It seemed that she resented not being invited. She came to remind them all that she was part of the family whether they liked it or not. Suzanne was wishing at that moment that R.J. had invited his sister to the wedding.

Suzanne tried to explain to R.J. that the only way to keep Angel away was to let her think you expect her to be there. Then she would have stayed away so that you weren't winning whatever battle was in her head.

R.J. and his new bride sat frozen with fear and embarrassment, not knowing what to do, but praying that someone did something quick. Ray couldn't bring himself to look at the person that his princess had become.

Aaron was the first to get to her. She hated and resented Aaron and always had. For some reason in Angel's twisted thoughts she believed that Aaron ruined everything. By the time Suzanne got to them, Angel was kicking and pounding poor Aaron with all her might.

He picked her up and threw her over his shoulder. As he started to go toward the front door, Suzanne steered him toward her old room. Aaron and Suzanne still kept Suzanne's suite for the nights they worked late. She instructed Aaron to throw the passed out Angel on the bed.

Suzanne could handle Angel, Aaron would have to go back to the reception hall and act like nothing happened. As far as R.J. was concerned all was well and this was still his magical night. There was no reason for him to be disturbed by his sister's actions on what was probably the most important night of his life so far.

Watching Angel sleep, Suzanne had to find out as much as she could about what was going on. It would be a good time to call Paul. How could he be her husband and let her get as bad as this? Why wasn't he doing something to help her?

Paul wasted no time telling Suzanne that Angel had walked out on him and Elizabeth. It had been some time since they were together. Long enough that he was able to go to court and get legal custody of Elizabeth. Angel didn't even bother to show up at the hearing.

Not that she would have had a chance. She was dangerous to Elizabeth and they all knew it. The only time she even showed up to see her daughter was when she was very drunk or wanted money. She was apparently living back at the house her grandmother gave her.

Mostly she gave an allusion of being alone; Paul had heard rumors... the kinds of rumors a mother shouldn't hear. Paul still paid her bills and sent her groceries every week, but he had quit giving her money a long time ago. He wasn't going to pay for her to drown in a bottle.

Suzanne needed advice and Paul could offer little. Angel was on a self destruct all Suzanne and the rest of the family could do was get out of the way and hope they didn't get destroyed with her.

Suzanne only had one last request, a request that was hard for her to ask... could Suzanne and the rest of the family see Little Elizabeth now and again. Maybe pick her up for a day trip or a family gathering?

Paul had to know that it would be important for Elizabeth to maintain family contact, to know her roots. Paul was very hesitant as he agreed to discuss it another day. At least there was hope, it was better than a straight out no.

For the moment Suzanne had enough to deal with. She promised to call Paul and keep him up to date on what they decided to do with Angel, as Paul promised to keep her up to date on Elizabeth.

Chapter Nineteen

Suzanne stayed by Angel's side the entire night. She didn't know what to expect with the withdrawal of the drugs. She knew how bad it had been with her alcohol withdrawal it had to be worse with all the drugs Angel had been doing for years.

Suzanne didn't want Angel waking up in a strange environment totally crashing down. During one of the many checks Aaron brought Suzanne a tray. He was running out of excuses but still needed to check on them. He knew how violent Angel could be and feared for his wife's safety and sanity.

Of course he never said those words out loud; he merely told her he missed her smiling face lighting up the room. They hadn't spent anything more than blinks away from each other since their marriage and he missed her. At least that was what he told her as he checked far too frequently.

There wasn't a night they had slept apart since they had married; it was an unspoken law in their marriage. Whatever else was happening in their day... their nights had to end together in each other's arms. Their marriage was strong and could survive this one night apart.

This would be a crucial night for Angel. She would need her mother even if she never her entire life admitted to it. Suzanne had no choice but to stay with her daughter to get her through this hell.

Suzanne had failed Angel many times in the past, but tonight she was going to be there for her. She had every intention of keeping her prisoner until she was sober and lucid enough to talk to her. It didn't matter how much she kicked screamed and fought she would not be deterred from saving her daughter.

Suzanne figured from her own experience, it would take at least three days for the D.T.'s to pass; then she had at least another two days of feeling rotten. That was to get the booze out of her system and get her to a point where she could converse.

God only knew what drugs she had in her system. Suzanne was a stranger to the drug world and couldn't begin to know what to expect. She quietly worried that perhaps she was in over her head. What if this was dangerous? What if she was putting Angel at risk?

All these questions rattled through her mind, haunting her, trying to convince her to not do this. When Aaron came back for yet another check, she gave him the contents of the bar. Suzanne had forgotten how much she once drank.

It was vital that it was all gone. Suzanne knew all too well how sneaky and frantic an alcoholic could get. She told him he had better count on her being with Angel for at least four to five days. Even that was a guess.

Aaron was more worried than he had ever been, he begged Suzanne to check Angel into a hospital. Suzanne wouldn't hear of it. She had made that mistake once before and she wasn't about to turn her back on her daughter again. Suzanne was determined to save Angel despite herself.

It was time for Suzanne to stand and fight. Fight for her daughter. She had to get her daughter past all the pain and hatred that took a lifetime to build up. It was time for both of them to start fighting the ghosts and stop hiding behind the past and all it's built in excuses.

Suzanne had almost put the reception out of her head when R.J. came to knock on the door and thank her for the reception. He had to say his good-byes; Aaron had surprised all of them with a honeymoon. It was something that otherwise would have been put off for an unlimited number of years.

As R.J. stood in the doorway watching his sister sleep, he was amazed at how harmless she looked. Suzanne begged R.J. to forgive and try to understand his sister. It was important to her that they didn't hate or blame her.

There were reasons why Angel was the way she was ... Reasons he could never begin to understand. The only thing he understood was that people had been making excuses for her as far back as he could remember. It was time his sister became answerable for her actions.

She brought pain and destruction everywhere she went and it was time for her to face the consequences of her actions. Everyone feels sorry for her when she hurts them. There is something wrong with that. She has to be made responsible for the pain she brings to everyone who loves her. It is time to stop crippling her by giving her pathetic excuses.

Angel spent most of the night lost in a fitful sleep. Suzanne remained by her bed, watching Angel thrashing and fighting the ghosts locked in her head. She wondered who or what it was that she was trying to fight.

In an attempt to help her Suzanne woke her daughter several times when the terrors seemed unbearable only to have her drift right back into them. Angel never seemed to wake fully or even know where she was. Suzanne worried about the drugs. There was no way of knowing what her daughter had taken or what the withdrawals would be.

When Suzanne tried to call a doctor for advice, the only advice was to bring her in to the hospital. Suzanne could not do that, she had to see her daughter through this. She had turned her back on her far too many times in the past. Suzanne would have to find a way through this.

The sun was barely up when Shelby showed up at the door. Aaron was sleeping in a chair in the livingroom; Suzanne was still by Angel's side in the bedroom. He brought them all an array of food and juices not sure what any of them would want or need.

For Angel he brought juices and broth, he was sure she wouldn't be able to hold much else. He walked to the side of the bed and wiped

Angel's forehead, he knew she would be very sick very soon. He was sure Suzanne had no idea what she was in store for. The only thing Suzanne was sure of was the fear that filled her heart. A heart that was breaking with every moment that passed.

One of Shelby's lovers had been a drug addict and he too thought he could nurse him off them. It was without a doubt one of the hardest, scariest times in his life. He prayed he would never have to see anyone go through it again.

He told Suzanne she could expect anything from sweats and chills to skin crawling with imaginary bugs. Angel could feel like she is on fire or that every bone in her body was going to break from the entire body aches of the withdrawals.

If none of that happens then the least she could expect would be dry heaves and deep body aches. "THE SICKNESS " as addicts refer, would cause them to hurt, and hurt bad. Reaching a point where they would say or do anything to make the pain go away ... that is depending on what she was on.

Shelby tried his hardest to think of all the drugs he knew about. Trying to give Suzanne hope, he named a few that had no withdrawal, at least not violent withdrawal. He couldn't help but think of the worst of the drugs, the ones that he was too scared to mention.

He had to talk her into doing this elsewhere. Some place secluded where Angel could be restrained if necessary. If Angel started yelling, fighting, or trying to get away, it wouldn't disturb the clientele. She knew he was right. What she didn't know was where to take her.

Aaron interrupted Suzanne he knew what they had to do about the situation. Suzanne agreed, there was only one place to take her. He had already received complaints from the night before.

The only place they could take Angel was their home. At least they were isolated so there was no one to disturb, and no place to run. It really was the only place that made sense. That is if Suzanne still insisted on no hospital.

Suzanne slipped her two sleeping pills, there was no way she wanted Angel to wake up in the car and try to jump out of the window. The first thing they did at home was to set up a bed in the basement. They had a little room for storage that had no windows and only one door in or out... with a padlock on it.

Suzanne prayed that it wouldn't come to that. Angel already had so many fears; Suzanne didn't want to add to them in any way. She needed her daughter to be sober enough to talk. Suzanne was determined that neither of them would leave until everything was settled. They had spent enough time running from each other.

Suzanne was both surprised and apprehensive when Aaron suggested bringing Angel to their house. Her daughter had openly hated and been disrespectful to him from the day they married. Suzanne was relieved that he understood but would not have blamed him if he refused to have anything to do with her.

Angel had never given way to misjudgment of a person and Aaron was a good example of misjudgment if Suzanne had ever seen one. She had misjudged him herself for years and finally saw him in a true light. Now hopefully they would all have a chance to see each other in a new light, Suzanne now had hopes of saving her shattered family.

It was several hours before Angel started to wake up, shaking from chills. Suzanne grabbed a blanket and wrapped it around her trying to hold her. Angel didn't want to be held, and she sure wasn't about to be held prisoner.

Angel wasted no time throwing out whatever threats she could think of. Right down to wanting Suzanne arrested for kidnapping. Suzanne wasn't so sure she would be arrested for kidnapping her own kid. Feeling pretty confident she made it more than clear to Angel she would have to figure out how she was going to get out to call the police.

With that Angel went crazy, spewing out a string of obscenities that Suzanne decided to ignore. Attempting to lunge at her mother Angel was forced to give up the fight as she began to vomit instead. Suzanne wasn't worried, at least not yet it would be days before she was strong enough to put up any kind of fight.

Suzanne took a cooled cloth to wipe her face, Angel swatted at her mother to stop. She didn't need her mother and certainly didn't want to be touched by her. Suzanne decided if that was what she wanted then that is what she would get.

Suzanne made her way to the door; Angel was like a cat, trying to get to it before her mother. That is until the dry heaves over came her, leaving her once again lying on the floor holding her stomach hoping the unbearable pain would pass.

Even writhing in pain it was obvious that Angel didn't want her mother anywhere near her. In time she would be thankful to her mother, she just didn't know it yet. Maybe in time she would not only appreciate her mother but thank her for all her efforts.

Aaron went to the hotel to hold things together. When he finally got home Angel was still ranting every bit as loud as she was when he left. It sounded like she had thrown every item that was in the room. They both wondered where she got the strength.

Suzanne tried hard to remember what she had left in the room then decided that anything that was smashed was not worth as much as her daughter. Things could be replaced, her daughter couldn't.

Determined not to go down to Angel until she was quiet, Suzanne could hardly stand it. She would not give in, not this time, even if it meant no supper. Like any other out of control child, bad behavior would not be rewarded.

Suzanne made her way quietly down to the basement not wanting Angel to know she was there, she sat with her back to the door, listening. She had to know her daughter was safe, even if she couldn't let her know she was watching over her.

Suzanne pressed her hands tightly over her face, trying to smother the sobs she didn't dare let Angel hear but could not hold back. Her heart broke as she was forced to face the mess she had left her daughter's life in. She swam in the guilt of a mother that knew she should have done better.

It was several hours before the Weinstein household fell into silence. Both Suzanne and Angel fell asleep where they crumbled in emotions with no more than a door between them. Aaron went to check on his wife, he was worried. Would his wife survive this? Would this push her back into the bottle herself?

He woke his wife begging her to come to bed. She could not; she had to take care of Angel. Suzanne made her way upstairs to heat up some broth and some juice not sure if her prisoner could even hold anything down. There was a very good chance that anything would make Angel start heaving again.

Suzanne opened the door as quietly as she could, not sure how close Angel was to it. Surprise would be the only way; they would have to sneak up on Angel so she didn't bolt as soon as the door opened.

It broke Suzanne's heart to see her daughter curled up in a little ball in one of the corners with a blanket wrapped around her. She looked so tiny and helpless, not much different than when she was little and would hide in her closet.

Suzanne could not help but wonder if now Angel lived in the house alone if she still hid in that closet. It was all so long ago and yet here it was still raw on the surface. Never were either of them allowed to forget or bury the past.

Suzanne set the soup on the table and sat on the floor beside her little girl making yet another attempt to hold her. This time Angel allowed the embrace. Suzanne began humming a soft song, the same song she hummed to her babies all those years ago when Anna and Angel were so little.

Angel's voice was no more than a weak whisper as she told her mother she remembered the song, not too sure where from. At least she was beginning to remember that was a start and all Suzanne would need to get to her and bring her back.

Angel looked bad; her hair had not been washed in many days. Between the withdrawals and the rages, her clothes were drenched in perspiration. Suzanne offered to take her upstairs for a shower if she could behave. She had to be trusted at some point; she certainly couldn't go forever without a bath. Suzanne hoped that her daughter was straight enough to appreciate that her mother was only doing this to help her.

Angel bolted, she was a wild animal caught in a cage, going in any and every direction desperate to out run and out maneuver her captors. It was Aaron who finally got hold of her and carried her to the bathroom, shoving her in the shower clothes and all. He turned the cold water tap on full hoping to cool off her hot temper.

Angel screamed a scream that would have woke the dead, making both Suzanne and Aaron thankful they had no neighbors within earshot. Bursting into uncontrolled sobs, Angel crumbled into a ball of helpless defeat in the bottom of the tub.

Trembling from the cold Angel tried her hardest to hold back the tears that were already escaping. Crying was what her mother wanted. Angel knew her mother was quite capable of using her weakness against her. It was vital she hide her weakness at all cost.

..." WELL MOTHER, IT ISN'T GOING TO WORK, SOMEHOW, SOMEWAY, I WILL FIND MY ESCAPE..." she simply had to be trickier about it. She would have to pretend to be playing her mother's little game. Eventually her mother would let her guard down enough for her to make her escape.

Suzanne pulled the shower curtain closed and stayed in the bathroom with her; talking to her, trying to keep her calm. Suzanne slowly got Angel out of the clothes that needed fumigating and would get to the garbage as fast as Suzanne could throw them there.

Suzanne slipped the warm flannel nighty over her daughter as though she was still her little girl. Angel appeared to have no fight left, she closely resembled the limp rag doll that she treasured when she was so little and helpless.

If the chills started again, Angel would be thankful for the warmth that only flannel can give. Suzanne loved wearing flannel nighties when she was little. The feel of it always made her think of being a little girl sitting on Daddy's knee before bed.

It was one of Suzanne's warmest snuggliest memories. She hoped that Angel could have the same little girl feelings as she snuggled into the warmth of it. The same safe escape she once had as her Daddy was still her protector and her knight.

Angel did seem calmer, quieter, somehow more accepting of the situation. Suzanne hoped it wasn't just the calm before the storm. Was all the silence simply Angel quietly planning and waiting for the moment of escape to present itself?

Suzanne hoped it meant that Angel had at least resigned herself to her fate. Aaron knew better and was determined to keep his guard up. He had not known Angel well or even allowed her to get too close, but he did know she was tricky and anything could happen if she were around.

The next four days were spent with Suzanne waiting on Angel hand and foot, hoping for a sign that she was coming around, that she would see the light, come to her senses. Suzanne was sure that as soon as the drugs and booze were gone, Angel would realize what she was doing to not only herself but little Elizabeth.

Every time Suzanne looked into her daughter's eyes she was met with loathing. She kept praying for some hint that her daughter understood that she didn't hate her. She prayed for some miracle from God that suddenly all would be forgiven, forgotten and all right between them.

That was the way it always happened on t.v... Wasn't it? Someone would start crying, confess how sorry they were, they would hug and it would all magically disappear ... not quite so easy in real life.

What is it inside Angel that kept her hanging onto her pain so tightly? It was as though she needed the pain to live, or was it make her feel alive. It didn't matter why she hung onto it. It was time to let go. If it killed them both, Suzanne was going to find a way to get past it.

After four nights of Suzanne sleeping on a cot by Angel's bed, Aaron was getting quietly impatient. He never said the words, but she could feel the front he put on sliding. On the fifth night she decided it was safe to sleep with Aaron, he had sacrificed enough and deserved to have a wife in his bed again.

It felt so good to snuggle in his arms. Suzanne had missed being held by him. They lay awake for hours, talking, mostly about Angel. Aaron was right; they couldn't keep her a prisoner much longer. She was sober and clean of drugs.

It was going to have to be up to Angel, there was nothing else they could do for her. Angel had to help herself; no one could save her if she wasn't going to save herself.

Suzanne only had one more thing to accomplish before she set Angel free. She had to find some way of getting Elizabeth for the day. Maybe that would be enough to shake Angel up, she had not been with her daughter completely straight in a long time. Suzanne hoped that straight Angel could open her eyes and see how much Elizabeth needed a mother, a straight and sober mother.

Angel had to stop floating in and out of Beth's life; she needed a full time mother at such a young age. It didn't matter how much Paul bought her or gave her, it wasn't the same as a mother.

Why did all that sound so familiar? People had given her the same lecture for years. There was no doubt that Angel would rub Suzanne's nose in that fact if she dared to tell her straight out the kind of mother she should be.

Suzanne could not believe how much Beth had grown. Had it really been four years already? She was an incredible beauty, every bit the beauty her mother had been and could still be again. The only way Paul would agree to this meeting was if he were there to.

He was worried about Elizabeth's vulnerability and Angel's instability; there was no way of knowing how either would react. Elizabeth hadn't seen her mother in some time, and she hadn't seen her grandma since she was a baby.

When they got to the house Angel ran to Beth hugging, kissing, crying and spinning her around like she couldn't quite believe Beth was there. Paul went with Suzanne and Aaron into the kitchen to discuss what to do next.

Paul asked Suzanne if she had been to Angel's house since Ray and Bev moved out. Angel hadn't been speaking to her since Ray's mother's funeral. Suzanne had heard rumors, none of them good. All of them broke her heart.

Suzanne asked Paul if they were a real married couple, if they were in love! Paul told her that they were married in name only, that when he looked at Angel he saw a little girl. The only reason they married was so he could take care of and provide for them both. He wanted Beth to have a father and a name in society.

He was the end of his family line, had no one to leave anything to or even cry at his funeral. When he died there would be a monthly allowance for Angel, enough she would be very comfortable but the majority of his fortune would go to Beth.

Suzanne tried to bite her tongue, it was Angel's life and she should stay out of it. Angel would never protect or defend herself; someone had to ask the questions. What would he do if Angel got strong and straight and wanted her child back?

He knew a child needed a mother and Beth was no exception. He could hear the way she cried quietly every night wanting her mother to tuck her in and hug her. It broke his heart to see how sad and lonely Beth had become.

When Angel allows herself to be she is a wonderful mother. Paul loved to see them together. But it never lasted long, still Angel can't stand the stability of a real family and has to go on a binder that often lasts several months. No child should witness a parent in that state.

Angel was welcome to come home and be mother to Beth at anytime. Paul held no grudges, she was welcome and could stay as long as she wanted or better... forever. That was all well and good, he would put no pressure on her.

However, never as long as he lived, would she take that child anywhere. Paul was getting angry with Suzanne's judgements... he told her to go to Angel's and take a good long look around before judging him. It wasn't a home; it was a flop house for every lowlife addict in town.

All he was doing was trying to protect Beth and keep her safe, from the environment that was so toxic to Angel. Someone had to love the child or she would end up as bitter and angry as both her mother and grandmother not to mention great grandmother.

Angel can't stand being in the house alone so she gets all messed up on drugs and then drags home any derelict that might follow her. If she has to sleep with them to keep them there, then sleep with them she does.

What do you think happens to a little girl in an atmosphere like that? Do you think Angel would be straight enough to keep that little girl safe? Or even make sure she was clean and well fed? Do you really believe after spending time with Angel that she will ever be a loving and responsible parent?

Suzanne had to know what Paul wasn't saying. She knew him well enough to know when there were undertones and unspoken words with hidden meaning. She had to know, what if... It could happen, Angel could turn her life completely around. After all wasn't that what happened to Suzanne?

Paul was adamant, it would never happen no matter how stable Angel became. Elizabeth would never be taken from him or his home. Angel had signed papers, as long as Paul was alive Beth would stay with him as her only and legal father.

Was Suzanne hearing this right? Had he bought both Angel and her child? Suzanne rose slowly she had to be eye to eye with Paul. She needed as much intimidation as she could muster up. It wasn't going to work, Paul knew her weak spots.

He wasted no time poking and prodding at them. How dare she be so self-righteous, at least he had always been there for Angel? That was a lot more than Suzanne could say over the years. She spent the last five days trying to be the mother she should have been all along.

Now she was getting upset... "YOU CAN NOT OWN PEOPLE ... SLAVERY WAS OUT-LAWED IN THE LAST CENTURY ... "No wonder Angel was such a mess,

Suzanne had always believed that Paul loved Angel unconditionally. Why couldn't he see the only person this was good for was himself? This was the ultimate of selfish acts.

Elizabeth was bound to spend her life longing and searching for her mother's love. Why couldn't Paul see... he wasn't protecting her he was scarring her...." YOU CAN'T DO THIS, YOU CAN'T!!... YOU JUST CAN'T ... PLEASE PAUL ... I BEG YOU THINK ABOUT WHAT YOU ARE DOING TO BOTH ANGEL AND ELIZABETH... "

Suzanne had to be calmer; she had to touch his soft side, hit on his good judgement. The real Paul had to still be in there somewhere. As Suzanne spoke she worked hard to soften her voice, to give it a tone of both compassion and understanding.

Only a calm level head would reach Paul, or so she thought. In reality, Paul was getting older and with age comes a kind of fear. For Paul it was a fear of being alone, a fear of never being loved.

He was right Angel had pushed away not only the family but all who got too close. Suzanne was as guilty as all the rest; they didn't have to let Angel push them away. Suzanne should have worked harder to force Angel to stay in the family. Suzanne placed her name at the top of the guilty list... That didn't mean Angel deserved any of this.

..." PAUL ... LOOK AT ANGEL AND BETH TOGETHER AND TELL ME WHAT YOU ARE DOING IS RIGHT ... YOU TOOK ADVANTAGE OF A SCARED CONFUSED CHILD... A CHILD THAT HAD NO ONE ELSE TO TURN TO ..."

Now it was Paul who was angered, she had used and abused him since the first day they met...." HOW DARE YOU MAKE ME THE BAD GUY ... ANGEL WAS A MESS LONG BEFORE I CAME ALONG ... I HAVE NOT DESTROYED HER, I HAVE SECURED HER FUTURE AND THE FUTURE OF HER CHILD ... I HAVE GIVEN THEM BOTH THE WORLD ..."

Paul was so upset that he could hardly speak. He had been there for everyone, for Suzanne, and for her children. When was it time for someone to give some of it back? When was it his turn to be cared for and protected the way he had always protected them? Didn't he deserve a thank-you at least?

He had given freely and expected nothing and asked even less, but now it was his turn. All he asked, all he wanted was to be loved and appreciated for all he had done.

" ... I HAVE NOT TAKEN ADVANTAGE OF ANGEL.. I HAVE TAKEN CARE OF ANGEL WHEN NO ONE ELSE COULD BE BOTHERED..."

Suzanne's heart broke, Paul was right they had all taken all he had to give and given back very little. But they had never asked him for any of it. It wasn't fair to expect them to pay such a high price for something he had given freely..."

..." AT WHAT PRICE PAUL?.. YOU MAY HAVE GIVEN THEM THE WORLD BUT YOU HAVE STOLEN THEIR LIVES, THEIR VERY SOULS... YOUR PRICE IS TOO HIGH..."

..." I CAN'T BELIEVE I AM EVEN HAVING THIS CONVERSATION...THIS IS INSANE ... SUZANNE YOU HAVE JUST SPENT THE LAST FOUR DAYS WITH ANGEL, HOW CAN YOU EVEN BEGIN TO FANTASIZE THAT SHE WILL EVER BE A GOOD MOTHER..."

Paul was dumbfounded. They should be all thanking him. They should be patting him on the back for raising Beth, for keeping her safe despite her mother. Maybe he couldn't save Angel but he could keep Beth from the same destiny that scarred both Angel and Suzanne.

..." MAYBE SHE ISN'T READY NOW, BUT SHE IS GROWING UP AND CAN SOMEDAY TURN IT ALL AROUND ... SHE DOES LOVE HER DAUGHTER AND EVENTUALLY I HAVE THE HOPE SHE WILL DO IT FOR HER, IF NOT FOR HERSELF..."

With that the discussion was over. Paul walked up to Angel and told her they were all going home. Beth got a huge excited smile on her face and hugged her mother even tighter. Angel followed Paul and Beth out like a puppy on a leash.

It broke Suzanne's heart to see what little fight her daughter had left. Here she was almost twenty-one, and she had a sad darkness on her face like she had already endured a lifetime of hardship and grief.

Suzanne wished there was some way she could help her, but even Suzanne knew there was no way. If there were something that could be done, Angel would never allow it. A small piece of Suzanne wondered if Paul would allow her to be straight and sober, maybe he liked to keep her worthless. Was that his way of stopping Angel from exercising her parental rights.

There had to be a way of stopping him. Maybe if Angel stayed clean for a period of time, she could go to court. Surely a mother had rights especially since Paul wasn't the natural father. Maybe that would be Angel's only hope. That is if ever she got away from Paul. From the looks of things she would never even question his authority.

As much as Aaron hated what Paul was doing, he couldn't see the sense in taking Beth from the only father and stability she had ever known. She had slept in the same bed her entire life. Uprooting her would be as bad as what Paul was doing. One fact that was true, they were both better with him than without him... for now anyway.

Lying in bed, safe in Aaron's embrace, Suzanne wished she could go back in time and fix everything that was wrong. Somehow, magically change Angel into a happy and secure child. If only Suzanne could erase all the things in her daughter's life that had caused her so much pain.

Chapter Twenty

The next day Suzanne picked up Anna and they were to meet Alice for lunch. It was the first time she spoke to her girls since she tried to rescue Angel. It felt good to gab and just have fun. It was a girl's day out.

Suzanne had come to enjoy the company of her adult daughters, she was proud of the kind of people they had become. They were so full of life and happiness. They had attained the kind of peace and contentment that Suzanne wished Angel could find.

Alice was brimming over with her secret and would burst if she didn't get it out. She was three months pregnant; she couldn't tell them 'til it was real and sure. She had given up all hope; the doctors told her it was impossible. This truly was a gift from God.

Alice had never been certain how she felt about God and religion, but this miracle would get her to church every Sunday. After that little announcement it would be hard to steer the conversation in the direction Suzanne wanted to go.

Anna had already given birth to her second son, so the sisters were immersed in baby talk and pregnancy woes. The girls laughed and giggled as they shared their stories. Suzanne wished she could let this be the afternoon. She hated to bring them down, or to spoil their day out.

Anna laughed as she told Alice she had better have the girl grandchildren in the family. Her husband had already willed all their children to be boys. Anna was pleased at the prospect of raising only boys it was so much harder and more complicated to raise girls.

With that Suzanne skillfully turned the conversation first to Beth and then Angel, the real meaning of this girl's afternoon out. She had to touch the girl's soft spot. It would be difficult, where Angel was concerned they only had hard bitter spots.

They both scowled neither wanted to discuss Angel or even acknowledge her existence. As far as the girls were concerned, they had no sister by that name. Angel was dead to them and the rest of the family.

Somehow, discussing Angel was being disloyal to Ray's wishes. But it was more than that; they believed that he was right in his decision to disown her, to banish her from the family. Suzanne had to beg them to even listen for a few short minutes. Mostly they hated the idea of ruining an otherwise perfect day.

She told them about the recent ordeal, how Paul had stolen Beth from Angel. Paul now owned them both and had no intention of ever letting them go or of letting them have any life outside of him. Both girls were getting angry and impatient; Suzanne kept talking for this was all too important. Angel had no fight of her own left, so she would need her family by her side. Suzanne had to get them to understand.

Anna was the hard nose, fully believing in what Paul did. Angel was irresponsible and always had been. If everyone hadn't made so many excuses for Angel maybe she would have grown up to be an adult, instead of a screw-up.

Alice was starting to soften, probably because of her own newfound miracle. She couldn't imagine carrying a child inside of her only to have it taken away. But then Paul wasn't trying to take Angel away from Beth but keep Beth and Angel safe.

Anna jumped right in…"ANGEL HAS MADE HER OWN BED… HER LIFE IS A MESS BECAUSE SHE MADE IT A MESS…" Suzanne had a sudden flash of deja vous, who did that sound like? How many times had she heard that in her lifetime?

Anna had trouble dealing with the grays in life. To her everything was black or white, right or wrong, and that was that, end of discussion. What she was most sick to death of were all the excuses everyone always made for Angel. No one could even say her name without following it with..." BUT "...

Suzanne hadn't asked for much over the years, as she sat she couldn't think of even once asking her girls for anything. She mostly let them live their lives without any interference. This time she had a request, an important request. She wasn't about to take no for an answer. The girls had to know this was important and she would never ask again.

Suzanne told the girls she wanted a family reunion. She wanted everyone together including Angel, Paul and Elizabeth. Even Ray and Bev would be invited.

She wanted to have it on the first weekend after R.J. got back from his honeymoon. Alice was excited right away, but Anna had one of her..." DON'T EXPECT ME THERE..." looks creeping over her face.

In the middle of the restaurant, in front of thirty people, both Alice and Suzanne dropped to their knees and begged Anna to reconsider. There was nothing like public embarrassment to break down stubborn walls. They kept begging 'til Anna relented.

She agreed to come only if they would get up immediately and stop embarrassing her. She had one stipulation... if Angel started her backward, farmer crap; she would have to punch Angel in the head.

Suzanne assured her that she wasn't like that anymore, that she had been humbled, beaten down by the world's hardships. Anna couldn't help but make Harp playing movements. She had been hearing the " OH WAH!.. POOR ANGEL SHIT " ... as far back as she could remember.

What Suzanne was praying for was that Angel would be sober and civil, but even more than that. It would take a lot of praying to just get her there. Suzanne knew she was going to have her hands full pulling this off, but she couldn't think of anything more important than her family being a family. Even Ray had agreed to come, not knowing about Angel possibly being there helped him agree.

Suzanne's newest resolution was to call all of her kids at least twice a week. Mostly they thought she was getting crazy in her old age. What it came down to was her new found respect for the life she was living, not to mention her own mortality.

Whatever she wanted to accomplish with her family, she had to start somewhere. She could never begin to undo all the pain and scars she had left for the past fifteen years of her selfish life, if she didn't at least make a start.

She didn't want anyone standing over her coffin crying about how much they hated her or wanting to know why Suzanne didn't love them enough. Suzanne was now well into her forties, there were no more guarantees in her life.

Every time Suzanne called, Angel hung the phone up on her. Suzanne was determined, persistent, and certainly not ready to give up. Even if Angel wouldn't talk to her she would know her mother tried. Sooner or later she would have to acknowledge her mother.

Suzanne had no choice, the days were closing in on her and still she hadn't managed to speak even one word to Angel. Her only option was to call Paul and beg him to find a way for the three of them to be at the reunion.

He did have some good news for her. Angel wasn't running she seemed fairly content. She was coming every day to be with Beth and coming clean and sober. Beth was happy to have her Mom back. Angel promised Beth she would make every effort to be there for her that she would always be there for her. There would be no more disappearing for long periods of time.

Paul believed every promise Angel made. Suzanne was pleased she was making an effort; whether it would last or not she would wait and see... there was no way of knowing

Anna, Alice and Suzanne busied themselves with plans for the reunion; they were baking cookies and cakes for a week. They made salads, meats and entrees of all kinds. Everyone was bringing something;

even RJ's wife was making one of those marshmallow, coconut things with all the whipped cream. Bev was doing a batch of fried chicken the old fashioned way and Anna had a cold glazed ham.

It was only two days away and still no word from Angel or Paul. She tried calling several times to see if she could at least pick up Beth but there was no answer; and Paul wasn't returning any messages left at his office.

All Suzanne could do now was wait and hope. She tried her hardest to hope when there was so little hope to hang onto. It all seemed so impossible she wished she had never set herself up for this agony. What made her think for even one instant she could pull all this off.

With or without Angel, the rest of them would be a family, a family that cared and could be one, putting away all bad feelings from the past. She had never had all her children and grandchildren under one roof before.

As she thought about it, she realized how much she had actually missed for all the years her children were growing, and becoming these wonderful adults that she now could know and enjoy. She was feeling pangs of guilt and regret that she didn't have more to do with forming them into who they had become.

The day of the gathering, Suzanne was scurrying around like a crazy person trying to make sure everything would be perfect. Suzanne wouldn't let anything go wrong.

Suzanne ran "to do" lists through her mind, over and over. She not only made herself crazy but Aaron and Shelby as well. Aaron decided to check on things at the hotel, since he had to take Shelby back anyway. He told Suzanne not to worry; he would be back long before it started.

In reality he wanted to give her some space until she calmed down a little. He couldn't stand it when she got this way and neither could anyone else. There was nothing to do but clear the way and get out of the line of fire.

Anna arrived early, which was no surprise to Suzanne. It was Anna's style. She had been reliable all her life..." BE EARLY OR DON'T

COME AT ALL..." Suzanne was actually relieved when Anna took over setting everything up, so Suzanne could grab a shower and change before anyone else came.

Suzanne was anxious to see R.J. and his new bride Carol wanting to hear all the stories of their honeymoon. She hoped they had taken a lot of pictures she wanted to share every moment, well almost every moment.

By the time she got out of the shower, she could hear them talking a hundred miles an hour all of them at once, chattering away. Suzanne went into her room to dress, feeling good about the excitement, and well being of her oldest and youngest child.

Alice and Stanley were next to appear. Suzanne loved the sound of the house filled with laughter and commotion. All her children together, full of life and excitement, enjoying each other's company. She felt a moment of sadness as she realized the loss of her Angel. Not gone, but not there either.

There was still a slim chance that Paul would talk her into coming. When she finally headed into the living room to greet everyone, she could see R.J. on the floor play wrestling with Danny junior. Alice was holding Brian in anticipation of her own bundle, which couldn't get here soon enough to suit her. Alice always did hate waiting, even at Christmas, weeks before the event she would be searching closets for hidden surprises.

As Suzanne stood with a tear of happiness and pride in her accomplishments of the day, she could hear a small voice behind her barely above a shy whisper... "HELLO GRANDMA!.." As Suzanne turned and saw Beth standing in the doorway, she couldn't hold it back any longer. Her face was drenched with tears of happiness that finally her entire family would be together.

Beth ran into Suzanne's arms trying to wipe away the tears with her tiny palms..." DO WE MAKE YOU SAD GRANDMA?..." Suzanne hugged her even tighter as she explained that they were happy tears.

They could never make her sad, she had never been happier. With that she broke one of her arms free to wrap around Angels neck. Still crying she whispered into Angel's ear..." THANK-YOU... THANK-YOU FOR COMING ... WE NEEDED YOU HERE... WE AREN'T A FAMILY WITHOUT YOU..."

Angel began crying in Suzanne's arms unable to say a word. Paul standing behind her grinned and mouthed a "hello" as Suzanne mouthed a "thank-you ". Suzanne knew Angel would never have come without him. Whatever he had to do to get them there, Suzanne was thankful.

Beth broke away from the embrace as soon as she saw Danny playing, wanting to play as well. They became instant best friends, chasing each other around the house, not bothering to wait to be introduced.

By this time Alice, Anna and R.J. were standing in line to greet Angel and Paul. At first, a little apprehensive, perhaps some would call it cautious, mostly they were simply unsure. They had learned over the years that Angel had many faces and personalities there would be no way of knowing whether she would hug or attack.

There was something different in Angel, a quiet sort of shyness, a fear or maybe it was guilt. She had hurt, embarrassed, and attacked, both physically and verbally, each of them at one time or another. She wasn't sure how much they hated her. She was extremely humble as she waited to see their reaction to her. To see if there was any forgiveness for someone who knew she didn't deserve it.

The other difference was sobriety. If ever she needed some liquid courage it was now. Most of her confidence and arrogance came straight from a bottle, preferably a brown bottle. Without it she was just a scared little girl. She looked so scared and helpless the family couldn't help but feel pity for her. Although pity was the last thing she wanted or needed.

What she wanted and needed from her family was forgiveness. She had inflicted each and every one of them with some form of abuse. Now looking through sober eyes, she hoped and prayed she would see hints of forgiveness in their eyes.

She looked so scared and so helpless they all moved forward to hug her all at once. She didn't have to say the words, she knew she was forgiven. Everyone held the embrace, crying in a huddled circle that filled the room with an overflow of emotions.

All except Ray that is, who sat on the couch, staring straight ahead, refusing to look in her direction, not daring to even acknowledge her existence. He was a rock, determined to show no emotion. Suzanne could see Bev nudging him, but he brushed her away and stayed strong.

Angel went over to her father cautiously begging him to forgive her. If he couldn't forgive then at least talk to her, yell at her, anything that showed he knew she existed. The silence between them was deafening and painful. Suzanne could hardly endure it, how was Angel going to get through this.

He got to his feet still staring straight ahead not once making any kind of eye contact, and walked out of the room. Bev got to her feet to go after him, Suzanne motioned her to sit. This was her mess to clean up and she would be the one to talk sense into Ray. It was a problem that came out of their marriage, one that had never been properly discussed or settled.

She followed him out to the end of the boardwalk where he stood alone staring out over the water. She knew him well enough to know it was only his pride making him act this way. She had no doubt that the man that sat awake many a night holding his Angel while she screamed through her latest of night terrors secretly wanted to hold his Angel again.

The man that spent every waking hour with her in the hospital and the same man that crawled into the back of a closet to hold and comfort her... DID LOVE HIS DAUGHTER. Maybe that was part of the pain, he loved her too much. So much that he didn't dare let her in to hurt him again. Perhaps he saw Suzanne in her, hurting him over and over.

When she finally got face to face with him, she could see a well of tears that took every bit of control he had to hold back unsuccessfully.

As soon as she saw his eyes she knew he wanted to give in, he only had to let himself...

" YOU KNOW THAT YOU LOVE HER ... ALL YOU HAVE TO DO IS FORGIVE ... IF YOU COULD FORGIVE ME, THEN SURELY YOU HAVE IT IN YOU TO FORGIVE YOUR OWN DAUGHTER..." Ray wondered what made her think he had forgiven her.

Filled with so much pain and heartache his was a heart that had too many times been shattered into bits. It was a heart that grew harder with each painful blow. Suzanne understood ... she did. He was afraid that he couldn't handle anymore pain. He was scared to set himself up for one more blow.

..." PLEASE RAY, SHE IS TRYING SO HARD... CAN'T YOU TAKE THAT STEP...? SHE'S YOUR DAUGHTER, YOUR BLOOD AND SHE ALWAYS WILL BE ...YOU CAN NOT TAKE THAT AWAY NO MATTER HOW MUCH YOU TRY ...!"

Ray still hadn't broken his silence. Suzanne was sure if he had he would have crumbled, silence was how he kept strong. She turned to go back to the house so she could leave him to think about it. She was sure that he would find the strength to try one more time to let his daughter into his life, he simply needed the time.

Walking down the boardwalk was Angel, coming out to fight her own battle, Suzanne swelled with pride. Angel not unlike her mother had always run from confrontation; now she would stand and fight the most important battle of her life.

As Angel got up to her father Suzanne turned to look up and mumble a quick prayer that she was sure couldn't hurt. She could hear Angel begging her father, tears in her eyes, a quiver in her voice ... " PLEASE DADDY...!? PLEASE ... JUST LOOK AT ME ... I AM TRYING TO CHANGE... TO BE THE DAUGHTER YOU WANT ME TO BE..."

Angel took a deep breath before she started talking again, what could she say that would soften his heart. There had to be a way of getting into his heart again. She would never hurt or disappoint him again if only he would give her the chance to prove it. He had hurt her as much as she hurt him and she was willing and ready to forgive.

"IF YOU CAN NOT FORGIVE ME, AT LEAST ... GIVE ME A CHANCE TO PROVE MYSELF... GIVE ME SOMETHING TO HANG ONTO... TELL ME THAT IN THE FUTURE... MAYBE...? THERE HAS TO BE A CHANCE...PLEASE DADDY!!.."

Without saying a word he reached out and held her in his arms. As he had when she was little, when he was her shining knight rescuing her in the middle of the night when all was so scary. To Angel she was that little girl again, a little girl safe in her Daddy's arms.

Suzanne returned to the house, leaving them alone. They would be all right now. There were still fences to mend but they had the tools and that was the beginning. The two of them remained on the boardwalk for almost an hour talking and holding each other. All was forgiven, at least for now and hopefully for always.

Suzanne now had the time to focus on other things. Like why hadn't Aaron come back, he was never late, that was his best quality. She was getting extremely worried, a worry that escalated every time she glanced compulsively at the clock. Something was wrong, it had to be, she could feel it. There was no shaking off the fear that she was becoming consumed in.

In all the years she had known him he had been reliable, without fault. Even before they were in a relationship, she knew where he was every minute. Time was a compulsion to him, he watched it carefully, never letting it either slip away or to loose track of it.

He knew how important this day was to her, he would never have done anything to add to the pressure she was already feeling. Suzanne gave the third degree to everyone not once, not twice but every few minutes. She couldn't help herself he must have called; someone must have taken a message.

No one knew him the way she did that was why they laughed as she grew more frantic calling the hotel. Even though they had said he left hours ago she had to call back, they must have been wrong. He had to be there, if he wasn't with her he had to be at the hotel. They assured her that not only did he say he was headed home but he was determined not to be late.

She called the hotel again this time to talk to Shelby. There was an emergency at the hotel when they got there, so Shelby volunteered to be the one to stay so Aaron could get back to her and the family.

He did have to make the bank deposits before going home to the madness. However the bank was only moments from the hotel, none of it made sense, he should have been home an hour ago. Now Suzanne could hear the panic in Shelby's voice. Something was wrong, something was very wrong.

When Shelby spoke to Aaron he was excited to be with her family. He was pleased they were all gathering. He would never have missed it. There was nothing he looked forward to more than playing with his grandkids.

Suzanne was determined not to give way to panic; she would not make herself crazy. He would walk through the door at any moment and then they would laugh about whatever the hold-up was. She had to convince herself all was well it had to be.

She would give him a little more time; it had only been a half-hour since the banks closed. Maybe he had a flat tire; maybe he broke down somewhere and was waiting for help. Everyone was content and gabbing, no sense panicking yet.

Suzanne had to catch R.J.'s attention with out alarming the others. She didn't want to alarm everyone more than she had already. She would feel foolish when he got home alright. But for now she had to send her son to look for him. She needed to feel like someone was doing something.

He was a man of routine. He always went in the same direction. If he had a flat he wouldn't even know how to change it. R.J. got in his car and drove in the direction his mother had instructed. Luckily Aaron was the kind of man who always went the exact same way.

He figured he would go all the way to the hotel then to the bank if he had to, determined not to return without him. It was the only thing that was going to calm his mother. He wouldn't dare return without him, not with the hysteria that she was working herself into.

Suzanne cursed Aaron a hundred times under her breath not meaning a word of it. She told herself that he would be a month sleeping on the couch over this, when all she could think of was wrapping herself around him and never letting him go.

On this of all days he decides to screw up for the first time. She still couldn't believe this was all happening. He knew how important the day was to her, why didn't he simply stay home. The hotel would have been fine without him.

R.J. hadn't driven far when he saw a number of vehicles pulled over on the side of the road. There were all the signs of an accident. He didn't have the time for this, he had to get to town, and there was no time to wait for an accident clean up.

The closer he got the easier it was to make out police cars, rescue trucks, and an ambulance. It had to be a bad one with so much rescue equipment involved. Slowing down to a crawl, he had to see the car.

It was hard to make it out; it had been almost completely demolished and unrecognizable. It was the same color as Aaron's; R.J. prayed it was all a coincident. He refused to let himself acknowledge the thought that crept in the dark corners of his mind haunting him.

He slowed down even more as he made his way closer, still praying under his breath. He knew his mother couldn't handle another heartache in her life. She liked to act like a hard nose but she was a weak muddle of emotions.

He stepped out of his car, parked as close as the police would allow him to get. Slowly he walked in the direction of the accident, half scared to look, not wanting to know but already knowing in his heart.

He stood frozen as they used the Jaws of Life to open the driver's door and pull out what was left of the man. The face was covered in blood, too covered to be recognizable. As he watched he saw the officer pull a wallet out of the back pocket.

R.J. tripped over the words that he searched to speak. He mumbled that he had been looking for his missing stepfather. R.J. could see compassion in his face as the officer began to read the blood stained I.D.

The officer was trying to be as gentle as he could and still confirm R.J.'s worst fears. It was Aaron Weinstein; he was still alive but barely. There wasn't much hope that he would last long. R.J. was on a full run back to his car as the officer yelled the name of the hospital telling him to hurry.

R.J. drove back like a maniac he had to get his mother to the hospital and fast. There would be no time for long drawn out explanations. He was never good at this emotional stuff. He usually joked his way through tense moments.

Suzanne knew the minute R.J. walked through the door that it was bad she had no idea how bad. He was trembling, ghost white, with perspiration pouring off him. He could hardly get a word out past Aaron's name.

Suzanne shook him as hard as she could. She had to know the worst and know it now. Was Aaron still alive? Where was he? She wanted to know details, to know what happened but she was too scared to ask too many questions, there would be time for all that later. Now she had to get to her Aaron and fast.

R.J. didn't have to beg her to come with him, she was already half way out the door and on her way to the car as R.J. attempted to give a quick explanation to the others. The only words he could get out were that Aaron was at the hospital and it wasn't good.

He could explain what little he knew to his mother while en route. They had to hurry; there was no time for conversation. As he drove he searched for the words he had to speak before they got to the hospital, he had to tell her something before they got to the smashed car that she was sure to recognize.

Driving down the road that wound its way down the hill toward town, he wished there was some way of getting there without going past the accident. She was sure to recognize Aaron's car and he hadn't even found the words yet to tell her what she was already guessing.

He didn't slow down or even turn his head as he drove her past the accident. It didn't matter. Suzanne screamed and covered her face with her hands. The car was completely destroyed. How could anyone have survived that?... She begged and pleaded for R.J. to stop, she had to see if it was him. As she pulled at the steering wheel R.J. tried to scream over her yelling.

He was not there, he was at the hospital he didn't have long they had to get to the hospital while he was still alive. The only thing all this hysteria would accomplish was getting them killed as well. She had to calm down; it wouldn't do Aaron any good if she was out of control.

Prayers started coming into her head. She made promises it would take a saint to keep, but she meant every word. If God would let Aaron live...She didn't care if he was a cripple for the rest of his life, or even if he was disfigured, she would take care of him. She just wanted him in her life any way she could have him.

..." PLEASE LET HIM BE ALIVE ... I NEED HIM..." She hadn't even told him that she loved him. She did love him. She loved him more than life itself. He was her life, she was nothing without him. The minute she saw him she would tell him she loved him.

She prayed he was in some kind of condition to let him know, so he could understand how much she truly did love him. She thought if only she could somehow get that into his head, he would live; he would live for her.

..." PLEASE LET HIM BE ALIVE... PLEASE LET HIM BE ALIVE ... PLEASE LET HIM BE ALIVE..." nurses were talking, doctors were talking, R.J. was trying to explain things to her as he dragged her down the hall to ICU. All she could concentrate on was a half prayer, half chant.

Suzanne didn't want to hear anything. She didn't want details, and she certainly didn't want to answer any questions. All she wanted to hear was that he was alive. If he was in surgery, there was still hope.

He was still alive and hopefully he would stay that way. He had to stay alive; she had to tell him she loved him. From now on for the rest of her days the people in her life would know she loved them, never again would she take the love in her life for granted.

R.J. wondered why hospitals had the most uncomfortable of furniture when there was nothing to do but sit and wait. He sat in silence as his mother stared at the operating room door, waiting for someone, anyone to appear. They needed answers. How long did they think someone could sit with no answers?

Suzanne appeared to be in some kind of shock as she sat with eyes fixed on the doors, not speaking or moving. Afraid if she blinked or looked away she would miss something. R.J. went to the cafeteria for coffee, but she couldn't take her eyes off the door long enough to sip it.

R.J. needed help he called the house for the girls to come. He was thankful when Ray explained that Bev and him stayed behind to watch the grandbabies while everyone else was on their way.

He had no idea how to act or what to say. If it was bad news that came through the door he would never be able to keep his mother calm, what could he say to comfort her. He was the family clown, the jokester, he wasn't good with sadness.

He felt nervous and overwhelmed just sitting beside her looking so morbid. He thought he should say something that would give her hope, but nothing appropriate came to mind. All he could think of was a handful of stupid jokes that he was pretty sure were not tasteful in this situation.

It didn't take long for reinforcements to arrive. The husbands stayed for awhile then went to Suzanne's to free Ray and Bev. Who would want to come to the hospital to show their support and their genuine caring for Aaron, all to show their support and love?...even Shelby wasn't long making his much needed appearance.

It was hours of waiting in silence. There was nothing anyone could say, nothing they could do... only wait and pray in silence. Occasionally a family member would harass a passing nurse or doctor but they had no answers.

A doctor finally appeared, after many long hours, his head was hung low, his hands rubbing his forehead like he had the worst headache in the world. As soon as he raised his eyes he asked who Mrs. Weinstein was.

Suzanne went to him not wanting to hear, she knew it was bad. She could feel the dread and the pity as soon as the doctor came out. Anna then Alice came over to hold her up, to give her the strength to hear what he had to say.

Starting the conversation with..." I AM SORRY MRS. WEINSTEIN..." she didn't need to hear the rest. She heard a scream that sounded outside of herself, as though it had come from someone else, somewhere else. Anywhere else was where she wanted to be; anywhere that she wouldn't have to hear what this Doctor that couldn't even meet her eyes had to say.

She knew it was her voice. It was as though she had left her body and was floating above. Somehow, she was watching herself crumble to the floor in a flood of hysterical weakness. It was Shelby that caught her and held her up.

The doctor walked over to R.J. and Ray, writing a prescription for sedatives for the day and sleeping pills for the night. He explained to them that it would be better if she slept for the next twenty-four hours.

Shelby had to carry her to the car and then into the house. It was Angel and Anna that got her changed and into bed, while Alice brought her juice to drink down a sleeping pill. She showed no resistance, she had left her body and was in a limbo state outside of all of this heartache.

Suzanne had no conscious idea of who was there or who wasn't, all she knew was that it wasn't Aaron. If she could get to sleep then she could wake up and discover it was all a terrible nightmare, the worst she had ever had. All she had to do was wake up from it.

It was Angel that stayed by her side, refusing to leave her for even a second. She slept in the chair beside her mother's bed. If anyone understood heartache, she did. Anna, Alice and R.J. could imagine, but they didn't know. No one knew like Angel and Suzanne knew.

They had been in pain their entire lives. Suzanne had, for a fleeting moment, escaped the pain with Aaron, as Angel had escaped with David, they were both gone, and the pain was back.

Suzanne wanted to go to sleep and stay asleep, never to wake again. Asleep she could feel Aaron in bed beside her, feel his embrace, and smell his cologne. As long as she could stay asleep he would be there with her. She had fought off sleep all her life and now she prayed for it.

As she floated off, she could feel the first kiss, the first embrace. Only this time it was different, this time she told him she loved him over and over again. She would never forgive herself for not telling him she loved him. In her sleep she could profess that undying love.

It was the men in Suzanne's life that took over the funeral arrangements, as Suzanne could not. Ray was a big help to R.J. and Daniel he had already buried both his parents and Suzanne's. Never did he think he would be helping to arrange a funeral for someone so close to his own age.

It had to be a closed coffin; there was no putting him back together. They would have a memorial service, which the girls handled. Ray had never seen so many people attend a funeral. Aaron had touched many lives and they all wanted to say good-by one last time.

Suzanne was a complete wreck, not speaking a word since Aaron died in the hospital. She had to be held up and guided through every step. When people came to her to give their condolences she nodded a polite greeting or weakly put out her hand to be shaken.

It was spooky, like she was a wind up toy, or robot on autopilot. It was pretty obvious that her mind had left her body. It was also obvious that when it returned she would be in a lot of pain for the loss of someone she married by accident. An accident she'd come to love more than anything else in the entire world.

Once they got past the memorial service everyone got on with their lives, leaving Suzanne alone, for the first time in her life, totally alone.

Suzanne took to her bed. For three days and three nights, she lay on her bed staring into emptiness, not seeming to focus on anything. Once in a while she would drift off and be with Aaron in some sort of dream state.

There was a time when she dreaded sleep, avoided it as long as possible. When she did give into it, it was usually more of a drunken stupor, so she could pass out instead of sleep. Now she wished for sleep, praying for it as hard as she could laying very still, waiting the moments for it to overtake her.

She couldn't pill herself to sleep, or drink herself to sleep. If she did she wouldn't dream. If she didn't dream, then Aaron wouldn't come to her. All she could do was lay and wait until sleep overtook her.

There were a few times when people came into the room, probably Well Wishers to check on her. She was sure it was someone important in her life, but she was out of her body, floating as she watched herself greeting people and people greeting her.

In the float she knew who everyone was, her children, her grandchildren, people she worked with, clients from the hotel, an endless stream of well wishers. But her body had no clue. It was merely going through the motions until she could get back to what was important, her dreamstate where Aaron would be waiting for her.

After the third day in bed, her children all came to her, all of them at the same time. She knew they were there but they were in the same distant fog that everyone at the funeral had been in. She knew they were trying to talk to her; she could see that their lips were moving, but she neither had the energy nor the curiosity to figure out what they were saying.

Didn't they know she was busy waiting for Aaron? She could feel them pulling at her, dragging her into the livingroom. Her body followed only because it was easier than fighting. Suzanne had no fight, all she could do was wait and go along with whatever they wanted.

They brought her something to eat; she stared. They brought her a drink she stared. They begged for her to talk to them. Suddenly in an almost robotic instinct, she got up, picked up the glasses on the table and headed to the kitchen.

Everyone sat watching, afraid to move or say anything. It was the first movement she had made independently since Aaron had died. It wasn't much but she was walking, and she was walking on her own. No one was helping her. No one was holding her up.

She guided her way to the kitchen. Everyone let her go. Maybe she was coming back to them. When she got to the kitchen she stood over the chrome sink and dropped the glasses. As they hit the bottom of the sink they shattered into pieces.

Suzanne stood staring into the sink as though trying to remember a bad nightmare that haunted her memory. Her hand, almost as if it were someone else's hand reached into the sink to pick up the pieces of broken glass which cut her fingers.

Everything was happening in an unreal kind of slow motion it couldn't be real. She watched the blood from her finger drip into the sink. As she saw her blood mingle with the glass the water, and the chrome; she could see Aaron's face in the blood....

Covered in blood, all broken as the glass was broken, Suzanne screamed and dropped to the floor as if she had melted, sobbing and crying in an overwhelming panic of grief that she could hardly bare.

Suddenly it all came into her head, the accident, the death, and the funeral. Flashing through her mind as though it were a movie on fast forward, a horror movie that she didn't want to see, but could not turn off.

Suzanne cried uncontrolled sobs of heartache as she was carried back to her room by R.J. and put to bed by her girls. It was too late, it was all too late. The tears were turned on and now could not be turned off.

It seemed like hours before Suzanne finally cried herself to sleep in total exhaustion. Her children all sat in the living room not knowing what to do. Their mother had always been so strong, so independent; she could handle anything.

They all loved their mother very much but they had lives to live. The farm, the dentistry, and the grocery store were not going to run themselves. It was finally decided that Paul could work from Suzanne's house for a while, so the three of them would stay.

Anna, Alice and R.J...." ASSURED "them that they would come and spell them whenever they weren't working. They all sat in silence for a few minutes, trying to figure out how long this would last, and if there was no change in her condition... then what?

After what happened in the kitchen there were no more peaceful rendezvous with Aaron in her dream world. Every time she drifted off to sleep she saw his face all broken and bleeding. She woke herself several times in a fit of sweat and tears. She was hurting now, and hurting bad. She had liked being on the edge of insanity. She didn't want to come back to all this pain.

Nothing she had ever been through in her life was as horrendous as the pain she now felt. She wanted to be with Aaron, she wanted to stop hurting, mostly she wanted to escape. It didn't matter, nothing mattered Aaron was dead...THERE!!.. She finally said it. It was the first time since his death that she knew he was really dead.

She had known he was dead; she simply refused to accept it. Now there was no denying it. She couldn't get it out of her head. She wished she could lie to herself. She wished she could go back into her comfortable daze where Aaron was alive and loved her.

Suzanne sat drowning in the depths of despair as she saw the sleeping pills the doctor had prescribed for her. Picking up the bottle she rolled it around her fingers as if it were a toy that she couldn't decide whether or not to play with.

As she sat fumbling with the bottle she knew what she was contemplating. She had done this dance before, only this time it would be different; this time she meant it. This time she wanted more than sleep and she wanted it to be forever. She didn't want to be there without Aaron. Aaron was the only one in her life that kept her safe and complete.

A warm breeze began to consume the room, a breeze that seemed to surround her like a gentle fog. Suzanne turned to look at the fog, to feel the breeze caress her. There was a familiarity in the fog, it was comfortable as though she had suddenly found her home again.

Smiling a gentle comforting smile, as she felt the fog surround her, she knew somehow that the fog was Aaron caressing and holding her. She could feel the same sense of warmth and security she always felt when he entered the room. He kissed her on the cheek, and smiled a sad smile, as he took the pills from her hand…

She knew this was all crazy but she didn't care. She was with Aaron again and that was all that mattered insane or not. She loved the feeling and didn't want it to stop. She made no attempt to dissuade herself from feeling and seeing what was going on around her. He told her he had to go ahead of her, he would miss her but he would be all right.

Before he left he had to come back to see her one last time. He had to be sure she was safe before he could go to his resting-place. He had to know she would be all right. He loved her even past the grave and would wait patiently 'til it was her time to come to him.

Her job was not finished on earth; she had children and grandchildren that needed her. What he needed was for her to be strong and survive this. He knew she could do it, she was the most incredible woman he had ever known and he needed her to continue with her spirit for him.

Suzanne could feel the tears stream down her face as she attempted to be brave. She uttered the words she had wished she said every day since she met him…." I LOVE YOU AARON… I ALWAYS HAVE…"

A gentle smile crossed his lips as he told her he had always known. If she wanted to show her love he needed her to go on with her life and make him proud. Tell all the grandchildren about him, not let him be forgotten.

As the fog started to fade away in the gentle breeze it came with, she could hear him whisper… "I WILL ALWAYS BE THERE FOR YOU … I WILL ALWAYS LOVE YOU…"

Shelley Cowell

Suzanne for the first time in a long time held her head high as she walked to the bathroom and poured the pills down the drain. She washed her tear stained face in cold water, took a deep breathe, and went into the front room to tell her children she loved them before it was too late.

The End

LaVergne, TN USA
01 October 2009
159522LV00003B/4/P

9 781434 317469